PRAISE FOR A COVERT AFFAIR

"Conant has written a book full of fascinating material about wartime and postwar America and how they intersected. . . . Conant doesn't disappoint in her picture of the whirlwind life of the OSS, created very much in the image of its founder, the maverick William J. Donovan. Her glimpses of how he overcame bureaucratic rivalries and turf wars are as exciting as her picture of life in the field, complete with dengue fever, cobras, and scorpions."

—*LOS ANGELES TIMES*

"*A Covert Affair* is a skillfully told tale of espionage, combining just enough background information with the right amount of boisterous anecdote to make the reader feel simultaneously amused and informed."

—*SALON.COM*

"The value of Conant's anecdotal approach is . . . in its depiction of ordinary relationships in extraordinary circumstances   of the way friendships, feuds, and romances develop in strange and secretive settings." —*THE NEW YORK TIMES BOOK REVIEW*

"Thoroughly researched, fluid, and compelling."
—*KIRKUS REVIEWS*

"A well-researched, entertaining, and fast-paced read."
—*LIBRARY JOURNAL*

Praise for *A Covert Affair*

"A great story for anyone interested in the early OSS days, in the Moral Operations (MO) program, in the OSS Far Eastern activities in Ceylon, China, and Indonesia. . . . Using the recollections of some of the participants and the voluminous and well-preserved diaries and correspondence of Paul and Julia, the author sets out a graphic picture of the adventurous lives. . . . A fascinating adventure tale."

—OSS Society Newsleter

"[Conant] has provided evocative vignettes of the lives and professional preoccupations of a small group of OSS members in Southeast Asia and a haunting reminder of the injustices and vicissitudes of life in the days of McCarthy—a cautionary tale."

—The New York Review of Books

"Before she mastered French cooking, Julia Child worked for U.S. intelligence, helping the Allied war effort and falling in love, too. Newly declassified documents inform this delicious exposé."

—Good Housekeeping

"Conant expertly describes the breathless excitement of the Good War and how these eager OSS members aided propaganda efforts in exotic locations."

—Boston Magazine

"Conant [has] found all the intimate details a writer could want."

—USA Today

"Conant's vivid tapestry of the 1940s skillfully interweaves interviews, oral histories, memoirs, and recently unclassified OSS and FBI documents with unpublished diaries and letters. The adventurous young OSS recruits spring to life throughout this meticulously researched, authoritative history."

—Publishers Weekly

"Conant has written a book full of fascinating material about wartime and postwar America and how they intersected. . . . Conant doesn't disappoint in her picture of the whirlwind life of the OSS, created very much in the image of its founder, the maverick William J. Donovan. Her glimpses of how he overcame bureaucratic rivalries and turf wars are as exciting as her picture of life in the field, complete with dengue fever, cobras, and scorpions."

—*Los Angeles Times*

"Conant writes in a breezy, amiable voice. . . . Nicely captures Julia's transformation into a cosmopolitan, intrepid, yet still cheerful soul. The account of how her friendship with the older Paul matured into romance is particularly good. . . . You can tell she had fun writing it, and the fun is contagious."

—*The Washington Post*

"Highly readable. . . . Conant's research is thorough. . . . Impressively, Conant manages to make the various storylines of this sprawling book coherent and engaging. . . . Even where the story digresses it proves interesting because of the many personal anecdotes that capture the drama and excitement of what it was like being part of early cloak-and-dagger operations."

—*The Washington Independent Review of Books*

"With this cast of characters, the story can hardly fail to be intriguing. . . ."

—*New Haven Advocate*

"Conant's extensive research reveals fascinating details about Julia and Paul long before they were the eccentrically cute couple from Cambridge who put on a cooking show."

—*The Kansas City Star*

"Jennet Conant is the perfect person to chronicle the weird, wacky world of World War II's Office of Strategic Services. Her eminently readable, though slightly florid, style matches perfectly the derring-do of the OSS in Ceylon, today's Sri Lanka; and her three earlier World War II books bolster her expertise on the era. . . . Conant cooked up a good book on the Childs without much cooking."

—*St. Petersburg Times*

ALSO BY JENNET CONANT

A

COVERT

AFFAIR

When Julia and Paul Child joined the OSS they
had no way of knowing that their adventures
with the spy service would lead them into a world
of intrigue and, because of one idealistic but
reckless colleague, a terrifying FBI investigation.

JENNET
CONANT

SIMON & SCHUSTER PAPERBACKS
New York   London   Toronto   Sydney   New Delhi

Simon & Schuster Paperbacks
1230 Avenue of the Americas
New York, NY 10020

First Simon & Schuster trade paperback edition November 2011

SIMON & SCHUSTER PAPERBACKS and colophon are registered trademarks of Simon & Schuster, Inc.

For information about special discounts for bulk purchases, please contact Simon & Schuster Special Sales at 1-866-506-1949 or business@simonandschuster.com.

The Simon & Schuster Speakers Bureau can bring authors to your live event. For more information or to book an event contact the Simon & Schuster Speakers Bureau at 1-866-248-3049 or visit our website at www.simonspeakers.com.

Designed by Nancy Singer

Photo credits appear on page 397.

Manufactured in the United States of America

10   9   8   7   6   5   4   3   2   1

The Library of Congress has cataloged the hardcover edition as follows:
Conant, Jennet.
 A covert affair : Julia Child and Paul Child in the OSS / Jennet Conant—
1st Simon & Schuster hardcover ed.
   p.   cm.
 Includes bibliographical references and index.
   1. Child, Julia.   2. Child, Paul, 1902–1994.   3. World War, 1939–1945—Secret service—United States.   4. United States. Office of Strategic Services—Biography. 5. Intelligence officers—United States—Biography.   6. Child, Julia—Homes and haunts—Europe.   7. Child, Paul, 1902–1994—Homes and haunts—Europe.   8. McCarthy, Joseph, 1908–1957.   9. Anti-communist movements—United States—History—20th century.   10. United States—Politics and government—1945–1954.   I. Title.
D810.S8 C3863   2011
940.54'85092273—dc22   2011002875

ISBN 978-1-4391-6352-8
ISBN 978-1-4391-6353-5 (pbk)
ISBN 978-1-4391-6850-9 (ebook)

To Betty

for all her stories

Thanks to the human heart by which we live,
Thanks to its tenderness, its joys, and fears,
To me the meanest flower that blows can give
Thoughts that do often lie too deep for tears.

—William Wordsworth

CONTENTS

A
COVERT
AFFAIR

1

SPECIAL INQUIRY

It started with the arrival of a telegram. Ever since the war, the thin slip of a letter had become permanently fixed in people's minds as a harbinger of death and disaster. Why Julia believed for one moment that it would be good news she could not recall—just that she had been so sure. The cable, which reached them in Bonn on Thursday, April 7, 1955, was addressed to her husband, Paul Child. The cursory message took the form of an urgent summons to Washington: REPORT SOONEST FOR CONSULTATION.

Julia had been over the moon. She knew exactly why Paul was being called stateside. They were going to make him "head of the department." She had even told him as much, her voice brimming with confidence and pride. Incapable of containing her excitement, she had been ready to celebrate then and there. It was silly of her, but characteristic, too. She had gone on happily speculating about the telegram the rest of the evening. Paul had eventually gotten caught up in her mood, his reluctant, mock impatience giving way to anticipation. This, at last, was his promotion, long deserved and long overdue. Then again, when had the State Department ever done anything in a timely fashion?

She supposed they should be grateful. Paul had never been particularly ambitious and because he had little patience with bureaucracy had remained mired in the middle ranks of the Foreign Service. He had never intended to pursue a diplomatic career and lacked the necessary instincts. He had simply been rolled into the State Department after the war and eventually found himself, along with most of his old department, reorganized into the newly formed United States Information Service (USIS).* His particular field, "visual presentation," which had once involved designing and running war rooms in such exotic locales as India and China, now encompassed such mundane matters as arranging press and special events for the agency's European missions. As Foreign Service jobs went, it was a somewhat unglamorous backwater, and it was unlikely he would rise very far. That suited Paul just fine, Julia knew. It meant he would have more time to devote to his artistic sidelines—the writing, painting, and photography that he found infinitely more satisfying. The job was just something he got on with, did well, and left on Fridays at five. Still, it was only right that after years of toiling under a succession of bores and simpletons (his current superiors were known to the staff as "Woodenhead the First" and "Woodenhead the Second," or WH1 and WH2 for short) Paul was finally going to get his due. Perhaps he would get to run his own show or, at the very least, be allowed to pick the members of his own team. There were few things more demoralizing, in Julia's opinion, than "working for people you don't admire."

It was just the morale boost they both needed. Six months earlier, Julia and Paul had been forced to leave their beloved France and, crueler still, an adorable apartment in the old port city of Marseille, because of an inane government decree that a diplomatic post in any given country could not exceed a period of four years. The three years they had spent in Paris directly after the war, followed by a fifteen-month stint on the southern coast, meant they had exceeded the limit. They had no choice but to pack up and go where they were told.

---

* The USIS is known domestically as the United States Information Agency (USIA), but for clarity and consistency will be referred to henceforth as USIS.

The transfer to Bonn could not have come at a worse time. Julia had been in the midst of testing recipes for a French cookbook she was contracted to write for the Boston publisher Houghton Mifflin with two fellow gourmands she had met in Paris. She knew that the new assignment for Paul not only would take her farther from her collaborators, but would remove her from the country in whose cuisine she should be immersing herself. As difficult as it had been for her to box up her kitchen in Marsailles, Julia understood that the move was infinitely harder on Paul. He had spent his formative years in France, and the language had become second nature to him, as had the internecine squabbling of the locals. The country had captured his heart long before it had taken hold of hers.

Leaving Paris for Marseilles had been a wrenching experience, but it was nothing compared to the jolt that Julia and Paul experienced upon learning they were being posted to Bonn. Paul was fluent in a number of languages, but German was not one of them. It was a poor use of his skills, and he was beside himself. While he had long since reconciled himself to the fact that few things in their government agency followed the dictates of logic, this yank of the chain was particularly galling. Julia could think of nothing to say to cheer him up. She had never set foot in Germany and was "horrified" at the thought. Her memories of World War II were too fresh for her not to dread the idea of settling in Bonn, which had temporarily replaced Berlin as the official seat of the government because it reportedly had less historical baggage. She could only hope she would think better of the new West German capital for having escaped the brunt of the Nazi boot. "To think of living in Germany," she grimly wrote Paul's family. "Will I ever get over the imagined smell of the gas chambers and the rotting bodies of the Concentration camps. Will we ever be able to learn the language in a couple of months?"*

Their first glimpse of their new home did nothing to lift their spirits. "Woe—how did we get here!" Julia scribbled in her diary on October 24, 1954, the day they arrived in Bad Godesberg, a drab residential dis-

---

* The eccentric capitalization and punctuation in all the letters are as they appear in the originals.

trict just south of Bonn. Flush with dollars from the Marshall Plan, the entire Rhine Valley had been rapidly rebuilt as part of the country's economic and industrial redevelopment, and it was full of blocky concrete office buildings and bristling with American soldiers. Julia and Paul were dismayed to find themselves back in the familiar embrace of the U.S. military, assigned to live in a segregated ("no Germans allowed!") compound called Plittersdorf on the Rhine, which its unfortunate occupants had dubbed "the Golden Ghetto on the Rhine." They had never cared for this part of army life—the rows of anonymous housing, streets crawling with jeeps and military policemen, and bars crowded with drunken young men in ill-fitting uniforms who wanted to be anywhere but there. Writing to her sister, Julia griped that she had "had enough of that meat-ballery during the war to last her a lifetime." Still, there were plenty of opportunities for escape. Paul's Foreign Service salary enabled them to live well, especially as the dollar was strong against the mark. Whenever possible, they fled across the river to Bonn, a picturesque university town that had been occupied by American troops toward the end of the war and had somehow managed to survive relatively unscathed, its medieval battlements and grand boulevards still redolent of Old World charm. There they could sample the solid regional fare, the sauerbratens and sausages, inevitably served with groaning plates of potato pancakes. Afterward, too full to go far, they would stop to recover at one of the pavement cafés along the banks of the river.

Julia and Paul, like most in their seasoned diplomatic circle, had always been guilty of a certain disdain for GI culture, but what had once been mild distaste had over time developed into a visceral aversion. They wanted no part of the martial fervor that arose in the shadow of the Soviet threat in East Germany. Bonn, the makeshift capital, seemed by virtue of its very impermanence to bring out the worst in its American occupiers, who were so conflicted about their objectives in the divided region that they appeared to be almost paralyzed. Caught between the menacing Soviet Union and Western Europe's fears of military vulnerability, Bonn was emblematic of the tenuous peace, and of the uncertain prospects for American forces and American dollars to achieve a united capitalist postwar Europe to deter the spread of Communism. Writing in *The New York Times,* Julia and Paul's friend Stewart Alsop observed that the U.S. diplomatic mission in Germany was "a peculiarly depressing place for a peculiarly American reason" and, in its confusion and excess of caution, was substituting "dogma for policy and the official line for serious thought."

Within weeks of their arrival in Germany, Julia and Paul had picked up on the atmosphere of distrust and unease. The place was rife with closed-door meetings, simmering tensions, and subterranean plots. They were on the front lines of the Cold War in Europe, though Julia could not help feeling that the chill in the air had its origin in the "rampant right wingery" that had seized their own country in recent years. In Washington, the mood was so changed that on her last visit home she had scarcely recognized the city as the same place she and Paul had lived in those first happy postwar years.

When peace was declared, Americans had celebrated their achievement. The GIs had triumphed over Germany, over Japan, and, in the bargain, over the Great Depression, and in the first glow of euphoria that victory had seemed complete. The United States, with its great economic and military strength, seemed invincible. During the late 1940s, while based in Paris, Julia and Paul had watched as their country's ascendance as a global power led to a new confidence in its role in international affairs, as well as a greater sense of its responsibilities in preserving the peace and shaping the future, and the corresponding spread of U.S. policy-making agencies and legations around the globe.

As the rewards of war failed to meet the impossibly high expectations, however, the euphoria had quickly faded. New fears about the nation's security had gripped the public. The tone of political debate in Congress grew sharply partisan and bitter, with the Republicans making the most of charges of Communist infiltration of the Truman administration, as though that could explain the failure to foresee what had happened with the Soviet Union and China. In the spring of 1947, in an effort to protect his administration, President Harry S. Truman established the Federal Employee Loyalty Program, a broad measure instituting background checks and screening procedures for all incumbent and prospective government employees. But instead of reassuring the public, the program helped legitimize the idea that international Communism posed a domestic threat. By the end of 1950, Alger Hiss was convicted of perjury, Klaus Fuchs confessed, and Julius and Ethel Rosenberg were arrested on espionage charges of passing bomb secrets to the Russians. Inevitably, in 1953, after years of relentless media coverage, the Rosenbergs got the chair. All of this seemed to confirm the existence of spies in every nook and cranny of government. Washington was awash in paranoia and suspicion.

Even more troubling than the hardening of ideology was the vicious Red-baiting of Senator Joseph R. McCarthy. To Julia, the whole government, spurred on by McCarthy's unscrupulous zeal, seemed consumed with hunting for subversives. Venting her anger in a letter to her family, Julia wrote that she could not help thinking that most McCarthy supporters, of whom she was afraid her "dear old Pop" was one, were "good-hearted but fat-headed people" who were hopelessly stuck in the past. For twenty years, her father's animosity had festered under the New Deal and the Fair Deal: "Roosevelt was, to him, the anti-Christ. Roosevelt was socialism. The enemy. He boiled and seethed with hatred." As far as she could see, McCarthy had tapped right into that source of hatred, fueling people's fears about the future: "Suddenly the new enemy is also Communism," she continued. "It is these nasty foreigners with their socialistic ideas, these nasty intellectual egg-heads, who *like* the foreigners, & who have always caused all the trouble. What we want is to return to 1925, when we had no world responsibility (presumably), and no truck with foreigners. We just want to live alone. McCarthy is the savior symbol."

The junior senator from Wisconsin's rapid rise to power was a recurring theme in the newspapers and Julia and Paul were riveted. They read everything they could get their hands on in Bonn, including the *Herald Tribune* and an edited version of the daily *New York Times,* and they beseeched family members to send articles from home. McCarthy had successfully made Communism a potent campaign issue, and he bullied President Truman into implementing an executive order to begin loyalty investigations of government employees. After the "fall" of China in October 1949, when the Communists led by Mao Tse-tung proclaimed the formation of the People's Republic, McCarthy and his allies had stepped up their ideological attacks. On February 9, 1950, in a speech before the Women's Republican Club of Wheeling, West Virginia, McCarthy had announced his crusade against government employees suspected of being members of the Communist Party, who were nevertheless "still working and shaping policy in the State Department." Julia and Paul had seen the headlines that followed, all of which focused on McCarthy's claim that he had in hand a "list of 205" names of traitors.

McCarthy's Red scare became a real cause of concern, alarm even, to State Department personnel. He had made the overseas information agency one of his targets and had vowed to root out "security risks." Hoping to appease McCarthy, President Dwight D. Eisenhower's new secretary of state, John Foster Dulles, had dismissed a number of high-level diplomats and had warned that anything less than "positive loyalty" from Foreign Service officers was "not tolerable at this time." Julia and Paul had been en route to Germany when they had heard about the flurry of coerced departures in Bonn. This had been followed by reports of books being removed from the shelves of libraries run by the USIS, known as America Houses, in a number of European cities. Dashiell Hammett's hard-boiled detective novel *The Maltese Falcon* was one of the many books McCarthy wanted "deshelved"—a neat euphemism for censored. In Berlin, a book entitled *Thunder Out of China,* written by their friend Theodore H. White, a *Time* magazine correspondent during the war, was found to be objectionable; it was removed and burned. Apparently White's sympathy with Mao and some of the Communist objectives made the book too dangerous for the eyes of impressionable Germans, the citizens of a country America was trying to turn into a unified democracy.

Julia and Paul learned from friends in Paris that Roy Cohn and David Schine, McCarthy's young assistants—the newspapers called them "the gumshoe boys"—had paid a surprise visit to the embassy there. Cohn and Schine had nosed around looking for dirt. Inevitably, they had rooted out a handful of employees who were disgruntled and interviewed them. One of Paul's former colleagues, Larry Morris, the Paris cultural attaché, had happened on the two men in his office one Saturday afternoon, apparently making themselves at home with their feet propped up on his desk. Incensed, he had demanded they remove their feet from his desk and leave. They had gone quietly, but not before holding a press conference during which they made all sorts of unsubstantiated charges—"vague, but dirty," as Paul put it. Naturally, no official at the embassy was given the opportunity to reply. Then Cohn and Schine announced that the next day—Easter Sunday—they would be questioning the ambassador, and wanted to meet with all the top USIS officers at 3:00 p.m. that afternoon at the library to examine the books on display. Everyone canceled his or her holiday plans and assembled at the library at the appointed hour, but Cohn and Schine never showed. Finally someone called the Hôtel de Crillon and discovered that the "two young bloods" had just risen from their beds and were eating breakfast in their suite. As far as Paul could tell, the only investigating they did was "during most of Holy Saturday night, among the naked showgirls of Montmartre."

Paul had seen only trouble ahead. Rumors about where McCarthy's tactics of intimidation—the book burning and finger-pointing—might lead had spread like wildfire through the diplomatic community. Paul was unnerved by McCarthyism and considered the senator to be "a desperately dangerous, power-hungry, fascist-operating bastard." He was less than sanguine about the new president's ability to stand up to the notorious demagogue. "Eisenhower appears to be trying to save the Republican Party at the expense of the country," he wrote his family in March 1954. "Sweeping the pieces under the rug in the plain view of the public won't disguise the disaster. He better hurry up and act or he'll find himself . . . eating out of McCarthy's hand."

Julia and Paul had watched with sinking hearts as one after another of the career Foreign Service officers they had served with in China, among them some of their closest friends, had been forced out, while still others quit in disgust. Anyone who had departed from the official line in the Far East, or had had the temerity to write a critical report, was being labeled un-American and blamed for having "lost China to the Reds." Somehow Mao's victory was now being seen as part of a master Kremlin plot, enabled by a band of Sinologists—known as China hands—who had conspired to undermine U.S. policy. "Quite a number of people were just ruined," recalled Julia. She and Paul had both served with the OSS in China and wondered if they should be worried, too. At the same time, it was difficult to judge to what extent some of the transfers and resignations being ordered from Washington were part of the normal changing of the guard and would have happened eventually, even without the buzz saw of McCarthy's Red hunt.

It was a point of personal honor with Julia and Paul that their colleagues could always count on their support. If loyalty was the burning question of the hour, they wanted to make it clear where theirs lay. When their old friend Haldore Hanson, a State Department official and longtime China expert—as a foreign correspondent in the 1930s, he had traveled the country by bicycle to cover the civil war—was accused by McCarthy of having "pro-Communist proclivities," they immediately sent him a note of encouragement. On his day before the Senate subcommittee, he denied any involvement with the Communists, stating repeatedly that he was "a loyal American." But as he later confided to Julia and Paul, he doubted whether his answer would "ever meet up with the charges." Even though the subcommittee found no evidence against Hanson, as a result of McCarthy's accusations his neighbors in Virginia had circulated a petition to drive him out, and one even labeled him a Russian spy. Hanson wrote to Julia and Paul that he had been "very touched" to hear from them, adding, "You have no idea what a few letters from friends can do for you in a time like that."

Hanson's letter depressed the hell out of them, but they kept it as a reminder of the perilous times they lived in. There was nothing they could do but keep their heads down and hope for the best. Writing to her sister, Julia confided her misgivings: "After the events of the last few years, I have entirely lost that nobility and esprit de corps. I feel, actually, that at any moment we might be accused of being Communists and traitors."

It was no wonder they seized on the telegram from Washington as a reprieve. Paul's orders to report to Washington meant that everything was going to be all right. He was going to get a promotion, maybe even

a new post. The Sunday Paul was scheduled to fly back to the United
States, Julia and a party of friends decided to see him off. They were in
a festive mood as they drove to the airport in Düsseldorf. The following morning, still feeling giddy, Julia decided to get dressed up and go
to a reception in honor of James B. Conant, the high commissioner for
West Germany.* Conant had overseen the end of the occupation and,
as a last act before his office lapsed into history, was formally recog-
nizing the beginning of rearmament. There would be champagne all
around—even if many in the room, Julia included, felt it was a bit premature for the Germans to be given their army back.

On Tuesday, another telegram arrived. It was from Paul. The first
words Julia read sent a chill down her spine: SITUATION CONFUSED.

Paul had landed in New York on Monday and caught the train
to Washington from Penn Station, arriving late in the afternoon. He
had wired her from the office first thing on Tuesday, after his trip was
starting to look like a wild goose chase. He had spent an exasperating
morning being shuffled from one office to another, where one bureaucrat after another expressed complete ignorance of and bewilderment
at the reasons for his return. One official finally let it slip that he had
been told to provide Paul with "a desk and telephone, nothing more."
No one seemed to have a clue what Paul was supposed to be doing or
how long he would be staying. Thoroughly disgusted, he had ended up
going out for drinks and dinner with two old colleagues, Mike Barjansky and George Henry, and they had spent much of the evening talking
over "the mystery" of why he had been sent for. Back in his room at the
Graylyn Hotel, Paul could not keep his growing anxiety at bay as he
wrote a long letter to Julia:

I thought Barjansky would be able to clarify the mystery. But
no. *On the contrary.* He was waiting for me to clarify it for him!
Ah me—what a muck-up! He thinks it must be something
special and secret, otherwise "they" would certainly have told

---

* James B. Conant was the author's grandfather.

him. . . . Mike says there was a definite instruction to mind his own business. He then, naturally enough, assumed I was a CIA agent all the time and that my job as Exhibits Officer was merely a cover, and that I was being hauled back on a secret mission. We were both astonished when each of us learned that the other knew nothing.

By Wednesday morning, Paul had begun to work out that the thirty-six hours of bureaucratic confusion were not simply a matter of crossed signals, but were part of a convoluted procedure conveying him toward some kind of "security investigation." By then it was also apparent that the cable demanding his presence in Washington had nothing whatsoever to do with his career advancement but had been part of a clumsy effort to provide him with a cover story. Although the "how" and "why" of it were still beyond him, Paul wrote Julia, "It appears to be (if the above assumption is correct) that they are actually trying to protect my reputation (and their own too, of course!) by all this secrecy—having, perhaps, learned from the public blare of the McCarthy proceedings, and the consequent adverse criticism of his methods, that unremovable smirches can be rubbed onto innocent persons." The labyrinthine maneuvering, he theorized in a later letter to his superior in Bonn, was in case they had uncovered a mess: "It would have served the Agency's interests not to have it bruited about. The investigation hinged on the standard guilt-by-association gambit, with all the potentialities that could spring from such a situation."

Before facing the inquisition, Paul telegraphed Julia, summing up his predicament: SITUATION HERE LIKE KAFKA STORY. He was being drawn inexorably into a drama not of his devising, one from which there seemed to be no way out. All the time, in the back of his mind, he could not stop searching his memory for a name, an assignment, even the most "tenuous connection," that might have inspired enough suspicion to warrant bringing him back from Germany for a security inquest. Nothing made any sense. "Why in Hell am I here at all?" he worried in a frantic note dashed off at 10:00 a.m. that morning. "This is curiously fantastic, unreal, frightening, and preposterous;

and I couldn't wish more that you were here to give me your invaluable moral support."

Resigned to the fact that he would have to "walk the plank alone," Paul reported to the Office of Security, where he spent the better part of the afternoon and evening being interrogated by two special agents, W. H. Sullivan and A. W. Sanders. A secretary, silent as the grave, took down a complete transcript of everything said. The two agents sat across the table from him, staring over a four-inch-thick dossier that had evidently been assembled with great care over a considerable period of time. Paul was informed that he was the subject of a State Department Special Inquiry, an official investigation into his character, reputation, and loyalty. Friends, relations, employers, and associates—from the distant past to the present—had been tracked down and interviewed.

As it turned out, the association that seemed to most interest the FBI was with one Jane Foster, a former OSS colleague with whom he had served in Ceylon during the war. This assumption was based on the fact that "a number of relentless and tricky hours" were spent in grilling him about Jane. They had wanted to know where, when, and how he had met her. How well had he known her? How often had he seen her? What had they talked about when they were together? Who were her friends? Where had she lived? What were her interests? After an exhaustive examination of that relationship, the interrogators had moved on, questioning him about other friends in the OSS and the Foreign Service, only to return to the subject of Jane Foster again and again in the course of the night. "I gather from the way they talked about her that she had fallen under suspicion of a connection with Communism," he later confided to a close colleague, Joe Phillips, the director of public affairs for Germany. "So they investigated all *Her* friends and acquaintances. My name appeared among the latter."

The "second suspicious thing" from his past, he wrote Julia, appeared to be the fact that he had at one time given the name of Morris Llewellyn Cooke as a reference. An old friend of his brother's, Cooke was an eighty-five-year-old liberal Democrat who had been a dollar-a-year man during FDR's administration. As far as Paul could tell, Cooke appeared to be in "bad odor" with the authorities and a suspect in some kind of right-wing "Republican-brand investigation." (Cooke was a member of the board of directors of the Independent Citizens' Committee for the Arts, Sciences, and Professions, an organization that the FBI listed as "Communist-controlled.") Paul told them that while he was acquainted with Cooke, he did not consider him "an intimate friend" and knew nothing about his political ideology. They worked away at Paul's connection to Cooke for at least an hour, asking about anything the two might have in common, including residences, work, ideas, projects, and travel. They asked if he was familiar with other colleagues of his brother and sister-in-law, and the FBI agents mentioned several names that meant nothing to him.

The third allegation Sullivan and Sanders had confronted Paul with was that he was "a homosexual." The minute the word was spoken, one of them rounded on him: "So, how about it?"

This caught Paul completely off guard. At first it had struck him as so absurd that he burst out laughing. Then he got angry. He demanded to know the name of his accuser. It was written in the Constitution, he argued indignantly, that he had a right to confront his accuser. The two special agents, whom Paul dubbed "the ultimate Kafkas," allowed as how they were not permitted to reveal anything. Paul was stymied. He had been a bachelor (more by circumstance than by choice, he liked to think) until the age of forty-four. Directly after the war, he and Julia, then thirty-four, had decided to throw caution to the wind and get married. As it turned out, their nine years of marriage did not amount to proof of anything. "Male homosexuals often have wives and children," the agents had demurred. Paul was dumbfounded. He found himself struggling to remain serious in what could only be described as a surreal situation. Finally, his voice heavy with sarcasm, he suggested that since he had a wife but *no* child, perhaps that let him "off the hook." The two agents remained stony faced. "If you want to have some verbal fun," he later wrote Julia, "try to prove sometime to two FBI guys that you *aren't* a Lesbian. How do you prove it?"

Unbeknown to Paul, a State Department investigation into his background in 1946, triggered by his application to work at the Pentagon designing intelligence installations, had raised questions about his sexual orientation. The report advised that at times in the past Paul had "given the impression of being bisexual," and the charge was noted in his file, cataloged along with countless others that raised questions about his character, politics, and patriotism. The records indicate that he was one of identical twin sons born to Bertha Cushing Child, a singer from Boston, and Charles Triplet Child, a scientist from Virginia who worked at the Astrophysical Observatory in the Smithsonian. Three weeks after the twins were born, Charles Triplet Child died of typhoid fever, leaving their mother as their sole means of support. She resumed her career as a singer, and the twins and their older sister were raised in a musical environment: little Charles played the violin, Paul the cello, and Mary (Meeda) the piano. Money was tight, so they were soon earning their way as the "Mrs. Child and the Children" quartet. The boys attended the Wilbraham Academy in Massachusetts, Boston Latin High School, and then the Park Lodge School in Paris. After high school, Charles attended Harvard while Paul tried an extension course at Columbia College before taking off for Europe. In France, both during his school years and later, Paul studied art, sculpture, and woodcarving and, according to the report, followed a "bohemian mode of life." As a result of his many years in Paris, he was thought to have "a free and easy approach to morals." He and Charles worked for a time as freelance artists and were characterized as intellectuals, "exceedingly left-wing," and allied to people of similar beliefs. One former neighbor described Paul as a socialist of the French school, "personified by the beliefs and teachings of Léon Blum."*

When the war broke out, Paul tried to get into intelligence work but claimed he was disqualified because of a partly blind left eye, the result of a boyhood accident. Then came a call from Washington that he might be of use to the government because of "certain abilities,"

---

* Blum was a leading figure in French literary circles, a Goethe scholar, a socialist agitator, and one of the heroic Vichy 80 who refused to recognize the authority of the Nazi-supported government of Marshal Philippe Pétain during World War II. He was three times prime minister of France.

which he later learned referred to judo, which he had been studying since the age of twelve. (He was a third-degree black belt.) Ultimately it was his talent as an artist that attracted the attention of the OSS, which hired him in 1943 to make situation maps, charts, and diagrams. While there were countless references from friends attesting to Paul's loyalty and integrity, describing him as a "solid citizen" and person of "high caliber," there were an equal number of reports expressing hesitancy about his brother, a painter, who was generally viewed as less stable, prone to sympathizing with the "underdog," and someone who could become receptive "to movements of a disloyal nature." Some of those interviewed maintained that Charles Child and his wealthy wife, Fredericka (Freddie), were "Communist sympathizers," although the record states there was "no actual proof" of any such activities.

Furthermore, Leslie Brady, Paul's superior at the American Embassy in Paris, while stating that he knew nothing derogatory about his moral character, indicated that he did not think he had "the proper temperament" to make a good public affairs officer with the USIA and considered him better suited to behind-the-scenes exhibit work. Brady explained that Paul found it difficult to deal with people who did not share his opinions, adding that Paul would become discouraged when he had to deal with foreign nationals who were not pro-American and "would make little attempt to influence these people to the American viewpoint." Brady described Paul as "moody" and "eccentric" and indicated that he thought he suffered from a "definite inferiority complex," apparently the result of having a twin brother who was a talented painter while he was "a frustrated artist."

As a result of lingering doubts about Paul's leanings, both political and sexual, it was recommended that his wife be investigated for anything of "a derogatory nature." According to her confidential file, Julia (or Julie, as she was known then) McWilliams was from a socially prominent Pasadena family, had attended school in California followed by Smith College in the East, and enjoyed an "excellent reputation." Her record was unblemished. Furthermore, she was known to be a close friend of the third Mrs. Harry Hopkins, formerly Mrs. Louise Macy, a fellow alumna of Smith College. Julia had been briefly employed at

Coast magazine in San Francisco, and in the advertising department of W. & J. Sloane in New York, before going to work as a file clerk for the Office of War Information in 1942. Her father, John McWilliams, recently remarried, was known to be a Republican, very active in civic affairs, and on the board of education. Overall, the family was considered to be "above reproach." A longtime neighbor testified that Julia; her sister, Dorothy; and their father were "as fine loyal Americans as possible." Investigators in Bonn turned up a coworker who reported that at times Julia could be more outspoken than her husband and had once referred to her father as a "Black Republican" and to members of her family as "stuffy middle class." The implication was that she felt her family had had "everything handed to them on a silver platter," had never done anything for themselves, and were therefore dull and uninteresting. However, the source did not consider her to be "left wing" and said he would classify her as a "Truman Democrat." As part of a routine "neighborhood check" in Paris, the concierge of the building where the Childs had rented an apartment was interviewed, and she reportedly stated that Paul and his wife appeared "devoted to each other and were always together." The concierge concluded by stating that she could furnish only favorable information about the couple.

Unfortunately, Paul's itinerant employment record, a long history of jumping from job to job, exacerbated the concerns about his character. It was, at the very least, suggestive of a troubled youth. One colleague in Bonn stated that Paul Child had once commented that he had "pretty much wasted his twenties" and only in his thirties had begun to settle down and apply himself. After dropping out of college, he had worked on the crews of freighters and tankers, picking up languages in the various ports of call. His linguistic skills led to teaching jobs, first as a tutor with a family in Asolo, north of Venice, and then at a boys' boarding school in France, in the Dordogne. The investigators could discover nothing about his life during this period. After returning to the United States, he worked briefly as an instructor in art and French at the Cranbrook School in Bloomfield Hills, Michigan. While there had been no complaints about him at Cranbrook, and he had been "highly regarded" at the Shady Hill School in Cambridge, Massachusetts, there had been "various instances" of questionable behavior at the Avon Old Farms School, an exclusive boys' academy in Connecticut. During his five-year tenure at Avon, Paul had instituted a photography club, provided nude photographic magazines as exhibits, and even endeavored to obtain a live nude model. Avon's dean had classified some of the photo exhibits as "obscene," and the magazine subscriptions had promptly been canceled. Paul Child's conduct, the dean reported, was "completely out of place" in a school for adolescent boys. Although he could not cite any particular manifestation of "homosexual tendencies," he stated that Paul had "these tendencies."

All of this material, some of it going back more than a decade, gave Sullivan and Sanders ample cause to press their case. They had to ask Paul about his homosexuality, they told him, no matter how embarrassing it might be for all involved. The "Kafkas" resumed their humiliating probe of the most private parts of his life, repeatedly reading something suspicious into his long bachelorhood. Just when he thought the two agents had exhausted the subject of his "homosexual tendencies," they commanded, without warning: "Drop your pants."

Paul just gaped at them. Was he supposed to prove his manhood with some sort of demonstration? He was so outraged, and so adamant in his denials—challenging the flustered agents to take down their own pants to see if it was possible to tell by "just looking"—that they finally let it go. In spite of this, a half hour later they asked unprompted if he had ever sought out psychiatric treatment. When he demanded to know "what in God's name that would prove," they said they thought that perhaps, long ago, he might have requested advice about "some little homosexual leanings."

Paul later wrote Julia that he had stood up to his interrogators and had assumed from the outset that the homosexual ploy—which he considered "fairly dirty"—was designed to unnerve him and compel a quick confession. He remembered that when their friend Charles E. "Chip" Bohlen was Eisenhower's ambassador-designate for the Soviet Union in 1953, McCarthy opposed his nomination, and when his attacks on Bohlen's performance at the Yalta Conference proved insufficient, he got the FBI to leak some suggestive stories raising doubt about

Bohlen's sexual persuasion. Bohlen was confirmed anyway. But to Paul, it showed that McCarthy and his henchmen viewed homosexuality, on their sliding scale of perversions, to be just a hair removed from Communism, and any such admission would have surely sealed his fate.

And so the questioning had continued, hour after hour. All the places he had lived. All the people he had known. All his colleagues since joining the OSS in 1942 and their names and addresses. There were more questions about his brother and sister-in-law: their interests and activities; the names of organizations they belonged to; the names of their friends and acquaintances. Questions about Julia's relations, etc., etc. His memory, not particularly good at this sort of detail in the best of times, occasionally faltered. Not that it mattered. He had nothing to hide. "They weren't brutal," he wrote Julia, "just very, very thorough." Their technique "was to take notes (in spite of the secretary), abandon a given subject for fifteen minutes, and then suddenly loop back and ask a question already asked, but in a different form."

Ironically, after having to defend himself against charges that he was sexually bent, he then had to convince them he had never bedded Jane Foster, despite the fact that she was an attractive woman—a high-spirited, golden-haired California girl who was reportedly one of the most memorable of the female OSS recruits to be flown into the Eastern theater during the war. Paul had spent an entire year in her company in Ceylon. Did he really expect them to believe that despite being billeted in the same barracks all that time he had never so much as made a pass at her? Paul patiently explained that while he and Jane were "very good friends," they had never been lovers. She was, in his words, a loose, warm, gregarious, and witty woman. Someone he found "fun to talk to." A "bold, free spirit" who was not regulated by traditions, the type of person "who might dine at six pm one evening and at eleven the next." He had escorted her to a number of dinner parties and dances on the post, and they had shared countless meals together, but that was as far as it went.

In the end, the two agents had just stood up, thanked him, and said goodbye. They were finished for the time being. They gave absolutely no indication whether they believed him or not. Their expressions gave nothing away. Paul, who had maintained his poise for most of the interrogation, finally lost it. He had had all he could take and gave full vent to his fury. The whole charade, he berated them, had been handled in an "amateurish" fashion. All the subterfuge had been for nothing because they had "left him dangling" without information for days, and as a result "practically everyone in the outfit was aware something was screwy." Bringing him back to Washington, he added bitterly, had been a pointless exercise, not to mention a fantastic waste of the government's time and money. Looking supremely unconcerned, the two agents replied that, far from being useless, the interview had proved "extraordinarily valuable," certainly worth the inconvenience and cost. With that, Paul was dismissed. It was 9:00 p.m. by the time he got back to his hotel and his letter to Julia. At the conclusion of his long, harrowing account, he had scribbled wearily, "The shape of the immediate future is—at the moment—totally unclear."

At first, Julia was unable to take it in. "Paul is being *investigated!*" she noted in her diary on April 13, the enormity of what was happening finally beginning to sink in. The very idea of a Special Inquiry was "inexplicably weird." Although it was utterly absurd that anyone could suspect her husband of being a Communist, she realized they could not afford to take the allegations lightly. Paul was afraid he might be in the "same position" as an old friend and colleague, Leonard Rennie, who was among a group of employees dismissed by the State Department as security risks. Paul had spent the weekend with the Rennies at their country home, and while their sympathy was well intended, it was of small comfort. They knew all too well the damage that even a hint of controversy could do, let alone a full-blown inquiry. He had been advised by a high-level USIS official by the name of Parker May to say nothing and wait. Patience would be in his "own interests." Meanwhile, he was not to engage in any real work, but to try his best to maintain the fiction that this was one of those run-of-the-mill "government mixups." If the FBI did not turn up anything incriminating, he would be given a clean bill of health and sent home.

Paul, of course, had no intention of keeping quiet. "As soon as he got out that first day, he went howling to everyone he knew," recalled

Julia, who had stayed up till dawn on Wednesday reviewing everything Paul had told her with a senior Foreign Service officer whom she knew they could trust. Between them, she and Paul knew a number of important people, and they both spent the next few days working the phones trying to find a way to remedy his situation.

Although Paul was confident he had acquitted himself well in the security interview and was still a "*persona grata*," he was not yet in the clear. He had been given notice that he could be reexamined at any time. He was not to leave town. The standard investigation lasted thirty days, and he had to sit tight until they were done. As a precaution of sorts, he asked Julia to make copies of his long account of his interrogation available to his two supervisors in the Bonn office. He wrote her daily. His affectionate letters, full of his usual chatty badinage about the poor food and soupy heat of Washington's Indian summer, belied his consuming doubt and anger. He cautioned her to postpone an upcoming trip to Paris in case she was needed in Washington at the last minute.

In one letter, he enclosed a *Washington Post and Times-Herald* article about the problems being caused by American postwar "hyper-patriotism," explaining that the extreme security procedures being put in place to safeguard against espionage were perceived by many leading lawyers and scientists as "harrying and constricting." The Washington attorney Harold Green, a former member of the Atomic Energy Commission's general counsel's office, also pointed to the government's "wobbly standards" in the present program: "Our criteria, for example, condemn the homosexual and pervert as security risks because of the risk of blackmail, but they are silent as to the married adulterer. We do not yet know who is the greater risk: the paragon of virtue who has a record of carelessness in locking classified material in his safe, or the chronic alcoholic who has a spotless record of security performance." Another story on the same page reported that the legality of the government loyalty-security hearings was facing a legal challenge in the Supreme Court because the proceedings "did not grant the accused the right to confront or cross-examine his accusers." At the top of each article, Paul scribbled "Julie! Julie!"

The waiting was agony, made worse by the fact that they were an ocean apart. She bombarded him with special delivery letters, telegrams, and telephone calls testifying to her unwavering love and support. "You are finer, better, more loveable, more attractive, deeper, nicer, nobler, cleverer, stronger and more wonderful [than other men]," she wrote. "I am so damned lucky even to know you, much less (or more) to be married to you." Privately, she felt fear bordering on panic. She was on pins and needles all the time. She was terribly worried about Paul's health. The FBI interrogation had been "a horrible experience for him." Every day he remained under suspicion was exacting a toll on him, emotionally and physically. He was having difficulty sleeping and was dependent on what he called his "goldfish"—tiny, brightly hued pills prescribed by a local doctor—for the little rest he got. His stomach, weakened by too many bouts of intestinal parasites contracted during the war, was in a dreadful state. She could not help thinking the worst. Paul could be fired or detained or dragged through endless months of loyalty hearings like some they knew. How was it that Jane Foster, of all people—smart, funny, talented Jane—had ended up on McCarthy's list of "Communists in the State Department"? Jane was a painter. She was not even employed by the government anymore. What, if anything, could she possibly have done to bring this calamity down on all their heads? The whole thing would have been laughable if it were not so terrifying.

On April 21, Paul was reinterviewed about Jane Foster, this time by one of USIS's own security officers. Paul again provided a detailed account of all his interactions with Jane while employed by the OSS in Ceylon, as well as every subsequent encounter. He again maintained that although the closest of friends they had never been romantically involved, and had kept up only an intermittent friendship. After the war, he had not laid eyes on Jane again until the spring of 1946, when he happened to run into her on the street in Georgetown and they stopped to have a brief conversation. That was the only contact he had had with her in the United States. He had next seen her in 1952, sometime after he had joined the staff of the embassy in Paris. At that time, he had met her husband, a Russian American named George Zlatovski. Over the next few years the two couples had occasionally met for dinner, though Paul estimated it was probably not more than ten times. He had last seen her and her husband in the fall of 1954, when they had spent a few hours visiting together. Neither she nor George seemed to be particularly interested in politics, nor had they ever expressed any interest in his government post or in USIS policies. They had never even given any indication that they were sympathetic with the Communist Party. No, he had never heard any gossip to the effect that they were Communists or Communist sympathizers. No, he had never seen any Communist literature lying around their apartment in Paris. Paul observed dryly that he had always thought Jane was "too disorganized to become interested in any organization."

The only question that gave him pause was the last one: Would he recommend Jane Foster Zlatovski as a loyal American who could be trusted with confidential information? Paul considered this for moment. He felt boxed in by the loaded nature of the question. He wanted to be honest without being incriminating. He had "no reason to question her loyalty," he ventured, adding somewhat hesitantly that he did not think he could trust her absolutely. When pressed, he explained that Jane was "a glib talker" and "somewhat irresponsible." As much as he hated to say anything against her, he would not trust her with confidential information because of her "indiscreetness."

At all times during his questioning, Paul tried to be perfectly frank, and to show by his attitude that he had nothing to be ashamed of or to conceal. He felt "untainted," he wrote Julia that weekend, because he was "completely cleared and completely blameless." Still, he could not let it go. The whole business ate away at him, poisoning his gut. "I'm afraid I hate the system," he agonized, wondering if he would ever again feel in control of his career, let alone his life. "What the Hell are they investigating Foster for, anyway? Or was that really a dodge to investigate me? Damned if I know." What he wanted, above all, was an explanation that made some sense of the whole thing, that would tell him what had gone wrong, so he would know how to go on from there. How else was he to avoid the pitfalls ahead? And protect Julia, himself, and his career from further harm? But clearly no such enlightenment would be forthcoming. He was on his own.

Paul had cooperated fully. He had told them everything he knew, which amounted to precious little at the end of the day. When he finished, he requested that a written clearance be placed in his permanent record. When informed that it would take time to process his clearance because of the thirty-day requirement for Special Inquiries, he went straight to the head of the USIS Office of Security and demanded that the rule be waived. He was advised that it would be wiser to wait and stick to protocol "so it wouldn't look strange." Paul assured the security chief that it could not possibly look any stranger than it already did. He also told him that if they kept him in Washington another month with nothing to do, then "by God everybody and his mother would know what was going on."

As soon as he received a copy of his clearance, Paul wired Julia: IN-VESTIGATION CONCLUDED SUCCESSFULLY FOR ME. He told friends he believed he had "weathered the storm." He was "almost a virgin," he wrote Julia, "a monument of innocence." No apology was forthcoming, nor did he expect one. Perhaps to make it up to him, the powers that be had decided to send him to Brussels so that he could pick out the site for the American exhibition in the upcoming 1958 World's Fair. It was a minor perk, given what they had put him through, but it was nonetheless a token of their esteem and Paul appreciated it. On April 26, he wrote Julia of his Brussels assignment, fairly crowing with triumph. Furthermore, he had applied for, and received, permission to fly back via Paris. If everything went according to plan, he would meet her there at the end of the month. At which time, he added, "I shall allow myself to be congratulated by a thoroughly prejudiced woman of my acquaintance."

As far as Julia and Paul were concerned, that put an end to the Jane Foster affair. They had no way of knowing then that it was far from over.

2
INITIATION

"Look, just what kind of organization *is* this?" Jane Foster was standing in the fingerprint room of the OSS's Washington headquarters, wiping her hands on an ink-stained towel. It was the fall of 1943, and the secretive new agency was only months old. She readily proffered the towel along with a conspiratorial we're-in-this-together smile that seemed to invite indiscretion. Her question hung in the air, the slightly mocking twinkle in her blue eyes daring anyone to answer. She was a slim, stylish blonde, her expensively tailored suit a cut above the boxy tweeds sported by the serious, efficient young women who typically populated Washington's wartime agencies. With a furtive glance back at the OSS personnel officer in charge of taking their prints, she confided in a low voice that it was her "first day, too," and then proceeded to pry all kinds of information out of Elizabeth "Betty" MacDonald, another fresh recruit, who had only just been warned not to discuss her new job with anyone.

"That was Jane," recalled Betty years later, with a shrug. "We weren't supposed to be talking, so of course we did. She had a great sense of humor, and was a bit irreverent. Well, more than a bit. Especially when

it came to anything to do with military protocol. She was always saluting the wrong people, or not saluting anyone at all. I liked her straight-
away. Everyone did."

Jane had the Irish knack for instant intimacy. Her vitality and
charisma drew people in, and before they knew it she had involved
them in some compromising situation or mischief of her own making.
Betty recognized her at once as "an unreconstructed rebel," attributing
both her charm and obstinacy to her Celtic blood. Jane was the classic
Catholic schoolgirl gone off the rails. An air of naughtiness clung to
her like an exotic scent. Everything about her was fresh and provocative, from the way she walked, talked, and dressed—a careless elegance
that together with her mussed curls always gave the impression of a late
night—to the way she picked a teasing fight with every man she met.

She impressed Paul Child, who was introduced to her at a party in
Washington earlier that fall, as "a wild, messy girl, always in trouble, always gay and irresponsible." Her spontaneity was part of her appeal, an
excess of energy and exuberance saved from the debutante cliché only
by her intelligence. From the nuns, she had learned to be deceivingly
modest. Conscious of always being the center of attention, she would
deflect it with a stream of wry, funny, self-deprecating stories that only
confirmed that she was the most fascinating person in the room. She
never stopped talking, making sly, hilarious observations about people
and then, as if to prove her point, dashing off devastating little cartoons
of them on whatever was handy, from a scrap of paper to the corner of a
tablecloth. Her caricatures were disconcerting. She would fix someone
with her baby blue eyes, and the subject would feel pinned to the wall—
pierced— exposed for all to see with a flick of her pencil. It was all part
of the performance: she liked to flaunt her cleverness. Boredom was the
only unpardonable sin. Avoiding it made her adventurous. And drove
her to extremes. Her snobbery was reserved for the dull or predictable.
She brought a heady air of playfulness to the most prosaic of gatherings, whether it was the morning staff meeting or the line at the lunch
counter. Her attitude always seemed to be "As long as we're here, we
might as well *enjoy* it. And anyway, it's never too early for champagne!"

She was impossible to resist. When Jane leaned in confidentially,

Betty found herself revealing more than she had intended. Jane quickly got her to divulge that she had been recruited by "whispered overtures," through a third party, who had expressed interest in her background. Betty had grown up in Hawaii, the daughter of two journalists, and just happened to be "on the spot" when a really big story came along on December 7, 1941. Her father was a veteran newspaperman named William "Bill" Peet, a sports editor with *The Honolulu Advertiser,* and her mother had been a columnist in Washington, D.C., prior to becoming an English teacher. A tawny, hazel-eyed brunette, with the lean athletic frame of an avid tennis player, Betty had worked her way up to society editor at the rival paper, *The Honolulu Star-Bulletin,* and had recently begun stringing for the Scripps Howard syndicate, writing feature stories about local events. The Sunday morning the Japanese bombed Pearl Harbor, she was still in bed. Her husband, Alex MacDonald, a police reporter, was barely awake and nursing a hangover. It was shortly after eight o'clock, and they were drowsily listening to the Mormon Tabernacle Choir on the radio when a voice broke in and announced: "This is not a drill. Pearl Harbor is under attack. This is not a drill." The news flash was quickly confirmed by a call from a local photographer, who told Betty he was heading out to check on the damage. As she and Alex hurriedly dressed, they heard the rumble of bombs and guns coming from Oahu's southern coast.

She told of driving fast toward Hickam Field, the largest army airfield in Hawaii. She could remember registering the lush green countryside flying past, the people strolling to church or out walking their dogs, when a bend in the road suddenly revealed the first signs of carnage. An open-air market had taken a direct hit. The horrifying tableau would stay with her always: flames and smoke pouring from the ruined shop stalls, the Hickam Field firemen pulling out the injured, and the badly burned bodies of the dead and wounded scattered all over the ground. A small girl stood dazed, still clutching a jump rope; all that remained were the charred ends in her hands. She died a short time later. What was weird, Betty recalled, was that in the middle of all the chaos there was a little boy sitting in a pile of Christmas presents, boxes and rolls of wrapping paper all around him, having what looked like a wonderful time. Her photographer, camera at the ready, yelled at her "to do something about the kid." The child's incongruous smiling mug was ruining the shot. On impulse, she leaned down and gave the boy a quick pinch, which started him crying. The poignant photo ended up running in *Life* magazine.

That was the beginning of her war. Betty was immediately assigned as a volunteer at a field hospital, where she saw the worst of the human toll—"terrible, terrible things." Her husband, who had been in the Navy Reserve, was in uniform by the end of the week. It was a frightening time. No one knew what was going to happen next. There were wild rumors the Japanese would be coming by sea. Then they heard that an invasion force might be coming in over the mountains. Betty helped string barbed wire along the sunny beach in Waikiki to keep them out. Martial law was declared. There were an immediate blackout and complete censorship. She had not been able to get a story out for weeks. Ironically, at the time of the attack she and her husband had been living at the home of a Japanese professor, Saburo Watanabe, and studying the Japanese language with the idea of going to the Far East as foreign correspondents. But instead of their going to Japan, Betty noted, "the Japanese came to us." As soon as things calmed down a bit, she started filing stories from America's first war zone.

Impressed with her work, Scripps Howard offered her a job in Washington covering Eleanor Roosevelt and the White House, and writing a weekly column called "Homefront Forecasts." Could she start right away? Betty was thrilled. This was the national press corps—the big leagues. At the same time, it meant leaving home and her husband. Sensing how much she wanted the job, Alex gamely agreed that it was too good an opportunity to pass up. He had accepted a commission from the Office of Naval Intelligence (ONI) and might be called up at a moment's notice and "sent off somewhere." Odds were, the war was going to separate them one way or another. Betty took the job, and a week later she left for Washington.

To her dismay, Betty found life in the capital pretty tame compared to wartime Hawaii. During an interview with a prominent Honolulu businessman, who was at a Department of Agriculture event she was covering for the paper, she admitted to being bored with the humdrum stories about food shortages and rationing. They got to talking about where they were on the day of infamy, and she told him about reporting on the aftermath of the devastating attack. When she mentioned in passing that she had been studying Japanese, he suddenly stiffened and his whole attitude changed. He demanded to know whether she had "ever considered working for the government." Would she like to make "a great contribution to the war effort"? When she nodded in the affirmative, he fumbled in his briefcase and brought out three government forms. Pressing them on her, he urged her to complete the paperwork and send it in at once. Muttering apologetically that he was not able to say more, he hastily departed.

Several weeks later, Betty was recruited by the OSS. All she was told in the initial interview was that because she had some Japanese she could be of help to them in their work in the Far East. Specifically what that work would entail, however, they were not willing to reveal. The only thing they could say with any certainty was that she would be going overseas. Betty told Jane this was the first time in her experience that an employer "hadn't described the kind of job [she] was being hired to do." That had started her wondering exactly what kind of organization it was, too. From the moment she entered the building on Twenty-third and E that brisk December morning, everyone had been very formal and closemouthed. Given that she needed to be issued a special pass to get in, she guessed it was not just another New Deal alphabet agency but was perhaps "something like the Pentagon."

Jane snorted, then shot a cautious glance at the fingerprint matron to make sure her outburst had gone unnoticed. She refrained from commenting on Betty's account of her "accidental" recruitment, but her eyes were bright with amusement. She arched her eyebrows theatrically, silently acknowledging what they both already knew: this mysterious crew had to be a secret service organization of one stripe or another. Jane was enjoying herself. She got a kick out of the shadowy agency's quasi-military methods and aura of clandestinity. The experience seemed comparable to an extremely elaborate sorority initiation, although she could not possibly imagine what they were looking for in the way of new pledges. She was terrible at following orders. She insisted she had to be one of the least likely, least disciplined females in all of Washington to mobilize for war. Jane proceeded to explain rather flippantly that she had been working at the Netherlands East Indies desk at the Board of Economic Warfare (BEW) when the OSS came calling that fall. She had immediately quit her job and joined up, "overcome by a great curiosity to find out how her knowledge of the Malayan language, her art training in France, Germany, and New York, and her four years in Java could change the Allied war effort in the Far East."

Jane was all breezy unconcern and coy asides, but underneath there was a confidence born of money and education. She was the only child of a wealthy San Francisco family, and, in spite of her travels and bohemian pretensions, it showed. Her father, Harry Emerson Foster, was a pillar of the community, a distinguished physician who was for forty years the medical director of Cutter Laboratories in Berkeley. Her mother, Eve Cody Foster, was a pampered fashion plate who found the demands of everyday life taxing, was frequently incapacitated by migraines, and depended on a phalanx of maids, cooks, and assorted servants to cope. After losing her devoted Chinese houseboy, Ming, to immigration authorities early in the war, she decided to give up any claim to domesticity, put all her antiques in storage, and moved into the Fairmont Hotel. Jane admitted to having been "outrageously" indulged as a child. She attended convent schools, supplemented by dancing classes, art classes, and horseback-riding lessons. Only the art took. She attended Mills College, where San Francisco's well-to-do sent their daughters, though her mother always maintained that too much education only "caused trouble"—which, in her case, Jane noted in a memoir, "was probably right."

Eager to break away from her doting parents, Jane took off for a grand tour of Europe immediately after graduation, with the announced intention of staying on afterward to "study painting in Paris." She sailed for the Continent in June 1935, with a gorgeous new I. Magnin wardrobe provided by her mother and a generous allowance of one hundred dollars a month from her father. Together with a small inheritance from her grandfather, it meant she could do pretty much as she pleased.

With typical bad timing, she picked that moment to go to Germany. Berlin was "silent and nobody laughed. Everyone looked worried and frightened and had reason to be." But she had an invitation to stay with a college friend, a German student named Anne-Marie, who had since married, as it turned out, an SS colonel. At first, Jane had found him and his officer friends, decked out at dinner each night in their full Nazi regalia, ghoulishly fascinating. As the weeks went by, however, she was increasingly appalled by their racist comments. Alarmed by the black-booted soldiers goose-stepping down the Kurfürstendamm, she cut her visit short. She and a girlfriend signed up for a ten-day Intourist tour of the Moscow Theatre Festival and hopped a train bound for Russia. They feasted on "three kinds of caviar for breakfast," saw plays morning, noon and night, and thought it was wonderful. Moscow was very dirty and poor, but at least people did not have the "wide-eyed haunted look" she had come to recognize in the streets of Berlin. Realizing that she could not remain in Nazi Germany—after an argument about Hitler, Anne-Marie's husband had hit her and locked her out of the house—Jane went to Paris and enrolled in art school.

Paris was heaven. It was everything she had hoped it would be and more, and she cursed herself for not having gone there directly. She stayed at the Cité Internationale Universitaire, Fondation des États-Unis, and studied under the French painter and sculptor André Lhote. Of course, it was impossible to escape the Nazi threat. In early 1936, Hitler marched into the demilitarized Rhineland in defiance of the Versailles Treaty. The French began to mobilize. Filled with sadness, Jane sailed home in May and resumed her art studies at Mills's summer school.

Still chafing at the familial bonds, Jane chose the time-honored route of romance to flee the nest. At a reception at the Institute of Pacific Relations, a foreign policy council favored by the local business and political elite, she met a handsome Dutch diplomat eight years her senior named Leendert "Leo" Kamper. Jane promptly fell in love, though, as she ruefully told Betty, it was unclear if it was with the strapping six-foot-two-inch Leo or some "romantic idea" of life in the exotic

Dutch East Indies. When his six-month leave was up, Leo returned to Java, and they made plans to meet in a few months' time and marry.

In October 1936, at the age of twenty-four, Jane sailed for Shanghai. A friend from convent school, Mary Minton, was married to an American naval officer stationed in China and had agreed to accompany Jane from China to Java. After several weeks on a small freighter in Southeast Asia, the two woman made their way to the port of Batavia, in Java. After a chaste betrothal period of three weeks (Leo's idea, not hers), Jane and he exchanged rings in Singapore and celebrated with a lovely lunch at the Raffles Hotel. Jane was not in Batavia long before it became apparent that she had made a mistake. She was not a good match for her conventional Dutch husband, nor did she fit in with conservative colonial Dutch society. She scandalized the neighbors by fraternizing with the natives, learning their language, and objecting to the harsh treatment of household servants. Homesick and unhappy, Jane returned to America after only eighteen months. Her excuse was an invitation from the San Francisco Museum of Modern Art to attend an exhibition of her paintings, but both she and Leo knew the marriage was over.

The divorce was tricky. In those days, both parties had to remain in Dutch territory for five months until the decree was final, so Jane decided to sit out her sentence in a popular artists' colony in Bali. She took a room by the beach, painted, and enjoyed the idle, sybaritic life of the other rich expatriates on the island. The enclave was a fantasy of freedom and a refuge for utopian romantics, aristocratic homosexuals, nudists, discontents, and runaway neurotics of all kinds. Most drank themselves into a stupor every night, and the small band of Anglo settlers earned a reputation for sexual promiscuity and low morals. Jane thought it was paradise—or at least everything the narrow-minded, stifling colonial Dutch outpost in Java was not. Five months quickly became nine, and she would probably have never left had the British not declared war on the Third Reich in September 1939. At her father's insistence, she once again headed home.

When her boat docked in San Francisco, her frantic parents were there to meet her. Once they had her safely back in their embrace, they were not about to let go. They expressed pride in the successful exhibition of her paintings but adamantly opposed her attempt to take a studio in the city. Taking a job was out of the question. Jane went back to school, beginning work on a postgraduate thesis on Java at the University of California. She found living at home suffocating, however, and it was not long before she felt reduced to being a child again, asking permission to go out for the evening. "My mother did not mind my going to the ends of the earth," Jane observed sardonically, adding that what she could not bear was any show of independence on her own turf.

When Jane heard that her friend Mary Minton was also back living with her parents (her husband had been transferred to Greenland), she got in touch and the two captives planned their escape together. In the winter of 1941, they moved to New York. A few months later, Mary went to Washington, and shortly afterward Jane followed. She scraped by doing freelance artwork until a friend from Java arranged for a job with the Library of Congress representing the Netherlands Information Office of the Dutch government in exile. She and her colleagues accumulated a vast amount of information on the customs and socioeconomic life of Indonesia but did relatively little with it. In time, the entire department was taken over by the Board of Economic Warfare and she became a newly minted economic expert (the war created a lot of overnight experts) and was expected to crank out analytical reports. She was put in a section called Reoccupation and Rehabilitation of Liberated Territories, where she wrote reports on such pressing issues as rice production in Indonesia and cheese production in Greece. When the OSS whispered in her ear, she, too, jumped at the chance to go overseas.

All this Jane sketched briefly between the fingerprinting and the swearing in. At the security office, where they had reported as directed, a grizzled second lieutenant, seated behind a large desk and sucking an unlit cigar, intoned, "You girls please raise your right hands and solemnly swear . . ." A large wartime propaganda poster of a huge pink ear hung on the wall behind him warning: "The Enemy Is Listening." They promised never to reveal what went on in the name of the OSS.

With that duty out of the way, the second lieutenant launched into a canned lecture on the need for constant vigilance. They were not to tell anyone, not even family or loved ones, where they worked or what they did. The security officer was very dramatic and to Betty sounded like he was reenacting something from the movies: there were enemy agents everywhere, you never knew who might be listening, one slip of the tongue could cost a dozen lives. "OSS is an undercover organization authorized by the Joint Chiefs of Staff," he continued. "We are anonymous. If people ask you what you do here, tell 'em you are file clerks. People aren't interested in file clerks—not enough to ask questions." He looked them over with distaste, as if pegging them as bad risks from the outset, and then dismissed them with one last weary exhortation: "Girls, for my sake, see if you can't set a good example."

They were both assigned to Morale Operations—the propaganda branch. The OSS initially comprised three branches: Special Operations (SO), the sabotage branch, which covered everything from blowing things up to carrying out irregular warfare in Axis territory; Secret Intelligence (SI), which dealt with espionage, i.e., infiltrating enemy lines and obtaining information; and Research and Analysis (R & A), which developed intelligence studies for operational groups and devised new methods of spying. As the organization grew in size and scope, other departments were appended, including Counterintelligence (X-2). Morale Operations (MO) was created in January 1943, and by March was ready for action.

Betty and Jane were told to report to their new CO at once, but, as they quickly discovered, this was more easily said than done. The first room they were sent to turned out to be an empty suite of offices that had been stripped of everything save for the telephone wires dangling from the walls. A passing workman explained that this was par for the course. The place was in a constant state of upheaval, and offices were always being moved from the Q Building to the M Building, and then moved again the next month. Staffers were always packing and repacking. Because the storerooms were also constantly being relocated, they took everything that was not nailed down. As Betty and Jane soon discovered, in the short time since its birth the wartime agency had ballooned in size to become a vast organization, filling five large office buildings that from the outside resembled ramshackle plywood sheds and were connected by a maze of stairs, passageways, and underground tunnels. The sprawling operation was scattered across a steep hill between the Naval Hospital and an old abandoned brewery, which explained the tantalizing aroma that wafted down the hallways. Q Building, where MO had recently been relocated, was at the foot of Foggy Bottom.

While they searched in vain for the MO offices over the next hour, wandering down long corridors lined with offices identified only by number and trudging past the Administration Building, where Colonel William J. Donovan had set up his command post, they compared notes. Between the two of them, they tried to form a picture of the organization that had plucked them from their safe but boring civilian jobs. They needed to know what they had gotten themselves into. Their new boss, the dashing Colonel Donovan, had received a great deal of flattering attention in the press. He was a much-decorated hero of World War I, holder of the Medal of Honor, millionaire Wall Street lawyer, and personal friend of President Franklin D. Roosevelt. "Wild Bill," as the newspapers had dubbed him, was a handsome bull of a man in his late fifties, with a swaggering self-confidence and intense personal magnetism that had helped propel his career. A great admirer of the British Secret Intelligence Service (MI6), he had spent time in England studying its organization and methods, and he managed to convince FDR that America, which had little expertise in espionage, would benefit from having the same kind of agency in the event of war. This led to the creation of the Coordinator of Information (COI), just five months before Pearl Harbor. Then, after eleven months of bureaucratic squabbling that was petty and protracted even by Washington standards, some of COI's functions were folded into the Office of War Information (OWI), and the OSS was formally established under the Joint Chiefs of Staff in June 1942. Donovan's ambitious plans for the OSS were doggedly opposed by OWI chief Elmer Davis and Foreign Information Service director Robert Sherwood, and it took a presidential executive order in March 1943 to clarify that OWI would be responsible for "white," or official, propaganda, leaving OSS nominally in charge of "black" propaganda.

Much of this had been outlined during Betty's and Jane's indoctrination early that morning. The OSS was authorized to collect and analyze strategic intelligence, and to plan and operate overseas. Their work would be used to support actual military operations and planned campaigns, as well as in the furtherance of guerilla activities behind enemy lines. They would be focused primarily on gathering pertinent information about enemy countries—everything from the character and strength of the armed forces and troop morale to internal economic organization, principal channels of supply, and relationship to allies. Their main job would be to collect intelligence, either directly or through various government agencies at home and abroad, and transmit it to the proper authorities. They had been assured that the heavy lifting—organizing guerilla resistance, arranging secret air drops, sabotage of enemy installations, and other forms of irregular warfare— would be left to those naturally inclined to and specifically trained for hazardous duty. This was fortunate, Betty wrote in an account of her wartime adventures, as they were both terrified "at the very thought of jumping out of an airplane."

It was widely known that the OSS was made up of a great many members of Donovan's high-powered firm, Donovan, Leisure, Newton & Irvine, along with what Jane termed "a large proportion of socialites," meaning Smith girls with gumption who could also type. There was also a wide variety of PhDs—everything from psychologists, anthropologists, linguists, and mathematicians to ornithologists—as well as an assortment of creative types, including artists, writers, journalists, inventors, and advertising men. Donovan had a penchant for hiring from the Ivy League and the Junior League, on the grounds that the well-off were harder to bribe, and a reputation for poaching talent wherever he could find it. He was "hardly beloved" by people in other government agencies because he was always raiding them for personnel, which was why Jane had taken the precaution of resigning from the BEW before jumping to Donovan's agency. The result was that the OSS had legions of critics, particularly among the old-timers, who were jealous of its power—Donovan reported directly to the president—and unlimited funds. They regularly derided his staff as a bunch of dreamers and bluebloods, and, as Jane put it, "sneeringly said that the initials stood for 'Oh So Secret' or for 'Oh So Social.'"

Just when Betty and Jane were about to give up and admit they were lost, they stumbled across the large, drafty room that housed the newly formed Far Eastern section of Morale Operations. Their CO, Major Herbert F. Little, was busy securing a large map of Manchuria to the wall, and he regarded them curiously from his perch atop the stool. A tall, balding man with a bemused expression, he was a British-born lawyer from Seattle who had traveled extensively in Asia in civilian life. Adding that they did not stand on ceremony at the OSS, he welcomed them informally by their first names and thereafter usually referred to them as "the girls." All women in the OSS were "girls," regardless of their age, rank, or responsibilities.

The major showed them to their desks amid a jumble of office furniture. He then led the way past a plywood partition to a small inner office, really just a step up from a cardboard box, where he proceeded to unlock a safe and remove a much-thumbed mimeographed document. Entitled "MO Manual, Revised," it was the handiwork of members of the original European Branch of MO, who had set down on paper the unorthodox means of warfare they had learned the hard way, largely from the German war machine that had applied them so effectively in the early drive into France. During the blitzkrieg, Nazi agents had softened the way for the advancing army by spreading false rumors—often in the form of forged leaflets and faked underground newspapers—proclaiming widespread German victories and forecasting the imminent collapse of England. It was a method of "sapping morale," they were told, an ancient practice that dated back to the sappers who breached fortress walls in medieval times, and "when done right was more effective than any modern weapon of war." The major then instructed Jane and Betty to familiarize themselves with the manual's contents and left for lunch.

The manual was their introduction to "morale operations," the art of influencing the enemy by means of psychological warfare, or PW. (Acronyms, they soon learned, were an integral part of the OSS mystique.) It dealt primarily with "black propaganda," which consisted of subtle lies, indirect rumor, and misinformation designed to deceive the enemy and its collaborators in occupied territories. As the MO bible stated:

> Morale operations include all measures of subversion, other than physical, used to create confusion and division, and to undermine the morale and the political unity of the enemy through any means from within, or purporting to emanate within, enemy countries; or from bases within areas where action and counteraction may be effective against the enemy.

MO operators, by means of black propaganda, could come up with countless possible ways to confound the enemy. They were constrained only by the limits of their imagination and any vestigial sense of decency. The standard methods included making contact with resistance groups, underground operations, and field agents, and employing them to spread rumors designed to have a demoralizing effect; or initiating the rumors themselves, spreading them via radio stations purporting to belong to the enemy, or putting out pamphlets ostensibly coming from within the enemy's own ranks. More cunning methods included creating exact reproductions of Japanese propaganda handouts and posters but tweaked ever so slightly to be damaging to, say, Indonesian attitudes or sensibilities. They could also play upon the enemy's emotions with deceptive reports of a discontented home front or wavering military leadership, or with exaggerated reports of U.S. intentions and capabilities. All this was laid out in the manual, along with the instruction that MO operators should carefully guard their anonymity at all times, should carry no evidence (in the form of documents or letters) that would reveal their true identity, and should always opt for civvies in favor of their uniform. As far as Betty and Jane could tell from their brief perusal of the MO handbook, almost any form of thoroughly amoral activity was condoned when it came to manipulating one's foe. The only thing that was absolutely forbidden, Betty noted, was to "blow cover."

They had just digested the section on "the preparation of incriminating documents" when their CO returned armed with a half-dozen telephones. Major Little proceeded to give them a crash course in MO work, embracing his subject with the benign enthusiasm of a dentist explaining the latest techniques in molar extraction. One way to disrupt Japanese relations with a puppet country like China, for example, would be to plant evidence of treason. "Our black radio net could send out 'compromise' code messages," he began, and then cheerfully elaborated all the different kinds of deceptive information that could be planted from this single scam. "We'd hint about puppet defection . . . Tell the Chinese the Japs are going to raze their city in the event of an attack. Tell the Japs their puppet troops are planning to revolt." Accustomed by now to a skeptical audience, he emphasized that all these ideas, even the most outlandish, were based on concrete intelligence reports. In the end, everything they came up with was run by a board of hardheaded experts—Harvard and Yale scholars, Naval Intelligence specialists, and State Department consultants—who signed off on the various projects before they were put into effect. If even one out of twenty wild schemes really worked, he maintained, "it saved lives." This was the MO mantra, repeated over and over again with the fervor of prayer: "If it worked, it saved lives."

Once he completed the mandatory lecture, Major Little introduced them to their fellow recruits, adding, by way of warning, "It takes all kinds to make an MO team." "It was an extraordinary cast of characters to be sure," Betty recalled, "rare, strange personalities selected at grabbag random from all corners of the world, for many reasons." A list of those she met that first day included "a Chinese artist, a Thai missionary, a newspaper reporter, a Shanghai businessman, a private detective, the producer of the Lucky Strike Hit Parade, a girl graduate from Hunter with a degree in international law, an Olympic broad-jump champion, a lawyer from New York, a dog fancier, a renegade American in British navy uniform who was also a black-belt holder in jujitsu, a traveling patent medicine salesman, and a Japanese-American who had fought with . . . Donovan and the Rainbow Division in World War I."

While Betty was busy getting acquainted with their new colleagues, Jane was summoned to Room 23 at 2:00 p.m. for a different kind of initiation. When she walked into the room, she found twenty or so officers seated around a long table. In the center of the table there was a large pile of weapons, only some of which she could identify: "pistols, machine guns, hand grenades, limpets, and other horrors." A young lieutenant, seated at the end of the table, began to disassemble a weapon, explain its function, and pass the parts around the table for closer inspection. Jane "understood nothing," but as the only woman present she was determined to keep up a brave front and "kept nodding merrily and murmuring, 'Very interesting, indeed.'"

As soon as the roundtable briefing ended, they were herded into a fleet of cars and driven to the plush Congressional Country Club, which the OSS had obtained permission to use as proving ground. It was time for a little target practice. Since she was a woman, Jane was issued a .32-caliber pistol and told to get acquainted with it. She was shown the difference between British hand grenades, which had long handles, and American ones, which were round as a baseball and theoretically easier to throw. "The first thing the lieutenant did was to throw me a live grenade," Jane recalled. She threw it right back at him and then made it perfectly clear she was "not having any part of the rest of the demonstration."

The minute they returned to Q Building, Jane sought out Major Little. "I did not join the OSS to handle lethal weapons I will never be able to use," she told him hotly, adding, "I'm resigning." When she had calmed down, the major explained that the small-arms session was "standard operating procedure" for new recruits and using a gun would not be a part of her regular job. Although it was small consolation, she learned that Betty had been allowed to skip the introductory course as, like many civilians in Hawaii, she had learned how to shoot in the months after the Pearl Harbor attack. The major also informed Jane that there were more "field trips" to come. The next day, she was slated to undergo three days of tests at Station S, the OSS's secret assessment station, in an undisclosed location. From guarded comments about S school in the corridors, Jane gathered it was a kind of mental-fitness clinic pioneered by the British War Office Selection Board, which staged similar examinations at country estates all over England in an effort to screen officer candidates from the pool of eligible young men. Persuading herself it would be a kind of fancy country weekend, Jane packed some of her most fashionable clothes to boost her confidence. She reasoned that she would be much less likely to crack under pressure in her favorite skirt, and a flash of leg might help distract the prying shrinks from what was really going on in her subconscious.

When the army weapons carrier, packed with twenty strapping young men in fatigues, pulled up in front of her little apartment on Second Street, Jane almost lost her nerve. It was with considerable relief that she recognized Betty, the only other woman on board, and she barely managed to repress an absurd show of warmth. They had been told in advance to use assumed names and not to "break cover," so she tried her best to avert her gaze. For most of the journey, she and Betty observed a nervous silence and gleaned little about their fellow guinea pigs except that they were destined to be parachutists.

They were driven to a charming old colonial mansion somewhere in Virginia, situated in the midst of a 118-acre estate that they later learned had once belonged to the Willard Hotel family in Washington. They had no time to enjoy their surroundings, however, as waiting for them on the portico steps were their chief instructors, both psychologists by trade. They were formally greeted by Dr. Henry A. Murray, director of the Harvard Psychological Clinic, and Dr. Richard S. Lyman, a professor of neuropsychiatry at Duke University. These two distinguished doctors, along with a team of graduate students, would be putting them through their paces with a rigorous series of tests specifically designed to evaluate OSS recruits' fitness for clandestine operations. The instructors wasted no time getting down to business, immediately explaining the daily routine, assigning rooms, and handing out schedules. Their days would start at 6:00 a.m. with breakfast; testing would commence at 7:00 a.m. sharp and continue until dinner.

The business of using pseudonyms presented Betty and Jane with problems right from the start. They were told the staff knew their true identities and had seen their files so that during the tests they could comfortably be themselves. The rest of the time, however, they were supposed to stick to their "student" names and the fake background stories they had rehearsed before arriving. The problem was, Jane had not expected Betty to be on the same course and for the sake of convenience had selected her name as a pseudonym and the cover story that she was a newspaper reporter. For Betty, this switch proved to be an insurmountable "mental hazard," and she constantly broke cover by responding whenever her name was called. For some reason, she could never remember to remain in character as "Myrtle," the ridiculous student identity she had adopted, and by the end of the course she had grown to loathe the name.

Over the next few days, they were given every conceivable test in an effort to chart their personality attributes: emotional stability, social relations, integrity, initiative, and leadership. There were some thirty-two different exams, beginning with the standard IQ and Rorschach tests, followed by Dr. Murray's own tricky little invention, the Thematic Apperception Test (TAT), a picture-interpretation exercise in which the subject is handed a series of provocative yet ambiguous images and asked to furnish his or her own interpretation, with the idea that telling one's own version of the story will draw out hidden thoughts and experiences. Jane naturally balked at this. As a trained artist, she lectured the doctor, she was not an appropriate subject for the TAT because, to begin with, she recognized all the pictures and could identify the artists who had painted them. "Besides," she later recalled arguing heatedly, "such subjects were not meant to tell stories. Painting was painting. Literature was literature. One art doesn't interpret another. A picture emphasizes visual qualities!" Finally, Dr. Murray was forced to give in. A compromise was worked out, and Jane's psyche was probed with five illustrations hastily clipped from a back issue of *Cosmopolitan*.

The recruits were also subjected to a series of "live" situation tests designed to evaluate everything from their observation skills to their leadership ability. For example, in one exercise they were told to search a room, then asked to evaluate the occupant based on his belongings. Betty, despite her best efforts, could not summon an image of the missing man from just "a half-consumed pint of bourbon, railroad ticket stubs from Cambridge, a suit from Brooks Brothers, neatly darned socks, and a copy of *Harper's*." In another scenario, they were given what Jane thought looked like an "erector set" composed of four poles and a number of planks; with two sergeants under their command, they were told they had fifteen minutes to build a shelter. Jane immediately begun issuing orders to her two sergeants, who either ignored her or willfully obstructed her at every turn. "After ten minutes, in utter frustration," Jane recalled, she picked up a pole and "started beating them with it." There were also physical tests. One afternoon, they were taken to a small stream on the grounds, pointed toward a knotted rope hanging from a tree, and told to swing themselves across the water. At that point, Jane rebelled. Shaking her blond head, she sat down on the bank and refused to move. Next they were instructed to climb the tree and remove some small cans, which purportedly contained explosives. Jane refused to budge. She announced that she was done. She was fully prepared to chalk up her short-lived OSS career as one of her many "brilliant failures."

The most disturbing aspect of the course was their assignment to compile as much information about the real identities of their fellow students as possible. "It was permissible to ferret out anything we could about our confreres," Betty recalled. "We could break and enter their rooms, listen at keyholes, question them at meals. At the end of our course we would be asked to evaluate one another in a confidential report to the faculty." Assigned to the same quarters, "a charming little colonial bedroom furnished with incongruous army cots," Betty and Jane immediately broke the S-school rule against fraternization and pooled their meager information. They were both so affronted by the idea that their male counterparts, segregated on the top floor, might attempt to snoop around their quarters that they considered "leaving Kilroy messages pinned to their dainties." The real measure of their naïveté, recalled Betty, was that when awakened later that night "by what sounded like an explosion, followed by a scream," they thought nothing of it. Jane sleepily dismissed the disturbance as a blowout, adding, with a yawn, "You'd probably scream, too, if *your* last good tire went blooie." It was a humbling morning for both roommates when they were informed that the blast was a demolition charge that had been set off in a nearby field to gauge their acuity. Their humiliation was complete when it was further revealed that their bedrooms had been wired for sound and all their whispered confidences recorded.

At the end of the third and last day there was a "graduation night" party. Some of the masterminds of the torture course came from OSS headquarters in Washington to help them celebrate. Among them was a very brilliant, very tall English anthropologist named Gregory Bateson, who was married to the even more eminent anthropologist Margaret Mead; their presence impressed all the recruits no end. Cases of liquor were brought out for the occasion, and they were told to help themselves to the generous supply of gin, whiskey, and bourbon. The free booze, it turned out, was a last test. "The idea," Jane learned later, "was to get the students drunk and see how they would react." If the intention was to loosen their tongues, the experiment proved a complete flop. The handsome parachutists all went straight to bed, and the only ones who stayed up and got drunk were the psychologists, accompanied by Betty and Jane. Needless to say, their covers slipped under the influence of alcohol. In the end, Betty reckoned they probably came through "slightly above par," since they ended up late that night making sandwiches for everyone, including "the staff, students, and lads on KP who joined the party."

When all the course work was finished, the recruits were given their final scores. Betty and Jane discovered they had done surprisingly well on some tests—Jane earned the highest marks for her ability to evaluate people—and very badly on others. The only other woman in the course, who went by the name "Annette," was the sole student to recognize the midnight explosion for what it was and to inquire about it the next day. (They later learned she was a member of the French Resistance; shortly after the course wrapped she was dropped behind enemy lines in Belgium.) Jane was certain the only thing they could have learned conclusively about her personality was that she was a "neurotic intellectual" and completely unsuited to the role of femme fatale, which she could have told them in the first place. Betty admitted to feeling rather deflated, having been informed by an instructor that she was an "open-face-sandwich" type and not Mata Hari material. They had not exactly covered themselves in glory, and on the ride back to town they could not help worrying that the psychologists' findings had been carefully noted in their files and would adversely affect their future wartime assignments.

It was relief to return to the relatively sane world of Q Building. After a few weeks, they started to get more of a feel for the OSS. For a large government bureaucracy, the place was conspicuously clubby, complete with nicknames and backslapping camaraderie. Anyone who showed up more than a few days in a row was hailed like an old fraternity brother. They decided the trick to sounding like a seasoned hand was to master the local lingo, which was easier said than done. To their untrained ears, OSS-speak sounded like a foreign language. As far as Betty could tell, the trick was to pepper your speech with as many obscure references and codes as possible, with the result that you were virtually unintelligible.

The OSS offices fairly hummed with a barely repressed sense of seriousness and self-importance, which was reinforced by the urgent clatter of the Teletype and the pressing business of the brass, who were usually flanked by aides. There was always the worry that Donovan would honor them with one of his "surprise inspections." The colonel was a commanding presence whether he was dressed in a Savile Row suit or in his starched army uniform, and for Betty and Jane these visits were always fraught, as they were never entirely clear on the rules for comportment for civilian recruits—"whether to salute or stand with hand over heart or sit quietly like a lady." Betty usually became so flustered she forgot even to shake hands.

They gradually mastered the layout of the MO building, but invariably got lost when venturing into one of the other branches. Once or twice they accidentally wandered into a restricted area and wound up being stopped by a guard and sent back where they came from. A wrong turn at the bottom of a stairwell or at the end of one of the long, badly lit corridors left you in uncharted territory. Hurrying to a meeting, Jane blundered into an office with walls covered in enormous maps, where she recognized Paul Child, who was leading a group of designers engaged in the most extraordinary work. One woman was making a series of meticulous drawings showing how to load, arm, and place a railroad booby trap. Another was sketching a series of demonstrations on how to detonate a petroleum arson bomb. A third was painting a series of wash drawings showing how to use an automatic searchlight buoy for shipwrecked sailors. Another three were clustered around a huge illustration of a bomb fuze-head. The far wall was covered with brightly colored diagrams and breakdown charts for combined night bomber operations for the United States Army Air Forces (USAAF) and the Royal Air Force (RAF). No one took any notice of her. Afraid she was on the verge of committing another security violation, Jane backed wordlessly out of the room.

In spite of all the secrecy attached to the work that went on—there were all sorts of signs on walls and desks reminding them to secure safes, file classified papers, lock doors, etc.—there was an ivory-tower unreality to it all. It had the lenient, idiosyncratic atmosphere of a small college, with the same tolerance for campus radicals, zealots, and oddballs. The OSS, for all its selectivity, embraced right-wing conservatives and Communists alike, as well as what appeared to Jane to be a disproportionate number of Irish Catholics. Every conceivable language echoed in the hallways. To find an adequate number of linguists, the agency recruited from strange corners of civilian life: missionaries were sought after for their language skills, specialized knowledge of remote regions, and network of personal contacts; explorers because they had traveled extensively and were self-reliant; exporters, traders, and journalists because they were men of initiative who felt comfortable in foreign environments.

The simple fact was that the OSS did not begin recruiting until after all the other services had had their pick of the field, so Donovan had been forced to scramble to find men and women with the very specific skill set the job required: the brains to solve problems on the fly, the street smarts to know when to lose the rule book, an underdeveloped sense of fear, and unlimited self-confidence. Of course, this same combination of qualities could be used to describe any number of dangerous crackpots, and critics charged that Donovan stocked his agency with some decidedly dubious characters in search of power and a draft deferment. There were even stories that the organization had brought in some "specialists" who would give any normal employer pause. "Safecrackers, criminals, people in jail—Donovan would hire anyone if he thought it would give us a leg up," according to Dan Pinck, who left college for the OSS at the age of nineteen and volunteered to serve behind enemy lines in China. "Why not, if we could use their skills?" Donovan, in Pinck's opinion, had only one goal—to defeat the enemy. Nothing stood in the colonel's way. He was not accountable to Congress; so as long as he had Roosevelt's support, "he could get away with it." Jane, who made no secret of her leftist leanings—including a brief flirtation with "Cadillac Communism" in her college days—and love of lost causes, fully embraced the OSS's maverick, eggheaded eccentricity as her own, declaring it "a weird and wonderful organization."

As the second anniversary of Pearl Harbor approached and found them still anchored to their desks, Betty and Jane could not help feeling mildly demoralized. When they inquired about their overseas assignments, no one seemed to know anything about anything. It was hard for them to believe, tucked away in their cubbyholes fifteen thousand miles from the nearest Japanese outpost, that the entire Washington organization was dedicated to dispatching agents by sea or air as quickly as possible. The bureaucracy seemed so large and cumbersome, with so many different OSS sections churning out ideas and strategies, and so many people tripping over one another with incoming and outgoing orders, all in support of a few teams, that Betty could not help thinking of it as an "elephant laboring to produce a field mouse."

For the rest of that fall, they struggled against the bureaucratic fatigue and cynicism endemic to government agencies, and continued their tutelage in the fundamentals of psychological warfare. Jane was assigned to the Southeast Asia sector and Betty to a cluster of desks that made up the Japan group. They immersed themselves in learning the "blackest of black" MO methods used in the European theater and spent untold hours analyzing the precise problems in deploying these methods against the Japanese, who were culturally very different and would require very different inducements to surrender. The MO staff included a nisei (second-generation Japanese American) named Tokie Slocum, who served as their resident expert, responsible for con-

juring up the mind of the typical Japanese soldier and assessing what
strategies would be most effective in playing on his emotions and superstitions and undermining his morale. To help produce MO material that targeted the enemy's weaknesses, they also studied transcripts
of prisoner-of-war interrogations from Burma and the Southwest Pacific, where General Douglas MacArthur's sea and ground forces had
had some success pushing back the Japanese. They concluded that the
main problem in waging thought warfare against Japan was cracking
through the "fanatical indoctrination" the Japanese received as both
soldiers and citizens.

"From a pathetically small amount of intelligence dealing with his
ideology and morale," wrote Betty in a wartime memoir, "we learned
that the Jap believed as doggedly in the doctrine of the Greater East
Asia Co-Prosperity Sphere as we did in the Atlantic Charter. He believed that Japan was engaged in a life-and-death struggle, and that the
armies of the emperor were champions of the downtrodden Oriental
countries which, until now, had been exploited by Western Civiliza-
tion." The Greater East Asia Co-Prosperity Sphere, announced in August 1940, embodied Japan's imperial ambition to create a self-sufficient
"bloc of Asian nations"—comprising Japan, Manchukuo and China,
and parts of Southeast Asia—led by the Japanese and free of Western
powers. The main impetus behind the policy was Japan's need for raw
materials—oil, rubber, tin, steel—to feed its war machine in face of the
U.S. embargo and to guarantee its access to new markets and new lands
for expansion. As a form of wartime propaganda, it appealed to the
Pacific nations' nationalist resentment of colonial rule and softened the
way for Japan's invading forces.

Japan had already been at war with China for more than six years,
occupying the richest provinces from Manchuria to the Yunnan border
in the south; defeating Singapore, Britain's fortress in the East; driving
the Dutch and French out of Indonesia; and in April 1942 chasing the
British out of Burma. The army under the British commander-in-chief
in the Far East, Field Marshal Archibald Percival Wavell, was defeated
and in disarray. The British troops reportedly believed the Japanese
to be invincible. As the American commander of Chinese troops in

Burma, General Joseph Stilwell was so disgusted with the British that he refused to fight alongside them on the grounds they were committed to a policy of inactivity. One of the few bright spots was the success of Major General Orde Wingate's long-range penetration units, which had proved that British Indian, Gurkha, and Burmese troops could penetrate Japanese lines and mount guerilla resistance.

All in all, it was a pretty dismal picture. Psychological warfare, the MO trainees were told, was one of the few ways to reach the people in these occupied territories and to counter the propaganda being sent out by Tokyo. "The Japs, we know, have been telling these people that, under the new Greater East Asia Co-Prosperity Sphere, they've attained independence," explained Major Little, "that they'll never again be under the British, or Dutch, or French. They've told them that the Atlantic Charter principles are empty words. They've told them that Asia is for Asiatics. Now—what can we tell them?" The problem was that the Americans could not simply counter with their own promise of freedom, because the British, Dutch, and French were still dreaming about returning to the "good old days" before the war. In Burma, for example, the "Greater East Asia Co-Prosperity Sphere" line was going down a damn sight better than their European allies' plea to the native peoples to protect the property they had left behind when they fled the advancing Japanese. So, until America and its allies were all on the same page in terms of political warfare, Little explained, they would have to continue to make the Japanese the sole target of all of their countersubversion.

One method that had proved effective against the Germans in Europe was "black radio," which involved creating stations supposedly manned by discontented rebels broadcasting from within Japanese-occupied territory and created the impression of resistance where there was none. This could be achieved either by jamming the Japanese signal or by using "ghost voices" to ruin an important enemy broadcast by creating static on the same wavelength. Even more devious were so-called slanted newscasts, slipped in so close to the enemy signal as to be confused with the genuine program but containing the slightest change in tone or emphasis, the ironic pause or well-placed snicker.

These subtle jabs could be directed at the lower echelon of the Japanese army or navy, where war weariness had set in and inefficiency and graft were rampant, or against home-front officials, cowardly bureaucrats, and black marketeers. This MO deception, when married to white propaganda, could be especially powerful, explained Jan, a courtly German American who was one of the last remaining members of the European MO branch. He went on, presumably by way of encouragement, to observe how "admirably adapted this technique" was to the feminine mind: "Who knows better than a woman how to use the poison darts of slander—the razor-edged rumor? Break a man with the twist of a phrase!"

Betty took offense at his suggestion that this was a talent all women had "inherited from Eve." She still had a reporter's instinctive suspicion of the high-pressure salesman and recoiled at what she saw as the same "cheap" advertising tactics used to foist products on impressionable minds. She also could not help wondering how well this form of propaganda, packed with hidden lies and verbal trip mines, would work against the Japanese. If the research she had seen was to believed, they were dealing with people who were "exasperated with a Marx Brothers comedy and went into gales of laughter when Clark Gable kissed his leading lady." Did MO really have any sound idea of what kind of subversive campaign would slow down a force of Japanese soldiers? Such soldiers had proved more than capable of using their own black propaganda when they led a banzai charge on Guadalcanal yelling "Down with Babe Ruth!"

After devoting two months to mastering the basics of MO work, Betty and Jane were eager to prove themselves ready to launch their own rumor campaigns against the Japanese. They had dutifully applied themselves to their studies; they had absorbed the contents of stacks of background papers. They had been introduced to some of the strangest characters and most harebrained schemes imaginable. The looniest proposal was for a "snake call," a small device that made a strangled *shhhhh* sound that was supposed to convince Japanese soldiers that they were surrounded by snakes, which—to judge by folklore—inspired inordinate fear and would theoretically cause panic, confusion, and surrender. This idea was proposed with utter seriousness by an elegantly suited older gentleman by the name of Mr. Earp, who waved an ivory cigarette holder about as he spoke, had logged time in the Orient, and claimed rare insight into the enemy. He wanted to put the gadgets, which he said could be bought at any sporting goods store for $4.50, into the hands of all Wingate's Raiders to blow as they "crept up on the Jap positions." With that, Betty recalled, he picked up one of the small black tubes and, puckering his lips, produced "a singularly unimpressive sound." Despite being relative novices, she was sure she and Jane could come up with something better for their boys than a whistle.

The same Mr. Earp was later responsible for one of the more embarrassing episodes in OSS history. He apparently did extensive research on Japanese superstitions and, citing old *Inari* fables that told of fox spirits with transformational powers and werewolf attributes, came up with the idea of inducing the Japanese to surrender by playing on their purported fear of foxes. His scheme called for American submarines to surface off the coast of Burma and put ashore thousands of foxes, which would then fan out along the beaches, scaring the Japanese out of their dugouts and sending them running for the hills. Earp must have been very persuasive, because Donovan, General Hugh A. Drum, and a handful of State Department officials agreed to observe a demonstration off Long Island Sound. Huddled on a barge and shivering in the predawn December fog, the dignitaries watched as the cage doors were opened and the animals, which had been dipped in phosphorous to make them easier to track, were dropped into the water. Despite Earp's assurances that the foxes would instinctively head for shore, they promptly swam out toward the Atlantic and disappeared without a trace. "The professor may have been an expert on Japanese superstitions," Jane noted, "but he was the class dunce on zoology." A furious Donovan called off the fox project, but it lived on, if only at bibulous OSS gatherings.*

---

* After the war, the fox project was cited in *The New York Times* as an example of the OSS's wartime ingenuity.

A chance remark over lunch a few weeks later convinced Jane and Betty that they had accidentally hit on their own formula for undermining the Japanese. They had been waiting in line at the OSS cafeteria when Jane, who always kept them amused with tales of her misadventures in Bali, told a funny story about a legendary "love curry" prepared by Indonesian women who wanted to exact revenge on their cheating men. According to Jane, wronged Indonesian women rendered their mouthwatering curries fatal by adding tiny, indissoluble hairs taken from the base of the bamboo plant. Some hours after a hearty meal, the tiny hairs would begin to work their way through the intestinal walls, causing hemorrhage and condemning the faithless lovers to certain death. When she finished describing the poisonous concoction, she grinned and added puckishly, "Why not revive it for MO?"

Betty agreed it was an ingenious method of dispatching the enemy. Together they spent the next hour plotting a "bamboo death" campaign. The deadly side effects of the curry could be presented to Japanese soldiers in Indonesia, Burma, and Thailand in the form of medical leaflets, purportedly issued by their own military high command. The plan, as outlined by Betty, called for exploiting the Japanese soldier's doubts about the food with further leaflets, which would "cast suspicion on native eating houses" and describe the symptoms of poisoning "in a general way that would lead him to believe that simple dysentery and indigestion were the beginnings of hemorrhages." As a crowning touch, Jane would use her artistic talents to do a series of medical drawings demonstrating "simple sabotage of the digestive tract, tracing the course of the deadly splinters into and through the colon walls with fluoroscopic clarity."

For the sake of realism, Jane announced they would need to pay a visit to Washington's Botanic Garden. She needed to get close to some bamboo plants in order to make sketches and take a few samples. While Jane gathered up sketch pads and pencils, Betty borrowed a large kitchen knife from the cafeteria and stowed it uncertainly in her purse. Happily, they discovered that the Botanic Garden was not busy on weekday afternoons, and they found no one in the sultry greenhouse that was home to rows of palms, tree ferns, potted orchids, and bamboo plants. Crawling on all fours, they began searching the base of the bamboo stalks for the tiny deadly barbs, but many of the plants were so old that when they peeled back the brown sheaths they found nothing but dust. Finally, they located a green shoot. Jane passed Betty the knife, and she began to scrape some splinters from the stalk. "We were flat on our stomachs in mulch and dry bamboo leaves," Betty recalled, "when we heard a distinct cough."

"Lost something?" The guard's steely tone, devoid of inflection, made it more of a statement than a question. Jane met his accusing stare and murmured something about "a school project," her blue eyes all innocence. It took some fast talking on her part—a barely plausible yarn about their being art students completing an assignment—to secure their freedom. The guard eyed them coldly, confiscated the kitchen knife, and escorted them off the premises. They returned to Q Building and never said a word to anyone about the ignominious end of their first jungle expedition.

3

LATE START

By Christmas 1943, rumors had begun swirling that a number of OSS personnel were headed to overseas posts. There was a buzz of excitement as staffers gathered in the corridors to exchange scraps of information. The word was that they were recruiting people for "five major rear echelon bases": New Delhi, Calcutta, Colombo, Chungking, and Kunming. The assignments were supposed to be a secret, but that did not keep the rumor mill from providing regular updates. Paul Child got a telephone call Christmas Day telling him to pack up and get himself on a plane to New Delhi, where he was to be the OSS representative on the staff of Admiral Lord Louis Mountbatten. He complained that the call was so sudden, coming just after he had forked up a "stomach-full of turkey," that it gave him a bad case of indigestion. He was also heard to grumble that because of the lasting influence of the British Raj on India, he was going to have to drop a small fortune at "Brooks Brothers in America" before he left.

Mountbatten was the name on everyone's lips. At the Quebec Conference that August, Roosevelt had met with Prime Minister Sir Winston Churchill to hammer out the details of their grand strategy against Germany and Japan. After hearing from their war chiefs, the two leaders agreed it was to time to step up operations in the Far East in order to cut Japanese supply lines, destroy their communications, and secure forward bases from which the Japanese mainland could be attacked. Field Marshal Wavell, both leaders agreed, was finished. What was needed was a new commander and a new combined operation. Roosevelt offered to let Churchill name one of his own as head of the new South East Asia Command (SEAC), and after some negotiation Mountbatten was named supreme commander and General Stilwell his deputy. During the meeting, it was also agreed that China would not be part of Mountbatten's mandate and would remain part of America's strategic responsibility. To safeguard China's interests, Stilwell would do double duty as chief of staff to Generalissimo Chiang Kai-shek and commander of Chinese troops in Burma and in Assam, India.

When Mountbatten visited Washington after the conference, he was greeted by a flurry of fawning press, who described the forty-three-year-old "boy" admiral—the youngest in the history of the Royal Navy—as a handsome, glamorous figure. Not everyone in the War Department was happy about the appointment, however, and P. J. Grigg, the British secretary of state for war, made no secret of the fact that he viewed Mountbatten as a rich playboy and not up to the job. The conservative Patterson newspapers, including the *Chicago Tribune* and *Washington Post and Times-Herald*, attacked "Dickie" Mountbatten as "a princeling" and were busy propagating alarmist rumors that the selection of the royal over the homegrown hero General MacArthur was another example of how Roosevelt regularly caved in to pressure from the British. The widespread skepticism toward Mountbatten, and his mission to reconquer all of the Crown's former territories—Burma, Malaya, the Dutch East Indies, and beyond—in a late-in-the-day effort to shore up the lost empire, led some OSS veterans to joke that SEAC (pronounced "See-Ack") stood for "Save England's Asian Colonies."

Over the next few months, Betty and Jane made it their business to learn as much as possible about the newly formed Southeast Asia theater, where their MO activities would be targeted. It was a "rather confused situation," as Jane put it, because while Mountbatten's SEAC command comprised all the territories that had once been British colonies, the Americans belonged to the CBI (China-Burma-India) theater of operations, informally known as "Confused Bastards in China." The CBI included China, while Mountbatten's Southeast Asia command did not. Go figure. Thus far, the CBI had been "the Cinderella of the war," its orphaned status reflected in the muddled state of affairs there. Militarily speaking, the CBI counted for little in the war. The big guns were Admiral Chester W. Nimitz's command in the Central Pacific and General Douglas MacArthur's in the Southwest Pacific. Stilwell's operation got the short end of the stick when it came to modern weapons and supplies. Stilwell earned plaudits from the press for his "fortitude in the face of adversity" and was routinely ignored by Washington. He was reputed to be a first-rate commander, but he was an aggressive, testy old professional soldier—having more than earned his nickname "Vinegar Joe"—and was consumed with hatred not only for the nation's enemies but also for some of its imperial allies, namely Britain and China, which he had been appointed to serve. He had nothing but scorn for Chiang Kai-shek, whom he regarded as an arrogant, unteachable Chinese overlord, and had an almost equal aversion for Mountbatten and his greedy colonial ambitions. As a result, Stilwell's command was riddled with feuds and bitter divides, and he was perennially rumored to be about to be replaced. From a political point of view, though, the CBI was "the most important," in Jane's estimation. Certainly it was where the greatest postwar changes would occur, which was the reason Donovan was so determined to establish an OSS foothold in the region.

The situation in India was especially complicated for the OSS because of the rivalry between British and American clandestine warfare organizations. Theoretically, they were all part of a unified command, but in the past Stilwell's and Wavell's operations had been "suspicious of—in fact, almost hostile to—each other," in the words of Albert C. Wedemeyer, the American general Mountbatten chose as his deputy chief of staff in New Delhi. It had gotten to the point where British authorities refused to have any working relationship with the OSS. The head of British intelligence there had reportedly told Donovan in no uncertain terms that the "door to India was closed" to the OSS, to which Donovan had replied, in his inimitable fashion, "Then we'll slip in through the transom." He got his chance with Mountbatten, who had pledged to foster Anglo-American cooperation and who took an interest in clandestine warfare. Donovan turned his not inconsiderable charm on the new supreme Allied commander and succeeded in getting his foot in the door to India. The story was that Donovan had won favor with Lord Louis by demonstrating his ability "to obtain New York theater tickets, to procure Cadillac automobiles, and/or to provide the services of Hollywood's John Ford to record SEAC's anticipated successes on film." The upshot was that Mountbatten consented to host a new OSS base in his theater. He would retain "full operational control" over the unit, though it would not lose its American organization or be integrated with a British unit. While the details were being negotiated, OSS personnel were marking time in Washington waiting for the "big show" to begin.

There were "other complications," as Jane put it, having to do with the growing professional rivalry between generals. The OSS was allowed to operate in Sumatra but not the rest of Indonesia—although it did so surreptitiously—because the bulk of the archipelago was under the command of MacArthur, who loathed Donovan "with a monumental hatred." The antagonism between the two was so deep that MacArthur had even sworn to court-martial any OSS member caught operating in what he considered his exclusive territory. Rumor had it that the feud had its roots in the fact that Donovan had won the Congressional Medal of Honor during the World War I, for capturing a German machine-gun nest single-handed, while MacArthur had been twice nominated for the award and twice denied, in the early days of World War II, probably because of the lasting controversy caused by his use of excessive force in dispersing the destitute veterans who had gathered for the Bonus March on Washington in the worst days of the Depression. His reputation was not helped any, according to Jane, when he left Corregidor in the Philippines for Australia but insisted on running the battle long distance, which resulted in commander Lieutenant General Jonathan "Skinny" Wainwright and his troops being captured by the Japanese. MacArthur meanwhile landed safely in Melbourne, taking with him on the PT-41 "his wife, his child, two Chinese amahs, and several trunks of personal belongings." While he eventually got the medal for his defense of the Philippines, it did nothing to lessen his antipathy for the much-decorated Donovan.

The situation in China, which America jealously guarded in the same way Britain did India, was even more of a tangled mess. The War Department had committed itself to a policy of "keeping China in the War" and providing the Chungking government, with Chiang Kai-shek as its president, with a major portion of lend-lease supplies. The OSS was officially committed to working with Chiang Kai-shek, but it was not clear which enemy the Generalissimo was more committed to fighting—the Japanese invaders who had laid waste to his country for seven years or his Communist compatriots in the north. As a result, the head of the Chinese secret service, General Tai Li—an infamous character who, legend had it, was "a blend of Himmler and the once-popular movie villain, The Insidious Doctor Fu Manchu"— was not exactly rolling out the welcome mat. Donovan had given Tai Li pretty much the same warning he had given Mountbatten, to the effect that the OSS would be coming in one way or another. But backing up that bluff was another matter. "We must take orders from the Chinese," Major Little told Betty, "and they are not too happy to have us snooping around behind the lines, possibly uncovering certain things about Communist and central government relations that would prove embarrassing." Frustrated by the separate, and at times incompatible, agendas that were holding up OSS operations, the major conceded that the waiting was hard on everyone. All he could do was ask that they "have faith." Progress was being made, and people would soon be shipping out.

He told Betty that they planned to send a small unit to Burma, where Colonel Carl F. Eifler had managed to establish an OSS base— Detachment 101—in Assam, on the northern border of the country. Eifler's outfit had already developed an effective field operation and was producing vital intelligence for Stilwell's north Burma campaigns. The 101 was also working with the British army staging counterattacks against the Japanese occupying forces, and training a guerilla band, the Kachin Rangers, to sabotage Japanese lines of communication and supply dumps. Major Little would be among the first to go, tasked with trying to smooth the way for MO in China. He was taking their MO colleague Charles Fenn, a thirty-six-year-old former Associated Press war correspondent who had covered the fighting in Burma and who would be sent into French Indochina to launch rumor campaigns against the Japanese. Tokie Slocum was leaving with another group to help organize and train the first contingent of Japanese interpreters, writers, and technicians going to India.

It was impossible not to be envious of the dear departing. Hungry for any news of MO personnel movement, Betty and Jane took to monitoring two listening posts—the 10:00 a.m. coffee line at the cafeteria and the ladies' washroom—both of which functioned as gossip clearinghouses in the Washington headquarters. By lingering in either of these two key locations, it was possible to pick up all kinds of extraneous bits of information. Most of the scuttlebutt tended to focus on the latest activities of the Hollywood director John Ford, head of the Field Photographic Unit, as well as other famous personalities who were moonlighting for the OSS. There were regular sightings of the actor Sterling Hayden in the building, usually at lunch with another VIP. And everyone, it seemed, had a Marlene Dietrich story. While gossip was strictly against the rules, it was inevitable, Betty observed, that with so much emphasis on responsibility and security the employees would find some way to release all the pent-up pressure. The occasional shared tidbit was their only vice. Jane put it best when she said that the OSS reminded her of a Quaker meeting she had attended where everyone was "bursting to blab."

Of all the chatty young stenographers, secretaries, and file clerks they befriended, their favorite was the immensely tall, exceptionally lively Julia McWilliams, even though she had what Betty termed a "highly developed security sixth sense" and never let anything slip. Julia, they both agreed, was the sort of "sensible, high-minded" woman who could be counted on to keep mum about the reports that crossed her desk. She worked in the Registry, a special office that functioned as the OSS "brain bank," the repository of all manner of highly classified information. She revealed little about her job, but Betty subsequently discovered that she held the keys to the OSS secrets that enemy spies would most like to get their hands on: "the distilled reports from the Research and Analysis branch; the real names of agents operating behind the lines; itemized amounts of expenditure for agent work, payoffs, and organization of undergrounds; locations of OSS detachments around the world, and implemented plans of operations of all branches bearing the Joint Chiefs of Staff stamp of approval." Julia always downplayed her position, admitting only that she had developed a "top-secret twitch" from handling so much sensitive material.

In the coffee line they learned that Julia was equally desperate to go abroad. Unlike Betty and Jane, Julia had never had the chance to travel outside the United States, with the exception of an afternoon jaunt over the border to Tijuana. At thirty-one, she was older than most of the other OSS girls and had been working toward her goal of "high adventure" since the war began. She was from an affluent, conservative California family much like Jane's, and her life after graduating from Smith in 1934 was filled with that pleasant whirl of social activities—golf outings, ski weekends, country club soirees, and balls—that is supposed to lead to a wedding. Julia, however, obstinately avoided marriage to the boy next door, Harrison Chandler, a wealthy heir to the Times Mirror publishing fortune, who was as handsome and decent as he was boring. She held on to the dream that something bigger lay in store for her, later admitting that her height might have given her an exaggerated sense of her own destiny.

Dreaming of a glittering literary life as a "lady novelist," she moved to Manhattan with two fellow Smithies in hopes of getting her start but never managed to interest *The New Yorker* in any of the reviews or short human-interest pieces she submitted. After a failed romance and faltering resolve, Julia returned to Pasadena and to what she termed her "social butterfly" years. An ill-fated stint as an advertising copywriter at the Beverly Hills branch of W. & J. Sloane—she was fired after only a few months—put paid to her ambitions for a high-flying career. Devastated by her mother's death at the age of sixty, Julia resigned herself to keeping house for her father and playing the part of dutiful daughter. She still dabbled in writing, penning plays for the Junior League and a monthly fashion column for a small California magazine called *Coast*, bankrolled by family friends, but it had become an occupation rather than a calling.

The war gave Julia a second chance to make something of her life. From an early age, a strong sense of civic duty had been drummed into her by her father, a major landowner committed to California's prosperous future, and she was immediately caught up in the patriotic frenzy that seized the country after Pearl Harbor. Everyone was being called to action—even women. Here was the opportunity to make a real contribution. She volunteered for the Aircraft Warning Service in her hometown of Pasadena, and then for the local arm of the American Red Cross. Determined to do more, she took the civil service exam. When all her married friends headed to Washington with their husbands, who had commissions waiting for them, Julia tagged along. She made up her mind to enlist. Tall, robust, and athletic, she judged herself to be exactly the right type for the Army or Navy Reserve. She was crushed when first the WACs (Women's Army Corps) and then the WAVES (Women Accepted for Volunteer Emergency Service) rejected her. The official explanation, according to the checked box on the standardized application form, was a "physical disqualification." While she joked that at six foot two she was apparently "too long" to serve her country, her unfailing good humor masked her deep disappointment.

By August 1942, she had settled for a job at the Office of War Information, arranged for her through family connections. At first the idea of working in the wartime capital seemed incredibly glamorous and exciting, and compensated in a small way for the fact that she was employed as a typist for Noble Cathcart, her cousin Harriet's husband. Bored stiff by the job at "Mellot's Madhouse," named for its maniacally hard-driving director, she persevered, furiously typing her way through ten thousand file cards in a two-month period out of sheer frustration. She told friends she would keep on hammering away, hoping her drudgery would be rewarded. She interviewed for a job at the OSS and made a "good impression," according to the unnamed officer, who described her as "pleasant, alert, capable, very tall." Four months later, her reputation for hard work won her a place on Donovan's staff as a junior research assistant. After she started, she often heard it said that the colonel's idea of the ideal OSS girl was "a cross between a Smith graduate, a Powers model, and a Katie Gibbs secretary." Julia could not help thinking that if she had only known that earlier, she could have saved herself a lot of trouble.

She was not in Donovan's office long before she got her first taste of the OSS's idea of "research," an elastically conceived job that covered hundreds of strange and esoteric occupations. Julia was loaned out for a year to the OSS's Emergency Sea Rescue Equipment Section, which she dubbed the "fish-squeezing unit" because of the series of stinky experiments they were running in an effort to develop a shark repellant to protect fliers downed at sea. The brainchild of Harvard zoologist Harold Jefferson Coolidge, a blue-blooded descendant of Thomas Jefferson, the Information Exchange of the Emergency Rescue Equipment Section (ERE), despite its more far-fetched investigations, managed to come up with some useful ideas for agent paraphernalia. (It helped speed the development of signal mirrors and exposure suits for floundering pilots.) Happy to be liberated from her typewriter, Julia threw herself into the inventive work of designing rescue kits, rising at the crack of dawn for her drive to the fish market to pick up the "fresh catch" for their tests.

For the first time in her life, Julia found a place where she fit in. Far from being a curiosity in her flat men's loafers and leopard coat, she had precisely the kind of social background and sophistication OSS recruiters looked for, along with a private income (from her mother's inheritance) that made her above reproach. Her height gave her an air of natural authority that, along with her ringing voice, helped her hold her own when dealing with her military colleagues. Always something of a tomboy, she impressed Lieutenant Commander Earl F. Hiscock of the Coast Guard Reserve—which eventually took over the unit—with her down-to-earth attitude, once turning over a wastebasket to serve as a chair in an impromptu meeting to discuss the frequent sinking of merchant vessels ferrying supplies to Europe. "Julia was a woman of extraordinary personality," recalled Jack Moore, an army private she met while in the rescue unit, who worked for Paul Child's graphics department. "She was not any kind of an American stereotype. By virtue of necessity—I mean, here is this six-foot-two-inch-tall American woman looking down on all the males she ever meets—she had to evolve a sense of herself that was different from the person who is a physically standard specimen."

In the fall of 1943, Julia returned to Donovan's staff and quickly progressed up the office ladder. In December she was promoted to administrative assistant in the Registry, supervising forty clerical assistants, typists, and stenographers. While she had worked her way to a position of greater responsibility, she was still no closer to her goal of active service. Unlike Betty and Jane, she had come into the OSS as "a plain person," and had "no talents" and no languages that would recommend her for an overseas position. Just when she began to fear she would spend the war as a glorified file clerk in Washington, she heard through the rumor mill that Donovan was looking for bodies to help organize and run the new OSS bases in India. Julia immediately volunteered. "The idea of going to the Far East appealed to me very much," she recalled. "The only way I could go was to go over in the files again, so I said, 'Well, I'll do the files again,' even though I had finally gotten out of them for a better position."

A few weeks later, she was handed a folder with her mimeographed travel orders for India. She was scheduled to leave on February 26, on a troop train out of Newport News, Virginia, for a weeklong cross-country trip to Wilmington, California, their port of embarkation. She would be accompanied by two OSS colleagues: Dr. Cora DuBois, a distinguished forty-year-old anthropologist, with the face and bearing to match, who would be heading up the Research and Analysis Division; and Eleanor "Ellie" Thirty, an eager twenty-two-year-old secretary. A petite, dark-haired beauty with wide-set eyes, Ellie had left the family farm in Rock Creek, Minnesota, to join the thousands of other young women who flocked to Washington after Pearl Harbor to work in the wartime agencies. Despite her youth, Ellie was surprisingly independent and resourceful. Against strict orders, she decided to keep a detailed diary of her overseas tour of duty with the OSS, writing in her own custom shorthand to safeguard its contents. She began by noting

that she, Julia, and Cora made for an incongruous traveling party—
they varied so greatly in size and age that they attracted amused stares
from the soldiers packing the train.

By her own admission, Ellie had "never been anywhere," and she
was thrilled when Julia offered to take her home to Pasadena for a few
days of sightseeing in California before they left the country. When the
trio reached Wilmington, they were joined by six other OSS women:
Virginia "Peachy" Durand, Rosamond "Rosie" Frame, Jeanne Taylor,
Virginia Pryor, Louise Banville, and Mary Nelson Lee. The women underwent a week of orientation, which consisted of training films, lec-
tures, and "boat drills"—so that if they ever had to abandon ship they
would not think twice about going over the side, via ropes—and farewell parties in town every night that left them absolutely exhausted. On
March 8, 1944, to the jaunty sound of band music, they boarded the
SS *Mariposa*, an elegant luxury liner that had been used to run tourists
from California to Hawaii before being requisitioned as a troopship,
and set sail for India. "We presented a picture beyond description," Ellie
wrote, referring to the ridiculous amount of military gear they were
expected to wear or strap to their bodies, everything from fatigues, gas
mask kits, and musette bags to steel helmets, "which, I must say, on
one's head, are the latest thing in chic!"*

The nine OSS women—"crows" in GI slang—were "a source of curiosity" on the tight ship with more than three thousand men, Thiry
noted in her diary. "We are also occasionally the object of wolf calls
and whistles. Julia launched a rumor that we are missionaries, which
has helped curb some of the outbursts." Of course, it did not help that
Ellie, Peachy, and Rosie took to spending the dull afternoons lolling on
the deck, their oiled limbs glistening in the sun. In the end, the bathing beauties created so much pandemonium that the captain had to
cordon off a section of the deck exclusively for the girls. They all had

---

* Ellie Thiry also wrote very long letters to her family, including "almost a manuscript"
about her voyage on the *Mariposa*, and asked her sister to share a carbon copy with "the
gals and guys" left in D.C.—a veiled reference to her OSS colleagues.

"man trouble" of one kind or another—thirty-one days is a long time to spend at sea with few distractions. All the same, Gregory Bateson, who was on the boat with them, and as an anthropologist was an expert in the mating habits of various species, declared Rosie Frame a practiced tease and "a little minx." Frame was the daughter of missionaries in Peking; she had grown up in China and spoke ten different dialects fluently. She had been working in the research department of the OSS in Washington and was in a hurry to get back to the country of her childhood and help the Chinese drive out the despised Japanese. Before the trip was over, she had caught the eye of Thibaut de Saint Phalle, a Franco-American naval officer recruited by the OSS to work behind enemy lines in France, who at the last minute had had his travel orders changed to the Far East. Rosie spent the month tutoring him in Mandarin and beating him at bridge, and in the process completely bewitched him. "Julia, Rosie and I played bridge all the way to India," he recalled. "I thought they were both wonderful."

Ellie, who was the oldest of nine, had no trouble keeping the boys in line. She quickly became one of the most popular girls on board, joining the ship's band, entertaining them all in the evenings by playing the piano and singing, and even occasionally performing in programs broadcast over the ship's "mikes." She also took the discomforts of their cramped living quarters in stride, writing that their cabin reminded her of her bedroom back home: "I never would have believed that 9 women could live together in a room that small—but we do and get along beautifully. We sleep in triple-decker bunks. There are 3 sets, with 3 bunks in each. I have a lower one, and Peachy has the one above. We each have 1½ drawers in the bureau—the rest of our junk we keep in suitcases under the lower bunks. Works all right." They all shared one bathroom and one john, and had to make do with a few cups of salt water for bathing, which made it difficult to get really clean. They washed their undergarments in the tub, stomping on them with bare feet, and then hung the dripping bras and panties on string all across the ceiling of their cabin, making it almost impossible to move. After two weeks, Ellie and Peachy were so desperate to get their hair done that they raided the men's barbershop and demanded service—a bold move that only two months before would have "sounded fantastic" to them. "We were watched by many GIs as we sat with our heads over the sinks, being scrubbed with Fitch shampoo and ice-cold water. Worked beautifully though—and hair got clean. We even persuaded that man to wash our faces and necks."

Julia, bored and restless after only a few days, offered to work for the *Mariposa*'s daily newspaper and soon knew more about what was going on belowdecks than anyone. She saw to it that each of them got a little write-up in the paper, along with a flattering sketch by one of the GIs. When they all got together in the evening, usually in various stages of dressing for dinner, they would smoke and chat, and try to pry the latest ship gossip out of their lanky girl reporter, whom Ellie Thiry described as "their representative" to the paper. "The times when we all get together in the cabin usually turn out to be quite hilarious," Ellie wrote. "Someone is always losing or misplacing something—and the main phrases used are 'I wonder where this or that has gone?' and 'Have you seen my comb?' or 'While you're up, will you pass me that ashtray?'" Those were the moments Ellie knew she would always remember when it came time to leave the ship. "We have almost gotten used to it as our normal way of living for the time being, and getting off will change everything, and we'll be starting over again. And we will miss a lot of new friends we have made."

As was usually the case when OSS colleagues went overseas, Betty and Julia were frustrated by the slowness of the mail deliveries and the fact that censorship meant they learned almost nothing of real interest from their friends' letters. By early April, they had it on good authority that after evading Japanese submarines, and a nauseating zigzag crossing, the group had landed safely in Bombay. There the women learned that during the month they had spent crossing the Pacific their fearless leader had changed his mind and decided to send them somewhere else. "Easter Sunday: Off the ship to encounter a real snafu," Ellie wrote. "Our orders were cut for Calcutta, but overnight our destination was switched to Ceylon. The Bombay U.S. military had not been notified, and to add to the confusion, they did not know we were women!" Temporary accommodations were hastily arranged, and the group spent the next ten days sightseeing and shopping while their new paperwork was pushed through. Rosie Frame left for New Delhi, where she would have to bide her time, as the American ambassador to China—who, rumor had it, did not want his wife to accompany him—had declared China too dangerous for American women. After what Julia described as a "killing train ride across India," tormented by the cinders and grit that poured in through the open windows and left them covered with dirt, they arrived at the Adam's Bridge Ferry linking India with Ceylon. The eight remaining women reached Colombo on April 25, wiring Washington of their arrival.

Fortunately, Betty and Jane did not have to wait long for their own marching orders. Mountbatten had decided to shift his headquarters from New Delhi to Ceylon, moving from the heart of India to the pear-shaped island at its southernmost tip. The OSS had to follow suit. The British, in a new spirit of cooperation—no doubt based on the calcu-lation that American money, equipment, and manpower would come in handy—had approved the establishment of an OSS intelligence-gathering base in New Delhi, as well as a plan to operate a small MO unit in Ceylon under the jurisdiction of a joint Dutch, British, and American psychological warfare board. Betty and Jane arrived at the office one morning to find a cable with their assignments waiting for them. Major Little had sent a wire stating that he had received approval for "number three air priorities for MacDonald to New Delhi, Foster to Ceylon."

Betty, who had managed to get her husband recruited by the OSS—which had jumped at the chance to get a Japanese-speaking naval officer—had to break the news that she was leaving again. Major Little had told her to expect a short stay in New Delhi before pushing on for Kunming. When Betty told Alex about her orders, he pointed to his own assignment papers, which had also come in that morning. He was to report to Detachment 505 in Calcutta. They embraced, then stood there looking at each other awkwardly, not knowing whether to be happy or sad. They had enjoyed only a brief reunion while Alex un-derwent his OSS training. Staff policy did not permit husbands and wives to serve in the same theater, so there was no chance of their being together. It was a hard-and-fast rule; any exception required a special dispensation from Donovan. By the time he got to India, she would be in China. "Just think," Alex told her, "we'll have only the Himalayas between us." They had no way of knowing when they would see each other next. Even this did not dampen Betty's spirits. "We were just so excited," she would recall. "After all the holdups, it was a tremendous thing to finally be going overseas." On his last night in town before leaving for an OSS training facility on Catalina Island in California, they went out and celebrated. When he bemoaned their long-distance relationship and lugubriously quoted *"C'est la guerre,"* they both laughed and drank to the future.

All the activity in the Washington headquarters shifted to getting people into the field. Every week, new appointments were announced, plans were approved, and the necessary equipment—agent radio sets, mobile presses, as well as weapons and ammunition—was acquired. The huge bureaucracy of the wartime agency was gearing up for action. A notice came through stating that diaries and journals must not be kept, that there had already been "problems," and this kind of "carelessness" could be a real danger to the war effort. Personnel were instructed to report for medical checks and begin the usual round of immunization shots for those headed to the Far East. Typhus, typhoid, smallpox, tetanus, yellow fever, and cholera—it was a Whitman's Sampler of deadly germs, courtesy of the OSS dispensary. They were warned that the injections would hurt like hell, and would probably be accompanied by swelling, aching, fever, chills, and, in some cases, wild, vivid dreams. They did not care. It was the first concrete evidence that they were actually on their way.

In the midst of frantic last-minute arrangements to rent out their apartments, have passport photos taken, and draw up wills, an adjutant informed them that they were being sent "back to school." They were expected to report to Richmond, Virginia, for a top-secret training course "designed to test students in operations of actual value in the field including cipher, clandestine meetings, tailing, interrogating, opinion sampling, and residence search." They spent the next three weeks in what Betty called the "never-never land" of secret OSS training schools, a series of safe houses scattered all over the Virginia area where they were taught how to make false documents, skulk around corners while following people, arrange secret meetings, and question suspects. At the end of the course, they were tested on their ability to successfully carry out these sorts of operations in the manner of an "active agent." Loosely speaking, the tests were designed to get the students into trouble and then see how they well they could keep out of it. Betty and Jane both thought they turned in dismal performances, though they fared better than some. In one final exercise, a group of young men led by Dr. James A. Hamilton, a Stanford School of Medicine psychiatrist working for MO, was supposed to break into a defense factory and then leave the premises undetected. Unfortunately, they were detected, arrested, and thrown into jail by the irate local police, who had not been notified of the war games. "It took all of Donovan's considerable influence to get them released," Jane recalled, "after they had spent a few uncomfortable days."

They still had to go through a Far East orientation seminar, extracurricular classes in everything from military protocol to sex, as well as a three-day crash course in small arms and OSS mechanical weapons. Standing on the country club fairway, pointing at the number three green, a ballistics expert patiently demonstrated the correct way to shoot a Colt .45 pistol "from the hip at a crouching position." Then he showed them the correct way to handle a Thompson submachine gun. With some fifty years of experience under his belt, the instructor, Lieutenant Norman Sturgis, made it look easy. In Betty's hands, however, the Thompson behaved "like a bucking fire hose." As soon as her finger hit the trigger she found it impossible to let go, and the force of the gun spun her around in a half circle so that by the time she had emptied the clip the entire fairway was "chewed with bullet holes."

After their last class, she and Jane giddily made their way to the ladies' room to repair their faces before heading back to town. Now that they were graduates of gun school, they were feeling victorious, smug in the conviction that they were ready to face any emergency. Moments later, they were rocked back on their heels by a loud explosion, and acrid smoke quickly filled the bathroom. It took them only a few seconds to recover their wits and another few to work out that the nasty little surprise had been triggered by the flush chain of the toilet.

"We had been introduced to our first booby trap," recalled Betty, noting that it was just a little OSS reminder that an agent can never be too prepared.

Thankful to have survived their postgraduate training, they were beginning to feel they would be lucky to get out of Washington in one piece. During this period, they also discovered they were to lose their civilian status. The OSS required its male operatives—those who were physically fit, of an age, and not yet drafted—to be classified as "specialists" and inducted into the U.S. Army, Navy, or Marines, and after the requisite training the men would emerge as officers with a rank and salary roughly commensurate with their previous professional qualifications. Similarly, it wanted its female personnel to be inducted into the WACS. The problem, as Jane understood it, was that the secretaries balked at becoming enlisted women because instead of the high salary they earned in civilian life they would have received the standard starting rate of sixty dollars a month, which was an insult to their pride as well as their pocketbooks. When push came to shove, and patriotism hit the pay wall, "the professionals stuck by the secretaries and voted overwhelmingly to remain civilians." The compromise that was eventually worked out provided OSS women with adequate pay and "assimilated military ranks," thus making them subject to military discipline (meaning they could be court-martialed) and the Articles of War (which meant they could not resign). In accordance with her civil service rating, Jane was given the assimilated rank of captain, while Betty was, as she put it, "a lowly second lieutenant."

On a stifling July afternoon a few days before they were scheduled to leave, a sergeant appeared outside Jane's office, unceremoniously dumped a massive pile of gear at the foot of her desk, and barked: "Foster, here's your overseas equipment." The army-issue kit consisted of a bedroll, a pith helmet with a small roll of green mosquito netting attached to the brim, fatigues, canvas leggings, gloves, dog tags, a rain poncho, a compass, a water canteen, a Hamilton wristwatch, two oral thermometers, and a portable typewriter. She was relieved to see she had not been issued the black "L" (for lethal) cyanide pills "to be taken in case of capture." Although the pills were legendary within OSS, she had never actually heard of anyone downing one and had no desire to have the poisonous stuff on her person in the event she fell into enemy hands. Last but not least, there was an Abercrombie & Fitch flight bag, though Jane worried that it was not nearly big enough to hold all her warlike equipment, not to mention a specially purchased tropical-weight wardrobe for the Orient that she was not about to leave behind.

Betty received the same parting gift from the OSS Service Office and faced much the same packing dilemma. Into an additional trunk that would be shipped by sea she crammed all the "operational equipment" that was deemed indispensable for MO selectees headed to India, including "several boxes of squash and tennis balls which the major wrote would be of value in trading with the British; trinkets such as lipstick and cigarette lighters for the 'natives,'" as well as "several long evening gowns which the personnel branch whispered were *de rigueur* at official functions; face lotions and potions for the rigors of the field; and a book that OSS Visual Presentation Branch sent around, entitled *This Is No Picnic.*"

Unlike Julia, who traveled to India on a slow boat, Betty and Jane were blessed with favorable air priorities. They would be flying a commercial plane bound for Miami, Florida, the staging area, where they would board the first of several transport planes for the long, circuitous trip. They were to keep this information strictly confidential. Dutifully, they told no one, not even family, of their plans. After trying and failing to find a suitably nondescript way to allude to her new post, Betty scribbled a postcard to her parents, telling them they "wouldn't hear from her for several weeks, but not to worry."

On the eve of their departure, Betty and Jane were handed special passports enabling them to pass through territories held by the British, French, and Chinese. They were told to be at the Washington airport a half hour before takeoff, where their major, just back from India, would meet them. And they were warned in no uncertain terms: *Don't lose your orders!* "Sew 'em in your corsets or something," the adjutant advised.

They did not get off to a good start. Early on the morning they were scheduled to leave for Miami, a sheriff showed up at the door of Jane's

apartment and announced his intention of arresting her for nonpay-
ment of back taxes. Indignant, Jane explained that she "did not mind
paying taxes" but objected to the fact that she "could not understand
how to make out the tax returns." She had even written a nasty letter to
the IRS along those lines, claiming that she "had heard President Roosevelt's speech about the American people having a right to an under-
standable tax law." As was her way, she talked a mile a minute, stringing
together excuses, anecdotes, and funny asides in one long, loopy tale.
The sheriff, charmed by her madcap volubility, and seeing by the GI
gear packed and waiting by the door that she really was heading overseas to serve her country, allowed her to catch her flight.

Things did not go any better once they rendezvoused at the airport.
Both Betty and Jane were under the impression, because their orders
were secret, that they would sail past the flight clerks with the rest of
the folks from Main Street and were shocked when the man behind the
check-in desk said in a bored drawl, "OSS girls bound for the wars, eh?"
and demanded to see their papers. When they parroted the rehearsed
response that they were merely research analysts in the employ of the
U.S. government, he snapped, "Don't give me any of that cloak-and-
dagger stuff" and pointed out that anyone carrying "shush-shush orders" and planning to travel halfway around the world at the taxpayers'
expense, was obviously OSS.

Embarrassed that they had managed to blow their cover before
even leaving the gate, they meekly hoisted their flight bags onto the
scale and said a silent prayer that the bags met the sixty-five-pound
weight allowance. Neither of their bags passed inspection. As a result
of what Betty called their "wishful packing," they were a good forty
pounds over the limit. When Major Little arrived at the airport a short
time later, she recalled, he found them sidelined in a small anteroom,
huddled over their "disemboweled flight bags, trailing stockings and
underwear." No doubt a veteran of such scenes, the major, she noted,
"patiently seated himself and held our jettisoned dresses in his lap
while he explained something about our overseas job." They only half
heard the last-minute advice he imparted, as their minds were on their
discarded finery, which they already missed.

They were billeted at the Floridian Hotel in Miami, a formerly grand establishment that had been requisitioned by the Air Transport Command and now catered chiefly to servicemen. The once-fashionable hotel retained its aura of luxury and elegance on the outside, with its huge pool and palm-fringed walks, but the illusion was shattered the minute they stepped into the spartan lobby. The army had placed its indelible utilitarian stamp on the interior, which now featured a PX in the nook once occupied by the gift shop, slot machines in the lounge, and crackling loudspeakers on the verandas announcing flight times. Only the prewar postcards for sale in the PX, Betty noted, "recalled the era when the Peacock and Crystal ballrooms were the last word in décor."

No sooner had they checked in with the corporal manning the front desk than Jane was handed a summons. Although Jane had thought she and the sheriff had ended on the best of terms, he'd sicced the law on her. The bottom line was that she was going to have to pay her back taxes before being allowed to leave the country. As she was not traveling with anywhere near the sum of money she owned, she had to call one of her closest friends in Washington, Charlie Flato, a former colleague at the OWI and discarded beau, and beg him to wire her five hundred dollars, promising that her parents would repay him. Flato obliged, of course, but not without having a little fun at her expense. Jane soon discovered that the hotel's services included the censoring of all phone calls, telegrams, and mail, because the next day she was called into the billeting office, where she was greeted by a half-dozen officers standing around grinning and "leering" at her. "One of them said, 'Here's a telegram for you and a money order.' The telegram read: 'Darling, forgot to leave this on your mantel. Love, Charlie.'"

Betty and Jane tried to make the best of their layover in Miami, but after a few days they tired of pretending to be tourists. It was just as well, as the last week of their stay they were confined to the hotel for "military security reasons," which put an end to Jane's shopping spree. By then they had been joined by two OSS colleagues, Marjorie Severyns, a bright, slender brunette who had graduated from the University of Washington a few years after Betty and had a degree in international law, and Lieutenant Edmund Lee, a security officer who they suspected had been sent along to babysit them. In his parting comments to them at the airport, the major had told Betty he would be sending Marj Severyns to help her set up the new MO unit in New Delhi and to keep an eye out for her en route. He had bigger things in mind for Jane, who was to be MO desk head for Malaya and Sumatra and would be working out of Ceylon.

When the Floridian's tinny PA system announced their flight—"The following will please report to the transportation desk at 1300 hours"—Betty was dismayed when Jane's name was not called. She waited, counting about twenty-three names in all, but Jane was not on the list. They knew they had different final destinations but had always expected to make the long, arduous Atlantic crossing together. Her excitement at finally heading overseas was dampened by the wave of doubt that washed over her at the thought of parting with the friend and comrade in arms who had been with her every step of the way during the seven months of training in Washington. "The prospect of splitting up was the only regret I felt at leaving Miami," recalled Betty, who had no way of knowing when they would see each other again. When she met up with the rest of their OSS contingent in the hotel foyer, however, she could not help laughing at the sight of Jane ransacking Lieutenant Lee's luggage in a last-minute effort to retrieve all the new clothes she had sweet-talked him into carrying for her.

Determined to be a good sport about being bumped, Jane accompanied Betty to the airfield to see her off. The next day she managed to get herself on a plane for Georgetown, British Guiana, the first of many stopovers on her circuitous route out east. Without fail, the flight officer at every fucling depot she touched down at from Miami to Colombo identified her as OSS at a glance and cut her orders without question, even though her passport bore the ordinary stamp "Jane N.M.I. (no middle initial) Foster, government employee." She was halfway to Ceylon before a grinning officer tipped her off that the trusty Abercrombie & Fitch flight bag on her shoulder was a dead giveaway. The identical khaki bag was issued to all agency personnel going oversees. They might as well have had OSS emblazoned on the flap.

4

A FINE SORT

After a series of hops in transport planes across India—touching down in Karachi, Agra, Bombay, and Madras—and getting lost in heavy fog over the Bay of Bengal in a C-47 that was rapidly running out of fuel, Jane finally reached Ceylon on July 12. While she was none the worse for wear, it was not a package tour she cared to repeat anytime soon. She had to keep shaking herself in order to realize she had survived the journey and was actually there. Major John D. MacDonald,* the commanding officer of the small OSS camp in Colombo, found her a bed for the night and filled her in on the events up in Kandy, the resort town in the mountains where Mountbatten had reestablished his command. Judging by the pea-soup quality of the air in the port city—her body was covered in a sticky film of perspiration seconds after landing—she could see why Mountbatten might want to seek relief at a higher elevation.

The news of their little OSS contingent in Kandy was not good. Shortly after Julia, Ellie, Cora, and company arrived, they all contracted

---

* MacDonald went on to become a best-selling mystery writer after the war.

dengue fever and were laid up in the hospital. "Breakbone fever," as Jane remembered all too well from her own bout with it in Batavia, was a painful mosquito-born viral disease that began with a high temperature that typically lasted three to four days. When the fever finally broke, it left its victims extremely weak and covered from head to toe in a nasty rash. Complete recovery took about two weeks. Another three girls had succumbed the day before, according to Johnnie (as Major MacDonald insisted on being called), and more were dropping all the time. It seemed to Jane that this lush tropical paradise, the fabled land of Sinhala kings and Kipling heroes, was full of hidden dangers quite apart from the Japanese, who were a good thousand miles away in Burma.

At eight the next morning, Johnnie put her on what looked like an old-fashioned toy choo-choo train, known as the SEAC Special, which the Americans affectionately called the "Toonerville Trolley." Although rickety in appearance, it would take her up the mountains to Kandy. The British had installed the narrow-gauge line back at the turn of the century, when their chief object was the expansion of trade and the tea merchants needed an efficient freight route from the Assam highlands to Bengal. It was now operated by Mountbatten's crew. Two antique engines hauled the daily load of passengers, a mixture of military personnel and colorful locals. The service was impeccable. The minute the little locomotive lurched into motion, waiters in starched military uniforms appeared with platters of eggs and bacon, along with toast and tea, as well as Indian gin for the old empire types ("I say, care for a drink, old bean?") who could stomach it.

It was a glorious four-hour journey, the train huffing and puffing its way up through steep mountain valleys and dense, verdant jungle, the brilliant green leaves on the coconut palms and giant acacia so shiny they looked hand-polished. They passed trees full of fruit bats the size of pigeons and pineapples as big as water buckets, and fields dotted with tame elephants both large and small helping to work the land. There were waterfalls, terraced rice paddies, rubber and tea plantations, little villages, and temples, the Buddhist monks outside in their brilliant saffron robes. In the stations, slim women in tight sarongs, babies casually slung on one hip, smiled and waved. Lest anyone mistake it for Eden, the roads were roaring with weapons carriers, trucks, jeeps, and command cars—all reminders of the ugly business of war and the burgeoning Anglo-American presence.

At noon, Jane arrived in the Kingdom of Kandy, which had been a planters' oasis before the war and was picture-postcard pretty with its eponymous lake and famed Temple of the Tooth, a shrine dedicated to Lord Buddha's preserved incisor. It was clear at a glance that her new home was no hardship post. Nestled high in the hills twelve hundred feet above sea level, the ancient upland capital was known for its temperate climate and was perceptibly cooler than Colombo. The air was sweet and fragrant but still so sultry it clung to her face like a damp washcloth. Jane was met by jeep and was whisked into the center of town. She was billeted at the Queen's Hotel, a great white wedding cake of a building in the British colonial style, the aging interior and period furniture redolent of faded grandeur. The shabbiness extended to the upper floors, but Jane was relieved to discover that she had a room of her own. It was not much more than a cubbyhole, furnished with a small dresser and a four-poster bed cloaked in the requisite mosquito netting. Due to the ancient plumbing, there was no running water in the rooms. She was informed that at six each morning, a Sinhalese boy would bring tea and a pitcher of hot water to splash into the basin.

She discovered that the hotel was teeming with WACs (members of the Women's Army Corps) and WRNS (members of the Women's Royal Naval Service) and all manner of female officers. She was puzzled by the presence of so many women until a cheerful WAC explained that most of the male officers were billeted across the lake at the Hotel Suisse. This setup was apparently established by the British authorities, who, with infinite foresight, deemed it undesirable to have their young colonels and old brigadiers (some of whom were now entering "their second youth") in close quarters with the opposite sex. Also billeted at the Queen's were Julia and the contingent of OSSers who had crossed on the *Mariposa*, including two male colleagues, Gregory Bateson and Paul Child. Jane was glad to see the two men's familiar faces, now sporting deep India tans, and the men seemed equally glad to see her.

She caught a ride with them in a jeep to their camp, which was located only six miles outside Kandy but ended up being a bumpy, half-hour trip on narrow, crowded roads full of Ceylonese drivers devoid of traffic sense. Beyond the gates of an old tea plantation lay Detachment 404, a group of primitive-looking structures that were scattered down the hillside from what must have been the original house on the estate, a spacious bungalow with palm-thatched walls and roof, now occupied by the detachment's commanding officer, Lieutenant Colonel Richard P. Heppner. The plaited-bamboo outbuildings, called "bashas" or "cadjans," were connected to the main building by narrow cement walks that, she soon discovered, became rivers of gurgling red-brown water and debris after every rainstorm. Bordering the tea fields were the grass huts that served as quarters for other officers and male civilians, as well as a thatched mess hall where lunch was served. Close by, a well-kept tennis court gave the encampment a touch of class. She had to hand it to the OSS, they really knew how to fight a war with style. The whole spread had the flavor of a titled Englishman's island retreat.

After being shown her MO cadjan, Jane was introduced to some of the more senior officers. The thirty-three-year-old Heppner, a junior partner in Donovan's law firm, was reportedly one of the OSS's bright young stars, a graduate of Princeton and Columbia Law School who had directed special ops in London and had participated in the North Africa invasion. In addition there were S. Dillon Ripley, a tall, attractive Harvard ornithologist who was head of the Secret Intelligence Division; Carleton "Scofie" Scofield, a psychologist from Yale who was the head of MO; Edmond Taylor, a well-known journalist and author of a book on psychological warfare called *Strategy of Terror,* who was in charge of coordinating Allied clandestine and propaganda activities in the theater; and John Archbold of the Standard Oil family, whose claim to fame was having explored, by plane, remote parts of Western New Guinea.

On learning that most of her female colleagues were still in the hospital, Jane decided it would be a good idea to pay a sick call. She had no fear of catching dengue fever as she believed that once having had it "one was immune." She took a jeep up to Kandy's hospital, housed in an old Franciscan monastery, and found them all prostrate in a row of beds in a large ward. Cora was "red from head to foot, even the whites of her eyes were red." In the bed next to her was Virginia Webbert, a girl from the Deep South with a lilting southern accent whom Jane had nick-named "the Magnolia Blossom," looking as pale and wilted as a day-old corsage. Two nights later, Jane came down with "violent chills and aches all over" and almost fainted into a plate of Chinese food at dinner. Some officers helped her back to the Queen's Hotel, but the next morning she joined her friends in the infirmary. (One's immunity, it turned out, lasted only a matter of months.) The U.S. Army cure-all at the time was the A.P.C. tablet—a mixture of aspirin, phenacetin, and caffeine. After being "stuffed" with pills for several days, she began to recover.

Jane soon discovered that the reason all the women fell ill with den-gue was that "the drains of the Queen's hotel had been neglected for years and were a perfect breeding ground for mosquitoes." The men, despite their deep tans, were not in much better shape. The whole of India was a bacterial breeding ground, and many of the original mem-bers of their OSS team, who had spent weeks if not months in Cal-cutta or Delhi before moving to Ceylon in April to set up camp, had contracted bacillary dysentery. By the time they arrived, they were all sick as dogs. Carleton Scofield and Paul Child had spent many days on their beds of pain, suffering an ailment popularly known as "Calcutta Crud" or "Delhi Belly." (The CBI was rife with pseudonyms for dysen-tery: in Burma, it was known as the "Rangoon Runs"; in Thailand, the "Bangkok Blahs"; and in Ceylon, the "Kandy Canters." The award for creativity went to the OSSers in China, who came up with the "Yangtze Rapids" and "Chiang Kai-shits.") They all had a hard time getting cured; they still tired easily and had lost a lot of weight. Paul reported having lost close to twenty pounds since arriving in India in January.

One of the most difficult aspects of adjusting to life in Kandy was reconciling their hotel's fancy appearance with the multitude of insects that infested their rooms. Even the intrepid Cora DuBois had devel-oped a raging phobia of cockroaches that kept her awake at night rigid with fear. It began after she was washing up one evening and reached for a towel to dry her face, only to have a giant, glossy roach skitter off the back of the cloth and across her cheek. Late that same night, clad only in her nightgown, she was sitting on the bed writing letters when a roach dropped from an envelope onto her thigh. She let out a shriek and jumped up, slapping at the cursed bug, but as she had her fountain pen in hand she ended up burying it in her leg, breaking off the point and covering herself in ink. Now when anything brushed one of her extremities, she became momentarily unhinged, shuddering and cringing and completely unable to control her horror for a long time afterward. Another one of the girls found a live tarantula on her dressing table, and when she screamed for the room-boy to kill it he responded in what must have been the local Buddhist fashion by covering it with a towel and then carefully shaking it out the window. For her part, Jane learned the hard way not to get up in the night when she once switched on the light to find a large lizard on the wall above her head. The lizard was a good five inches long and reacted to the sudden glare by making a disturbing noise Paul later likened to a spoon scraping the bottom of an aluminum pan. After that, she stayed safely cocooned in her netting and did not stir until she heard the room-boy at her door with the early tea.

Jane fell into the habit of meeting Paul for a proper breakfast every morning in the hotel dining room, where they established their own private table. An austere-looking bachelor in his early forties, Paul was finicky and set in his ways but endowed with an engaging, slightly offbeat sense of humor. After discovering they both hated pre-coffee prattle, they settled into a routine of sharing the full English buffet in companionable silence, each happily engrossed in *The Ceylon Times*. Neither of them would "utter a word" until the plates were cleared and the papers thoroughly digested. They looked for all the world like an old married couple. One morning as they were breakfasting, they glimpsed "an apparition," as Jane put it, "a buxom girl, very sexy in a tight black satin dress and black satin high-heeled shoes, with long red fingernails, plus a high Pompadour hairdo." General George E. Stratemeyer, the Far East Air Force commander, was so transfixed by her appearance that he just sat there "drooling egg down his chin" as she sashayed past his table. Paul looked up over his glasses and broke his silence for the first time. Inclining his head slightly, he murmured, "Ah, the Black Tulip!" Jane smiled knowingly at the reference to the Alexandre Dumas novel about a fierce competition to grow Holland's most coveted flower. From then on, they referred to the bodacious OSS assistant by that "Dumas title," and on such a slender reed a mutual understanding was formed.

Paul had only recently written to his twin brother, Charles—who had landed a cushy job in Washington as advisor on art and music to the Department of State—complaining about the paucity of female companionship in Kandy. He was "lonely," and he longed to meet a woman who was his equal, "an intimate, intelligent, and understanding companion." Paul saw himself as a connoisseur of the fairer sex and lamented that his high standards only exacerbated the problem: "I am really spoiled for other women and I realize it over and over." For seventeen years, he had been involved with a woman named Edith Kennedy, living with her first in Paris and then in Cambridge, Massachusetts. She was twenty years his senior and tremendously dynamic and sophisticated. He regarded her as the great love of his life and was devastated by her death from cancer in 1942. By the time he joined the OSS, he had recovered sufficiently to date Jeanne Taylor, a young graphics designer in his department, and had reluctantly bidden her adieu before shipping out.

Very much on the prowl for a new girlfriend (confessing that he had more or less given up hope of seducing Nancy Toyne, the sometime mistress of his married friend Tommy Davis, whom he had met in Delhi), he sent his brother long, highly descriptive letters analyzing all of the available women, commenting on everything from their appearance and figures to their subtlety, individuality, and allure. While Paul technically honored the OSS injunction against keeping a diary, he wrote his brother that he considered his letters an "extension of his journal," explaining that he jotted down notes during the day and "treasured up" anecdotes and apt phrases for the finished product, which he considered every bit as much as an art as his painting. When not discoursing on his health—he suffered from a host of ailments, from bad migraines following a serious car accident before the war to an array of allergies, an ulcerative stomach, sleeplessness, hives, and other nervous disorders—he elaborated his "dream" type of woman. She was a "Zorina," in honor of the famous ballet dancer Vera Zorina, who possessed, besides beauty and a goddesslike body, "what is lacking in this warring, man-ridden world: a sense of the continuity of life and perpetual sympathy, fellow-feeling, and consolation." Since arriving in Ceylon, Paul had accompanied Julia and a flock of chattering girls on a day's excursion to the cave temple at Dambulla, but he was not particularly taken with any of them (not a Zorina in the bunch). In the narrow margin of one letter, he scribbled an aside that Julia had a "somewhat ragged, but pleasantly crazy sense of humor." Most of the OSS girls were "soft-headed dopes," who, he wrote, "with their uncomprehending sex appeal and limited understandings, have almost no magnetism for me, except in a very surface fashion."

Then, on July 27, Paul wrote Charles that he was pleased to report the arrival at last of "a new and interesting gal named Janie," adding that they had immediately bonded. "She's an artist, intelligent, talkative, and a comfort to me."

After their acquaintance had stretched to several weeks, he sent his brother a long letter about his new friend, filling several pages with descriptions of her delightful, if slightly mad, character and antics. "Janie is sweet and warm," he began, singing her praises. Though not conventionally pretty, she had a freckled, piquant face "with lively attractive blue eyes and a ready grin." Comparing her to the much-admired wife of a friend, he wrote, "Many of her phrases and attitudes are exactly those of Margaret Gerard. The difference is great, however, as Janie is undisciplined emotionally, and though she has a better mind her feelings are always crashing around. She is sloppy physically, and given to wild hair and a messy room," though some of this could be forgiven on the grounds that she was "a true Bohemienne."

Their instant camaraderie was rooted in shared intellectual passion. They could talk for hours about art, books, and politics, and she could more than hold her own on any topic. She was still curious about life and had the gusto and force of character he admired in a woman. He found her an immensely attractive, talented, and stimulating person, despite her various eccentricities. Shortly after arriving, she had rescued a tiny chipmunk, which had fallen out of a tree; improvised an incubator; and lovingly nursed it with milk administered with an eyedropper. She called it Christopher and carried it around in her pocket. She's "a fine sort," Paul assured his brother. "She adores animals and people, draws with great style, and is worldly and often witty."

Deeply fastidious by nature, his behavior modified at all times by a certain discipline and sense of decorum, Paul could not help but marvel at the breathtaking spectacle Jane made of herself. She was a lusty, independent creature, the sort who spooned her soup too noisily, slept outside because she loved the smell of the flowers, and clambered on top of an elephant with the gleeful abandon of a toddler mounting a rocking horse. Her capriciousness, like that of a spontaneous child, was both disarming and slightly alarming. To illustrate his point, Paul wrote of a "typical Janie gambit":

> She began telling me about a dinner-party she went to last night, starting with a wild spate of description, about the middle of the evening, not identifying anybody, with loose narrative threads flying all over the place. I said, "For God's sake Janie, wait a minute. Go back to the beginning and give me the full history." *"Oh,"* says she, in a heavy Russian accent, *"so you vant the story of my laif? Vell, mister, I vasn't always a prostitoot . . ."* And I got ten minutes of charming and funny *histoire,* invented on the spot, and growing by leaps as she got her mind into the new idea. This, while she sat on the bed, skirts up to her hips, a chipmunk sitting on her shoulder, and drinking from a bottle of 3.2 beer.

In the meantime, various men dropped by Jane's room, including a young Malaysian who apparently spoke no English and a strapping Australian flight lieutenant whom "she had apparently collected somewhere or other in the last week." While they endeavored to have a conversation in a pastiche of Malay, English, Australian Cockney, and, of course, her faux Russian, a steady stream of servants came in bearing cups and teapots and black-market scotch, apparently procurable at five minutes' notice from the Malay doorman downstairs. All around them lay dozens of Jane's ink drawings spread out to dry, covering every surface and a good part of the floor, along with half-written letters, blouses, negligees, and other intimate gear tossed carelessly about the room. "The funny mistress of five or six accents," Jane regaled them all with the story of her dinner party, successively taking the part of a lecherous old Oxonian who was trying to pinch her bottom, a drunk Ceylonese official, and a dry old colonial widow with a lorgnette. She topped off her performance by claiming that by the end of the dinner, pretending to be drunk herself, she shocked them "with descriptions of her early life (this in a thick brogue) in a family of 15 Irish in which the mother fought over the back of the fence with another lady."

Paul was alternately drawn to and repelled by her whimsicality and wantonness. At heart, he knew himself to be far too shipshape a personality to put up with such prodigality for long. They were such opposites that any initial spark of sexual attraction he may have felt soon faded, though a certain fascination remained. To Paul, marooned in Ceylon, starved of company and conversation, Jane was like the circus coming to a remote town. She restored his good humor and revived his spirits. While he found their rundown hotel, with its incompetent staff and terrible service ("they make you wait three days for toilet paper and soap!") wildly infuriating, she dubbed it "SNAFU Mansions" and laughed at its inadequacies. Similarly, the British-dominated war zone's thickets of red tape that drove him to distraction, to say nothing of the "the stupid, arrogant, stubborn" stiffs the British called officers, were for her a source of endless amusement. For all her flightiness, there was seemingly nothing she could not get done by sleight of hand or obtain, if occasionally at shocking black-market prices. She always knew exactly whom to cajole, bully, or bribe. When in a particularly black mood he decided to demand a raise from the OSS, it was Jane who helped him craft "a masterpiece of a memo," having at some time in her the past made "a special study of the loopholes, strictures, and legal verbiage of the Civil Service."

Even in the narrow confines of the camp and hotel, she regularly managed some mischief. Every other day brought a new Janie escapade, another epic triumph or near disaster. The whole chaotic comedy of her life, he wrote his brother, was enormously diverting:

Yesterday her chipmunk fell out of the hotel window onto the slanting iron roof over the servants' quarters, one story below. This roof is about forty feet above the ground but she was out of the window like a flash and down the drainpipe to the roof, her mind wholly on her pet. Picture to yourself the horror of the several stodgy British military characters who, hearing an unwonted scrabbling and clucking on the roof, looked out, and there saw Janie on all fours, a banana in each fist (for bait), chasing a squirrel, and alternately cursing and cooing in English and Malay. She's the type who finds herself in such crazy situations all the time, as if by some Natural Law.

A few days later, as they were leaving the dining room, Christopher escaped from her pocket and disappeared under Stratemeyer's table. Jane, in hot pursuit, dove under the table and, not seeing her precious pet, started feeling up the general's pant leg. Stratemeyer ducked his head under the tablecloth and demanded, "Young lady, may I ask *what* you are doing?" Grinning like an embarrassed schoolgirl, she replied, "Looking for my chipmunk, General." Just then she spied the little devil cowering by his shoe, crammed it in her pocket, and rushed from the room. After that, she stopped carrying Christopher around, and locked it in her office at night, where she made it a bed out of a typewriter cover.

Jane had a long history of such misadventures. She liked to tell the story of how she ended up babysitting a nine-week-old panda in Shanghai, going to absurd lengths to make sure the little black-and-white bundle of fur was out safely of harm's way. The bear belonged to Mrs. William Harvest Harkness Jr., a wealthy American socialite whose explorer husband had captured it during an expedition in western Szechuan province and planned to sell it to Chicago's Brookfield Zoo for a large sum of money. Her husband then died, leaving her to complete the mission. The problem was, Ruth Harkness had taken ill and needed someone to help take care of the cub, which she named Su-Lin, Chinese for "a little bit of something cute," and kept in a wicker laundry basket in the corner of her room at the Palace Hotel. The other problem, according to Jane, was that Mrs. Harkness needed to keep a low profile, "as it was forbidden, even in those days, to export pandas from China, although it was probably the best known 'secret' in all of China at the time." Naturally, Jane volunteered to give the baby panda its bottle and burp it by walking up and down the hotel room and repeatedly slapping it on the back. Every time the cub belched, Jane recalled, "Mrs. Harkness would emit a croak, 'Thank God,' and fall back on her pillows." Eventually the lady was well enough to travel, and with the help of Madame Chiang Kai-shek, who, in return for what Jane suspected was a hefty commission, helped smuggle the small creature out of the country.*

Julia, too, found Jane's stories "fascinating," and she looked up to her adventurous friend despite her occasionally "scatterbrained" behavior. "She was terribly funny," said Julia. "All kinds of ridiculous things would happen to her. Everyone adored her because she was just so amusing."

It did not take Jane long to become a popular figure in Kandy. She had a special faculty for making friends in high places, so that almost at once she seemed to know all sorts of important people in both the American and British commands. She was the only female member of their OSS unit to be honored with an engraved invitation to one of Mountbatten's elegant dinner-jacket affairs. Lord Louis and his staff had taken over the King's Pavilion, a delightful miniature white palace that had been the summer residence of the colonial governors. The royal residence had originally been built in 1829 for Mountbatten's godmother, Queen Victoria, in the event she graced the island with a visit. (She never did.) Famous for its airy style and the graceful proportions of its architecture, from the regular colonnades to the wide, graveled drive that led to its imposing arched entranceway, it was said to be the finest structure in all Ceylon. The manor house was surrounded

---

* Su-Lin made headlines when she arrived in New York in 1936, carried not in a cage but in Mrs. Harkness's arms, the first giant panda ever to be captured alive and safely brought back to the United States.

by ornamental gardens and extensive grounds, including a golf course that went down to the sea, and save for an array of flags and a few military trappings appeared to be a throwback to the heyday of British colonialism. The fast-growing HQ was informally laid out along roads named Fleet Street, Ludgate Circus, Times Square, and Broadway to reflect the Anglo-American spirit of the enterprise, with a lavish array of thatched messes, clubhouses, and living quarters situated along the banks of a river. The supreme commander—"Supremo" in the local shorthand—had arrived at his idyllic new headquarters that April, and he had immediately decreed Kandy "probably the most beautiful spot in the world."

The OSS bashas were just beyond Mountbatten's gardens. The juxtaposition of the two headquarters provided a ready-made drama for Jane quite apart from the war itself, and she reveled in the expertly contrived entertainment. The admiral's fledgling command was already earning quite a reputation for luxury and high living and had come under fire from the home office for its extravagance. There was the small matter of carving an airstrip out of Kandy's misty mountains, and the staff—Mountbatten had originally planned to make do with 4,100—was reportedly growing by leaps and bounds. (The final tally would be nearly 10,000.) Drawn mostly from British aristocracy, they were an impossibly well-groomed lot in their trim khaki uniforms and could be seen coming and going in their shiny staff cars or saluting in stiff parades worthy of Buckingham Palace. "Lovely Louis," Jane recalled, using the American general's nickname for him, "liked to be surrounded by handsome men and beautiful women." The women, many of them titled, were mostly WRNS or FANNYs—members of the First Aid Nursing Yeomanry Corps. The latter outfit, according to Jane, was ostensibly an aid organization dating back to World War I but had, over the years, become an auxiliary of British intelligence. Hence, beware of beautiful FANNYs!

Despite her anticolonial prejudices, which shone through in her constant mocking of the declining empire and her Marxist cracks about "the mangy British lion," Jane was allowed entrée into their social enclave. She was the only American invited to join their Shakespeare group, and at their amateur theatricals the British would roll in the aisles at her pronunciation of words like "clerk" and "Berkeley." She met Mountbatten on several occasions and considered him the most charming man she had ever met, recalling, "He had the great and wonderful gift, during conversation, of making you feel that all his life he had been waiting for your pearls of wisdom, and he was sincere, for the moment at least." Perhaps it all came down to her being such a determined flirt, but as a result of her close contacts among the khaki-clad set she knew more about what was really going on than almost anyone on the island. Guy Martin, another Donovan lawyer turned OSS lieutenant, was not surprised at Jane's progress. She was "the jolliest girl on land and sea," he said, and "the only Communist with a sense of humor."

Every morning at eight sharp, Paul, dressed like a British major in shorts and an open-neck bush jacket with rolled sleeves, herded them into a weapons carrier outside the Queen's Hotel, which ferried them to the OSS camp. Their little group usually included Jane, Julia, her roommate Peachy, Cora, Ellie, Gregory Bateson, and a gaggle of secretaries. Bateson, whom Jane once accused of "having a genius for making the obvious obscure," was a rather batty, absent-minded English academic. Moose-tall and gangly, he had a huge head and sparse hair, and went about in a pair of abbreviated American shorts, his sadly inadequate wool stockings bunched around his ankles. He was not only an Oxford PhD but had lived for years in remote regions with native tribes, and had absorbed altogether too much of their habits and cultures. He was forever urging them to go crocodile hunting, and spoke with nostalgia of this great sport, having last indulged in it in some far-off section of Sumatra. He reminisced about "bagging the beasts" in very deliberate, richly accented English, which Paul described as a cross between "an Oxford don and the-visitor-from-Mars." Julia had quite a crush on him, but it may simply have been because at six foot six he was one of the few men who towered over her.

While in Ceylon, Bateson came up with the bright idea of turning the great Irrawaddy River in Burma a putrid shade of yellow. The Irrawaddy, a mighty river some thirteen hundred miles long, was a way into Burma and of great strategic importance. He had stumbled across a Burmese legend that, roughly translated, promised, "When the waters of the Irrawaddy turned as yellow as the *pongyis'* [monks'] robes, the foreign enemy will leave Burma." While the "foreign enemy" in the legend was almost certainly the British, Bateson was confident that the term could apply to the Japanese as well. Used as part of an MO whisper campaign, he argued, the ghostly yellow river would be a sure sign to the superstitious Burmese that the Japanese had to go and would incite insurrection. He applied for and received permission from P Division (originally the Paranormal and Psychic Phenomena Division of Naval Intelligence, it became the covert psychological unit of OSS, code-named "Delta Green") and with great difficulty procured several cans of a yellow oil designed to create "slick smears" for downed planes trying to attract rescue teams. Just before arranging for the Air Force to drop the dye into the river, he tried pouring a sample of the stuff into his bathwater to see how it worked. It immediately sank to the bottom of the tub, producing no telltale smear. Unfortunately, on closer inspection, the instructions on the can read: "For use in salt water only."

Bateson was by no means the only "mad scientist" who cooked up disruptive schemes and noxious weapons to use against the enemy. The OSS brains in the Department of Research and Development produced a glossy magazine devoted to the subject, which personnel in Ceylon received on a monthly basis. Jane could not help poring over each new issue, which had "the fascination of a repellant object." One of the nastier weapons, she recalled, was packaged in ordinary cans of pork and beans, which the Japanese would find in a bundle of rations and presume had been dropped into the jungle for American soldiers. When the Japanese tried to open them, however, "the cans would explode in their faces." Studying this catalog of wicked devices, Jane observed herself beginning to undergo that change from rookie to hardened field veteran, barely flinching at the sound of ack-ack guns coming from next door, where soldiers practiced shooting at a towed target.

Jane's office cadjan was a palm-thatch hut, a tropical version of army prefab, with a cement floor. Each room merited one 25-watt bulb hanging from the ceiling; as Paul drily observed, they affected the afternoon gloom about as well as a birthday candle. From her open door she could see papaya trees and coconut palms and up the hills to the green rice paddies. The hut's windows were bare, with wooden shutters that were never closed except when the rain was too heavy. This was just as well, as she heard that the previous week a young British naval commander who saw a six-foot-long cobra in his cadjan dove out his open window and escaped with only a sprained thumb.

Her hut contained her desk, for Indonesian and Malay affairs, and the desk of Captain Howard Palmer, a twenty-seven-year-old Harvard Law School graduate who represented Thailand. A large, jovial fellow, Palmer had been born in Bangkok to missionary parents, had lived in Thailand until the age of nine, and spoke fluent Thai. Off in one corner, surrounded by charts, was the MO desk for Burma. They shared the space with Liz Paul, their assistant, a pretty twenty-five-year-old graduate of a secretarial school in New York. This close cohabitation resulted in a confusion of noises from typing and dictation to snatches of overlapping conversations, all of which was hugely distracting, as was the presence of vociferous coolies, engaged in some mysteriously unending construction work, who just stood outside and stared and stared at her until someone shooed them away.

Paul Child's cadjan was the best in the compound. He called it his "palazzo." He had the large center room to himself, and he had made it comfortable and quite attractive, with big maps covering the walls and bulletin boards with up-to-date news clippings and radio monitorings as they came in, so that everyone went there to visit or just to sit and relax. The two side rooms were occupied by Heppner's deputy, Lieutenant Colonel Paul Helliwell, and Ellie, who did Paul's secretarial work. Paul was in the midst of designing and building an elaborate war room for SEAC but was so swamped with presentation work—such things as operational phase charts, diagrams and military models for the OSS, and, for Mountbatten, a large decorative map of his command—that he was way behind schedule. After months of complaining, he had been assigned additional staff, and in late June, Jack Moore had arrived from Washington. Paul had also found himself blocked at every turn by the Royal Engineers, who were in charge of all construction on the island and had not been informed of OSS's plans. The Royal Engineers controlled access to all the necessary materials, and the carpenters and electricians, and despite being a royal pain had to be placated. Paul eventually discovered the fastest route to their heart was "by drinking a lot of weak whiskey and slapping a lot of weak backs," and as a result his new building was finally under way.

Jane settled down to her MO work as best she could with the limited means at her disposal. Their OSS unit in Kandy, joined by other bases in Ceylon, was responsible for mounting operations in Thailand, Malaya, Sumatra, and the part of Burma not covered by Detachment 101's Kachin Rangers. The Japanese occupied Burma, posing a threat to India, as well as Malaya and Holland's Indonesian empire. Thailand was a nominal Japanese ally under Japanese military occupation. India and Ceylon remained under British control, and while they more or less cooperated with the Allied war effort, there were aspects of the old colonial rule that were unpopular. A sore point for OSS personnel stationed there was that Britain had yet to renounce its imperial claims on any part of Asia. Jane's assignment was twofold: "to undermine the Japanese army and, second, to turn the native populations against the Japanese and their collaborators." After seeing the "excellent examples" of subversive leaflets and cartoons she had done in Washington, Heppner had specifically requested Jane be assigned to Ceylon to expand their output of MO materials discrediting the Japanese.

She began by scouring all the latest intelligence reports from occupied territories, looking for anything she could use to deceive, mislead, or frighten the enemy, such as the names of Japanese military personnel or their Malay and Indonesian collaborators. She enlisted the help of Julia, who had assumed her duties as head of the Kandy Registry and was responsible for keeping track of all the intelligence reports. Blessed with "a phenomenal memory," Julia dug out everything they had in the archives, but it was "unfortunately scanty" and unpromising. Relying on her own ingenuity, Jane tried devising schemes that might stir up native hostility against the enemy. "I would look into space, sometimes for hours," she recalled, "and dream up a leaflet, a pamphlet, or a broadcast, saying perhaps that certain collaborators were lining their pockets while their wives were sleeping with the Japanese." To her dismay, some of the early leaflets she had printed up were not as effective as they might have been because there were no native Japanese speakers on the staff. Their two nisei translators had such flawed grammar and old-fashioned idioms that their efforts did not fool anyone, least of all the enemy.

The distribution of the black propaganda in the occupied territories was carried out by agents working for Detachment 404 and the Americans. The best agents, Jane decided, were the Chinese Communists. They were devoted to their cause—defeating the Japanese and Chiang Kai-shek's Nationalists—but as the former were the greater immediate threat, they were perfectly willing to help finish them off first. Whereas the natives, either the Malay or the Indonesians, "could have cared less. One colonial power was like another to them." As a result, the Americans secretly employed the Chinese Communists, all the while remaining scrupulously anti-Communist. Jane regularly used Communists to carry MO leaflets into the Malay jungles or to penetrate the coast of Java, because the British subs did not want to get in that close and none of their people would touch it for fear of detection. "We would parachute to the Chinese guerillas, when we could, printing equipment, radio transmitters and, sometimes, the finished product"— including, in once case, Jane's own "crudely printed pamphlet on how to derail trains."

Nothing about the work was easy—from producing the fakes to making sure the deceptive materials were properly disseminated. Everything in Kandy was messy, opportunistic, and too fluid. After several frustrating weeks, in which Jane began to wonder if her efforts had succeeded in harming the Japanese in any way, she voiced her doubts to Alec Peterson, her opposite number in Mountbatten's command. "Why don't we just give them guns?" she blurted out, thinking how much easier it would be if the guerillas could just shoot the Japanese.

"Because we'll only have to fight them after the war to take the guns away from them," he replied with the maddening we've-been-through-this-all-before composure of a seasoned campaigner.

Feeling that all her efforts had come to nothing and that she was "wasting the taxpayers' money," Jane dashed off a letter of resignation to her boss in Washington, effectively firing herself and her staff of two. She got back "a blast" by return mail, reminding her that she was subject to the Articles of War and that resignation was "tantamount to desertion." (It was not the first time she was thus threatened, nor the last. Jane maintained that she was probably the "most-threatened-with-court-martial person" during the war.) After that incident, Liz Paul would often try to put the brakes on Jane's excesses, asking gently, "Are you *sure* you want to say that in your report?" or "Is that *really* the way you want to put it?" Jane's blunt retort never varied: "What do *you* think?"

Jane was hardly the only one increasingly skeptical about the prospect of an effective OSS show in SEAC. At the Monday morning staff meeting on August 14, Heppner gave them all a pep talk about operations and then brought up the array of obstacles that blocked them—the lack of personnel, supplies, and transport. Everything was in short supply, almost laughably so. They scrounged for everything from fuel to office supplies and were reduced to carefully saving their paper clips. Things could only get better because they could not get any worse. Carleton Scofield left the meeting feeling completely "disconcerted" and complained to his diary, "What's wrong—too many people here, yet not enough really to do anything. How would I change it? I don't know!"

Then there were the many personality conflicts and Allied policy differences, along with London's failure to articulate its policy toward Thailand, as a result of which the OSS had to try to guess the British attitude to Thai independence from cables and the casual remarks of various officials. In a memo to Washington, Heppner complained of constant meddling by the British intelligence—"SOE [Special Operations Executive] is getting in our hair more and more"—and warned of the dangers of being vulnerable to "the wiles of the British":

> The point should be made unequivocally to all involved that all British endeavors in Thailand up to the present time have resulted in complete failure. These operations were carelessly devised and hopelessly executed. We, ourselves, were not connected with these attempts. As for our own activities, we are

conducting operations there which have much better propects
for success.

There were rampant suspicion of SEAC's actions and a fear, shared
by General Stilwell, that the OSS would succumb to what Ed Taylor
termed "the contagions of Western colonialism." The primary concern was that their British rivals would shut off OSS links to high-level
contacts in Bangkok and then isolate the leaders of the Thai resistance
from any liberalizing U.S. influence, rendering them "little more than
native mercenaries of British imperialism." Taylor even worried that
the hostilities might reach the point where OSS's role would be reduced
to "a single head or coordinator responsible to Delhi (Stilwell) instead
of Kandy (Mountbatten)," thereby dooming Detachment 404. After an
aborted mission to bring the Thai regent, Pridi Phanomyong (known
by his OSS code name, "Ruth," after Donovan's wife), out of the country, a failure blamed on adverse weather as well as a blatant lack of British cooperation, Scofield lost all patience with the conflicts of empires.
"Damn it, why are we here?" he ranted to his diary. "The Dutch are
afraid, and the British haven't given us a break yet. Sometimes I can't be
sure who the enemy is. Almost every British officer or civilian I've dealt
with has been OK, but institutionally they seem to want to get us out.
All right, I'm for pulling out."

Echoing his frustration, Cora DuBois, the head of Research and
Analysis and the most senior OSS woman in Ceylon, fired off a cable
to her chief in Washington on August 24 complaining about being
"poorly staffed," adding pointedly, "It may be an impertinence to tell
you that SEAC is the largest unexploited colonial region in the Far
East and therefore a potential bone of contention between us and colonial powers in the future." Her focus was Thailand, which she argued
was strategically of vital importance to Japan, as the crossroads for its
troops traveling overland between Burma, Malaysia, Indochina, and
China, and would be politically of equal importance in postwar Southeast Asia. She was a lean, owlish-looking woman whom Jane persisted
in calling "Herr Doktor DuBois" behind her back because of her odd
way of peering over her glasses and asking about arcane facts and fig-

ures during meetings, as if the others were in the front row of her lecture room and had not come prepared.

DuBois was both brilliant and highly competent, qualities not always found in OSS officers. In a sharply worded memo to the camp's young CO, Dick Heppner, she faulted the unit's bureaucratic waywardness and went so far as to suggest that integrating her branch into every phase of operational planning might improve matters: "At present I feel that each branch operates in relation to any one project as though it were an isolated abstraction. The tendency for responsible people to gallop madly all over the countryside should be controlled administratively." Heppner responded by noting sulkily in a progress report to Washington that, despite her many talents, DuBois could be "tactless" and "overbearing" and that her manner resulted in "the usual problems with army officers being placed under a woman's command, which causes trouble."

Far from leading a coordinated effort with the Dutch and the British, the Americans were, Jane liked to joke, completely "uncoordinated." As she explained in a letter to Betty, Ceylon was an Elysium so far removed from the realities of war that while everyone had an academic interest in what was happening, they found life far too pleasant to do anything too drastic about it. "To those red-blooded Americans who signed up to fight somebody and arrived in Ceylon to find themselves pinioned beneath P Division directives, the SEAC situation was just another form of British tyranny—frustration without representation," she wrote. "But to the Americans with a planning-staff mind-set and a penchant for major and minor intrigue, Ceylon was the palm-fringed haven of the bureaucrat, the isle of panel discussions and deferred decisions." On the more trying days, she would quietly sing a parody of "Oh, What a Beautiful Mornin'!" written by two war correspondents, which included countless ribald stanzas:

> Oh, what a wonderful theater,
> Oh, what a beautiful place.
> We love political warfare
> We don't fight; we just save face.

Heppner attempted to improve matters that autumn by dispatching Ed Taylor and the recently arrived Alex MacDonald, both journalists, to set up a new propaganda workshop dedicated to OSS operations in Thailand. Taylor had an overconfident, almost cocky manner, but it was hard to argue with his authority as he had successfully matched wits with Nazi propagandists as the leader of the OSS's European psychological warfare branch. The new shop was based down in Colombo, within an adobe compound the OSS maintained downtown in the port city. Grim-faced Gurkha soldiers guarded the entrance. Jane was assigned to go with them, and to focus on black propaganda ideas for Indonesia, which was also under Japanese occupation.

Their new team included three Free Thai students who were training to be OSS operatives. The three had escaped the Japanese and had been helped out of Bangkok by OSS field agents. They reported that the political situation in Thailand was deteriorating rapidly. Japanese forces had shut down all Bangkok radio broadcasts, and had replaced them with their own war news broadcasts, created by Thai collaborators, over Radio Tokyo. Most of the student operatives' days were spent listening to Thai-language broadcasts out of Tokyo, analyzing the content, and suggesting counterpropaganda ideas.

The Japanese, of course, did counterprogramming almost exactly like their own and meticulously reported all of the Allies' failures for the edification of their listeners and the Tokyo rear echelon. Japanese even had plans for a secret black radio station, to be called Free Ceylon, aimed at inciting the Indian population. Ed Taylor had urged their team to "put their imagination to work" in trying to sabotage the Japanese radio propaganda. They gathered the first morning and sat around like "Madison Avenue ad men," Alex recalled, "and ran a few ideas up the flagpole."

They agreed that in order to win the propaganda war, they needed to produce their own insidious anti-Japanese broadcasts, copying the exact form of the Radio Tokyo programs, and pipe them back into Thailand. Their strategic purpose, MacDonald instructed his Thai apprentices, was to counteract the Radio Tokyo line that Japan was winning the war and that Thailand, as a passive ally, should join with the empire in its goal of a "co-prosperity sphere" in Southeast Asia. But they would have to be subtle in their subversion. Most of their simulated programs had to consist of straight news, picked up from a variety of overseas broadcasts, with just a twist of their own—usually a "regretful" report of Japanese setbacks in the Pacific. One of the Thai students, who was twenty and had been studying architecture at Harvard, also masterminded "official" Japanese pronouncements worded in a way guaranteed to offend the Thais. The broadcasts—exactly imitating the style of the programs put out by the Japanese high command but with material designed to infuriate the native population cleverly inserted— would create distrust and dissension. The ultimate goal of the team's black radio scheme was to stir up resistance against the Japanese occupiers, aid the Thai underground, and enlist sympathy and even support for their own side. The additional challenge they faced was somehow to dissociate themselves from the attitudes of their colonialist allies, but this was not always a practical, let alone easy, policy to uphold.

Heppner had also banished their printing unit to Colombo, which Jane interpreted as another attempt to keep their MO work out of the sight and mind of the higher command in Kandy. A lot of Regular Army types, as well as the naval brass, viewed psychological warfare as a dubious Washington-spawned branch of the intelligence services, had no idea what it really meant, and wanted nothing to do with it. Their bafflement led to either ridicule or a lot of annoying questions that could not be answered. Hence MO offices were usually hidden away in some dark corner of the OSS compound. In Colombo, their "MO-tel," as it was called, was on empty stretch of white beach on the outskirts of the city, at the end of a lonely road, beyond a stockade and barbed wire fence, and camouflaged beneath a green canopy of ancient palm trees. There was a cluster of nondescript thatch-and-plywood outbuildings, with the print shop set the farthest back from the beach to protect the equipment from the ocean spray.

Whenever Jane dropped off her painstakingly prepared black leaflets to be typeset, she felt as if she were sneaking off to a house of ill repute in the seedy part of town. It was thirty miles from the headquarters in Kandy and on the other side of the island from Trincomalee, the

British naval base. Of course, it was also possible that because of the undercurrent of distrust, the OSS might want to keep the MO production sequestered from British intelligence. It was an open secret that the two dueling cloak-and-dagger agencies were keeping an eye on each other's methods of operating with an eye to getting a political and economic leg up in postwar Asia. "Each side cheated to about the same degree," according to Ed Taylor, "and usually with a certain gentlemanly restraint." At times, he recalled, his "resources of ingenuity were severely taxed to produce for [their] SEAC superiors an innocent explanation for the presence of some accidentally discovered OSS intelligence team or guerilla base in an area where no such operation had yet been authorized; fortunately, the same occasion was usually exploited by one of [OSS's] British rivals to 'surface' some equally unsanctified activity of its own, so SEAC could give its retrospective blessings to both."

All OSS personnel in SEAC had been warned to be on guard against any interagency deception. The British considered this sort of trickery a classic secret service tradition and had been known to plant spies in U.S. bureaucracies to sift through information. Julia was told to protect the Registry's secrets from prying officials from outside agencies. There were rumors that one fair-haired British femme fatale was specifically targeting "high-echelon personnel" in Kandy, but there were so many decorative blondes on Mountbatten's staff it was impossible to guess her identity. OSS security even had the temerity to suggest that OSS female personnel were particularly at risk because gullible American girls were "easy targets" and tended to go to pieces "at the first sound of a British accent."

Jane did her best to contribute to this spirit of virtuous intrigue. She suspected that her British friend Alec Peterson, who worked in Mountbatten's headquarters, was probably MI6 and engaged him in some minor cat-and-mouse games. They would often meet up on weekends for dinner and dancing at the Silver Fawn (more commonly known as "the Septic Prawn"), one of Colombo's nightclubs for officers that was enjoying a booming wartime trade. On these occasions, she would slip into the new black silk cocktail dress she'd had made locally (if her mother could only see the tailors in Ceylon!) and black high-heeled sandals brought from the States. She would always bring along a bottle of "operational scotch," and after they had both had a drink she would attempt her own sub-rosa maneuvering: "OK, Alec, let's get it over with. When are the bombers going over?"

"On the twentieth."

"Would you drop some of our leaflets?"

He would sigh and, more often than not, agree. Scofield repeatedly reproached her about being "too friendly with the British," Jane recalled, "but reluctantly kept supplying the operational scotch."

At the end of a particularly hectic week, Ed Taylor, the camp bon vivant, announced that he was organizing a big party "to celebrate the dark of the moon"—though clearly any excuse would do. It was the first real party since Jane had arrived. They all went to the Kandy Club for dinner and dancing—Ed, Jane, Paul, Julia, Scofie, Cora, Gregory, Virginia, and others. And, saints be praised, there was something closely approximating a bar, offering gin martinis, sherry, brandy, and scotch. Everyone had too much to drink, and one or two disgraced themselves, but no one was in any condition to be telling tales.

On the jeep ride home, Jane searched the night sky for the Big Dipper, knowing that, like everything in this part of the world, it would be upside down. Back in her room at the hotel, her head fuzzy with the effects of alcohol at that altitude, she discovered that some indefatigable monks were, as Paul put it, "hell-raising" at the Temple of the Tooth next door. Small lamps were burning in the niches in the old wall outside, and the smoky air was pungent with the smells of incense and coconut oil. There were drums beating, flutes wailing, and dozens of beggars bleating. This exotic scene, so characteristic of Ceylon, was wasted on her. She wished they would just shut up.

5

INSTANT FAME

Thank Buddha, it was the third day of sunshine in a row. They were just emerging from a second wave of monsoons, the bedraggled survivors of weeks and weeks of daily drenchings. Sitting in her office cadjan, Jane had come to recognize the now-familiar signs of the coming onslaught: first came the roaring sound, steadily gathering force as it tore through the jungle; the sky dimmed; a violent wind whipped up and filled the air with the smell of rotten leaves; then came the slashing rain. It came in sheets and blew in through the open doors and windows, scattering her papers and sending rivers of muddy water across the ground outside. Then, just as suddenly, it stopped; the sun came out, and everything steamed. The air felt fresh and cool, though the humidity still soaked her cotton blouse and left it plastered to her back. Thousands of insects began to buzz; birds trilled; and, as Somerset Maugham put it, you could practically "see the herbage grow before your very eyes." Then it rained again. In the past, both the British and the Japanese had maintained that it was impossible to fight during the wet season and shut down operations from April to October until the weather improved. Jane thought it an eminently sensible point of view.

The new SEAC commanders, however, saw no reason to let a little mud and malaria get in their way, and as a result it had been an unusually busy autumn in their corner of the war.

Jane was laboring in her Colombo office when Ed Taylor phoned down from Kandy, his voice uncharacteristically strained. "Donovan's here," he announced grimly. "He'll be down to your place at ten tomorrow morning. I hope you've got something to show him."

The OSS director, who had recently been promoted to major general, was on one of his swings through Southeast Asia and was headed their way sooner than expected. Donovan always traveled with a large entourage—assorted branch chiefs from Washington, Far Eastern theater officers, and a gaggle of bright young aides—that he referred to as his "flying circus." His visits tended to be fast and formal, resembling a "quasi-royal procession," and they inspired much scurrying about and nervous twitching throughout the theater. They also led to the most appalling displays of brown-nosing among their more sycophantic colleagues, some of whom could not get down on their knees fast enough when the great man appeared. Alex MacDonald called their small MO team together and warned them to be prepared. "It meant we had to clean up everything," recalled Jane, "and make ourselves look terribly efficient, and draw up charts to show what we were doing and what we were planning to do."

The next morning, the general arrived at ten sharp, wearing an overseas cap and slightly rumpled khaki uniform without medals, escorted by Heppner and another officer. Donovan took a keen interest in the black radio operation and was gracious with their three young Thai students. Nodding his silvered head in approval when MacDonald finished showing him their setup, he said, "Sounds promising. Get it going. But you'll have to get closer to the action." Turning to Heppner, he ordered, "Send them up to Detachment 101 in Burma and order equipment for them out of Calcutta." Then Donovan turned to Jane, who was on the verge of saluting when he extended his hand. "How about Indonesia?" he asked her. "Got anything going here?" As their team leader, MacDonald "groaned inwardly." He was all too aware of what Jane had going.

Assuming a look of bland courtesy, Jane led the way toward a separate room at the far end of the cadjan dominated by a long table where
several young Ceylonese women were busily working. Everywhere on
the table surface were open boxes of SilverTex condoms. The women
were expertly stretching the rubbers, prying them open, and stuffing in
wadded-up pieces of paper and little yellow pills. They would then blow
into the opening until it was partially inflated, quickly tie off the end,
and toss the condom on the growing pile.

Donovan looked at Jane inquisitively, a bemused grin on his round,
ruddy Irish face. Knowing he was a great believer in inspired amateur-
ism, she plunged ahead, hoping to make a convincing case for her MO
scheme: "They're messages to the Indonesian people urging them to
resist the Japanese. OSS officers are being taken over to Malaya and
Indonesia by submarine to recruit native anti-Japanese agents. I've arranged for the OSS men to release thousands of these at sea along the
island coasts. The Indonesians who pick them up will know they have
friends outside to help drive out the Japanese. The messages are in both
English and Arabic," she finished, adding that the pills were the "highly
prized" antimalarial preparation Atabrine.

"Hmm," Donovan muttered, fingering one of the inflated rubbers
doubtfully, as if trying to image the reaction of the locals when they
saw what the tide had brought in. "It seems a long shot. But keep it
going. Keep it going." He gingerly replaced the balloon in the bouncing
pile with the others, gave Jane a weak smile, and departed. As soon as
Donovan's jeep was out of sight, Alex turned to Jane and wrapped her
in a hug that was part congratulations, part relief. Not long thereafter,
he and his black radio team departed for Chittagong, near the border
between India and Burma.

The condom caper became Jane's claim to almost "instant fame"
in the CBI theater, according to Betty, who happened to be on temporary assignment from Calcutta to help coordinate the black propaganda campaign in Burma. Naturally, the story got better as it made
the rounds, in part because of an incident that had occurred a few days
before Donovan's visit. Jane, at a loss as to where to find the necessary
waterproof containers to float her MO materials, had as a last resort

turned to the OSS camp's resident doctor. Navy Commander Willis Murphy had met her for what he understood to be an office visit. When she indelicately requested that he issue her a large quantity of prophylactics, his eyebrows shot up, "Jane, really!" At her cheerful "Yes, Murphy, about five hundred," he had dropped his stethoscope and looked at her in complete disbelief. She loved telling people it had taken several minutes to persuade him they were not for her "personal use" and repeated the story vivaciously at endless cocktail parties.

Betty was gratified to see that six months in the jungles of Ceylon had done nothing to diminish Jane's incorrigible flamboyance. When the Calcutta intelligence chief suggested someone go on an "errand-boy visit" to check out the neighboring MO operation in Kandy, Betty had immediately put her name forward in hopes of seeing her friend again. They drew straws and she won. Looking out of the C-47's window as they taxied down the tiny Colombo landing strip, she immediately spotted Jane, flouncing along the hot tarmac in a light gingham dress and sandals, "the same freckled, friendly face, the same broad grin."

Before they were even out of the terminal, Jane rounded on her, accusing Betty of being a spy from the Calcutta office "on a boondoggling hejira to the Land of the Lotus Eaters." Was Betty planning to expose their MO staff as "a bunch of charlatans," Jane demanded, "taking their ease in thatched bungalows by the sea and sleeping the war away under the influence of siren songs?" Had it not been for the familiar mocking twinkle in her blue eyes, Betty would almost have thought her serious.

Jane filled Betty in on their suspicious little island community as they drove to the Colombo MO-tel, skirting the main part of the city, which appeared to Betty, after filthy, overcrowded Calcutta, "so clean it had a freshly washed feel to it." They settled in the main lounge, looking out on the sparkling Indian Ocean while two beautiful Singhalese boys in orange-and-green sarongs served tea. Jane told her she would learn everything she needed to know the next day when they drove up to Kandy to meet with their acting chief, Carleton Scofield. He was temporarily in charge, since their handsome young boss, Dick Heppner, had departed for Kunming. Heppner had been designated strategic officer for China and promoted to the rank of colonel. His replacement, Colonel John

Coughlin, a West Pointer, was expected any day. A new contingent of OSS secretaries had come from Washington, which meant people were finally getting the help they needed. Julia's new assistant, Patty Norbury, had arrived in the nick of time. The Registry was booming, the file cabinets were full to bursting, and poor Julia, in her own words, had "reached the saturation point." Because of a hitch in schedules, Jeanne Taylor, the graphics designer Paul had so eagerly awaited—for both personal and professional reasons—had not arrived until December 29. Instead of being welcomed by Paul, all she got was a nine-page memo with instructions because he, too, had been ordered to Kunming.

Jane's main purpose in gossiping about all the personnel changes was to gauge Betty's knowledge about the altered situation in China and the future of the OSS mission there. Everything was very uncertain and unsettled. In October, Chiang Kai-shek had repeated his usual imperious demand for Stilwell's removal but this time made sure he got his way "by holding a dagger at Roosevelt's back," threatening to make a separate peace with Japan unless Stilwell was removed and the control over all the booty—in the form of the guns, gasoline, wireless sets, and supplies—coming into China was turned over directly to him.

Vinegar Joe had never hidden his contempt for the greedy warlord, whom he derisively called "the Peanut" and loathed for pocketing American money and doing nothing to throw his deteriorating Kuomintang armies against the Japanese while keeping his best divisions in the north to blockade the Chinese Communists. All the while, the Allies were spending vast sums in support of the Generalissimo, constructing air bases for bombing the Japanese mainland and building a road from Burma at the cost of a million dollars a mile. According to Jane, "Stilwell knew Chiang was completely corrupt and was selling supplies to the Japanese to enrich himself, his family, and his clique, and hoarding the rest to use against the Communists." It got to the point where Stilwell could not stomach Chiang's procrastination, lies, and shams, especially as the supplies being flown into China over "the Hump," a treacherous wind-battered stretch over the Himalayas, came at a terrible price in terms of American lives. So many planes went astray that there was a mutiny in the Air Force, as pilots balked at taking their "101 boom-booms" over the Hump when they knew perfectly well where their cargo was headed.

In the end, Stilwell was sent packing, with the small comfort that it took three men to replace him: General Albert C. Wedemeyer was moved to Chungking, Lieutenant General Raymond A. "Speck" Wheeler replaced him at Kandy, and Lieutenant General D. I. Sultan took over the Burma campaign. Jane rather sympathized with "the old sourpuss," as she called Stilwell, who stormed around Ceylon in his scruffy jeep like a bald, scrawny John Wayne character. She had even let him twirl her across the dance floor at a couple of big functions at the Queen's Hotel. There was a wonderful story that the first time Stilwell flew over the Hump into China he was napping on a lilo (inflatable mattress), but when the aircraft climbed to eighteen thousand feet and the cabin pressure dropped, the lilo suddenly burst. Vinegar Joe hit the deck hard, woke with a start, rolled over, and drew both revolvers. He was ready to shoot the first thing that moved. Fortunately for his fellow passengers, a second later he passed out from lack of oxygen. For all his hell-for-leather cowboy zeal, Stilwell was a Yankee and an intellectual, who had first gone to China as a young military attaché and had learned both Mandarin and Cantonese. Jane believed he had a genuine liking for and understanding of the Chinese—no one in his command was allowed to use the common military slurs "gooks" or "chinks"—but he just could not come to terms with the Peanut.

Jane and Paul had spent a sad little early Christmas together, knowing that they were about to go their separate ways. His affection for "the chipmunk chaser" had deepened over time, and her name was a happy constant in letter after letter: Janie was helping him to organize a party, had accompanied him on a visit to the studio of a local artist, was just up from Colombo full of gossip about the triangular affair of close friends. She had been asked to decorate the enlisted men's mess hall for the holidays and as usual had gone the extra mile, painting a fabulously tongue-in-cheek mural over the bar in their club depicting half-naked native women waiting on a soldier lazily reclining on a mound of pillows. She had devoted all her spare time to the project, and Paul was unabashed in his admiration.

He was not in love with her, but she assuaged his feelings of loneliness and emptiness more than any other woman he had met since coming to Ceylon. She was simply "fantastic," he wrote his brother, and would always remain a dear friend. He added that he had whipped out a little "jewel" of a watercolor as a birthday present for one of the other OSS girls but on second thought decided to keep it as it seemed too good to part with simply "as a casual, friendly gesture." Then, in a letter five days later, he noted, "gave the little painting to Janie, as a Christmas present." In a remarkably complacent aside, he mentioned that Julia had given him a Zippo lighter, "though where she ever got it," he wrote, "I don't know." He seemed far more impressed with the coveted bit of GI paraphernalia than with the woman who had procured it for him.

Paul spent his last evening in Ceylon with Jane, and after dinner they went back to her hotel in Colombo and talked long into the night. He felt "shaky" about his new assignment. It was not the prospect of building another set of war rooms for Wedemeyer so much as the proximity to danger that filled him with apprehension. He worried that once the Allies opened the Ledo Road, a vital supply road connecting Assam to Kunming for the first time, the Japanese would have to act to knock out the American wartime base. He did not understand the logic ("of course, I am not a military man") of setting up an establishment in a place that was so obviously and one-sidedly threatened and feared they would all be "running like hell within 60 days." It had all combined to make him more tense and fretful than usual.

That night, he shared thoughts and feelings he probably never would have "except that all the elements of the time and place bent themselves toward sympathetic understanding, and even to bits of self-revelation":

> Janie's hotel, a strange place, far out of town and once the seat of a certain colonial elegance, no doubt—but now distinctly mouldy and passé. However, Janie's room is in what was probably once a cellar storeroom and it has a little corridor outside leading directly onto a grassed and balustraded terrace shaped like a piece of pie. . . . We took two chairs and a little table out there and sat, facing the sea (only 50 feet away) with a strong wind in our faces, most grateful after a sweaty day, and drank

gin and fruit juice. There was a brilliant new crescent accompanied by the evening star hanging like a lamp just above it. For
an hour or two I felt really relaxed and smoothed out and fine
and was able to forget the fox gnawing my entrails.

After Paul's departure, Jane was delighted to have Betty with her.
The morning after she arrived, they drove up to Kandy in a jeep, along
with "the Black Tulip," her MO colleague Howard Palmer, and Julia's
new assistant, Patty Norbury. On the three-hour drive up to OSS headquarters, Jane played tour guide and kept up a bantering commentary
on the local sights: "And there's a famous footprint at a pilgrim station
near here. The Brahmins say it's the footstep of Siva. The Buddhists say
it was made by Buddha; the Mohammedans, Adam. And now that the
Americans are here in Ceylon," she continued, "the gag is, of course,
'George Washington *stepped* here.'" It was Jane at her silliest and most
fun, and Betty laughed in spite of herself.

During the long ride, Patty Norbury told them the reason she had
volunteered to come to Ceylon was to try to find her fiancé, Lieutenant Roy Wentz Jr., who had been stationed with the Tenth Air Force
in Burma. He was reported missing after his plane was shot down in a
bombing mission over Rangoon. Everybody had told her he was dead
and to move on with her life, but she would not give up hope. She was
determined to find him or, failing that, to at least learn with certainty
what had happened to him. "I took this job with OSS to be as close to
Burma as I could," she told them. "I watch every report that comes over
my desk from our men in the field. One of their jobs is to report on Allied prisoners of war. Some day, someone will pick up Roy's trail." She
added softly, "You see, no one ever saw his plane go down, no trace has
ever been found of the crew."* Her honesty and good cheer in the face

---

* Norbury eventually stumbled on a clue to her fiancé's fate in an OSS agent report. Roy
Wentz had been captured by the Japanese and was interred in the Insein prison camp
near Rangoon. After Burma fell, he was released, seriously ill and wasted to ninety-five
pounds. Patty was reunited with him in Calcutta in May 1945, and they were married a
few months later.

of tragedy was like an unspoken rebuke to all their petty complaints and discomforts, and quite silenced the party for the remainder of the trip.

By the time they reached Kandy, it was starting to drizzle. Jane deposited Betty at Scofield's office and went in search of one of her Thai agents. The boy, nicknamed "Chop," weighed only eighty-five pounds and had been smuggled out of Bangkok in a rice basket. "Chop says he has worms again," Jane told Betty. "He's something of a hypochondriac. Doc Murphy slips him an aspirin, and he's fine again for weeks."

Over their afternoon tea the previous day, Jane had explained that one of her more time-consuming duties was "the care and training" of a half-dozen native agents—Batak, Malay, Thai, and Karen—used in OSS intelligence-gathering missions. She and Howard Palmer looked after them as best they could, catered to their various needs and whims, and attempted, with varying degrees of success, to "shield them from the cruel white light of reality." This was more complicated than it might seem, as they suffered from all kinds of fears, superstitions, and complexes. Her two Malay agents, Hadji Muktar and Abdul, a former university student and a village schoolteacher, were particularly sensitive and rank conscious.

To bolster their esteem, Jane went to great lengths to obtain special privileges for them, including the right to eat in the officers' mess. She came to regret it. When she went down to work in Colombo, the officers there refused to eat with her "zoo," as they called the various native agents. Moreover, each of her charges had different dietary habits and taboos ("Hindus no beef, Moslems no pork, Buddhists no meat at all") that resulted in "culinary chaos." For that matter, Bataks had a quaint habit of practicing cannibalism, roasting the enemy for religious ritualistic reasons, but human flesh was definitely not on the canteen menu. Jane was appointed the Muslim agents' "official taster," but no matter what she said, Hadji persisted in badgering her about the possibility that this or that dish contained pork fat. Finally, they were forced to eat in an area of the mess hall that was cordoned off from everyone else. Even though Jane and Howard would have much preferred to dine with their friends, they always made a point of sitting with their agents "so no one's feelings would be hurt."

The youngest of the group was Danny, a seventeen-year-old Karen student who had been captured by the British in Burma after he had fallen during a desperate attempt to flee. He had sustained a concussion but was convinced the headaches and dizziness were a sign that he was going crazy. Nothing the OSS camp psychiatrist said would persuade him he was sane. Further complicating matters, Danny was unaccustomed to wearing Western-style clothes and at the first opportunity tended to strip off his shirt, cap, and tie. Once, according to Jane, he had showed up at the open-air movie in Kandy and began to remove his pants in front of an amazed audience. They had quickly bundled him off to the camp, and they kept a close eye on him after that. Howard had hopes of one day employing Danny as a radio announcer for the Chittagong black radio station, but the young man still had a long way to go.

A Batak agent who was presented to Jane shortly after she arrived in Kandy also proved to be a handful. "Nick" (his real name was Chabudeen) had been captured by a British submarine off Sumatra and was turned over to the Americans after being interrogated at Trincomalee. The questioning seemed to have wounded his soul, and thereafter he "wilted whenever anyone spoke sharply to him." He, too, developed a variety of physical and mental ailments, and Jane, the only one fluent in Malay, was kept hopping between doctors and dispensaries. On one occasion, after Nick collapsed, she tried to translate his strange affliction for Dr. Murphy: "He says he's emptying out blood."

"Which end?" the doc inquired without interest.

Nick was admitted to the British hospital for observation in the event that he might have ulcers. With her usual disregard for protocol and procedure, Jane snagged him a bed by claiming he was an American sergeant, filling out the forms herself, and made him promise not to speak to anyone. The ruse backfired when a nurse at the hospital rang her in the middle of the night—"the mute 'sargeant' had written her name on a piece of paper and must see her at once." Jane had to throw her clothes on and jeep the seventeen miles out to the infirmary. It turned out that Nick thought that the hospital was some form of house arrest and had become extremely agitated. "They don't like me here," he insisted, almost falling into her arms. "They want me to die. They are starving me to death. They are feeding me only milk." Jane managed to settle him down after explaining that no wanted him to die and that milk was the prescribed treatment for ulcers. Three days later, he was back on his feet and begging Jane to drive him to a mosque so he could pray and give thanks for his recovery. That was the second OSS jeep she had to requisition on a shaky pretext to keep Nick contented. Theoretically the OSS boys were going to launch him deep into enemy territory with a handset to spy on the disposition of Japanese troops, but Jane thought he would be terrified at the very idea of such an assignment.

The majority of their native agents were obtained by British submarines during "snatch sorties." Snatching, according to Jane, was a method of collecting intelligence: "The subs go over to the mainland, wait around for a native fishing junk to appear. It's a case of sighting ship, sinking same, and snatching survivors." The captors were brought back to Trincomalee for questioning. If they were deemed of value, they were trained as agents. If not, they often ended up doing odd jobs and living in internee camps.

In general, she continued, the native agents in Southeast Asia did not have a "subversive bone in their bodies" and could not understand why OSS involved itself in such elaborate black propaganda schemes. "They favor the direct approach to propagandizing their own people. They can't understand why we just don't drop leaflets into occupied zones telling the natives how bad the Japs are." For example, Sam, one of Howard's agents, a high-ranking official in the Thai government in exile, was hopelessly obliging. He had been brought in with the idea that he could provide advice on how to slant propaganda targeting the Thai population, but he had "a sweet habit" of agreeing with every proposed program, so that it was impossible to determine which ideas were more promising than others. Jane told Betty that the boys who taught Sam to play poker discovered this habit the hard way because "they never knew when he was bluffing. With every hand he drew he smiled and muttered: Good—good-good!"

During her meeting with Scofield, Betty learned that Alex was making progress at Chittagong. The small, 5-kilowatt radio station had been erected just outside a Royal Air Force (RAF) camp in the Burma bush, but with their technical staff recalled to Delhi to run the powerful All India Radio, the British had offered the antenna to OSS. Alex had immediately been dispatched to check out the site's possibilities for black radio warfare. The plan was for their MO-SEAC black radio station to operate under the cover of the Japanese radio station JOAK, going on the air just seconds before and only a hair's-breadth turn of the dial from the Tokyo team's frequency. They hoped that if they slipped their black broadcast in so close to the Japanese one, listeners in Thailand searching for news would accidentally pick up their signal and mistake it for the real thing. In the beginning, they would go on twice daily. They had no idea how big an audience they might net: "It could be just a few listeners; it could be thousands." Alex decided to make their young Thai Harvard student their announcer. He was a mere waif, but he had a strong, confident voice that was tailor made for counterprogramming, and he would boast arrogantly in his perfect Thai of Japan's ultimate goal of subduing all of Asia.

Their first trial broadcasts succeeded in duping British direction-finding units in Burma, which reported picking up the signal of a "Jap" station operating in the jungle. Their black radio propaganda also paid dividends: a Bangkok newspaper reprinted part of the test news program that had been beamed to Thailand. The fake story described damage inflicted on Japan by Allied bombing raids and the resulting instability of Japanese markets. The Bangkok paper had swallowed it whole, crediting the report to the "Siamese Hour" over JOAK Tokyo. Scofield told Betty that she would need to start churning out ideas for radio scripts. "When the station starts operating," he added, "we'll broadcast all hours of the day and night."

It was not until months later in Bangkok that Alex MacDonald would learn how effective his "sneak broadcasts" had been: "The Thai foreign minister told [him] that one day the Japanese ambassador in Thailand had come storming to him to report the 'enemy' operation and called on the Thai government officially to expose and denounce the airwaves intruder." The minister assured him that this would only serve to make the broadcasts that much more popular with the Thai people.

When Jane took Betty back to the Queen's Hotel, they ran into Julia McWilliams and Gregory Bateson having drinks on the porch. Betty had always liked Julia. She admired her dedication and absolute discretion but had always wondered at someone her age, and with her obvious capabilities, being stuck behind a file cabinet. Looking at her now, Betty immediately saw that running the Kandy Registry had injected Julia with a new self-confidence. Julia, with her high security clearance, was in charge of the OSS camp's "nerve center," according to Fisher Howe, who headed the maritime unit and was privy to virtually every top secret, including "highly sensitive" plans and operations. "You can be an able and effective intelligence officer but not be undercover, and we were not," recalled Howe. "But she was very effective in the job she had."

The job itself was laborious and, at times, maddeningly dull—accessioning, cross-indexing, circulating, and filing the thousands of dispatches, orders, and espionage and sabotage reports that flowed in from Washington and OSS field operations all over Southeast Asia—but it carried with it a grave responsibility. In September alone, Julia plowed through 365 pouches from Washington, which were broken down into about six hundred classified intelligence inputs that had to be filed and then stored under lock and key in the Registry. After much trial and error, Julia developed what she hoped was a "fool-proof locator system," with master cards on each current field operation including the names of all the agents and student recruits, and their various code names. The nightmare was that the theater commander, Air Force, OWI, and other branches all had their own systems. Julia vigorously campaigned for them to settle on one uniform procedure so their documents could be related and communications streamlined.

She was known to relieve the tedium by making fun of OSS's obsession with opaque codes, once writing to the Code and Cipher Branch to air-pouch a little black book, "one of those you have giving people numbers and funny names like Fruitcake #385," and adding, in a deprecating tone, "frequently we find references to them here and no one knows who on earth is being referred to." In case the paranoid denizens of the Cipher Branch mistook her flippancy for a lack of caution, she concluded solemnly, "This document will be kept very securely in a fire-proof Mauser safe, and will be available to no one except Col. Heppner." Over time, her droll style became immediately recognizable to her OSS colleagues, as did her refreshing attempts to cut through the red tape. One urgent request for information from headquarters in Washington contained this memorable postscript: "If you don't send Registry that report we need, I shall fill the next pouch to Washington with itching powder and virulent bacteriological disease, and change all the numbers, as well as translating the material into Singhalese and destroying the English version."

Thinner and browner, Julia exhibited a new directness and ease—especially around men. The nervous giggle that had once punctuated her sentences had been replaced by a loud, whooping laugh that was contagious. Always warm and engaging, if a bit awkward at times, she had morphed into the social butterfly of Detachment 404. To Guy Martin, she appeared "exuberant and extraordinary socially outgoing—if you put her with a hundred people, by the end of the afternoon she would know fifty."

During the time Betty spent in Kandy, she, Jane, and Julia went on a number of sightseeing trips around Ceylon. One afternoon, they went elephant riding, and it transpired that the large male pachyderm carrying Julia got a three-foot erection. "Julia was so embarrassed," recalled Betty. "She was just beside herself. It was her time of the month, and she didn't want anyone to know. We all thought it was hilarious—who knew elephants had such sensitive noses! But whenever anyone mentioned it she would blush and get terribly flustered." It did not stop them from teasing her relentlessly, but Betty remembered thinking that "in some ways Julia was not as mature as she might have been."

Betty could see by the way Julia lit up around Paul Child that she liked him. "It was already obvious," she said. While it was true that Julia found him extremely intelligent and attractive, she also confided to her diary that he was taciturn and remote, "not an easy man." Much as it pained her, she also knew she was not his type. She had watched him flirt with Jane and Peachy and was aware that he liked "a more worldly Bohemian type." She had learned enough about him to know that he was widely traveled and highly cultivated, and that he sought out similarly capable, adventurous companions. With her, Paul was chatty and chummy. They often went to dinner and the movies and on occasional day trips with others from their little group. But that was as far as it went. She was afraid that was as far as it would ever go.

While she commiserated with herself ("Wish I were in love, and that what I considered *really attractive* was in love with me"), Julia was not one to mope. She hid her disappointment and soldiered on. Perhaps hoping to be seen in a new, more alluring light, she gave Paul a photo of herself posing on her cot in an elegant dress and pearls, smiling up into the camera, one bare leg coquettishly crossed over the other. If there was any implied invitation in the photo, Paul missed it. He sent the picture straight on to his brother with the explanation that it was an interesting interior shot of their quarters. Identifying the female as "Julia, the 6′2″ *bien-jambee*," he continued in a pedantic tone, "The room is a typical 10 × 18 with its coir matting, woven cadjan walls, wooden shutters, and army bed with folded-up mosquito net above."

Julia was not wrong in surmising that Paul did not reciprocate her romantic feelings. He thought of her as "a warm and witty girl" with long legs and a good if relatively unexercised mind. The perfectionist in Paul found much to analyze and to critique, as was his habit when describing available women to his married twin. He cringed at her uninformed, simple-minded pronouncements—"She says things like this, 'I can't understand what they see in that horrible little old Gandhi'"—and mannered, "overstressed" way of speaking that led to "gasping when she talks excitedly." He saw Julia as the typical product of her Pasadena childhood, "safely within the confines of her class and station," with the predictable limitations in terms of knowledge, culture, and sophistication. He also saw how badly she wanted to break away from the controlling influence of her father. He theorized that she was "in love" with her father in the classic Oedipal formulation (if in an entirely unconscious and harmless way) and had spent her life deferring to him "for much of her thinking and acting."

At thirty-one, Julia was "a grown-up little girl." He was genuinely fond of her, and he empathized with her predicament, but only up to a point. "She is trying to be brave about being an old maid," he told Charles, adding that he felt sure she would marry him "but isn't the 'right' woman from *my* standpoint!" Her virginity put him off. Her "wild emotionalism" and "slight atmosphere of hysteria" got on his nerves. He could sense her sexual shyness, the neophyte's frustration: "I feel very sorry for her because while I see clearly what the cure is, I do not see clearly who will apply it."

Having carefully considered the matter, he concluded that she was altogether too inexperienced and overwrought for a randy old goat like him—"it would be too much for Dr. Paulski to risk attempting." Julia had potential, he continued, but was in need of "training and molding and informing." She enjoyed good food, art, music, and literature and would doubtless develop a taste for the finer things if they were in her orbit. She was eager and pliable, but just thinking about all the work it would take made him tired. Referring to his earlier treatise on the Zorina, Paul reminded his brother that his ideal type was confident and refined, someone "who has been hammered *already* on life's anvil and attained a definite shape."

As for when his dream woman would appear, Paul was still in the dark. After a deep malaise following the death of Edith, his long-time lover, he had sought the advice of an astrologer. Her name was Jane Bartleman, and he was so impressed with her powers of foresight that he paid her more than one call in Washington before going overseas. Paul had written down her prediction word for word and pinned all his hopes to it. He quoted bits of it often in his letters to his brother, as if convincing himself of its truth, almost willing it to happen. The New Year, Bartleman had advised, would bring "many changes, sudden moves, unexpected shifts," and with them heavier professional responsibilities. There would also be great changes in his personal life. He would fall "heavily in love." The woman in question would be "intelligent, dramatic, beautiful, a combination of many facets," someone who can keep house, yet is a modern woman." As Bartleman's predictions about the path his career would take had always been "on-the-button," Paul took heart that her promise of romance would also prove true.

In the meantime, he would have to make do with his little fan club. Not long after departing for China, he wrote Charles that he had received the "best birthday present imaginable" in the form of a batch of mail, his first since leaving Ceylon, including greetings from "my three Jays"—Jane, Julia, and Jeanne. In another letter, he good-naturedly scolded his brother for having trouble keeping track of the many girls mentioned over the months of correspondence—"Your confusion concerning . . . Janie, Julie and Peachy is prob'ly natural: only names to you"—adding, "I suggest you adopt the system I used when I read *War and Peace*; keep a chart."

Although married, Betty was not insensible to her friends' plight. She, too, felt the nagging loneliness when she returned to her room at night and no one was there to warm her bed. There was small comfort in the wedding band on her finger. Her long-distance relationship with Alex seemed more painfully stretched and tenuous with every passing month. The war had disrupted all of their lives, and there was a natural tendency to look for affection and tenderness close at hand. Under the stress of work, and the instability of their surroundings, all kinds of alliances—however impetuous and fleeting—developed. In contrast to Julia, who had confided a degree of anguish about her situation, Jane was suspiciously silent on the subject, all the while appearing more carefree and buoyant than ever. If she read her friend's character correctly, Betty had to hazard a guess that Jane was enjoying the attentions of someone in Ceylon—someone whose identity she had her own reasons for wanting to keep secret. Betty could well imagine why.

When confronted, Jane confessed all. Shortly after arriving in Kandy, she had met a thirty-seven-year-old American navy officer by the name of Manly Fleischmann, the handsome son of a Jewish father and Quaker mother who had in adult life opted to become Episcopalian. He was a Harvard graduate and a successful lawyer in civilian life, "but not one of Donovan's." In 1943, he joined the OSS and was sent to Mountbatten's theater in Ceylon. He led a hundred-man mission to Japanese-occupied Burma, where he helped direct espionage operations behind enemy lines. He was in Colombo organizing additional intelligence-gathering schemes, and he boasted that he had recently managed to enlist a Burmese postman to steal Japanese mail sacks and rifle the contents for war plans, the disposition of troops, and other helpful bits. Jane liked him right away. He was brilliant and witty, if "a bit of an intellectual snob." He joked that he and Jane were the two smartest people in the OSS but that sometimes he had his doubts about her.

He was married, of course. Worse, he had a child. When he and Jane realized all too quickly that what had begun as a roll in the hay had turned into a full-blown affair, they agreed they would "be true to each other" during the war but would make no claims on each other when it was over. For the time being, however, they were very much a couple, enjoying all the conjugal benefits without the complications of the Real Thing. Jane liked pretending to be the captain's wife and keeping house, at least in their little Sinhalese home port. No model of domesticity, she admitted that every time he got promoted she would endeavor to sew another stripe on his uniform, "unevenly, of course." None of this came as a shock to Betty. "There was a lot of that sort of thing going around," she said years later with shrug. "The war was hard on a lot of marriages."

Manly was often called away on missions to India, Burma, and Assam. In his absence, Jane kept up a pretense of going out with other men but in practice kept to a "virtuous" monogamy: "No one else ever crawled under my mosquito netting, except [her chipmunk] Christopher." They kept up a funny, fond correspondence, trusting the services of an odd selection of "fleet-footed couriers, firemen, and tourists who plied the Colombo-Arakan route" to be, in his words, their "Cupid's messengers." He would write her when he expected to be coming her way so she could arrange to be free, making almost no effort to disguise his lascivious intent from the army censors. After one reunion, he wrote, "I can hardly tell you how much I enjoyed our brief interlude. I am bound and determined that they will never say that all work has made MF a dull boy, and my ruthless will is now fixed on a repeat junket ere many moons."

Jane tried to be discreet for obvious reasons, not the least of which was that "the U.S. armed forces did not officially recognize sex." After receiving one of her messages, Manly teased her for going to absurd lengths to safeguard their privacy. "It is not necessary to enclose them in stamped, air-mail envelopes," he wrote. "My ancestral blood boils at this proof of your Basically Bourbon nature. It is such conduct that makes COMMUNISTS, or worse." They thought they had everyone fooled until the morning Manly crept out of her bedroom at the Queen's Hotel and across the lobby with her "red-and-white dressing gown trailing from his back pocket." He was halfway in the jeep when his GI driver pointed out the incriminating peignoir.

At the end of two weeks, Betty's TD (temporary duty) was up, and Jane drove her to the airport for her flight back to Calcutta. Tired of teary goodbyes, they made funny faces and grinned back and forth foolishly. It was easier to make light of the occasion. Betty would shortly be headed to Kunming along with a number of their colleagues from Detachment 404, including Paul, Julia, and Ellie. With so many of her old pals gone, Jane was in need of new playmates. It was the only way to endure the ludicrous monotony of life in Kandyland. She soon found pleasant diversion in the person of Peggy Wheeler, an OSS colleague she had befriended in Washington, who was the administrative secretary to Colonel Coughlin, along with her father, "Speck" Wheeler, who was now the top American commander in the theater. Peggy, by virtue of being "the only child and the apple of her father's eye," as Coughlin wrote in a cautionary memo to Donovan, had rather unusual status and privileges. "While an ardent supporter of OSS," she saw all incoming and outgoing messages from Washington—except those marked "eyes only"—and it was understood, Coughlin added, that Wheeler would "depend on her to keep him informed."

Jane immediately endeared herself to the general by persuading Peggy to abandon her tiny room at the Queen's Hotel for his much-larger suite at the Hotel Suisse across the lake. In recent months, conditions at the Queen's had gone steadily downhill. In addition to the dicey plumbing, the power was frequently on the fritz. They had all grown accustomed to running up and down the stairs carrying flashlights, trying to dress and apply makeup by the light of one spluttering candle, and more or less camping out indoors. Peggy had at first refused to leave, gamely insisting she would stick it out with the rest of her OSS pals. Jane finally convinced her to go by arguing that if she moved in with her father it would be to their advantage, as she could then invite them all over for hot baths. Even Peggy could not counter the obvious wisdom of this argument, and she relented. As a result, Jane enjoyed her first really good scrub in months and swore she emerged several shades lighter.

Wheeler, the new deputy supreme Allied commander, was rumored to have an entertainment allowance of ten thousand dollars, and he was generous with his hospitality. Jane was frequently invited to the general's dinner parties, and she enjoyed being wined and dined at Uncle Sam's expense. Wheeler was a top army engineer, intelligent and humane, and was popular with both his fellow officers and the troops. As a young West Point graduate he had worked on the construction of the Panama Canal and had spent the better half of a century tackling the army's heaviest jobs, building roads, railroads, harbors, and dams in almost every part of the world. He was the kind of tough-minded pioneer they could count on to get it done, no matter how hellish the conditions.

Stilwell assigned him the tremendous task of completing the Ledo Road, a two-hundred-mile lifeline hacked through jungle and swamp, connecting India and China. After the Japanese cut the Burma Road in 1942, the Allies were forced to airlift the majority of war matériel to the Chinese over the Hump, so establishing an alternate land route from Assam to Kunming was a priority. Wheeler directed fifteen thousand American soldiers and some thirty-five thousand local laborers, laying down a winding double-track road across steep mountain passes, roaring torrents, and sheer drops. The worst section, a series of hairpin turns following a narrow trail across the Patkai Range, was nicknamed "Hell Pass." Altogether, it was an amazing engineering feat. The job won him an oak-leaf cluster for his Distinguished Service Medal, and the British named him an Honorary Knight Commander. Touched as he was by the honors, Wheeler confided to Jane that the work he was proudest of was the salmon ladder of the Grand Coulee Dam on the Columbia River. Apparently, a side effect of this great barrier taming the river had been that the salmon could no longer swim upstream to spawn, so Wheeler, with his customary ingenuity, had conceived of a series of steps that the fish could traverse.

Tall and lean, with a bristling mustache and horn-rimmed glasses, the general, Jane thought, looked like a "straight-backed Groucho Marx." He had punctilious but easy manners and a nice dry sense of humor. The story was that on his first visit to Burma, Wheeler asked Lieutenant Colonel J. H. Williams, aka "Elephant Bill," the famed British elephant wrangler, how long the gestation period was for a baby elephant. Two years, he was told. A little while later, he saw a teak forest and commented on how convenient it was that teak—a valuable wartime resource used for everything from the decks of combat ships to docks—was in such ready supply, and just "rolled into the river and floated downstream." He was informed that teak had to be dried for three years before it would float. That evening, he observed to his British counterpart: "If it takes two years to produce a baby elephant and three years for teak to float, I have a feeling things are not going to happen very rapidly on this front."

Despite his daughter's job, Wheeler took a dim view of the OSS and the inexperienced civilians it attached to the military units of SEAC and elevated to positions of authority. For the most part, Jane recalled, he viewed the OSS as "a useless organization" and its employees as "a bunch of mavericks." Peggy and Jane would protest ("as loyal OSS types"), but to no avail.

Wheeler's suspicions were frequently reinforced by the odd behavior exhibited by some of Donovan's more eccentric ivory-tower types. In one unfortunate incident, S. Dillon Ripley, one of the country's outstanding authorities on birds of the Far East, was shaving in his basha prior to joining an outdoor cocktail party already in progress on the other side of a row of tea bushes bordering his hut when he caught sight of a rare *Picus chlorolophys wellsi* (a small green woodpecker). In midlather, sporting only a bath towel, he grabbed his gun and rushed out to bag the specimen for the Smithsonian. As he ran to retrieve the bird, his towel gave way, leaving the thirty-year-old Ripley exposed to all the festivity, which was being hosted by Wheeler. It was at this point that the general noticed the OSS intelligence chief—who at six foot three and a half was an arresting sight in the nude—attracting the attention of a number of officers and ladies, mouths agape and martinis in hand. Not the least bit put out, Ripley dressed and rejoined the party a few minutes later, whereupon he "modestly advised Mountbatten, who had greeted him a trifle coolly, that the Picus, though up to then unrepresented in his collection, was not unknown to science." Ripley's contacts and experience in the region may have made him useful to Donovan, but his civilian garb, languid air, and frequent birding expeditions into sensitive border areas were an endless irritant to the military. According to Jane, Wheeler "never forgave the OSS for harboring such characters."

Wheeler, who liked to go exploring, frequently organized weekend trips with his daughter and Jane. He would forgo his big staff car for a smaller model, still helmed by his driver, Tex, and sporting pennants with three stars. Whenever their sightseeing sorties took them near one of Ceylon's secret airfields—there were a surprising number—he would insist on making a detour so he could inspect the layout and workmanship. He would stride out across the landing strip, survey the length and breadth of it, then get down on his hands and knees and sniff the ground like an old hound dog trying to pick up a scent. After a few good whiffs, he would stand up and pronounce his opinion of the runway. The problem with most of the makeshift airfields in the CBI was that they became unusable during the monsoons, the planes just sank into the mud or slippery red clay. The Americans sometimes used pierced-metal plates to surface a portion of the landing strips, but the plates were heavy and loud and still needed proper drainage. The best all-weather airstrips were made of bithess, a locally made burlap soaked in tar that made it both waterproof and durable, but even those were uncertain in heavy rains. Whenever the tarmac met with his approval, Wheeler would clamber back in the car and tell Tex, "Get the Commander. I want to congratulate him on the quality of this airfield. A very professional job."

By March 1945, the entire Ledo Road was open to Allied traffic, which was critical to opening the way for future victories in the last campaigns of the war in Burma. In the weeks that followed, U.S. troops recaptured Bataan in the Philippines, Corregidor, and finally Manila. Meanwhile Lieutenant General W. J. Slim and the British Fourteenth Army, together with combined SEAC forces, pulled off a series of daring maneuvers, recapturing Meiktila, Ramree, and then Mandalay. The rest of the Burma coast was easily taken all the way down to Rangoon, with the Japanese retreating rapidly to the southeast into Thailand. It had been a race with time all the way to beat the Japanese before the spring monsoons turned the roads back into a sea of mud. In the interior, the OSS Detachment 101, made up of 300 OSS officers and 3,000 Kachin natives—mostly naked and armed with everything from knives to obsolete U.S. Army rifles—engaged the enemy in fierce guerilla warfare. These Kachin Rangers finished the Japanese army, routing a force of 10,000 and killing 1,246 while losing only 37 of their own. In recognition of their outstanding record, the heroic Kachin Rangers were awarded the U.S. Army Distinguished Unit badge. Alex MacDonald, who had been serving with Detachment 101, shared in the presidential citation.

Mountbatten, Wheeler by his side, came up from Kandy to lead the elaborate celebration to mark Burma's official Liberation Day. The Burmese public gave the magnificent military procession, complete with seventeen-gun salute, a polite if restrained reception, understandably unsure what designs their "liberators" might still have on their country. Unfortunately, the march past included a goose-stepping contingent of the Burma National Army—created by the Japanese to fight the old colonial rulers—led by the Burmese nationalist hero Aung San, still sporting the uniform of a Japanese general, which sent a decidedly mixed message about Burma's political future. On a dais erected in the shadow of the huge gold-leafed Shwedagon Pagoda, a Buddhist temple whose glistening spires dominated the skyline of Rangoon, Mountbatten delivered a formal address that was read out simultaneously throughout the whole of the SEAC command, lauding all the troops who had fought in Southeast Asia. Halfway through his speech, the monsoon struck. The loudspeakers just managed to carry his voice above the rain, but the Royal Air Force flyover was ruined. The planes, barely visible above the clouds, were prevented from passing directly overhead for fear of clipping the top of the pagoda.

6

THE GREAT WHITE
QUEEN OF BALI

Jane spent most of the spring of 1945 commuting back and forth between Kandy and Calcutta. Much to her dismay, she had been promoted and reassigned to the MO station in India. The triumphant end of the Burma campaign passed in a blur of work and travel. There was a tremendous sense of exhilaration among the uniformed boys in Kandy—victory was in sight, in the Pacific as well as in Europe. Germany was finally faltering, caught between the advancing Russians on one side and General Eisenhower's armies on the other.

The dramatic pace of events made it hard to stay focused. Jane was bored by her administrative chores, and she found Calcutta wretched beyond belief, "a sad, ugly city." It deserved its reputation as the "cesspool of the world" and was hotter than any place she had ever known and rank with contagion. "The Americans were strictly forbidden to eat in any Indian restaurant and the MPs enforced this regulation," she recalled. "Nor was this prohibition unreasonable, because there were roughly 3,000 people dying in Calcutta each week from cholera, typhoid, and other diseases." It did not help that the OSS had leased a house for their headquarters in the Kallighat district, not far from the place by the Ganges where the bodies were cremated. The staff would go to lunch at the Great Eastern Hotel with all the well-dressed Brits, stuff themselves silly, and then on the way back to work would be "confronted with all the dead, swollen bodies in the street." Despite the unbearable stench and misery of the city, she dreaded the return flight to Ceylon even more. She dated her fear of flying to those terrifying eleven-hour trips across the flat red plains of India. "Something was always happening to the 'war wearies,' either an engine or a wing was apt to fall off." She lived to tell the tale, but "many others didn't."

Jane had been on her way to the OSS headquarters in Calcutta when the driver of her command car had turned to her sorrowfully and said, "I'm sorry that your president is dead." She had dismissed him sharply, certain he must be mistaken. It was not until she reached her office on the afternoon of that early spring day that she heard the stunning news: the commander in chief had died of a cerebral hemorrhage at his retreat in Warm Springs, Georgia. "Roosevelt had been president practically since I could remember," Jane recalled. She could not "imagine another."

She was also in Calcutta the following month when Germany submitted its unconditional surrender to General Eisenhower. The next day, May 8, 1945, was V-E Day. A group from the office had organized a party for that evening. Giddy with excitement, they carried on noisily late into the night and got rather loaded. Jane and a Russian-born colleague began a tipsy rendition of "The Internationale"—the Communist anthem—belting out successive choruses in the original French, followed by German and English, with her colleague finishing with a rousing solo in his mother tongue. Their performance outraged John Archbold, who turned to them "purple with rage" and demanded, "How dare you sing that subversive song?" On sober reflection the next morning, Jane recognized that it had been perhaps less than diplomatic to choose that particular clenched-fist salute to serenade "an heir to the Standard Oil fortune."

The end of the war was in sight, but much of Asia was still in the clutches of Japan's large, well-equipped military machine. Malaya, Sin-gapore, Thailand, and Sumatra were all still under Japanese occupa-tion. The elation at OSS headquarters was also tempered by news of the grievous losses incurred in taking Iwo Jima and Okinawa. It was a grim indicator of the hard fighting to come. It was impossible to know how long the Japanese would continue to resist. Prime Minister Kantarō Su-zuki had announced that Japan would fight to the very end rather than accept unconditional surrender.

Back in Kandy, Jane resumed her MO work and continued to run the Indonesia desk. She was sorting through a stack of routine intel-ligence reports handed over by the British, most of which were unim-portant (which was why they were handed over in the first place) when she stumbled on a message concerning their Batu agents. At present, OSS had five men operating in the Batu Islands, off the coast of Su-matra, whose job consisted mainly of radioing local weather updates to their bombers based in India. The message, in Malay, was scribbled across the back of a report on rice supplies in Sumatra, which had been lifted from a sunken Japanese patrol boat. After translating it, Jane re-alized that the author appeared to have knowledge of the capture of three of their native agents. Once she had verified the report—two of the agents had managed to escape and were thought to be in hiding—she immediately brought it to the attention of their colonel.

Jane had expected the OSS to send out a rescue party at once. In-stead, Colonel Coughlin took the matter-of-fact line that little could be done at this late date. It was the view shared by the rest of her col-leagues, who reasoned that "the war would be over soon and nobody was anxious to risk his life at such a time." Always quick to identify with lost causes, Jane could not leave it there. She felt "a strong sense of re-sponsibility for the fate of two agents being hunted down somewhere in the Batu Islands." Her feelings, a potent mixture of self-righteous anger and remorse, came to a head when she discovered that the reason their plight had not been discovered earlier was due to the "negligence and/or stupidity" of the major in charge of monitoring their radio commu-nications, who had failed to report their coded distress call. "Knowing him," she wrote furiously, "he was simply drunk at the time."

Galvanized by her sense of outrage, Jane mounted a second charge on Coughlin. She finally convinced him to take action by arguing that the OSS would never get another native agent to work for them if they made no effort to recover the missing men. "Rumors were already rife in the Trincomalee camp," she added, "that we were abandoning agents to their fate."

Jane assumed responsibility for organizing the operation, which took a bit of doing. No American ships were available for the mission, but the British were finally persuaded to send a destroyer to transport the American landing party. Jane petitioned to go with them, badgering her boyfriend, their chief of operations, for permission. He wisely passed the buck to Coughlin, who refused to authorize having a woman join the dozen American commandos aboard ship. Apparently there were strict rules about such things. In the end it was decided that Gregory Bateson, the only other Malay speaker, should head the landing party. While Jane did not doubt Bateson's genius (his Irrawaddy scheme had been "on a par" with her condom caper), she was not convinced he was the best man for the job.

The landing party took off, and Jane was left in Kandy to wait and worry—an absurd, unendurable state. After ten of the longest days she could remember, the unit received a radio flash that the ship had come under fire from a Japanese patrol plane. Jane suffered paroxysms of guilt at the idea that she was the one who had sent them all to their deaths. Fortunately, a short time later the destroyer "limped back" to Colombo. Jane was in the officers' club when Bateson loped in, dirty and unshaven but otherwise no worse for wear. Jane threw her arms around him. After planting a big kiss on his bristly cheek, she gushed. "Oh, Gregory, you don't know how glad I am to see you back."

"Of course you are glad," he replied gruffly. "You did not want *me* on your conscience for the rest of your life, did you?"

They never did track down their missing agents. The landing party managed to locate the charred remains of their camp but then lost their trail. When Bateson's photographs were developed, Jane was thoroughly annoyed to discover they were "mostly devoted to the defecation and nursing habits of the natives." It was nice to see that the rescue mission did not get in the way of his real work. "Gregory, ardent anthropologist that he was, would go ashore at every possible place and take pictures. It was important to him, it seems, to find out which breast the mothers used for nursing and with which hand the natives wiped themselves!"

On the morning of August 6, Jane was in her MO office, where she now shared a desk with Bateson, when a voice announced over the army loudspeakers that "an atomic device" had been dropped on Hiroshima. They were having coffee at the time, and they both just froze, cups in midair, and stared at each other in mute astonishment. There were no whoops of joy, no jubilant slapping of backs or pounding of shoulders. The voice, crackling and distorted, went on to describe the earlier secret trial explosion in Alamogordo, New Mexico. As she listened, trying to absorb the news, Jane tried to picture in her mind "a vast eyeball-searing yellow desert with huge orange suns blazing and, in a corner, a small steel structure, twisted, crumpled, and torn, and not a living thing around." It was a terrifying image—one she knew she would "never put on canvas." All the while, in the background, she could hear Bateson banging away on his portable typewriter. Finally, unable to stand it another minute, she snapped, "Gregory, what in God's name are you typing?"

"I'm writing about the future of life insurance in the atomic age," he replied, and went back to typing.

Two days later, the Soviet Union declared war on Japan and invaded Manchuria. The next day, they heard that a second atom bomb had been dropped on Nagasaki. On August 14, Japan accepted the Allied terms of unconditional surrender. Jane picked V-J Day in the betting pool and won a case of scotch. "How we celebrated on that case of whiskey," she recalled. Later, she lay awake in her bed at the Queen's Hotel listening to the drunken revelry of the British and American troops, the occasional "shrill whistles" of the MPs piercing the night.

On August 20, Colonel Coughlin sent a message summoning Jane to his bungalow at six that evening. That worried her. Usually when the colonel made an appointment to see her it meant she was going to be hauled over the coals. "I quickly made my *examen de conscience* as I had learned to do at the convent," she recalled. "What sin or breach of discipline had I committed now?" Expecting to be "bawled out," she felt a flutter of trepidation as she stepped onto his veranda. She relaxed as soon as she heard the reassuring *tink* of ice cubes and spotted the coffee table laden with drinks.

The colonel greeted her warmly but wasted no time getting to the point. They wanted her to volunteer to stay behind and go to Java immediately after Japan's formal surrender and report on the transition. "Volunteer" was OSS code for joining an operation that might be dangerous, and Coughlin made it clear he could not order her to go. It had to be her choice. Since the Japanese occupation of what was officially termed the Netherlands East Indies (NEI) in March 1942, news and intelligence in that part of the world had been hard on the ground, and no one knew exactly what to expect. Coughlin added unnecessarily that she had been singled out for this assignment because she was fluent in Malay and was probably more familiar with the complex political situation than most. If she accepted, she would be promoted from field agent to MO representative.

He then proceeded to give her a brisk assessment of the little they did know: In the frenzied period just before the Japanese surrender, the nationalist leader, General Sukarno, had assumed the presidency of the newly formed Republic of Indonesia. Since then, his followers had been helping themselves to large quantities of arms and munitions from the Japanese, more or less with their blessing. "The Indonesians were in full revolt against the return of the Dutch," according to Coughlin, while the Dutch were determined to take back their rich colony and reinstate their sanctioned indigenous queen. At the same time, "there was reported to be, in Central Java, a large contingent of the Kwantung army, a Japanese division from Manchuria but recently transferred. They were untried and undefeated in battle, and there were rumors they would not accept surrender. Would [Jane] be willing to go despite the danger?"

Ready and willing, was her immediate reply. An uprising here or there did not frighten her. ("What could possibly happen to Mrs. Foster's little girl, Jane?") Truth be told, she was "delighted." They had already sent her MO colleague Howard Palmer to Bangkok, making use of his language skills to report on Japanese activities. He had been sent in to replace John Wester, who had cracked under the pressure of his clandestine assignment and been secretly flown out in a state of delirium. Palmer had spent the last months of the war holed up in the former royal palace, secretly radioing out intelligence reports to Ceylon. Jane had assumed all along that she might be called on to carry out a similar assignment. Just before Betty had left Kandy, Jane had divulged her "confidential plan" to infiltrate a small Indonesian island by submarine. She would be deposited on an empty stretch of beach, plunge into the jungle, and long after the fighting was over emerge as "the Great White Queen of Bali." At the time, Betty had no idea whether or not she was serious. With Jane, "you could never tell."

Clearly pleased she had agreed to go, Coughlin got down to the details. Jane would have three principal duties: first, to help supervise the repatriation of American military and civilian prisoners of war; second, to make a formal record of their war crimes testimony; third, and most important, to file daily reports on the domestic political developments in Indonesia to OSS headquarters in Washington. With the war over, Coughlin had formulated a plan by which the organization would continue to operate and begin phasing into a "peace-time covert intelligence agency." His OSS field teams were expected to begin "covert development of contacts productive of political and economic intelligence essential to the State Department and other federal agencies faced with future responsibilities in Southeast Asia." Once in Java, Jane would continue cultivating agents, observers, and other valuable sources of information.

Major Robert Koke, head of the OSS station in Batavia, would be heading up her team. He and his men would be stopping in Singapore before continuing on to Batavia. The American military mission, headed by Major Frederick E. Crockett, would be traveling directly to Batavia on a Royal Navy cruiser. Once again, because of her sex, Jane would be barred from joining them on the ship. Instead, she would bring up the rear and fly in on the first American plane into Java.

"Here's luck!" the colonel told her as he refilled their glasses, adding blandly: "In Java, you'll have to go in uniform and carry a pistol."

He would cut her orders in a few days, and she would have to get outfitted. She might also want to brush up on her shooting skills. In the meantime, after she had cleared her desk, she was entitled to ten days' leave.

Dazed and happy, Jane lifted her glass. She had missed out on her "cherished wish to see the liberation of Paris," she told herself, but she could still see "the liberation of Indonesia."

Coincidentally, Jane already knew Bob Koke, along with his wife, Louise. Before the war, they had run the popular Kuta Beach Hotel in Bali, and she had stayed with them for a month while waiting for her divorce decree. Bob was a tall, lanky American from Santa Barbara whose bronzed skin and laconic manner disguised a real intelligence. He had worked for MGM studios in Hollywood and had the odd distinction of having introduced surfing to Bali. Louise, an artist, was rumored to have run away from a rich husband to be with him, and the couple had been an amusing addition to Bali's tiny expat community. Because he was fluent in Malay, Bob was now with the OSS; he had been on a number of missions with Manly.

Warmed by the alcohol, Coughlin became almost chatty. Some OSSers considered the thirty-seven-year-old, six-foot-five West Pointer "a martinet" for being such a stickler for army protocol—"He made the GIs wear their caps on the way to the latrines"—though Jane considered him a fair and intelligent man. Dropping his usual stiff demeanor, he spoke candidly about the postwar power struggle.

Since the Japanese occupation, the major resistance movement in Indochina had come from the Communist guerillas, whose members were mainly Chinese and who the Americans had been all too happy to aid in their efforts to pin down the Japanese. In exchange for this uneasy alliance, the United States had agreed to help establish decolonized protectorates, or "trusteeships," after the Japanese defeat, with the hope that these would eventually evolve into independent democratic nations. But Roosevelt's distaste for colonialism—prompted in part by his fear that "1.1 billion enemies are dangerous," as he told one reporter after Yalta—had faded in the last months of his life as the British became increasingly obdurate about not sacrificing their interests in Southeast Asia.

After FDR's death, and faced with the Soviet Union's rising influence, Truman decided to reverse the policy. The New Deal idealism of Roosevelt and Donovan, which viewed the struggle against colonialism as part of the struggle against tyranny, was out of vogue. Doubting that the Indonesians were ready for independence, Truman took a hands-off approach that yielded control to the colonial nations. The American Chiefs of Staff approved the idea that United States would be released from the responsibility of "mopping up" the Japanese forces in the area. At Potsdam, it was decided that Allied authority in Indonesia would be shifted to Mountbatten's command, which would be widened to include Thailand (formerly Siam), the Netherlands East Indies (Java), and the southern half of Indochina. Mountbatten was expected to restore order, begin the arduous task of rebuilding the devastated territories, and prepare their return to the old order.

In practice, this meant Truman was now tacitly supporting the Dutch and French efforts to regain their overseas territories, and the United States would look the other way while the British attempted to make Thailand a disguised colony. These activities went directly against the various new nationalist movements that had sprung up in the occupied territories and were even now gathering force in the immediate postsurrender excitement and confusion. Coughlin confided that only that morning he had received a coded message from Jane's buddy Howard Palmer concerning "the Draconian Thailand peace treaty drafted by the British," which the Thai emissaries were being pressured into signing at a luncheon at Mountbatten's headquarters. This was particularly frustrating, as the Americans viewed Thailand as a fairly progressive, orderly little country, capable of running its own affairs and contributing to the political stability of the region. Coughlin had made straight for the governor's palace, where he had little difficulty persuading the Thai emissaries to hold off signing anything until Washington was consulted. (Jane later heard that the result of Coughlin's intervention was "a protest" by the American government and "the quiet shelving of the treaty.")

There was also the very real concern that if the British attempts to reassert their influence went badly, the Soviet Union, which had no direct role, might try to woo the Communist rebels. In French Indochina, the Communist leader, whose nom de guerre was Ho Chi Minh, had declared himself head of an independent Vietnamese republic. Regardless of their personal feelings about the rights of these colonies to control their own destinies, and the aspirations of their peoples, the Americans were there in a severely limited capacity, and were responsible to the British. The best hope was that the former imperial powers could be encouraged to accept the fact that these territories were on the road to self-government, and further American pressure would help improve the treaty terms. Either way, America was determined to remain outside the negotiations. It was a messy, muddled situation, to say the least, one that was bound to make Jane's OSS mission that much more complicated.

The ten days' leave was a gift. It was the end of summer, the end of her sojourn in Ceylon. Jane and Manly took full advantage of their last few days together, escaping to an elegant British government rest house on a pristine stretch of beach on the southern coast of Ceylon. "There we swam, sailed, bronzed ourselves, lazed, and collected exotic shells," she recalled. "It was a bittersweet parting between me and my lover, as we knew it was all over." They had made a pact; the only problem was that she had not counted on falling in love with him.

When the time came for him to leave, she prided herself on not making a scene, unlike the night she threw the *pot de chambre* at him. For once out of clever things to say, she walked him to his jeep in silence and bid him a stoic farewell. The State Department had offered him the prestigious post of general counsel to the Foreign Liquidations Committee, so he would be around for a few more months arranging the sale of its military surplus to the Indian government. In his usual easygoing way, he quipped that he only took the job so he could get a ride home on an airplane instead of a slow boat. Then it would be back to his law practice and his wife in White Plains. There was something about the calm, unharassed way he laid all this out that made it hurt more. After he left, feeling badly in need of inspiration, she "sat on the beach and read Buddhist literature in English translation."

He sent a chasing note of farewell from Burma, asking her to stay in touch. "Well, kid, I guess this is it," he wrote, laying it on in his best hackneyed GI style. "It's goodbye, then, to the things we've always dreamed of, you and I. Makes a fellow kind of wonder, don't it? . . . Things have been dull indeed since you left the jeep last Saturday but are due to liven up plenty without any further delay whatsoever. You may not hear from me for some little time, but don't forget that mail gets through to him very easily indeed. . . . We fighting men appreciate a word of cheer from the home folk now and then, let me tell you; makes us think what we're coming back to—and with me that's Scott tissue, when, and in the quantities, I want it. . . . Goodbye, Lotus Flower." He signed the note "Love, a Friend of the Republic."

A few days later, a GI drove over from Kandy with Jane's travel orders. On September 15, she flew from Columbo to Calcutta, landing at an airport with the disturbingly suggestive name of Dum-Dum, where she transferred to a huge four-engine C-54. It turned out the only other passengers were the newly appointed prime minister of Thailand and two of his cabinet ministers, fresh from exile in India. The plane landed in Bangkok long enough for them to get off and then continued on to Singapore with Jane as its sole passenger. The empty cabin was somewhat eerie, and she took frequent swigs of the cheap Indian gin she had poured into her canteen for just such exigencies.

Bob Koke, his brown surfer's body as trim and elegant as ever in wartime khaki, met her at the airport and took her to a large house that served as the OSS headquarters. She was not in the least prepared for what happened next. Saying he had "a lovely surprise" for her, he led the way upstairs. "There, under a mosquito net, was a naked male body with only a sarong over him," Jane recalled. "I could not see his face, but, when Bob shook him and he turned around, there was Don Hubrecht." A close friend of theirs from Bali, Don was the scion of a wealthy Dutch family—his father was the Dutch ambassador to the United States—and he had been picked up by the Japanese before he could slip away. She had heard he was in a prison camp in Central Java along with her former husband. She had assumed that Don, not blessed with Leo's keen instinct for survival, had died long ago, succumbing to malnutrition and dysentery like so many others. She hugged his thin shoulders, exclaiming, "Don, I'm so glad you're just alive."

"Jane, those are the nicest words anybody ever said to me," he replied.

They had gotten Don out only that morning, rescuing him from an internment camp in Singapore. He told her that Leo had been held in the same location until the Japanese ordered him to work on the Burma–Thailand railroad as an interpreter. As far as he knew, Leo was still alive. He suggested she look for him in Bangkok or Saigon. It seemed that her ex-husband was a natural leader and had proved "something of a hero" to his fellow prisoners. They had made him their "spokesman," and he had used his Japanese to ingratiate himself with the camp commander and help secure them extra rations and other privileges. Leo had showed them all how to weave hats out of palm fronds and insisted everyone wear them as protection against the tropical sun. "Jane, if you could have seen him in that damned hat," Don said, doubling up painfully with laughter. "How could you have married him, with your exaggerated sense of humor?"

Koke would tell her later that another acquaintance from her Bali days, a cantankerous hotelier called Manxy, was also rumored to have escaped the hands of the Japanese. Manxy's real name was Muriel Pearson, and she always claimed to have come by the nickname because she was from the Isle of Man. Don had bankrolled her small Beach Hotel ("merely because he found her so amusing") and had even bought her a bright yellow Rolls-Royce, the only one of its kind in Bali. "She was pure Celt," Jane recalled, "with periwinkle blue, slightly crossed eyes, short and dumpy." According to Koke, Manxy had recently resurfaced in Surabaya in East Java, where she was broadcasting for the radical guerilla armies under the name of K'tut Tantri, though the Allies had dubbed her "Surabaya Sue." There were all kinds of rumors that she had survived the occupation by offering herself as one of the so-called "comfort women" to the Japanese officers, but no one knew if there was any truth to the stories. Perhaps whatever abuse she had suffered at the hands of the Japanese had sparked her revolutionary fervor, for she was known for her bloodcurdling speeches for the cause. No sultry Tokyo Rose, she was a passionate and committed player in the propaganda war, her nightly broadcasts rallying opposition to the Dutch and British colonial rulers and support for the Indonesian revolution. It was a weird, improbable metamorphosis for the plump, gypsy-like woman with long batik dresses and dyed-black hair Jane had last seen arguing with impecunious guests on Kuta beach.

The flight to Java the next morning proved to be another of one those trips that wreaked havoc on her nerves. It was not exactly reassuring when the navigator emerged from the cockpit carrying a map and asked if she could help them locate Batavia. The Japanese still controlled the airport, so there was no radio contact, and consequently they were "flying blind." Her extensive travels in Indonesia during her married days had done nothing for her grasp of aerial geography, so in the end they had to resort to the rather primitive method of staring out of windows on opposite sides of the plane. When they finally sighted land, the navigator announced his intention of buzzing the Allied POW camp to buck up the prisoners and let them know the cavalry was coming. With a little effort, she was able to help him pinpoint the location with information she had from captured enemy documents. He flew in so low that it terrified her, but she quickly realized his instincts had been right: "We could distinctly see the poor men, naked from the waist up, barefooted, wearing ragged shorts, waving and screaming and jumping up and down." Afterwards, one of them said to her, "Ma'am, we never saw anything as beautiful in our lives as that big bird with the U.S. Air Force insignia."

There were scores of armed Japanese soldiers roaming the airfield. They looked "surly" but did nothing but stare as she hurried past. She took a jeep to the Hotel Des Indes, which was guarded by more Japanese soldiers. It was September 16, a month and a day after the capitulation of the Japanese emperor, yet to all appearances nothing had changed. The Japanese military, which had been in control during the wartime occupation, was very much in control of the peace. Japanese patrolled the streets, imposing "security measures" against the rebellious natives and insisting that all Allied personnel remain within the Des Indes and its eleven-acre enclosure. If they left, they had to be escorted by the Kempeitai, "the dreaded Japanese Gestapo." The Japanese attempted to further restrict their activities by stating that they, the Japanese, could not be held accountable if Allied personnel ventured into certain "un-safe" areas. The ambiguous nature of this warning opened the way for all manner of mischief on the part of the Japanese, who, as far as Jane could tell, "occasionally seemed to forget that they had lost the war."

If it had been possible immediately upon Japan's surrender to send the British occupation force to Java, the Allies would not have been in quite such a mess. As it was, the shortage of available ships delayed the landing of troops for six long weeks, leaving the conquered Japanese temporarily in control and providing the Indonesians with the perfect opportunity to seize the reins of power. As a result, much of the internal government of the country, especially the services, was now being run by Sukarno's Indonesian republic. The only thing that seemed clear to Jane was that the situation in Batavia was dangerously confused and bordering on "explosive."

HMS *Cumberland* had dropped anchor in Tanjung Priok harbor the day before, carrying the first postwar Allied Military Mission to Java. The military mission, totaling fifty in all, including a small force of Royal Marines and civilians and headed by Rear Admiral W. R. Patterson, deputy to Mountbatten, was to negotiate with the Japanese for the carrying out of the surrender terms and to disarm the Japanese as soon as British reinforcements arrived. Also aboard the *Cumberland* was Dr. Charles van der Plas, representing the Netherlands and chief of the Netherlands Indies Civil Administration (NICA), organized to ad-minister the colony. Major Crockett, who led the four-man OSS team, made up the U.S. part of the mission.

The major had no command function and had a carefully defined humanitarian mission: to see to the release and repatriation of Ameri-can personnel. Freddie Crockett, a trim, alert man of middle age, was tough, very self-assured, and a good raconteur. He was classic OSS. As a twenty-one-year-old Harvard graduate he had become an expert sled-dog driver and joined Admiral Byrd's famous expedition to Antarctica. Predictably, in Donovan's pipe-smoking old-boys' club, he was a long-time pal of S. Dillon Ripley, the Harvard zoologist who had been Jane's intelligence chief in Colombo. Crockett had gotten rich prospecting for gold in the southwest, and he and his anthropologist wife had organized a series of expeditions (with Ripley) to the islands of the South Pacific and western Pacific in the mid-1930s, concentrating on New Guinea. He had spent most of the war building runways in Greenland. He knew little about Java, did not speak the language, and was more than happy to give Jane a free hand in negotiating with the Japanese. He was especially tickled by the fact that the Japanese officers felt that dealing with a woman was beneath their dignity, saying each time he sent her in, "That'll l'arn 'em."

Their first task was to get the four to five hundred American POWs—including army, navy, and air force personnel, along with some two hundred civilians—out of Java. Most of them were from the 2nd Battalion, 131st Field Artillery, the so-called Lost Battalion, or were survivors of sunken cruisers from battles in the Java and Coral Seas. Twice a week, a U.S. Air Force plane would make the trip to Singapore, each time carrying as many people as it could hold. American POWs had priority, followed by American civilians. The British took care of flying their own people out in their own planes. Jane's unit had no authority to fly out non-U.S. personnel, which unhappily left the Dutch internees stranded until their government sent planes. While the Japanese, who still controlled the airport, did not interfere actively in the evacuation efforts, small, unexplained problems cropped up with suspicious regularity. "The pilots had an unusual amount of trouble, with the engines sputtering and misfiring all the time," she recalled. Later, the Americans found out that the Japanese had "the nasty habit of putting sugar in the gas tanks."

While they waited for the U.S. Air Force DC-3s to return, Jane's OSS team went into the camps and did what they could for the men while taking down their statements of war crimes. "The prisoners were really in pitiful shape," she recalled. "We would interview them one by one and give them food, scotch, and cigarettes." A young American naval commander, appointed by the Japanese to be the head of the POWs, was so emaciated he was down to almost half his normal weight. He was a tall man, and his skin "hung on him in folds," reminding her of a baby elephant she had once seen in Ceylon. Even though he was "yellow from malaria," nothing the flight surgeons said would induce him to leave until the last other POW was on the plane out.

Jane worked twenty hours a day, listening to the prisoners' descriptions of forced labor, grueling conditions, degradation, meager rations, and poor medical care, along with mental and physical torture, routine beatings, and occasional beheadings by samurai sword. Some had survived forty-two months of captivity and told of watching friends die slowly. What emerged from their stories, she noted, was that the inhumanity of Japanese guards was "not due to a deliberate systematic policy of extermination," as with the Nazis, but was more apt to involve individual acts of cruelty. For example, the deprivation suffered by the prisoners was in some sense shared by the common Japanese foot soldiers, as they were issued the same frugal rations. The difference was that the prisoners, weakened by disease and despair, could not live on "a bowl of rice a day."

Despite the litany of horrors she transcribed daily, Jane refused to give in to the hatred of the Japanese that seized so many of her colleagues. She had spent too many years in Asia to blacken an entire race as evil because of the excesses of war. As far as she could see, the "obvious criminals" of the Kempeitai had fled Batavia to escape the Allies, and most of the remaining Japanese they encountered were "simple soldiers and officers who had not taken any part in the atrocities."

A case in point, she believed, was the decent, hardworking Japanese army officer who had been assigned as aide-de-camp. "Poor Captain Oshida!" she recalled. "We communicated in Malay, of course. I would say to him, 'Captain Oshida, I need a fully furnished house by nine o'clock next morning for the Air Force personnel coming in to pick up prisoners. I want a housekeeper and a cook for it, enough food for six men, two cases of real scotch, and a Cadillac. And you'll get another Cadillac for our use by three this afternoon.' Captain Oshida would bow and say, 'It will be done, *Nonja*,' and he would always come up with the necessary."

One day, she happened to observe one of their POWs—a small-time crook named Tommy who had been hanging around Southeast Asia when the Japanese interned him—giving Oshida two cartons of cigarettes. Astonished, she had taken him aside and demanded to know what he was thinking. "You don't mean it!" she told him. "You want to give cigarettes to a Japanese?" Even though he had spent three and a half years in a prison camp, Tommy was still good-hearted enough to spot "a nice guy" when he saw one. Seeing Oshida's face light up with joy and gratitude at Tommy's unexpected generosity, Jane reflected, "It was my first experience of the phenomenon that former enemies who had got to know each other personally had less resentment towards each other than those who had never had any contact."

The women POWs, many of them Dutch refugees from Malaya, were kept in a separate camp composed of small huts surrounded by barbed wire. The conditions were unbelievably squalid. One of the first women Jane interviewed was a gaunt twenty-five-year-old American who had been newly married to a Dutch executive with Shell Oil when they were caught and interned by the Japanese. Intelligent and articulate, the women was able to give Jane a calm, collected account of her four-year ordeal at the camp. "Some of the Japanese treated us very well and some were simply indifferent," she told Jane. "But we had a commander who was a sadist, and, whenever there was a full moon, he would go crazy, order the women out and beat them." The only good thing she could say of him was that none of them was ever raped.

Her clothes had long since disintegrated. A primitive bra and the briefest of shorts hung from her bony frame, both garments painstakingly pieced together from old sacking. While still in Ceylon, Jane had read in the intelligence reports that the women prisoners in Java had no clothes, so before leaving she had taken up a collection among all the OSS women, filling three large body bags (the kind used for corpses) with their castoffs. Jane gave this woman all the best things from her friends in Ceylon, as well as many of her own clothes. It was a poor excuse for a trousseau, but the woman needed something to wear when reunited with her liberated husband in Singapore. "She was practically a young bride," recalled Jane, who just wanted to help her "to look pretty."

Like the young naval commander, the woman insisted that Jane see to the old and sick first and adamantly refused to leave the camp until the others had been moved out. The worst off was Sister Muriel, a seventy-year-old Protestant missionary who was lying semiconscious on her side on the floor. She was covered in lice and sores and had the swollen belly and skeletal limbs that Jane recognized as the classic signs of starvation. The woman was urgently in need of medical care, but Jane was not authorized to remove any of the female prisoners until all the POWs had been airlifted to Singapore. Those were the British orders, and the Japanese had no reason to countermand them on her say-so. But the sight of the nun's frail body curled up on the floor defied all reason. Remembering the small .32 tucked away in the shoulder holster under her left arm, Jane took it out and strode off in search of the Japanese camp commander. Confronting him with the old woman's precarious health, she told him flatly, "I'm taking Sister Muriel out."

"You're not without the express permission of Admiral Cunningham," he retorted.

With a kind of desperate bravado, Jane countered, "Don't you dare tell *me* what I'm going to do or not do!" She waved the gun back and forth, keeping it a good foot in front of her in case it went off accidentally. "This woman is dying," she insisted. "I'll wait for no permission, and if you persist in this attitude, I'll put you down as a war criminal."

They tried to stare each other down for a few moments, and then the commander, for whatever reasons of his own, decided to let her go. Jane whisked the old woman into the Cadillac and took her straight to the hotel. On the recommendation of the flight surgeons, she doused her with DDT and scrubbed her from head to toe in the shower. She had been warned not to give the woman too much to eat too quickly, so she fed her a small meal of a banana and a bit of rice. Exhausted, Jane tucked her in the spare bed next to hers and then collapsed. She got little rest, though, as Sister Muriel carried on thanking the Lord and singing hymns all night. Luckily, Jane found room for her on a plane leaving the next morning.

Most of her time and attention those first few days was focused on the POWs, but Jane could feel the political climate subtly shifting, particularly in Batavia. She had not been back to the quaint Dutch town since since skipping out on her marriage six years earlier, and the colonial outpost looked much the same, with most of the fighting having been pushed beyond its broad, tree-lined boulevards and handsome, white-stuccoed buildings. Its citizens had clearly been through the war, however, and Batavia had emerged from its tropical languor, its streets now roiling with riotous crowds steeped in the hatred born of oppression and racial bitterness. Three and a half years of Japanese occupation and intensive anti-Western and anti-imperialist propaganda had made an impression.

The Indonesians had greeted the Allied mission with cautious optimism, though it was clear from the first that they resented the presence of the Dutch and the English, which smacked of a return of their old colonial masters. The red-and-white nationalist flag was flying over every building where the Japanese and Allies were not in residence, and as far as Jane could see it was "the only flag of any kind in evidence." Everywhere they went, the once-familiar streets were covered in revolutionary slogans: "Government of the People, by the People, for the People" and "Life, Liberty, and the Pursuit of Happiness." These legends and many more, lifted from the Gettysburg Address and the Declaration of Independence, were crudely painted in three-foot letters on buildings, buses, and the sides of houses all over downtown Batavia. The nationalists had established their own newspaper, *Soeara Indonesia Merdeka* (Voice of Free Indonesia), and a radio station that broadcast anti-Dutch programs.

As a precaution, Jane had painted big American flags on the sides of the Cadillac they drove to the camps, because it was obvious that "Americans were the only Allies liked by the Indonesians." The Indonesians thought the Americans were their liberators—not the English or Dutch. The United States had defeated the Japanese and would now help them secure their independence. "In the event," Jane noted, "they thought wrong."

Four days after her arrival, she filed her first impressions to her control, Lloyd George, the civilian reports officer assigned to funnel her intelligence to OSS Washington. Stating that in the past few days the political situation had grown "increasingly tense," Jane summarized recent developments, drawing on intelligence gathered by both herself and her main local contact, an Indonesian OSS agent* code-named "Humpy."

---

* Most such agents were Indonesian Communists in exile.

The city is full of rumors, many over-exaggerated, and all difficult to check. The three opposing forces—the Allies, the Japanese, and the Indonesian nationalists—are largely unaware of each other's intentions. The Japanese, being under orders, seem to be the only ones who have a definite program of action; they are required to keep law and order, and to facilitate Allied demands. To all appearances they are complying to the "letter." However, incidents are reported hourly. Dr. van der Plas, ranking Dutch official, has been temporarily removed to the HMS *Cumberland* in protective custody. On September 17, a group of nationalists attacked Tjideng internment camp (European women and children) and two Japanese guards were reportedly killed by the nationalists; a policeman was beaten and then jailed by the nationalists after trying to break up a meeting; a Japanese ordered a nationalist flag removed from a building and was killed by the crowd.

The two main sources of tension appeared to be public resentment of the Allies' dependence on the Japanese for maintaining order and the Dutch intransigence in regard to Indonesian demands, but Jane foresaw far more serious problems. She identified four main areas of potential conflict. First, it was clear that throughout the Indies, but particularly in Java, "the great mass of the people are violently anti-Dutch." Second, her "Source" ("Humpy") maintained it was certain that the Indonesians wanted "nothing short of independence." Although the Indonesians disliked the Japanese intensely, they cared for the Dutch even less. The view held by the educated classes was that they had always known the Japanese promises were "phony," but at least the Japanese had declared Indonesia independent, which was more than the Dutch were willing to do. Third, the Indonesian president, Sukarno, and his vice president, Mohammad Hatta, had been the two chief "Japanese puppets" during the occupation. One of her sources had confirmed reports that the Dutch planned to execute both men as traitors who had collaborated with the Japanese. Both men had run afoul of Dutch authorities before: Hatta had been exiled and Sukarno jailed for inciting Indonesians to riot against their colonial masters long before the beginning of the war. Meanwhile, their supporters were ready "to resist by force of arms a return of Dutch rule." There were secret political meetings every night, caches of weapons all over, and the organization and training of an armed force.

While Sukarno was still at large, on September 19 he managed to organize a mass meeting of his followers in the Koenigsplein, the main public square in front of the Governor-General's Palace. Afraid the rally might touch off an uprising, Admiral Patterson ordered the Japanese military police to stop the meeting. When the Japanese advised that this might prove even more inflammatory, Patterson commanded them to make sure the meeting was conducted in an orderly fashion. The rally came off as scheduled and was a completely peaceful gathering. Sukarno briefly addressed the crowd, and they all sang "Indonesia Raja," the new national anthem, and shouted *"Merdeka!"* (Freedom!). Even though Sukarno stated that although united in their desire for independence, the Indonesians wanted no bloodshed, the nervous Europeans sent in troops. "With a supreme lack of political acumen the Allies, i.e., the British and the newly liberated Dutch, had the Japanese tanks surround the rally with their guns," Jane reflected later, "which certainly made a very bad impression on the Indonesians."

Her fourth point, and the one she knew was of keen interest to Washington, concerned the collaboration of the nationalists with the Japanese. To Jane, it looked as though the position of the Japanese was "ambiguous" at best:

> On the one hand they are reported to be depressed and demoralized as they are afraid they will not be able to keep order or protect Allied nationals (Source; Col. Dewer). On the other hand, the situation is one which they have been advocating and preparing the Indonesians for throughout the whole war. Source maintains that they are at present providing the nationalists with money and arms, and the nationalists are awaiting word from the Japs to side against the Allies when the occupation forces arrive.

Jane added that she herself had observed Japanese officials riding around in cars flying the nationalist flag. Based on all the intelligence she had gathered, Jane concluded, "It looks as if [the Japanese] are playing the double game: promoting strife subversively and at the same time making sure they are not held responsible for it by cooperating to the fullest extent with the Allies and obeying implicitly all Allied demands."

Jane attached a separate memorandum outlining practical concerns relating to her agent (Humpy). She included details of how he had secretly slipped back onto the island, sustained an injury in the process, but still managed to make his way to Central Java, where he landed a job as a driver for the Kempeitai. He knew a great deal about what was going on, and what is more had a number of contacts who he said would be willing to work for them. Crockett had recommended, and she concurred, that Humpy be sent to Singapore and interrogated by Major Koke. She added that he wanted to leave Java, as he had blown his cover on a number of recent occasions, including coming to the hotel for their first meeting, and felt that his position there was "precarious."

Ten days after they arrived, Crockett declared their quarters too cramped and commandeered the Governor-General's Palace. Admiral Cunningham had decided to remain on board his ship, so the place was up for grabs. A huge, marble colonial mansion, it held out the promise of living in "royal splendor." Just before they were scheduled to move, however, they all ended up barricaded in the Hôtel des Indes—"waiting (like dopes) for all hell to break loose," Jane reported to Lloyd George. She noted that the property request (i.e., the task of protecting American property belonging to former POWs) that came through that day was "practically laughable," given that they "couldn't even find out what was happening in the street let alone in Pladjoe."

She reported that the POW situation was under control. All the internees had been brought out, except for a few who were remaining by choice and were being taken care of. The outer islands had not been "cased completely," as their C-47 junket plane had been grounded, but it would get done. She indicated that she had not finished the POW depositions, explaining that the delay was due to the fact that they had no confidential secretaries and she had to type up all the classified material herself. "All in all the thing is like a stage set by Dali, and I expect the Rockettes to dance out of Des Indes dressed as Kempei," she wrote. "And we wouldn't be a bit surprised."

A group of British and American journalists arrived and managed to arrange a conference with Sukarno. Jane and Major Crockett attended the no-holds-barred question-and-answer session. The nationalist leader proved to be a cool customer. He had an answer for everything. One correspondent asked him what he meant when he had said in a radio broadcast six months earlier that he, personally, "would drive the British and Americans back into the sea if they tried to invade Java."

"The broadcast was prepared by the Japanese," Sukarno replied with equanimity. "There was nothing I could do about it."

"What was your attitude toward Allied fliers forced down over Java?" asked another correspondent. Jane had heard terrible stories about the fate of Allied planes lost over the jungle. In some cases, patrols reported finding the fuselage intact with all of its occupants butchered by Indonesian guerillas, leading some pilots to say they would prefer to pull into a high dive and "finish the job quickly."

"I wasn't able to take care of them," Sukarno, unruffled, explained. "I had no underground organization, no way of acting."

The reporter pointed out that there had been underground organizations in Thailand and Malaya, not to mention most of the European countries that were occupied during the war, that they had all managed to aid Allied fliers, and that people in those countries who had cooperated with the enemy to the extent Sukarno had were now on trial for their lives. At this, Sukarno shrugged and spread his hands.

Afterward, Crockett met with Sukarno and informed him that the American headquarters was "neutral" and he could call on them whenever he had a problem to discuss. The major reminded him that he had "no authority to act" and should be considered only as "blotting paper," willing to listen and absorb anything he had to say. Sukarno called the next day and continued to do so, coming himself or sending one of his cabinet members almost daily over the next few weeks.

Jane began work on a detailed account of their interviews with Sukarno and his four cabinet members, outlining the organization and aims of the Republic of Indonesia and setting out its policies, constitution, and aims, as well as how it might react to British and Dutch military intervention. But even as she compiled her report, British and Indian troop-carrying planes and ships were converging on Java. These were the advance echelons of the forces under Lieutenant General Sir Philip Christison, Patterson's replacement and the newly appointed Allied commander in chief for the East Indies. Shortly before his arrival, Christison held a press conference in which he outlined his military mission in Java. When asked about a possible hostile reception, he responded that he had no reason to expect any such thing. He had been told, he said, that Indonesians "liked the Dutch." It was frightening that anyone could be so misinformed.

Despite her official status as an observer, Jane was incapable of remaining a neutral. She was so eager to show Washington—and the world—that Sukarno's new government was capable of running the country that when he complained in one meeting that their efforts to restore trade were being blocked because no British or Dutch ships would carry Indonesian goods, Jane again took matters into her own hands. The first American merchant-marine freighter had just arrived at Tanjung Priok harbor, delivering a load of army trucks. Jane tracked down the captain and asked him to take a shipment of raw Javanese rubber that was ready to go. At first he refused, protesting that his ship was not equipped to handle the cargo, but when she ordered him to do it, he reluctantly complied. She patrolled the dock, pistol in hand, making sure they loaded the huge consignment. Although she meant well, she later heard that during the journey back to San Francisco the rubber had melted in the hot sun and had to be scuttled before it sank the vessel.

With the arrival of the Dutch forces, under Lieutenant General Ludolph Hendrik van Oyen, the mood in the city changed dramatically. The incidents of violence increased, and Dutch troops, armed with machine guns and automatic rifles, guarded the entrance of their headquarters, located next door to that of the OSS unit on Oranje Boulevard. Crockett recorded his observations of the deteriorating situation: "There began to appear in the streets roving patrols of trigger-happy Dutch and Ambonese soldiers. They shot at anything that looked suspicious, and when hunting was poor, they were not above forcing an Indonesian house and dragging off, without charges or warrants, some or all of the inhabitants." The major was particularly disgusted by the fact that the undisciplined Dutch troops were making use of American trucks, clearly marked with the U.S. insignia, which they had somehow hijacked from a recent lend-lease shipment. They were mounting machine guns on the trucks and mowing down civilians. He suspected it was a device to imply that the Americans were in sympathy with the Dutch.

For her part, Jane thought the newly liberated Dutch soldiers were "truly clinically crazy." ("Who wouldn't be, considering that they had all been prisoners of the Japanese?") They were so jumpy they let fly when they heard a twig snap. The British and Indian troops who had been sent in to keep a lid on things until the Dutch took over made no secret of the fact that they hated their jobs and could not wait to leave. Jane kept radioing back that Washington needed to know there was absolutely "no chance of a compromise." The Dutch expected to get back their most valuable colonial possession *"status quo ante bellum."* The State Department response was to tell the Dutch "to paint out the 'U.S. Army' markings on our trucks."

There were almost daily reports of ambushes, clashes, and search and seizures. The Indonesians understood that these tactics were designed to humiliate and intimidate their people with an eye to stirring up unrest in the native population. On the morning of October 9, Sukarno and Hatta, along with a contingent of cabinet ministers, came to the American headquarters to see Crockett. They were accompanied by Mohammad Diah, editor of the newspaper *Merdeka,* and his wife, who served as interpreters. Sukarno demanded to know whether the United States was prepared to do anything. When the major tried to sidestep the question diplomatically, saying he had "no information as to the official U.S. attitude," Sukarno put to him a question he could not easily answer:

"But do you, personally, Major Crockett, think it is fair of the Dutch and the British to continue to expect no resistance from our people when we have been provoked almost beyond endurance by their tactics?" What Sukarno and Hatta wanted was what the United States had given the Philippines: an assurance of future independence, with a set date and a program for achieving that goal. At the very least, they felt they had a right to state their case to the United Nations.

Bob Koke, who was just back from Singapore, took the opportunity to ask about the notorious Bali hotel proprietress turned radio propagandist Surabaya Sue, who seemed to be working as a spokesperson for his administration. Sukarno responded that she might have to be sacrificed in the event a settlement was reached. "Her days were numbered as an employee of his government because she would be of no value broadcasting against the Dutch and British [from] whom at that time he wanted some sort of recognition," Koke recalled. Sukarno went on to say that if he and his party did not get some voice in the government, or some recognition, they would have no choice but to fight. Jane turned away. How sad that Manxy, who had somehow found her way from that backwater in Bali to a position of some prominence in Indonesia's independence movement, would end up a victim of her own romantic dreams—a vision of herself as some kind of noble revolutionary avatar.*

Two hours after the meeting, they were returning to their headquarters after lunch when they heard the single sharp retort of a car backfiring. In the next instant, Jane heard a burst of machine-gun fire from across the street. She ran to the door and was just in time to see a fat Dutch guard emptying his submachine gun into an old jalopy with its top down, spraying the car and its four occupants with bullets. Just as she rushed out, the car veered off the street and slowly came to rest against a tree.

As she approached the car, she could see two young Indonesian

---

* In fact, not only did Surabaya Sue survive, but her influence increased as the revolution progressed in 1946 and she became a de facto public relations officer for Sukarno's fledgling government.

boys covered in blood. But the Dutch guards had not finished their target practice. She vaguely registered what "sounded like the buzzing of a swarm of bees" overhead when Koke yelled, "For Christ's sake, Jane! Hit the ground." Van Oyen's guards were still punishing the stalled car with submachine gun and automatic rifle fire. Koke was yelling at her, "Crawl on your stomach and get behind that tree!" Jane obeyed "mechanically" but in her panic got turned around and ended up stumbling behind a big banyan tree facing the Dutch yard. Koke shouted, "You dummy! Crawl to the window and jump in!" Covered with mud and blood, she made a mad lunge for the headquarters window and heaved herself over the three-foot-high ledge, landing hard on the stone floor and painfully skinning her hands and knees—her first "war wounds," as she ruefully called them.

It was all over in a matter of minutes. A lieutenant from the British garrison came out and confronted the Dutch colonel in charge. "What the hell do you think you're doing?" he demanded. During an angry exchange, the details of the incident were unraveled. The lieutenant established that it was a car backfiring, and not a shot, that had instigated the shooting spree. The absence of weapons in the car confirmed what they already knew—that unarmed civilians had been gunned down. The boys' crime had most likely been their proudly displaying the red-and-white flag of the Republic of Indonesia; it was still flying from their battered little car. "The lieutenant insisted, with considerable heat, that the guards hold their weapons at parade rest," Crockett recalled, but as soon as he left they returned them to "the alert position." An ambulance came and took away the wounded boys, one of whom clung to life until the next morning. Their two friends in the backseat miraculously escaped without injury.

Five days later, martial law was imposed. The Allied Military Administration of Batavia, as it was known, was established on October 14, and it imposed heavy penalties—including death—for anyone possessing arms, striking, or rioting. The only people allowed to carry arms were "members of the Allied forces." In order to avoid further violence, Sukarno ordered all Indonesians to stay off the streets after dark. By 8:00 p.m., Batavia was a ghost town except for the roving Dutch guards.

To be out past curfew was tantamount to suicide. Machine-gun fire ringed the town at night, and the next morning the bodies of the dead floated down the wide canal that ran through the center of town. Each side accused the other of atrocities. The Western press corps, which as far as Jane could tell spent their days holed up at the hotel "swilling whiskey and never going out to see anything for themselves," filed stories based on handouts from the British and Dutch reporting that a Red revolution was going on and the streets of Batavia were running in blood. The last part was true enough, Jane observed, "but it was Indonesian blood only." Realizing that the newspaper stories would terrify her parents, she radioed the State Department asking someone to call and reassure them with whatever stock phrases they used in these eventualities.

The State Department sent over a Lieutenant Colonel Kenneth Kennedy from military intelligence to assess the situation in Java "in light of the Indonesians' ability to resist the return of the Dutch authority." Jane arranged through her underground channels to visit the Indonesian president in hiding and acted as Kennedy's secretary and interpreter to conceal her OSS connections, but noted in her report, "we are of the opinion no one was fooled."

After meeting secretly with members of the Indonesian cabinet, Kennedy reported that Sukarno and his followers were willing to cooperate with Allied forces as long as no Dutch troops were landed but that if even "a single Dutch unit" was included, the Indonesians would "immediately and violently oppose them." His findings echoed Jane's as to the attitude of Sukarno and his cabinet toward the Allied occupation, their commitment to independence, access to small arms and some military training from the Japanese, and determination to fight the Dutch. Kennedy, however, did not see the situation in Java to be as dire. He concluded that while the Dutch would face "some sporadic fighting," it would be largely the work of "extremist elements seeking to encourage the lawless elements of society." He did not believe the Indonesians were sufficiently trained to offer "serious resistance to a modern army," though he indicated that the Dutch were in over their heads. "It is the opinion of the Observer that unless some third power aids the Dutch in repressing the revolt it will be impossible for the Dutch to defeat completely the forces of the Indonesian Republic."

Meanwhile, there was a serious food shortage in Batavia. Jane and her OSS colleagues were subsisting on C rations and booze. Bizarrely, while there was little in the way of fresh fruit or vegetables, the market stalls were stuffed with the most magnificent flowers. If only the blooms were edible! Sukarno had declared an embargo on all foodstuffs entering Batavia and intended for the Allies. He had paid a courtesy call to American headquarters to explain that the embargo was intended to send a message to the British and Dutch that the Indonesians wanted their independence. He added that they had nothing against the Americans and would be happy to make an exception in their case. Jane, acting as translator, had communicated his message to Crockett. Although "salivating at the thought of fresh food," both she and Freddie agreed they had to refuse his offer. The major had politely declined, explaining that they were under British command and it might prove politically awkward.

The embargo was extremely effective because the port was desperately short of food, and while the Allies held Batavia and most of the other cities, the countryside, along with most of the roads, was in the hands of the nationalists. Officials of the Republic of Indonesia reported growing restlessness and impatience on the part of the masses, particularly the youth movement, who were anxious to retaliate against the Dutch, and feared that their people would soon "get out of hand." It was impossible to know whether this was a threat to force negotiations or the truth. "Incidents continue at a great pace," Jane wrote in a classified OSS situation report on October 15. "Soekarno [the spelling then in use] is reported to be spending most of his time traveling around the island endeavoring to calm and hold back the people."

General Christison, who had taken over the Governor-General's Palace for his own use, invited her for tea in her former elegant digs. The invitation turned out to be "an undisguised request for information concerning the nationalists." Nevertheless, she found him to be a charming man, and he listened with interest as she told him that negotiation was the only way to avoid conflict. He was "quite appalled at the deception of the Dutch," Jane recalled, and appeared to have "complete contempt" for their conduct and lack of realism. As he later put it, "the Dutch remedy [was] force and still more force, to teach the 'natives' a lesson."

The following day, she was asked to brief General Slim, commander of the Allied land forces in SEAC, upon whom Christison clearly wanted to impress the strength of the nationalist movement and urgency of the situation. As Jane later noted in her report, the British "knew all too well of the Dutch provocations" (the use of American and British equipment and uniforms, etc.) and desire to involve the British deeper so that they would commit more troops to the area. The Dutch did not have enough men to take their errant colony by force. They needed the British to help prolong martial law in order to give them time to ship in more troops from the Netherlands, and hoped that in the interim the independence movement would lose steam or even collapse from exhaustion.

She concluded her secret report to Washington by stating that in her opinion the situation in Indonesia had reached "a complete stalemate" and that time was essential:

> [The nationalist movement] is well-organized, disciplined, armed at least for guerilla warfare, and above all, unified. The economic weapons at their command are enormous and they are well aware of them. It is the culmination of twenty years of rising nationalist spirit and the Japanese merely gave it an impetus and opportunity. If the movement is put down by force it will rise again. . . . It is no longer a matter of military occupation for the surrender of the Japanese and the release of POWs and internees; it is a serious political situation which may have far-reaching consequences for the United States. It may be that the impasse has gone too far even now, but certainly the only chance of a peaceful solution is recognition of the problem by the United Nations.

Jane's grim view was underscored by Crockett, who provided Washington with his own blunt assessment of the volatile situation in Java. He blamed the Dutch administration's "brutal conduct" and bungling efforts to restore colonial rule for squandering any possibility of compromise or a solution. Days after he left, the British ordered the Japanese to wrest control of the city of Bandung, seventy-five miles southeast of Batavia, from the nationals. This meant the disarming of the Japanese was moved still farther into the future, and the out-of-control fighting would continue to spread across the country. It took almost three weeks for British and Indian troops to quell ferocious Indonesian resistance and reoccupy Surabaya in November. The intransigence of the Dutch officials spelled inevitable disaster. "The situation could obviously go nowhere except from bad to worse," Crockett later wrote in a scathing indictment of the United States' policy of noninterference published in *Harper's Magazine*. "Without mediation, there is usually violence. One Javanese town was wiped off the map. When that didn't produce the desired results, the British tried again with another town. Presumably, the process could go on endlessly." The problem, simply put, was that no one wanted to get involved. "The peoples of Southeast Asia are now looking to the United States—and to the United Nations organization. The chips are down. What they are waiting to find out is: were the lofty pronouncements of the Allied war leaders about self-determination and independence promissory notes, or were they propaganda?"

The truth was, the revolution was on before Crockett's plane cleared the island. The remaining members of the small OSS unit had moved into the house of a prominent business executive, but the shooting in their neighborhood grew worse with every passing day. Washington sent orders that Jane had to be transferred someplace safe. She moved into a hotel and was assigned a second-floor room that was guarded by Dutch soldiers around the clock. She could hear "the rattle of machine guns and the boom of mortars all night long." Before returning to their base in Ceylon to report, Crockett had instructed her, "Jane, have your pistol with you at all times and sleep with it under your pillow." She could not help being reminded of the classic scene in old black-and-white films about the British Empire, "when the 'natives' go on a rampage and a white planter says, 'Take this gun, Sybil, and save the last bullet for yourself.'"

Early one morning, woken by the sound of gunfire, she crouched on her small balcony, pistol in hand. Peering down through the pearly dawn light, she saw a "fat Dutch sergeant" raise his gun and take aim at boy on a bicycle. The shot echoed in the empty street and rocked Jane back on her heels. It was cold-blooded murder. The senselessness of the act filled her with rage. "What a boy was doing on his bicycle at that time of the morning, I do not know," she recalled. "The boy fell off, twitched for a few seconds, and lay still in a spreading pool of blood. I have never in my life come so close to killing someone. I aimed at the back of the sergeant's thick red neck, only a few feet below me so that even I could not miss it, but somehow I could not squeeze the trigger." She went back inside and curled up on her bed, feeling very small and "an awful coward." The next morning, the boy's body, lying by his bicycle, was still on the road bordering the canal.

In late October, a cable came from Washington ordering Jane out of the country: GET FOSTER OUT OF JAVA. The gist of the message was that she was to be evacuated from the danger zone because the State Department was concerned that it would make "an unfavorable impression" on the U.S. public if an American woman was killed in Indonesia.

That got her back up. "Public opinion be damned!" Jane fumed after the radio officer had finished reading her the message. "What kind of an impression do they think it will make on *me*?" She made some more noisy objections, but Bob Koke cut her off, stating that he was the top-ranking American officer in Java and she had no choice but to obey orders. She would have to leave for Singapore with him that afternoon. In a conciliatory tone he added that she could always come back later "when things quieten down." Jane laughed and pointed out with a kind of amazed bitterness that things were not likely to "quieten down for years." Annoyed and exasperated, Koke threatened her with court-martial. Jane just laughed again. She had been threatened with that before, she replied, and—this last with a sneer—"by bigger brass than you."

"OK, Jane," he said, sounding pained. He knew her too well to try to argue. "But come to Singapore for my sake or I'll be in trouble."

As soon as they landed, she fired off a furious cable to headquar-

ters in Kandy: HAD NOT BARGAINED FOR SIT-SESSION IN
SINGAPORE.

The reply was designed to put her in her place: PEACE   OF
WORLD WILL NOT—REPEAT NOT—BE ENDANGERED BY YOUR
REMAINING IN SINGAPORE FEW HOURS.

7

CHICKENS COMING HOME TO ROOST

Jane had scarcely enough time in Singapore to catch her breath before receiving orders to go to Saigon. She had done good work in Java, and OSS Washington wanted a comparable report on the revolution under way in southern Indochina as the French scrambled to pick up the pieces of their old empire. Jane spoke French but knew none of the local languages, and she had no background in the region and no expertise to fall back on. Coughlin had confidence in her, however, and felt she knew how to get on in that part of the world. Not that she objected to going to Saigon, far from it. She loved the jolly provincial town, the capital of the richest of all French colonies, with its beautiful green parks, open-air cafés, and famous Cercle Sportif, where the smart set had gathered on the terrace to sip *citron pressé* and watch the tennis. She had expected to find the city in ruins, based on what she had heard, and was surprised to find it much the same as she remembered, if "slightly shabbier." The airport was an absolute shambles, but Jane was so relieved to be on the ground she hardly noticed. It had been another appalling flight. The C-47's engines had shuddered and coughed alarmingly ("the remnants of sugar in the gas tank"), and they flew very low over the flat country the whole way, the plane just skimming the brown-and-green-counterpane squares of the half-drowned paddies below. It would have been picturesque if not for the prospect of going nose first into the rice.

From the little Jane knew about the situation in Saigon, she had a depressing feeling of déjà vu. It seemed that nationalistic fever was catching. Unrest was spreading across the old imperial territories of Southeast Asia—Thailand, Ceylon, Malaya, Burma, Java, and onward. In Indochina—actually encompassing Annam in the east, Tonkin in the south, and Cambodia and Laos in the north—French rule was threatened. The native peoples had heard about the coming Philippine independence and were less than happy about returning to the yoke of colonialism.

Sensing a power vacuum after the sudden Japanese surrender, the Viet Minh had rushed to declare its sovereignty by staging what it called the August Revolution. On August 22, 1945, the Viet Minh organized an Independence Day celebration in Saigon, mirroring the uprising in Hanoi the week before, which would lead to the establishment of the Democratic Republic of Vietnam by Ho Chi Minh. The Viet Minh, which had forged close links with the OSS during the war by providing information about Japanese troop movements, were hopeful of American support because of FDR's rhetoric about self-determination and the United States' promise to liberate oppressed peoples. But as far as Truman was concerned, the die had been cast at Potsdam, where it had been decided to temporarily partition Indochina at the 16th parallel. The British, always willing to play the heavy in matters of the Crown, had agreed to occupy southern Indochina until the French could send forces to reclaim it and reestablish the monarchy. North of the 16th parallel, Chinese forces under Chiang Kai-shek would assume control from the Japanese. To Jane, it seemed like another confusing mess. For better or worse, her assignment was to observe the French reconquest and report on the political trends.

In the beginning of September, British Major General Sir Douglas David Gracey and his crack Indian 20th Infantry Division had arrived in Saigon and immediately ordered the provisional nationalist Viet Minh government to suspend business. Gracey enlisted the surrendering Japanese to help keep the peace, allowing them to resume their posts and take back their guns in the process. Once again, this struck the natives as the worst kind of double-cross. Gracey also released and rearmed the French POWs, who promptly went on a rampage. The violent reprisals quickly led to all-out conflict with the Viet Minh. The native Annamese, professing their willingness to die for liberty, retaliated, shooting up homes, burning shops, and ambushing foreigners. The depth of their sentiment was reflected in their slogan: "Death to all Europeans." In the Saigon suburb of Tan Dinh, a frenzied mob attacked residents in the French-Eurasian district of Cité Hérault, taking more than three hundred white and Eurasian men, women, and children hostage. Approximately half the hostages were slain during the predawn hours, while the remaining half were released after being beaten and tortured.

The next day, September 26, the OSS chief, Lieutenant Colonel A. Peter Dewey, was shot and killed at a roadblock after reportedly being mistaken for a French officer.* The roadblock, a barrier of tree limbs and brush, had been erected just five hundred yards from the OSS headquarters at the Villa Ferrier. Dewey, who was driving, had slowed down in order to maneuver around the barrier when without warning a hidden light machine gun opened fire. Dewey took a bullet to the left temple and died instantly. Another OSS officer, Captain Herbert J. Bluechel, managed to escape from the overturned vehicle and made it back to the OSS headquarters. During the fierce exchange that ensued, six Viet Minh were killed by the OSS pinned down inside the Villa Ferrier. After several hours, the Viet Minh called a truce and attempted to negotiate an exchange of the dead. The exchange was about to take place when two British Gurkha platoons arrived to save the day.

---

* A. Peter Dewey is often cited as America's first fatality in the Vietnam War.

The Viet Minh grabbed their dead comrades and fled in Dewey's jeep. His body was never recovered.

Before his death, Dewey had managed to air-pouch a comprehensive report of the complex political maneuvers in southern Indochina. He had been sent to Saigon on September 4 to head an eight-man POW evacuation unit charged with taking care of American prisoners and CIs (the critically ill), investigating war crimes, and carrying out other OSS instructions. While there, he had radioed the first account of what had happened in Saigon on Independence Day. Dewey was sympathetic to the Viet Minh's aspirations for independence, and in the days that followed he had been deeply disturbed by the French troops' provocative attacks on the Viet Minh, which he believed had most certainly led to the shocking Tan Dinh massacre.

He and his OSS team had witnessed savage French reprisals—gangs of French troops roaming the streets searching for Viet Minh to set upon and thrash with sticks and bare fists. Viet Minh sentries had been shot execution style. Too outraged to let it pass, Dewey attempted to lodge an official complaint with General Gracey, whose forces stood idly by "apparently enjoying the sport." Gracey responded to the American's protest by declaring the OSS officer persona non grata and ordering him out of the country. Dewey was on his way to the airport to catch his flight to Kandy when his jeep was ambushed. His last prophetic report, received two days before he died, described the beginning of a war: "Cochinchina is burning, the French and British are finished here, and we [the Americans] ought to clear out of Southeast Asia."

News of the brutal murder flashed around the world. Dewey was a bona fide American hero and had been handpicked for the Saigon mission. He was the ideal OSS man: the son of an Illinois congressman, he had majored in French at Yale and seen action in France against the Germans before being recommended to Donovan by a family friend. As head of an OSS team, he had parachuted behind enemy lines in southern France and spent six weeks transmitting crucial intelligence on German troop movements before escaping by way of a six-hundred-mile trek through enemy territory. Dewey was in Saigon representing "American interests," and hard questions were asked about how he came to be shot in the head at point-blank range after only three weeks in the country.

There were rumors of plots and subplots. The twenty-eight-year-old Dewey, who had no previous experience in the East, had reportedly exceeded his mandate and, acting independently, made contact with the extreme left-wing leaders of the Viet Minh independence movement—activity the British had repeatedly warned him against and perceived as nothing short of subversive. Suspicions about who ordered his killing led to bitter recriminations, with everyone pointing the finger at someone else: some Americans blamed the British Special Operations Executive (SOE), the British blamed the Japanese, and the French naturally blamed the Viet Minh. After a period of diplomatic turbulence—Mountbatten threatened to recall Gracey but never did—Dewey's death was officially blamed on a case of "mistaken identity." If the jeep he had been driving at the time of the incident had been displaying an American flag, per General Gracey's instructions, then "the shot would not have been fired." In an attempt to mollify the Americans, Ho Chi Minh sent a letter to President Truman expressing his condolences and making it clear that he disapproved of the killing.

By the time Jane reached the wartime capital on October 22, Gracey's troops were embroiled in a protracted guerilla war with the Viet Minh. There had been a series of violent incidents in recent weeks and British troops had retaliated, with orders to punish the offenders on the spot. General Gracey had decided that the Japanese were "not doing their stuff" and declared his men would "take strong concerted action and shoot armed Annamese on sight." The only result had been considerable casualties and loss of Allied prestige. The French forces had started to arrive and had brazenly occupied all the major buildings in Saigon, but were not yet strong enough in number to completely disarm the Japanese and take control. Meanwhile, the French colonials blamed the Japanese for stirring up trouble and accused them of arming the natives, inciting them to riot, and even joining in posing as Annamese.

"Basically, the situation in Saigon was like that in Batavia," Jane wrote. "The British were in control of the city but the Viet Minh held the countryside and the roads. The French had been let out of the camps and, after internment, deprivation, fear and undernourishment, were not normal, any more than the Dutch." Why exactly the top brass thought she would be safer in Saigon than in Batavia, she would never know.

The British were now in the position of having to help the French forcibly subdue the natives—the same Viet Minh who had allowed them to land without bloodshed only a short time before. As Jane reported to Abbot Low Moffat, head of the Division of Southeast Asian Affairs at the State Department, the British botched the job. According to a memorandum of that conversation, "[Miss Foster] felt that General Gracey had acted with much less circumspection at Saigon than General Christison had demonstrated at Batavia." Furthermore, Gracey "admitted that he had violated his early promise not to intervene politically in the affairs of Indochina, giving as his excuse that when he made the promise he did not appreciate the strength of the Annamite movement."

Jane spent ten days reporting on conditions in Saigon and came away convinced that the nationalist sentiment of the Annamese was far stronger and more widespread than previously believed. "It was apparent that the nationalist movement in South Vietnam was less well-organized than it was in the north," she observed, adding that the nationalists nevertheless had "an administration of sorts functioning outside of the areas held by the British and French forces." The Viet Minh were nationalists first and foremost, though they were buttressed by Communist support. Both professed to be pro-American but were really just virulently anti-French and were hoping the United States would help them gain their independence. Moreover, it was clear that the Chinese were enjoying their newfound importance as a world power and were backing the nationalist movements in both northern and southern Indochina. The British and French were trying to reassert military control but with little success. At present, there was an impasse between the Allies and the Viet Minh, with time and numbers on the side of the native forces. It was shaping up to be another prolonged, bloody struggle. "Boycotts and guerilla operations against the French could easily continue for years to come," Jane noted, "and guerilla warfare is in the prospect for an indefinite period."

Jane's observations were very much in line with the attitudes of her OSS colleagues and were echoed in briefs and memorandums filed by other members of the OSS mission in Saigon. In a signed affidavit dated October 25, 1945, Major F. M. Small wrote: "The general situation in Saigon reflects an intense desire on the part of the Vietnamese (Annamese) for independence and through hatred of them for the French and any other white people who happen to be in any way supporting or sympathizing with the French. The hatred of the Vietnamese for the French has been brought about by the not too enlightened policy of the French, which has been to exploit the Vietnamese to the greatest extent possible and treat them more or less with contempt."

Small shared Jane's view of the Vietnamese resentment of the British for protecting French interests and by extension the growing resentment of the American military in Saigon as long as the Americans appeared to align themselves with British and French policy. He also stated unequivocally that Gracey's mishandling of the French POWs was "the single immediate contribution to the intensification of the Vietnamese animosity to all whites in Saigon, and thus directly contributed to Dewey's death."

Ironically, the official American policy at the time, to the extent that there was one, was not unfavorable to the Viet Minh. Jane surmised that part of this benevolence ("on the part of some of the big shots at least") was motivated largely by economic interest: with the British, French, and Dutch on the verge of being kicked out of their resource-rich colonies, the Americans could swoop in and take over those markets. Yet not even this rationale was allowed to impinge on the silence that was preserved on all long-term political issues in Asia that might involve offending the Allies. At the same time, the European division of the State Department was arguing that a strong recovered France was vital to postwar Europe; it insisted, as Moffat later put it, that "to get the French back on their feet we should go along with practically anything that the French wanted."

So despite some misgivings, Washington went on supplying the

French with new American-made military equipment. The foreign correspondents in Saigon were reporting that most French officers carried American .45 automatic pistols, and the poorly blocked out U.S. Army insignia was still visible on many of their jeeps and trucks. It was likely that this would create the impression that Washington tacitly approved of the French policy, which would do nothing for America's reputation in the region in the years to come.

Jane was billeted at the Hotel Continental, which was full of Allied officers and intelligence units, as well as the remaining members of Dewey's beleaguered OSS mission. The classic French colonial–style hotel, located at the end of rue Catinat, had been built at the turn of the century by a home-appliance tycoon who wanted to provide luxury accommodations for wealthy tourists after their long cruise, and Jane had stayed there on her first jaunt to the Far East. These days the hotel was generally referred to as "Radio Catinat" because it was the favorite hangout of the foreign press—*The New York Times* had its bureau on the first floor, *Newsweek* on the second—and was awash in rumors and speculation.

On her first day there, she ran into Edgar Snow, a celebrated war correspondent and the author of *Red Star over China,* a book about the early days of the Communist movement and the rise of Mao. He still had the aura of a glamorous boy reporter, though he looked tired and older than his forty years (successive bouts of dengue fever, malaria, and scurvy will do that). Snow was working on a series for *The Saturday Evening Post* on the aftermath of the war in the East. A staunch anti-imperialist, he made no secret of his sympathy for the Annamese, and he obstinately inserted his political views into his dispatches. He was an adventurer—a romantic at heart—and more moral than ideological. Jane liked him and considered him "the best journalist" she had ever known.

The violence continued unabated, so that it was next to impossible for Jane to do any real reporting, let alone produce her daily crop of intelligence telegrams. Saigon was besieged. One afternoon, while she and Ed Snow were having a drink together at a sidewalk café, some Viet Minh came by and began lobbing hand grenades in among the tight cluster of tables, sending everyone diving for cover. Days later, she and Ed were walking down rue Catinat when they came upon a Viet Minh who had just tossed a grenade into the window of the French Information Office. An outraged French housewife, who had been waiting in line at the neighboring bakery, had cornered the culprit and was viciously assaulting him. At any time of day or night, they would hear explosions followed by the low, mournful whistle of the ambulance and the racing sound of police and military vehicles on their way to the devastation. For a short time, the streets would remain deserted. Even the ubiquitous *pousse-pousses* (rickshaws) would make themselves scarce. Then people would drift slowly back and it would all begin again, the turmoil of a new day. Menaced by all the explosions, Jane spent most of the time confined to the hotel with the other reporters.

By the end of the month, they had both had enough and took the same plane to Bangkok. Ed spent the whole flight with his head bowed over his baby Hermes typewriter furiously pounding out his story on Indochina. When she tried to assemble her notes, Jane found she had only a few scrawled pages and ended up relying on Ed for "practically all" her information. She attached the few pages of foolscap to her lengthy report on Indonesia. Ed later wrote that when he spoke of what he had witnessed in Saigon to General Douglas MacArthur, the veteran soldier responded with surprising feeling: "If there is anything that makes my blood boil, it is to see our allies in Indochina and Java deploying Japanese troops to reconquer these little people we promised to liberate. It is the most ignoble kind of betrayal, Snow, and it puts our cause in jeopardy everywhere in the Orient."

At Bangkok's Don Muang Airport Jane almost fell into the open arms of her pal Howard Palmer. Young Palmer had become famous in OSS circles for a stunt that had taken place a few months before the end of the war. The regent, Pridi Phanomyong, leader of the Free Thai, who risked his office every day by working with the OSS, had warned that Palmer, for his own safety, needed to be moved out of the house where he had set up his secret radio station. Arrangements were made to smuggle him to a new location, and he was put on the floor of an official Thai limousine, covered by a blanket. The move proved, in Howard's words, "as secret as La Guardia going to fire." Halfway across town, the limo got stuck behind a parade in honor of the Japanese emperor's birthday, and when the driver honked to clear the road, the horn stuck. The honking continued as Howard, sweating in the back, pleaded with the Thai driver to stop politely entreating the horn to "shush" and pull out the goddamn wire. Finally, at an intersection, an irritated Japanese officer raised the hood and silenced the horn, and the car proceeded to its destination without further incident.

Howard had established a new OSS headquarters in an old palace on the outskirts of the city called Suan Kularb (Garden of Roses), a vast European-style chalet of stucco and stone, with a brightly colored tile roof, marble pillars and turrets, and all the fairy-tale trimmings. The palace was set back from the road in the middle of a large compound that showed signs of neglect, as did the bedraggled rose bushes lining the long graveled drive. Still, Jane had to hand it to Howard, he knew how to pick his hideouts. She was disappointed to learn she would not be staying in such majestic surroundings until she heard Alex MacDonald complaining that the OSS headquarters was as crowded as a college dormitory on homecoming weekend. Among the many lodgers were several agents from the Thai underground, as well as Ed Taylor, who had flown in from Rangoon in mid-August to oversee the evacuation of the American POWs. As a favor, they grudgingly agreed to make room for Ed Snow.

It turned out Howard had arranged for Jane to have an elegant pavilion all her own, a smaller, gingerbreadish affair in the Dusit district, the official part of town. Bangkok was full of palaces—winter and summer palaces, city and country palaces—all built by the old kings of Siam for their extended families. Pridi, courting favor with the Americans, had made some of these royal residences, complete with their large household staffs and chefs, available to the OSS. It helped that Palmer's father had been dean of the Bangkok Christian College before the war and was an old friend of Pridi. Howard had clearly taken full advantage of the catering; he sheepishly admitted to having packed on fifteen pounds. Jane noticed he had taken to wearing floppy Chinese trousers to accommodate his new girth.

As soon as she was settled, Jane began making inquiries all over the Thai capital in an effort to locate the camp where Leo was being held. In the end, the Swedish consul general directed her to a Japanese internment camp on the outskirts of Bangkok. Once again, Jane found herself confronted by a mulish Japanese commander who refused to release his prisoner without the consent of the British authorities. "But I had Howard with me," she recalled. "We put on our usual 'we own the world act' and succeeded in getting Leo out and only Howard knew he was my ex-husband." Unlike the POWs she had helped evacuate in Batavia, Leo was in fairly good shape. He had been housed in an old villa with a small group of Dutch prisoners and had not suffered unduly. Although thinner and sprouting less hair than when she had last seen him, he had managed to triumph over his circumstances with his usual "stern self-discipline." She had never doubted it for a minute. His first words upon seeing her were "Of all the millions of Americans, they had to send you!"

She took Leo back to her palace and let him get cleaned up. She found him some clothes to wear and even managed to wangle the use of a jeep. That was about all the succor she was prepared to offer her ex. They went for long drives, took in a few gaudy temples, and talked about their wartime experiences. He still thoroughly disapproved of her. Tiresomely earnest, he considered the OSS inept for employing someone with her radical views, and he made it clear he would have preferred being rescued by the military. The war had not mellowed Leo. Nothing would. His government made arrangements to evacuate him to the Netherlands. He was made a colonel in the Royal Netherlands East Indies Army and dispatched to Japan as a member of the Dutch delegation of the Far Eastern Commission. It was only much later that she learned that Leo was not a diplomat as he had always led her to believe. His dull-sounding desk job—head of the Japanese Section of the Bureau of East Asiatic Affairs of the Netherlands East Indies Government in Batavia—was actually a cover for a Dutch counterespionage organization. All the time they had been married, he had been secretly monitoring the subversive activities of Japanese and Chinese Communists in Java. Boring, balding old Leo was a spy.

Bangkok made for a lovely change from the chaotic and threatening atmosphere in Saigon. Jane was enjoying palace life. It was wonderful to indulge in a spell of luxury after so many weeks of hardship. "There was no shooting," she recalled, "my war was over, my revolutions were over." The palace Howard had put at her disposal was opulent, with gleaming polished floors, overstuffed Victorian furniture, and ancient Siamese objets d'art—every precious item stamped with the royal arms of Thailand. Knowing her proclivity for mischief, he had threatened her with court-martial if she tried "to swipe anything." Jane could not resist taking one small memento but for Howard's sake settled for some sheets of royal stationery.

Despite the heavy presence of British occupying troops, Bangkok was bursting with an uninhibited gaiety. Unlike the situation in Indonesia and Indochina, here the Free Thai government was in charge and had made speedy work of disarming the Japanese. The new government had been rewarded by the United States' reestablishing relations and agreeing to vote for its admission into the United Nations. If only Britain's demands for a settlement could be modified—among them monopoly rights to Thai oil and timber, rubber, and rice exports; control of shipping; and commercial aviation rights—there was hope the country could escape colonial, if not economic, bondage. The British bitterly insisted they only wanted their due: Thailand had aided and abetted the Japanese during the war and reparations were owed. Still, hopes seemed to be high. The streets were crowded with people chattering and laughing. Their good cheer was infectious. Jane ran into OSS colleagues and friends from all over the CBI. She caught up with Alex MacDonald, who was a member of the Thai mission, and exchanged news of Betty. Alex, who shared Jane's sympathy for the anticolonial movement, agreed to talk to Ed Snow on background and helped him arrange interviews for his *Saturday Evening Post* article "Secrets from Siam."

The tiny shops were filled with an array of luxury goods, the shelves crowded with things Jane had not seen since leaving the United States. Silk stockings, for example, were so plentiful the soldiers were using them to clean their guns. There was an astonishing amount of jewelry for sale, superb and quite cheap, and she would have "bought the place up" if she had had the money. Even Ed Snow was tempted. Buying anything turned out to be a challenge for Jane, for not only had she not been paid for several months, but the Japanese occupation yen she had been given for expenses, while still in circulation, was worthless. No self-respecting shopkeeper would touch the defeated currency, instead rattling off a long list of what was acceptable, everything from Dutch guilders and Indian rupees to francs, pounds, and the rare American dollars. Not to be cheated out of her first real shopping expedition in more than a year, Jane begged Ed to part with some cash and convinced Howard to extend her a small loan from the OSS reserves he kept in a safe in his office. She picked up some small treasures, a few rings and silver belts, but her best find was "a sixteenth-century, solid bronze head of Buddha, weighing fifteen pounds."

Just before she left Java, OSS brass had advised her that the organization was being restructured into oblivion and would limp along as the Interim Research and Intelligence Division until its wartime function ended on the last day of business in December 1945. The news had thrown her for a bit of a loop. Who exactly was she working for, or, more to the point, whose eyes would be perusing her eyes-only intelligence reports? Was it all going straight to the State Department, or would it be crossing other desks along the way? "We are all slightly confused as to where our stuff will eventually land," Jane had radioed Lloyd George. In the meantime, there was a serious shortage of personnel in the intelligence sections. With Cora DuBois recalled home, there would be no one left in Kandy to receive their reports and translate them into a usable form. Jane had "slews of material" to pouch to Washington, but it was all in Malay or Dutch or French, and she was afraid it would never get read.

Unable to extend her pleasant interlude in Bangkok any longer, Jane packed her meager belongings—she had given away almost all her clothes to the female POWs—and made plans to return to Calcutta, where she would make arrangements for her transportation to the United States. Her last days were caught up in the social whirl of victory celebrations. Pridi gave a lavish dinner party featuring a full orchestra and the Royal Siamese Ballet. The Thais were generous hosts: the liquor flowed freely, the food was plentiful, and scores of waiters danced attendance. No one seemed to notice the absence of the prima ballerina, who, in a diva display worthy of Nijinsky, pulled a no-show at the last minute.

Jane felt rather detached from the festivities but could not hide her amusement at the ceremony in which the regent decorated General Stratemeyer with the Order of the White Elephant, Third Class. For some reason, the name of the award struck her as hilarious—"it was so fitting." Suddenly she was laughing uncontrollably. The effort to choke back the mirth that came fountaining forth earned her a reproachful glance from Howard, "although he, too, was turning pink." Then it was Howard's turn to be honored. Jane watched with something akin to motherly pride as the general awarded him the Silver Star and the regent bestowed another medal, both of which she judged "richly deserved." Still, she could not help thinking they were all white elephants now and there was nothing the Thai people—or, for that matter, most of the old empire's inhabitants—wanted more than to see the back of them.

Waiting on the runway of the Bangkok airport after several failed attempts to gain sufficient altitude, Jane was doing the complex figuring on the odds of her surviving another run on one of the "war wearies." It was a relatively short flight to Singapore, but the prospect did not look promising. After some debate, the crew decided to inspect the engines and discovered a dead raven in one of them. Sure it was a sign, Jane refused to get back on board. Howard had to "physically push" her onto the plane. Once she got to Calcutta, she put her foot down. She declined a priority flight to Washington and instead took the first troopship headed for New York. It would take a month, but at least she would make it home in one piece. Shortly after they set out, the ship's captain, on hearing she was an artist, asked her to paint a large canvas to serve as a kind of banner when they pulled into New York harbor. The USS *A. W. Greely* would be one of the first ships returning from the China theater, and he wanted to make an entrance. She submitted a series of sketches, and inevitably he chose the one she liked least: "It showed a huge G.I. in a rickshaw pulled by an Asian in a conical hat.

The G.I. had a cigar in his mouth and had his feet up. Around the rickshaw were little Japanese soldiers running in all directions, with the flag of the Rising Sun lying in tatters."

For most of the thirty-day crossing, Jane worked on the enormous painting, which covered a six-hundred-square-foot stretch of canvas. When they reached New York harbor on December 6, the captain draped it triumphantly over the side of the ship. The phalanx of photographers on the dock captured it in all its glory, and it received more publicity than any other painting Jane had ever done. It made her "shudder" just to think of it.

A handful of friends were at Pier 88 to meet her. She could tell by their raised eyebrows and slightly dismayed expressions that she must look a sight. It was an icy mid-December morning, and she was dressed in her threadbare tropical uniform—a khaki shirt and skirt, tightly belted because it was now two sizes too large, WAC shoes, and no stockings. One of the Red Cross girls on the boat had lent her a sweater. As soon as she could, Jane telephoned her parents in San Francisco. When the exclamations of joy had subsided, her mother, who always had her priorities straight, asked, "Darling, do you have clothes?"

Over the next few days, Jane went on a shopping binge using her mother's charge accounts at Bergdorf Goodman, Bonwit Teller, and Henri Bendel. On December 11, armed with a new Mark Cross bag, she took the train to Washington. She reported to the old Q Building, where the remaining operational part of the OSS was still located. Much had changed since she had left for Ceylon. Most of "the heavy-duty thinkers" in the R & A divisions had been assigned to the State Department, while the so-called "thin rapiers of steel" in the operational units had been transferred to the War Department.

A wave of nostalgia hit her as she negotiated the familiar maze of corridors and peered into offices filled with cardboard boxes, and she stepped blindly into one long room only to find herself suddenly face to face with a group of her old colleagues: "No longer in khaki outfits with sleeves rolled up and with black sweat stains under the arms and on the backs, but in beautifully tailored winter uniforms. Each chest was displaying rows and rows of ribbons ('fruit salad,' as it was called then) and each shoulder was sporting a shiny new eagle of a full (or 'chicken') colonel." Even Bob Koke, who had scarcely bothered with shoes when she first knew him on Kuta beach, was all spit and polish. She felt a great rush of affection for them—her "comrades-in-arms." In the difficult, sometimes dangerous times over the past two years, they had been her blood brothers, her closest friends, "her family." To cover up her unaccustomed sentimentality, she leaned against the door, folded her arms, and announced in a droll voice, "Well, well! As the Chinese say, the sky is black with chickens coming home to roost."

Jane handed in her assessment of the situation in Indonesia—a fat document that she had labored over for many hours on the ship, writing and rewriting it until she was satisfied. She had always been given free rein in expressing her opinions about the military and political disarray she had witnessed, and she felt no need to hold back now, despite the wider distribution that her final report would probably receive. The long voyage had given her time to summarize the trend of developments and crystallize her thoughts about the lessons of the U.S. experience there. The Allied victory over Japan had not restored the prewar order in Indonesia or, for that matter, in most of Southeast Asia. Dutch rule was most likely doomed, and the French were under attack in Indochina. The Philippines and Burma were preparing for independence, and even India, with all its explosive potential, was on the road toward a similar goal. It spelled the end of European domination in that part of the world. "The Japanese had planted a time bomb in Southeast Asia, which was nationalism, through showing that the white man could be defeated by a yellow people," Jane wrote. "All the troops, shipping, arms, and supplies would be unable to suppress the nationalist movements." This thesis was supported by some thirty pages of research consisting of a chronology and her detailed analysis of day-to-day events. What she could have added, but did not, were these lines from a Kipling ballad: "Then, underneath the cold official word: / 'This is not really half of what occurred.'"*

---

* Rudyard Kipling, "A Legend of Truth."

The minute her report landed on the desk at headquarters, it was stamped "Top Secret." It struck her as laughable that anything so painfully obvious could be considered confidential.

She was asked to stay on in Washington for another day, as Undersecretary of State Dean Acheson wanted a chance to debrief her. Jane found Acheson to be "a gentleman of the old school"—conservative, European-oriented, but very competent. He listened to her attentively, questioned her closely, but did not argue. After spending several hours with him, she was asked to report to the State Department's Abbot Low Moffat, head of the Division of Southeast Asian Affairs, an anticolonialist who was a holdover from the Roosevelt/Donovan years. Also present was John F. Cady, a Burma analyst for OSS during the war who had been transferred to the Office of Intelligence Research for South Asia, and Richard Allen, representing North European Affairs. As by that time departmental personnel from the European side determined policy—the Russian threat had clear priority—while the old CBI hands were comparatively unimportant, Allen's was the loudest voice in the room.

Jane again described the situation in Indonesia and Vietnam as it appeared to her and patiently answered their questions. It soon became clear that Allen had an issue with the whole idea of Indonesian independence and found it suspect. He argued that Indonesia could never be a unified nation ("there are about a thousand islands and they all speak a different language") and was still very much a Dutch colony. Jane politely pointed out that she had traveled through all of the larger islands and that all the inhabitants spoke a lingua franca—Malay.

"Sukarno is a traitor and a Japanese collaborator," Allen objected.

Jane tried to explain that it was not as black-and-white as that. It was not at all clear that Sukarno deserved to be classified simply as a puppet quisling of the Japanese. He had a long prewar record as a champion of Indonesian independence. It was true that the Japanese, once they saw that they could not win the war, had tried to turn the Indonesians—along with other colonial Southeast Asian peoples—against the Allies, including the United States. This shift in policy had changed the Japanese propaganda complexion. The Japanese had actively encouraged the anti-Dutch nationalist movement led by Sukarno, but their endeavors had met with relatively little success. Jane knew that some nationalist leaders in other countries—Dr. Ba Maw of Burma, for one—had collaborated with the Japanese more than they had any excuse for doing, but in her view Sukarno did not fit that mold. She firmly believed he was anti-Japanese at heart and that he had had no choice but to cooperate with the occupying Japanese army. "Sukarno has always been a nationalist, who has agitated against the Dutch his whole life," Jane said heatedly. "To him, Dutch and Japanese overlordship is the same thing."

It came to her that this man Allen was not befuddled, as she had first thought, but obstinately wedded to his own view of America's strategic links in the Pacific. Moreover, he did not share her moral reservations about America acting as a handmaiden to the mercenary colonial powers. It was clear to her that the State Department view was that American interest lay in the maintenance of the British, French, and Dutch colonial regimes, especially if that meant those regimes would be better and more cooperative allies to the United States. The State Department was in favor of liberalizing the regimes only insofar as it made them easier to maintain and would check Soviet influence in stimulating revolt. In the meantime, nothing would be said or done that might compromise relations with the Europeans at such a sensitive time.

After a series of back-and-forth exchanges that escalated into a sharp disagreement, Jane lost her temper. "I've just come back from there," she snapped. "Are you interviewing me because you want me to tell you something or do you just wish to be confirmed in your preconceptions?"

That sour note ended the interview and brought her OSS career to a close. She had typed a letter of resignation and submitted it with her report. A few colleagues tried to convince her to stay on, but she would not hear of it. Her duty to her country was over, and she wanted to get back to painting and her "real life." Bob Koke even offered to put her name in for a meritorious service decoration, but Jane just snorted in disbelief. "Don't you remember that afternoon in Batavia?" he prompted, referring to her heroic plunge through the OSS headquarters window in a hail of bullets.

"If medals are being awarded for stupidity," she replied with a wry grin, "I'll accept one."

Even as she said it, at the back of her mind she was already thinking that she might write a book about the revolution in Indonesia. She pictured the bloodied bodies of the two boys slumped in the front seat of the jeep. Her exposure to the indignities and miseries underlying the confrontation with the Dutch had made an indelible impression. It would take time to absorb fully, yet she was aware she had registered with dismay a kind of arrogance in the State Department's view of Southeast Asia that was in itself a form of imperial droit du seigneur. She felt weary and unaccountably sad. All she wanted to do was to get home to San Francisco in time for the holidays. Even though she had sworn never to take another airplane as long as she lived, she crossed her fingers and caught a flight to the coast.

8

WHISPERS IN THE WILLOW TREES

Chungking reminded Paul of Paris in winter, only without the amenities. The first few weeks of 1945 were bone-chillingly cold, the sky was a relentless gray, and the rain never stopped. He slept in long underwear and socks beneath three wool army blankets and could not get warm. He arose at dawn "more icicle than man" and sat huddled in his overcoat, his breath fogging in the raw morning air, blinding himself working on charts, maps, and diagrams by the light of a feeble Chinese candle, which consisted of a small cup of water and fat with a string in the middle. The electricity was intermittent at best due to the pitifully short supply of current produced by the power station, which ran on Szechuan brown coal and could not begin to keep up with the demands of the large and growing U.S. military contingent.

When the Japanese army captured Hankow in 1938, Chiang Kai-shek had moved the seat of his government to this city in the remote western province of Szechuan, and it had effectively become China's wartime capital. It was teeming with soldiers, diplomats, and members of the international press. Paul had done in Chungking exactly what he had done in Kandy—scrounged for men and materials, bossed coolies, and somehow built a war room—before being pulled away and asked to construct three more war rooms in the same theater. Leave it to the army to punish a man for doing the impossible. Still, Wedemeyer had apologized for pushing so hard, assured him he had "a terrific reputation" among all the generals—American and Chinese—and recommended him for promotion. "Balm in Gilead, by God," Paul wrote his brother. "I stand modestly to one side, swollen head slightly averted, awaiting a wreath of laurel."

After four months in China, it was still the stench of the country that Paul minded most, a mixture of mud and sweat and shit that permeated the air. (Human feces were used to fertilize everything from crops to neighborhood vegetable patches.) The Chinese looked like dolls in their heavily padded coats and straw sandals, only their bright red apple cheeks visible beneath snug caps bearing the blue-and-white Kuomintang star over the visor. The living and working conditions were beyond terrible, made worse by the scores of rats that infested the city. They ate his paints and modeling clay, and regularly chewed through the telephone lines at night. Because of the time pressure, Paul had spent most of his time jumping back and forth between job sites, his army jeep plowing through bomb-battered roads of liquid mud and spraying the oozing slush on the local populace, who crowded the streets with their rickshaws, black pigs on ropes, varnished parasols, and steaming baskets of noodles. With the approach of spring, the top layer of muck had begun to dry and turn to dust, and they were all covered from head to toe in the brown filth, the grit clogging their nostrils and coating their faces and the roofs of their mouths. "It's dirty beyond belief, utterly inconvenient, full of disease, misery, corruption, and mystery," he wrote Charles, "but I love it."

The workload was as unrelenting as the rain. One of Paul's assistants cracked under the strain and took to "bawling like a baby" at the first cross word. He was too young and too green for the job. Washington had to be scraping the bottom of the barrel to be sending kids like that into the field. Despite being desperately shorthanded, Paul had been forced to send him back to the States. At times, he was so tired that he himself entertained childish fantasies of faking a breakdown or illness—"of becoming magnificently and continuously sick"—in order to get shipped back with a Section 8. Though back to what, he did not know. He had "no home, no dame, and no dough to speak of." Where would he go? What would he do? It was silly in more ways than one. The average rotation overseas was eighteen months, which meant his time would have been up soon enough except that Wedemeyer had decided he was indispensable. There was nothing to do but slog on and get the job done. One of the few ways to relieve the pressure was to indulge in the local firewater, a home-brewed gin made by a White Russian named Morisov. The stuff was sold in two-and-a-half-gallon crocks, and it was "not too bad." At any rate, it warmed the blood.

Chungking offered precious few diversions, but it had one chief attraction in the form of Rosie Frame. She was OSS, a "mishkid" (child of China missionaries), and had traveled over on the *Mariposa* with the rest of the gang. Frame had been involved in various black propaganda work in New Delhi along with another young OSS recruit named Joy Homer, descendant of the famous painter Winslow Homer and a room-mate of Betty MacDonald. In the winter of 1944, one of their opera-tions—aimed at identifying an enemy agent in the Chinese diplomatic community—had taken a violent turn. When the suspected agent was identified as a beautiful nineteen-year-old Chinese woman who was betrothed to an American army major, Rosie and Joy were assigned the job of infiltrating the Chinese Embassy. As they were both fluent in Mandarin, they were asked to attend the girl's engagement party and eavesdrop on the guests to see if the bride was close to anyone on the Chinese delegation staff. Almost immediately after the party, the bride-to-be "disappeared," and OSS relations with the Chinese community in New Delhi became strained.

Fearing for their safety, both Rosie and Joy asked to be issued hand-guns but were refused, even though their MO chief, Oliver Caldwell, endorsed their request and was armed himself. Then, one night on her way home, Joy was run down by a car on a narrow New Delhi street.

Julia McWilliams and Paul Child both served overseas with the OSS's Detachment 404. They met in Ceylon and did most of their courting in China, but Paul would not agree to marry the "6′2″ *bien-jambée*" until he had seen her in civilian clothes. He finally relented in Maine in the summer of 1946: he was forty-four, and she was almost thirty-four.

2

Jane Foster, a beguiling
blond OSS officer who
first caught Paul's eye in
Washington, D.C., in the
fall of 1943, was "a wild,
messy girl, always in
trouble."

3

OSS officer Betty MacDonald,
who specialized in black
propaganda, with the canine
patrol guard she shipped
home from China as "K-9
First Class Sammy." Reared in
the company of spies and GIs,
the spaniel had a taste for gin
martinis.

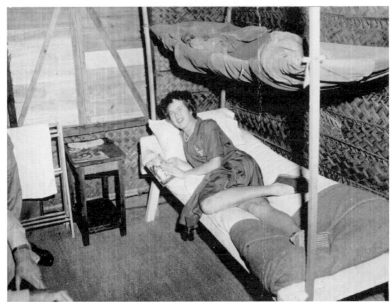

Julia striking a coquettish pose on the cot in her bamboo hut in Kandy. She hoped the photo would give Paul ideas, but instead he forwarded it to his brother as an interesting example of the local architecture.

OSS personnel at work in the Research and Analysis section of the Kandy field station, housed in an old tea plantation, where unwanted visitors included lizards, tarantulas, and six-foot-long cobras.

Lord Louis Mountbatten, the supreme commander of the China-Burma-India theater of war, paying a visit to the primitive OSS camp in Kandy. Behind him Detachment 404 commander John Coughlin looks on, along with Lieutenant Commander Edmond Taylor.

Major General William J. ("Wild Bill") Donovan, director of the OSS, recruited what one employee called "rare, strange personalities" from every walk of life, including academics, journalists, assorted criminals, and Communists.

7

Lieutenant Colonel Richard Heppner, the brash young head of Detachment 404, complained of constant interference by British intelligence so much that at times it was hard to tell they were on the same side.

8

The Queen's Hotel in Kandy, a Victorian relic, was a breeding ground for mosquitoes, so Julia, Jane, and the other OSS women billeted there promptly contracted dengue fever.

The charming Mountbatten, who Paul Child called the "one hero" in his life, selected the King's Pavilion as his elegant headquarters, and decreed Kandy "probably the most beautiful spot in the world."

General Joseph Stilwell (*far right*) scowling as he poses with Mountbatten, who is flanked by Generalissimo and Madame Chiang Kai-shek, and Lieutenant General Brehon Somervell in Chungking, the wartime capital of China. Stilwell had nothing but contempt for the corrupt Chinese Nationalist leader and the imperialist ambitions of the British.

The OSS headquarters in Kunming was as bare bones as a cavalry outpost, consisting of a few two-story buildings scattered on a dirt parade ground. Paul described the atmosphere as "rather like a party which has gone sour."

Betty MacDonald standing with colleagues in the doorway of the flooded MO print shop during the historic 1945 flood in Kunming. The camp's well-fortified walls turned the OSS compound into a three-foot-deep lagoon, and they were forced to commute between buildings in life rafts.

14

15

(*Clockwise from top left*) John Carter Vincent, John Service, John Paton Davies, and Owen Lattimore were among the veteran Foreign Service officers—known as "China hands"—Senator Joseph McCarthy blamed for having lost China to the Reds.

16

17

18

McCarthy investigated Communist sympathies in the movie industry and succeeded in jailing the "Hollywood Ten"—including the screenwriters and directors Samuel Ornitz, Ring Lardner, Jr., Albert Maltz, Alvah Bessie, Lester Cole, Herbert Biberman, and Edward Dmytryk—shown here on their way to federal court in Washington, D.C., to face trial on charges of contempt of Congress for their defiance of the House Un-American Activities Committee.

David Schine (*left*) and Roy M. Cohn (*center*), who Paul called "fascist bully-boy types," with McCarthy during a subcommittee hearing in 1953.

After a bumpy courtship, Julia and Paul were not about to let a pre-wedding car accident keep them from exchanging vows on September 1, 1946.

Dick Heppner and Betty MacDonald also married in the summer of 1946, and were thrilled that other members of their detachment had found happiness after the war.

22

The Childs in their grand "Roo de Loo" apartment in Paris with their cat, Minette, who was the beneficiary of many of Julia's early failed soufflés.

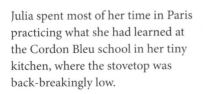

23

In a pointed repudiation of the charge of homosexuality, Julia and Paul boldly posed naked in a tub of bubbles for their 1956 Valentine's Day card.

Julia spent most of her time in Paris practicing what she had learned at the Cordon Bleu school in her tiny kitchen, where the stovetop was back-breakingly low.

24

Jane Foster returned to painting after the war, and Paul envied her small studio in Paris, where she sometimes produced a picture a day.

Jane's woodcut of the U.S. Board of Passport Appeals in Washington, D.C., which in March 1955 turned down her passport application on the grounds that she "followed the Communist party line."

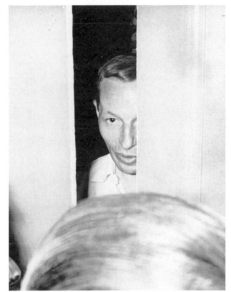

Jane's husband, George Zlatovski, peeking through the half-open door at the mob of reporters outside their Paris apartment the morning after they were indicted as Russian spies.

Jane had expensive tastes in everything from clothes to restaurants and always lived beyond her means.

The beautiful Martha Dodd and her wealthy husband, Alfred Stern, threw fabulous parties in their penthouse apartment in the Majestic that attracted such notable leftists as Lillian Hellman, Paul Robeson, Margaret Bourke-White, and Clifford Odets.

The mysterious Boris Morros, a Russian-born Hollywood producer, posing here with Ginger Rogers, was secretly working as a double agent and spent twelve years helping the FBI corral Soviet spies.

Jack Soble, in handcuffs, and his wife, Myra, being led by a federal agent, pled guilty to "receiving and obtaining" U.S. defense secrets and testified that Jane and George were members of their Soviet spy ring in return for a more lenient sentence.

Jane's self-portrait, drawn after her first breakdown in 1955, while she was in Cornell University Hospital in New York hiding from "the men in gabardine coats."

Betty never believed Jane was disloyal but had her doubts about George, who she visited in Paris in the early 1980s and again found to be "a strange man."

After they left the Foreign Service in 1961, Julia and Paul settled in Cambridge, Massachusetts, where they lived happily for the next thirty-two years, but they never forgot the friends who were not lucky enough to escape the McCarthy era unscathed, and they remained passionate Democrats.

When she regained consciousness, she was able to state positively that the driver was Asian, which convinced Caldwell that she had been deliberately targeted by the Chinese Embassy. So-called taxi accidents had been arranged before to discourage foreign interference. In the end, the OSS succeeded in exposing two embassy officials who had been transmitting secrets to the Japanese, but the investigation had to be abandoned to avoid embarrassing an ally. Joy's injuries proved so serious she had to be sent home for further medical care.* Rosie was transferred to Chungking, where she discovered that General Tai Li's secret police had her marked down as a "dangerous thinker." Rosie handled the arrangements for all the meetings between the Chinese government and the American ambassador Patrick J. Hurley, an unpopular figure she and her OSS colleagues dubbed "the albatross."

Paul was immediately taken with the bold, spirited Rosie Frame. She was a most alluring spy, with her pert nose, dark glossy hair, and inviting smile. He felt her to be a natural sensualist, "with an eager mind and an eager body." This was a woman to be both admired and desired. He threw himself into a "passionate friendship" with Rosie, writing his brother that she had "real brains," and "many elements" he would want in a wife. He filled pages and pages with rhapsodic descriptions of her "Junoesque figure" and "wonderful and complex personality." At twenty-seven, she was too young for him and not as completely formed as he might wish an intimate companion to be, yet she was a woman of "real taste and interesting ideas, untrammeled by tradition." He pursued her doggedly, knowing it would probably not lead anywhere, as she was seeing an OSS captain named Thibaut de Saint Phalle, the scion of an aristocratic French family that was now penniless. However, she glimpsed him only occasionally between highly secret missions behind Japanese lines, and Paul took advantage of his rival's absence to press his suit. When she finally spurned his advances, Paul was disappointed but not destroyed. Julia, who had just arrived in Chungking, was as always

---

* Joy Homer never recovered, possibly due to complications from her diabetes, and she died a year later in the United States at the age of thirty-one.

"a great solace." "Paul Child was a rather curious man," recalled Thibaut de Saint Phalle. "He could be very difficult and dour. And sometimes he was not very nice to Julia, but she was always very nice to him."

In early April, Paul was sent to Kunming, the old capital of Yunnan province in southwestern China, where it seemed he was to spend the rest of the war in "the underside of the world." In a country rich in cultural delights, Kunming was by all reports as barren and depressing a place as could be imagined, little more than a dreary American supply depot. The U.S. Fourteenth Air Force under Lieutenant General Claire L. Chennault was based there for operations, and planes came and went from the busy "Roger Queen" airport (Kunming's code designation) day and night, ferrying American equipment to the Generalissimo's army in training, as well as to OSS teams at guerilla outposts and airstrips across the China theater. When he deplaned at the airfield, one of the first things that he saw was a sign that read, "China is no place for the timid."

Given the lousy advance billing, Paul was completely unprepared for the beauty of the medieval fortress city and, visible in the distance, the blue-rimmed mountains, which were "incandescent and dreamlike." Like frontier towns in the Old West, Kunming was a crossroads, the end of the Burma Road and the beginning of the unknown, and there was a wild quality to the place and the people that Paul found exciting. He loved "the look of China," the bustling confusion of local characters and color that passed through the stone gates: "the Mongolian ponies, with loads of dust-laden vegetables, that plod along with their eyes shut"; the tall, shaggy Tibetans and brightly costumed tribal outlanders, "their babies' heads done up in silk scarves like melons in exotic bags." He and his staff were warned to take care when wandering beyond the city's heavily guarded gates into the countryside and vast fetid fields of millet and rice. OSS personnel had been attacked repeatedly by Chinese government troops posing as bandits and stripped of everything they had on them, from money and documents down to their shoes and wristwatches. The winding alleyways of Kunming's "Thieves' Row" were full of stolen American gear for resale alongside the usual tawdry black-market goods.

The OSS compound consisted of a fenced-in area with a half-dozen two-story buildings scattered on a dirt parade ground. A number of people from Paul's old mob at Kandy had preceded him there, including Dick Heppner, who looked "slightly disintegrated" from overwork and fatigue, along with Betty MacDonald, Peachy, and Ellie. Julia was on loan from Chungking to help set up the new Registry, containing reports of the OSS's current and planned guerilla operations. The place was as primitive as any cavalry outpost and certainly as poorly equipped. They lacked almost everything they needed to function, including such basic necessities as tables and chairs. He held his first morning conference sitting on the floor. Six coolies in blue uniforms persisted in hollering at each other through a hole in the ceiling as they attempted to hook up the electric wiring. Because of the Chinese carpenters' passion for Ningbo varnish, all the rooms were submerged in a damp Victorian gloom that was singularly depressing. "The atmosphere is rather like a party which has gone sour," noted Paul in his daily letter-cum-diary. "The guests are sitting bored stiff, far apart, sticking it out until it becomes possible to leave and go home."

The mood was not helped by the realization that the war, only a few mountain passes away, might descend upon them long before the bureaucratic gridlock eased sufficiently for anyone to issue the order to retreat. Recent Japanese troop movements indicated a possible drive toward Kunming and other points along Chiang's southern flank, but Heppner, lacking anything resembling a clear policy, had his hands full trying to figure out exactly what the OSS should—let alone could—do about any of it.

The China theater was a tangle of internecine international political struggles and divergent war objectives. Wedemeyer's primary mission was to assist the Generalissimo's ragtag peasant army in fending off the advancing Japanese. But as the war progressed and the Pacific became the primary theater, China was becoming increasingly important as both an intelligence base and a launching ground for covert operations in Indochina. Chiang wanted more support to combat a feared Japanese offensive; the retreating French in Tonkin were clamoring to be rescued; and Mao Tse-tung's Communists in the north were demanding a coalition government and greater cooperation in fighting a common enemy. Was the OSS supposed to help the French escape into

China? Was it supposed to assist the Communist guerillas, as many of them had done in the European theater? And what to do about the many rumors of the widespread corruption of Chiang's Kuomintang government and persistent whispers that Chiang had entered into negotiations with the Japanese to restrain his military forces in exchange for permission to hold Chungking and concentrate his strength in southwest China for postwar purposes?

Julia's Registry "bulged with reports about the incompetence of the Chinese military command." OSS demolition teams reported finding large ammunition dumps that held tons of arms and supplies, all being secretly hoarded by the bungling Chinese troops even as Japanese troops camped less than twenty miles away. The OSS teams were forced to destroy large stores of the valuable equipment only hours before the advancing Japanese could stumble on the treasure trove and use the equipment against the Americans.

Mr. Ma, a refugee from the Shanghai literary set who had been recruited by MO, lectured them about the deteriorating military situation. He explained that the Chinese government troops were losing control over the country and that various minority factions, backed by warlords, were threatening insurrection. Generalissimo Chiang Kai-shek's popularity was fading. People were losing faith in the Kuomintang because of the increasing government monopoly of all business and the extreme corruption and inflation. According to Ma, their resident philosopher, "appeals from the Kuomintang were sometimes like 'whispers in the willow trees.'"

From time to time, OSS teams would report armed clashes in the area as local factions jockeyed for position. "The warlords were always shooting at each other," recalled Betty. "But we never really felt scared. We had pretty good protection, and the Flying Tigers [Chennault's fighter planes] kept the Japanese at bay."

As Betty soon observed in her MO work, "the Chinese never followed the rules." Smuggling was a way of life. They brazenly peddled state secrets and were equally overt about trading everything from information to arms with the Japanese. Everything was for sale. Itinerant merchants, passing from Japanese to Chinese territory, paid a fixed tariff to both sides. This underground economy "knitted all factions together in common trade and exchange of necessary commodities," Betty noted, "and only the Americans seemed to disturb this odd status quo when they became too inquisitive observers, too energetic saboteurs."

In the course of its intelligence-gathering missions and guerilla operations, the OSS adapted to the thriving black-market culture as befitted the occasion. Julia was shocked the first time she saw one of their Chinese informants being paid in opium, staring in disbelief as Betty cut a thick slice from what looked like a loaf of Boston brown bread that she then carefully rewrapped and returned to the Registry safe. Julia soon learned that opium was the preferred currency, and she became adept at doling out the sticky intelligence payroll. Even when liberally rewarded with what the OSS termed "operational supplies," many of the Chinese guerillas were reluctant or inept fighters, and complaints from the field were frequent. One exasperated team captain complained that his Chinese conscripts had no concept of "ambush discipline," and that they often exposed the presence of OSS sabotage teams by detonating explosives "for the sheer pleasure of hearing them go *Boom!*"

When at their wit's end, they could always refer to the pearls of wisdom contained in the OSS booklet on the China theater: "Lack of patriotism on the part of many Chinese may discourage you. Remember that their social system has been built on a strict loyalty to family rather than state."

All this contributed to the state of utter confusion that characterized life in Kunming. Every meeting adjourned with the idea that the day's issues or resolutions needed further review at Chungking levels, the official seat of Allied high command, where Heppner kept his OSS office, close to Wedemeyer's headquarters and Chiang Kai-shek's center of government. In the meantime, brass was pouring into their little backwoods corner of the country. They were tripping over generals, senior staff officers, strategists, and tacticians, along with representatives of rival intelligence apparatuses, all of whom had their own elaborate schemes and agendas. And that was before taking into account Chiang's people, who had to give official "clearance" to any proposed OSS operations, and plotted over cups of tea, aided by polite but sly interpreters. "The warp and woof of war-in-China is complex beyond belief," Paul observed:

The inner workings, the who-influences-who's, the deals, the sleights of hand, the incredible chicaneries, the artistic venalities, the machinations and the briberies. Some facts are so incredibly romantic and sinister that only hearing hundreds of verbal reports from the mouths of the horses themselves finally convinces me of the dreadful reality of the under-the-sea war—the war of back alleys, back rooms, big parties, magnificent whores and equally magnificent blackmails. It almost becomes the "real" war, of which the news-war is only the surface expression.

The chances for honest-to-God peace in China seemed almost impossible. Even with the European part of the war officially over, the action in their part of the world seemed to be amplifying. "Here all is preparation," Paul reported to Charles with dismay. "Building up, plans for months ahead, materials and personnel being striven for and allocated, anticipated dangers faced."

With the prospects of going home anytime soon growing dimmer, the small OSS contingent dug in for the long haul. Their first experience of a Chinese spring made it more bearable. The mild weather lifted their spirits, and the gradual change of season and shy rays of sunlight made for a delightful change from the endless midsummer furnace of India and Ceylon. The plum trees blossomed, and jasmine and mimosa scented the air. They shed their heavy wool uniforms for lightweight khaki (unlike in India, everyone wore fatigues here, even on their days off) and organized sightseeing excursions, picnics, and boating parties on the lake. With the exception of the occasional movie on the compound, and the crowded, tacky Tennis Club, one of the few American nightspots, there was little entertainment except what they made for themselves.

Paul, intent on exploring the area despite the warnings, organized "photo-walks" with the girls. They went up to the West Gate, where they could look down on a rolling sea of tile rooftops in the town below, or four miles out to Jialing, where they could go down to the river and watch the junks being rowed by twelve-man crews chanting songs as they passed. Julia was thrilled by the sight of a flotilla of baby ducks being guided by a young Chinese duck herder, who had no trouble keeping his charges in line with the stern flick of a long willow stick.

One Sunday afternoon, Paul managed to snag a jeep and a bottle of mulberry wine, and he and Julia "struck off into the great unknown":

> The weather was incredibly inspiring: hot sun and cool air, spar-kling sky, breeze enough, scattered cloud. The great mountains lay around us like back-broken dragons. God, what a beautiful country—the mud villages with their green-tiled towers, the flocks of black swine, the blue clad people, the cedar smoke, the cinnamon-dust, were all eternally Chinese and connected us with the deep layers of past time. We saw a beautiful red sandstone (Avon color) bridge set in the midst of a paddy field. The stones were all wind-worn like the *tourelles* at Neuvic, so they looked like soft loaves of bread. We sat on it and drank our wine, and got sunburned, and looked at the mules going over it, and relaxed, and life came right for a spell.

Although it was "a good afternoon," these platonic outings did little to assuage the deep loneliness that assailed him. He did not lack for company, but it was the true companionship—the deep connection that came with a long-term, committed relationship—that he craved. Paul was increasingly consumed by the fear that he was fated to spend the rest of his life alone. He had been in the Far East for more than a year, and his sense of frustration and unfulfilled need were beginning to take a toll. "Perhaps you will never know what it is to feel profoundly lonely," he wrote his twin, who was happily married with a brood of three. "Well, you become empty, unbased, and bereft." Paul regarded his brother, Charles, and his wife, Freddie, to be joined at the hip, and routinely addressed them in his letters as "Chafred." The latest cause of his discontent was Marjorie Severyns, a striking twenty-five-year-old green-eyed brunette from Yakima County, Washington. She had recently come from Delhi, where she had manned the MO office with Betty MacDonald, and had been asked to help set up their intelligence

office. To Paul, everything about her—from her trim frame to her perfectly tanned skin—seemed to exude the best of the American West,
and she bowled him over with her health, beauty, and stamina. He had
never been one to believe in "love at first sight," he told Charles, but
now he knew himself to be "a victim." Here was his Zorina, a "superior
spirit," at last and *enfin:*

> I've talked to her once—at table—but we sat for an hour after
> the meal was over and then walked through some rice paddies
> for another half an hour, both reluctant to stop. I feel strongly
> drawn to her and she to me. She understands *double enten-
> dre,* and suggestion, completely, which makes conversation
> creative. . . . She has a first class brain and is widely informed,
> wonderfully quick, subtle and humorous, but very earnest
> about life and its problems and possibilities. You begin to love
> women like that the moment you see them, almost.

Paul's feelings intensified in the weeks that followed. "Marjorie continues to be an unusual and darling human being," he wrote, adding
that the situation was not particularly hopeful as there was a long line
of suitors ("all wolves") beating a path to her door ahead of him, including a tall, young United Press reporter named Al Ravenholt who was
movie-star handsome. The competition for women in their conglomer-
ate American outpost was "ferocious." There were at least forty men for
every woman, and the most fetching (Peachy and Rosie) were reportedly dated up to three weeks in advance. Ellie Thiry was already being
monopolized by a Major Francis Basil Summers, a dashing British army
intelligence officer who had been on the stage in London before the war
and positively reeked of derring-do. Summers had spotted Ellie standing next to Julia at an officers' club party their first night in Kunming
and announced then and there that he was going to marry her.*
     "A good many of the men here are extremely attractive, compe-

---

* He proposed by giving her his signet ring, and they were married in London in 1946.

tent, experienced, and interesting, as you can imagine they would be in such a place at such a time," Paul fretted in a letter to Charles. "Even the snaggle-toothed, the neurotic, the treacherous, and the dim-witted among women are hovered over by men, as jars of jam are hovered over by wasps." When it came to someone as lovely and beguiling as Marjorie, that hovering-over turned to "an angry roar."

The danger and isolation, together with the confined nature of their existence within Kunming's tall walls, conspired to bring people closer together. "We were pulled together by circumstance," recalled Betty, and inevitably quite a number "paired off."

Betty had fallen in love with her handsome CO, Dick Heppner, during the year they spent in Ceylon, and by the time they reached Kunming there was no longer any point in trying to hide their relationship. Everyone knew everything about everyone else in their tiny circle. After work, she and Dick often went for long walks in the ancient cemetery just outside town, trailed by his adopted little cocker spaniel puppy, Sammy. As they made their way among the grave mounds and crumbling monuments, Heppner poured out his anxiety and guilt about all the young men he sent into the field and feared would not come back. "We talked and talked and talked," said Betty, "he was terribly worried." She had not seen Alex for many months, and had no idea where he was or what he was doing. Heppner had not seen his wife in Washington in over two years. "We did not know what was going to happen next week or next month," she added. "Everything was uncertain. It was like being in limbo. And we were all very lonely."

By mid-May, Paul's infatuation with Marjorie had him in a state of acute misery. He had courted her patiently and tenderly, twice invited her to dine in his rooms, read to her, written intimate letters (she never answered them) and a love poem, all to no avail. If Marjorie was not the long-awaited wonder woman of Bartleman's predictions, "how could it be any *other*?"

With what he saw as almost "calculated perversity," the pattern fate had laid down for his emotional life was repeating. Once again, as in Dehli those many moons before, his friend Tommy Davis had arrived on the scene and turned the head of the one woman on whom Paul's heart was set. Now that he had tired of Nancy Toyne, the glamorous, married Tommy had moved on to Marjorie, who appeared all too amenable to his attentions. "So now, as before, I am twisting over the fire," Paul wrote Charles. "I find it hard to sleep, food nauseates me slightly, and my mind virtually refuses to remain on anything but my personal problems." He did not blame Tommy for his predicament; it only added "a drop of gall to the mixture." That did not make it any easier to watch them together—laughing as they bicycled to work, holding hands as they crossed the compound, cooing and cuddling like newlyweds.

Sick with jealousy, he sent Marjorie a letter confessing his torment ("all the classic symptoms") and asking for her understanding if he seemed cold or distant. She had warned him she would not be able to reciprocate his kind of love, but the interdiction came too late. He penned another poem—not written to or for anyone—but designed only to help purge the bitterness that curdled his soul. This he forwarded to his twin with a full account of his suffering:

> These prison-wires strung round my bones
> Bear cryptic messages from the heart.
>
> Wasteland, wasteland—never a bush—
> No gushing coolness under the rock,
> Devoid of butterfly and buttercup.
> Vacant as an idiot's eye.
>
> These pipes, pulsing in my flesh,
> Water no garden, fertilize no flower.
>
> Bitter, bitter on the sand is love.
> Love lost, love never gained, love unfulfilled.
> The teeming world is lonely as a mooreland,
> As a bird in the middle of the sea.

Paul had no choice but to retire with grace. He wrote Charles that he was swearing off young girls for good. He had finally learned that it would never work. ("I know too much and they don't know enough.")

In the meantime, he hated his life. He had no gusto for anything—not eating, or painting, or reading. Not even the articles about V-E Day that Charles had sent and the realization that war was really over in Europe could cheer him up. The days dragged by monotonously. He devoted himself to his job with great determination and rigidity. He slept, ate, and worked. Work was his great escape. He would have preferred love, but "the work was available." He had dinner with Tommy, who was soon heading off on a mission, and Julia, who had been transferred permanently to Kunming. They drank copious amounts of vodka, made by yet another White Russian. "We talked about the future, which is futile, and the past, which is even more futile," he reported. His spirits were very low. He had heard that two officers he was fond of had been killed in one week. It was "hard to take."

In July, Jeanne Taylor arrived from Kandy, and she and Julia did their best to cheer him up. Paul wrote Charles that their intellect and humor were "morale-building," far more than the latest bulletin from Jane Bartleman, who had told him to expect "a year of plugging still to come." One night Paul and the girls went to dinner with Al Ravenholt, who regaled them with the story of his big scoop—when CBS correspondent Eric Sevareid's plane went down over the Hump and everyone was desperate to find out what had happened to him and the crew. Ravenholt had beat out all the competition by raising Sevareid on his walkie-talkie and reported to the world that they had all parachuted to safety in the Burmese jungle. Julia surprised them by capping his story with an amusing anecdote. The OSS officer Duncan Lee had gone down in the same plane as Sevareid and had told her that the newsman had been cool-headed enough to rescue one item before he jumped: a quart of gin he had promised a friend in Chungking. "He was terribly conscientious about it—and delivered it intact," continued Julia. "Didn't touch a drop during the two days he was walking through the jungle." Although she insisted it was true, no one believed her.

As the night wore on, they found themselves in the same long room—separated by a pink silk screen—as a Chinese general and his party of friends. The Chinese got very drunk, particularly the general. "It was fortunate our two gals were tough and worldly," Paul noted in his first cheerful letter home in weeks. "There's something about a Chinese general vomiting a few feet away that might otherwise have taken the fine edge off the bowl of eels and garlic we were eating."

A few days later, Paul reported that he, Julia, and Jeanne, along with two other guys, had spent a pleasant weekend together. They had all packed into a jeep and driven forty miles up the Burma Road, where they turned off and headed up into the mountains to a tiny hotel with hot spring that had been built by Governor Long Yun of Yunnan province in 1943. The resort was called Wenjen and was a favorite of off-duty GIs as well as high-ranking members of the Kuomintang, who came to partake of the curative benefits of the radium baths. They all soaked in the steaming water that bubbled up from an underground stream, meekly choosing one of the more temperate baths after the moon-faced manager warned that only hardened veterans—those who stayed for more than a week—could brave the premium pools. These, he boasted in his incongruous English, were "hotsy totsy." Afterward, Jeanne recalled a glowing, pink-skinned Julia declaring: "Do you realize that if everyone in the damned war had a Sani Hot Springs bath every day, it would be over by now?" That night, Paul and his two male colleagues piled into one bedroom, while Julia and Jeanne shared another. The next day they all went for a long walk in the pouring rain along fields of ripening rice and up through a trail of thick pines to a monastery. The mountains looked magnificent cloaked in a heavy mantle of gray mist. Looking down on the emerald green valley, Paul again felt inspired by the beauty and drama of China.

Paul did everything with Julia that other couples did without acknowledging that they were one. They planned their days off together and went on hikes in the hills, jeeped to the Black Dragon Pool temple to collect rare stone rubbings, and went sampaning at twilight on the lake. They went on shopping trips, explored the crowded flower markets, and visited out-of-bounds Chinese restaurants where they sampled the different cuisines—Fukinese, Pekinese, Annamese, Szechuan, and Cantonese. He applauded her adventurousness in bypassing the flown-in American chow available at the Red Cross canteen to join him in these forbidden feasts, in which they binged on steamed dumplings, crisp duck, mixed green vegetables, and succulent baby frog legs swimming in sweet-and-sour sauce. Invariably, the outings were followed by bacillary distress (dysentery), which might as well have been on the menu and was, as a consequence, a major topic of dinner table conversation among Chinese and Westerners alike. Paul took pleasure in helping to educate Julia's meat-and-potatoes palate, and he looked on with real pride as she became a champion chopstick wielder. "They were an odd couple, but it turned out to be a very good match," recalled Thibaut de Saint Phalle. "Julia did not feel she was very beautiful and was delighted to be with someone like him. Paul felt he was in charge of her, and she let him think that, and they were very good together."

Over the course of these outings, Paul began to see Julia in a new light. He was impressed with her competence in riding herd on a staff of ten assistants and "running a very complicated operation with great skill." He also liked that she was gutsy; he observed in a letter to Charles that she was "a wonderful 'good scout' in the sense of being able to take physical discomfort, such as mud, leeches, tropical rains, and lousy food." She seemed completely "unflappable," as in Betty's account of their white-knuckle flight over the Hump—when the lights began to flicker and the plane bucked and rolled through lightning and icy rain, and she looked over to see Julia calmly reading a book as though she had made the Himalayan run a million times. "The China theater was a lot rougher than Ceylon," acknowledged Betty. "Julia rose to the occasion. It brought out the best in her."

All the time Paul and Julia spent together did not go unnoticed. "They were always together," recalled Betty, laughing. "We were all rooting for a romance. We watched their relationship develop day by day." They lived in very close quarters, and everyone could see exactly what was going on, even though the couple in question remained clueless. Most evenings after dinner, Paul would head to Julia's room, taking his artwork, along with favorite novels and volumes of poetry. Though he had earlier complained to his brother that part of his problem was that he "never liked the idea—which is so appealing to many men—of Man the Sculptor, molding and shaping a woman to his desire," Paul had made rather a project of Julia. "He sort of took her on like one of the trainees in his design section," mused Betty. "He would read aloud to her for hours. Everyone knew she was completely mad about him. I don't know why it took him so long to get it."

Recent experience, however, had taught Paul caution. He had opened his heart to Marjorie only to be ruthlessly cut down. In retrospect, he realized that he had taken too much for granted. He had been so sure that he recognized her as "the one" Bartleman had promised that he had forged ahead too quickly, and the intensity of his feelings had probably frightened her off. Never again would he "plunge head-first into the Pierian Spring."

In the meantime, everything in Kunming was in flux. The rice harvest had begun in anticipation of the approaching monsoons. A late summer crop of peace rumors had everyone riveted. Rosie's intelligence team was trying to track down the source of "a great whisper campaign" that the Japanese had put out peace feelers. With the tide turning against Japan in the Pacific, it was believed that a handful of Japanese officials in Switzerland were attempting to negotiate for an end to hostilities through the OSS organization in Europe. Even their OSS detachment in Kunming was in transition. They appeared to be headed for one of those dreaded periodic reorganizations that sent people whirling off in all directions never to be seen again. Jack Moore, the faithful assistant who had been with Paul since Washington, was being sent to another part of China. Already several people had come by to bid Paul farewell, apparently taking for granted that his present position had also run its course. He found himself trying to pare down on belongings in order "to be light for any eventuality."

As if that were not enough to deal with, they were all a little on edge due to the cholera epidemic that was upon them. The summer rains had brought flooding of dramatic proportions, and with it disease. The overflowing canals immersed low-lying roads and submerged the paddy fields, in some areas creating small islands where the peasants continued "placidly hoeing crops, amid the rushing brown waters." The new restrictions prevented OSS personnel from going into town, and brought Paul's regular forays to Chinese restaurants to an abrupt end. It was the glorious sense of freedom as much as the flavorful food that he missed. It was only the communal mess hall for the foreseeable future, and SPAM in all its many incarnations, but he would "rather stay alive and be bored."

Betty's MO group had been working for months on leaflets warning the Japanese that "something terrible was going to happen in August"— all part of an effort to soften the enemy's morale prior to the American invasion—so that when it actually happened it came as a shock. One of the MO teams, allowing for no cease-fire in the war of subversion, decided to capitalize on the news by putting an extra out on in the streets of Hengyang trumpeting a bomb so powerful that it had blown away the city of Hiroshima. "Until that time the people of Hengyang had accepted every MO fabrication as gospel truth," Betty recalled. This time, however, they just shook their heads. Such a weapon was simply not to be believed.

They scarcely had time to absorb the terrifying reality of the atom bomb when Mother Nature, in a demonstration of her own terrible power, brought torrential rains down on their heads for days on end. The canals and marshes burst their banks and turned the rice paddies into dark, threatening lakes. The boiling brown water swamped Kunming and, thanks to a well-fortified surrounding wall, turned the OSS compound into a three-foot-deep lagoon. They were forced to commute from building to building in bright orange inflatable life rafts taken from the airplanes, rowing past floating office equipment and assorted military bric-a-brac. In some places, the engineers managed to rig rickety pontoon bridges out of gasoline drums and planks, but about half the time people slipped and fell into the drink. At first, the absurdity of the situation inspired a certain sense of adventure and hilarity. Betty and Julia were intentionally "dunked" more than once by gallant colleagues extending a helping hand. When the water level rose, GIs in hip boots were brought in to rescue secret documents and perishable gear and carry it to higher ground. After a few days, it ceased to be fun. Everything they owned was soggy, dank, and mildewed. "All the toilets and cesspools are flooded, of course," Paul noted dolefully, "and the amenities of life are impossible to preserve."

The rising tide drove colonies of large, voracious rats out of the ditches and up into their compound and workrooms. Nothing was safe from their ravenous jaws. One morning Paul discovered that the pack of Lucky Strikes he had left on his desk the previous evening had been devoured. All that was left was a few strips of silver paper and a scattering of rat turds. A young major took to hunting the vermin "as a purely sporting proposition" and knocked off fifteen to twenty a night with his .22 rifle. After days of putting up with Paul scoffing at his stories of the rats' formidable size, the major brought in proof in the form of a bucket of rat carcasses, soaked in gasoline per the medic's orders to kill the fleas and lice. Paul measured the biggest one and found that it was, incredibly, twenty-two inches long, not counting the tail. "That's a big rat," he wrote Charles, "as big as a beaver, damn near."

It was the worst flood in a generation. The dislocation experienced by OSS personnel was nothing compared to the havoc the deluge wreaked on the surrounding countryside. Betty recalled Chinese villages of mud huts "melting like chocolate," the owners looking on helplessly as their few humble belongings were swept away by the current. Farmers drowned in their own paddy fields. Corpses drifted by on the swollen river. Everyone who could fled to the hills, carrying what they were able to in bundles slung on shoulder poles or dragging their belongings on overburdened carts. It was only when the rains stopped that the full horror of the disaster became clear. As the water seeped away, the edges of town filled with washed-out refugees. There were long lines of coffins in the street. Many had been built crudely and with such haste that they were too short for the occupants, whose pale, waxen feet stuck out. Sturdier models boasted a live rooster tied to the top or even K rations, to help speed the departed on their way. Paul was struck by the resilience of the Chinese, "a tough people who never know when they're licked." As soon as the sun peeked out, they were busy laying wheat and rice on their roofs to dry and digging under the muddy water for cabbages and onions.

The flooding had scarcely begun to subside when the second atom bomb brought the capitulation of the Japanese. "The sudden ending of the war was taken in stride, with no noise, and work going on as unremittingly as before," Paul wrote Charles on August 16. "There is work for us to do, of a less violent kind than before, although some violence is still ahead."

The cataclysmic events of the previous week had completely altered the situation in China. Two days after the Hiroshima bomb, Russia had declared war on Japan and launched a massive offensive into Manchuria. The incoming Russian soldiers only added to the Pandora's box of pressures and factions in a country torn by years of fighting among the Japanese, Chinese Nationalists, and Chinese Communists. As both the Nationalists and the Communists began moving in to take over the towns and cities formerly occupied by the enemy, tensions escalated. The warlords, many of whom had been playing both sides against the middle, now saw which way the wind was blowing and quickly realigned themselves with the Kuomintang against the Communists. The confusion and uncertainty led to sporadic fighting. Determined not to be drawn into the middle of a civil war in China, Washington instructed the OSS to avoid getting involved in the internal conflict. At the same time, however, Wedemeyer's troops were ordered to help "sustain" Chiang's government and aid it in establishing its authority over the countryside. More significantly, U.S. forces were to allow Kuomintang troops to accept Japanese surrenders. It was all too clear to the many OSS intelligence officers scattered throughout China and Indochina that this dream of American "neutrality" was an impossibly fine line to walk and was doomed from the outset.

In the days that followed, OSS headquarters in Kunming went into overdrive. Eight mercy missions were launched to protect the twenty thousand American and Allied POWs and the roughly fifteen thousand civilian internees being held in camps from Manchuria all the way to Indochina. The immediate concern was for the safety of the prisoners in the event that the defeated Japanese chose to ignore the imperial cease-fire order or, worse, chose to inflict reprisals on their captives. Betty's MO unit began churning out leaflets advising the Japanese that the OSS teams parachuting in were there "for humanitarian reasons only." All the frantic preparations—for rescue operations, food and medical drops, and evacuation—had to be undertaken despite further flooding, sodden runways, and weather delays caused by low ceilings and poor visibility. Adding to the drama was the uncertain fate of the six-man OSS team dispatched to Mukden in Manchuria to rescue General "Skinny" Wainwright, who along with his men had endured more than three years of brutal captivity since the surrender at Corregidor in May 1942. After thirteen nerve-wracking days filled with wild rumors that the Japanese had murdered Wainwright, the OSS team flashed the news that they had plucked Skinny from the POW camp at Hsian and were bringing him back to safety.

The chaos in the countryside was spreading. There were reports of Soviet troops raping and looting. The OSS "mercy missions" in Mukden were treated very badly, and OSS officers were held up by Chinese troops and robbed of all their arms and valuables by drunken soldiers whose leaders claimed they were "out of control." There was no redress of any kind and no apologies, and then they were unceremoniously kicked out. The mood in China was changing fast. Even in Chungking, the Chinese troops were becoming increasingly antiforeign and uncooperative. For the past six months, the Soviets had had secret agents in China working hard against U.S. propaganda and intelligence activities and clearly intended to do whatever suited their own interests. The Chinese attitude was that the U.S. presence had served its purpose but now they wanted to be in control and to put the Americans in their place.

By late August, OSS field teams were facing growing conflict with Communists in North China. One rescue party, including a young intelligence officer named John Birch, a Georgia Baptist missionary fluent in several Chinese dialects, encountered a belligerent Communist detachment, which Birch may have further inflamed by addressing the soldiers in what his men later described as a harsh manner. He was warned by his Chinese deputy that this was a dangerous approach but reportedly snapped in frustration, "Never mind, you don't know what my feelings are. I want to find out how they intend to treat Americans. I don't mind if they kill me. If they do they will be finished for America will punish them with Atomic bombs." When he later squared off with one of the Communist officers, who refused to allow the OSS team to continue on to the Allied POW camp near Suchow, a furious Birch attempted to force his way. The Communist officer ordered his men to disarm the OSS team. Birch resisted and he was shot and the rest of the party taken prisoner. Birch was then brutally bayoneted to death, his face mutilated beyond recognition. While many at OSS headquarters in Kunming believed Birch that overzealous—the official investigation concluded that his conduct had shown "a lack of good judgment"—his senseless death after the war was deeply disturbing to the American personnel stationed in China.*

Heppner, just back from a quick trip to Hanoi, informed them that OSS was beset with problems there as well. Thousands of still-armed Japanese soldiers were "keeping order" in French Indochina, Paul reported to his brother, adding that Heppner expected there would be civil war there soon, too. The French refused to recognize the new Republic of Vietnam, and because they suspected that U.S. policy was tacitly favorable to the independence movement, they were working with the British to push hard for "the restoration of white supremacy in the Orient." The French were more and more openly anti-American and were using agents, wearing stolen U.S. army uniforms, to provoke brawls and disorder to discredit the OSS teams. British agents near Saigon were illegally dropping arms to French guerilla forces, which were using them to pummel the Annamese and put down the independence movement. As a result of the British and French propaganda, U.S. prestige in French Indochina had deteriorated rapidly since VJ Day. If OSS activities in that region were to be curtailed as rumored, the situation would get worse. "It discourages the Hell out of me," Paul concluded. "The people behind these sorts of activities have learned nothing about the necessity of cooperative efforts along international lines—only how to be more and more skillfully bastardly."

The streets of Kunming were littered with red paper victory signs and exploded firecracker casings. Some of the signs were in English and bore inscriptions which read "Thank you President Roosevelt and President Chiang!" and "Hooray for Final Glorious Victory!" and "Let us now fight for Peace as we fighted [sic] for War!" Paper dragons sixty feet long were whirled through the alleyways, followed by civilians with flutes, gongs, and drums. For the first time since all the "victory hul-

---

* Years later, an extreme anti-Communist group decided to make Birch a martyr for its cause and in 1958 appropriated his name, calling itself the John Birch Society.

labaloos" had begun, the sight of the happy crowds and cheerful ca-
cophony of the firecrackers and instruments gave Paul the feeling that
"perhaps the God damned war is really finished."

The handing out of medals, by both the Chinese and American
military, added to the feeling of finality. Paul was unexpectedly pleased
with the parachute wings—embossed gold embroidery worn on the
right breast of his new wool uniform—that he was awarded by the general of the Chinese Commandos in gratitude for the part he had played
in helping to train the first unit of Chinese parachutists. Heppner presented Julia with the Emblem of Meritorious Civilian Service for her
service as head of the Registry of OSS Secretariat, citing her "important work at registering, cataloging and channeling a great volume of
highly classified communications. Her drive and inherent cheerfulness,
despite long hours of tedious work, served as a spur to greater effort
by those working with her." Morale in her section could not have been
higher.

After the high excitement of those early days, the weeks that followed were a letdown. Most of them were emotionally unprepared for
the abrupt end of the war. "There was a sudden vacuum which peace
had brought," recalled Betty. "Up to now there had been purpose, urgency, importance in doing what we were doing. Now things suddenly
had no meaning."

The OSS staff would soon go back to their drab civilian lives. They
would go back to ordinary desk jobs they barely remembered after
years of excitement and adventure abroad. And back to wives who
seemed like strangers and children they scarcely recognized. The long
months of separation had left Betty estranged from her own husband.
Alex had written from Bangkok to say that he wanted to remain in
Thailand to start an English-language newspaper there. Betty knew she
would not be joining him and would have to break the news that their
marriage was over. Dick Heppner had been away from home for years.
What would he be returning to? And, more to the point, what did the
future hold for their relationship? Betty could not help feeling dazed by
the turn of events and more than a little depressed. "I was in love," she
admitted, "and we didn't know what we were going to do."

Everyone was making preparations to leave. Tommy Davis had come back suddenly and announced he was returning to the States. He was in a very bad way. A burst ulcer and the subsequent hemorrhaging had nearly done him in, and he was being sent home on a special plane. The OSS brass had decided to "pitch-fork out most of the dames," so Betty, Julia, and Jeanne were all awaiting their travel orders. Marjorie was staying on, however, and joining the staff of *Fortune* in Chungking. Al Ravenholt, who was one of the four reporters assigned to cover the signing of the surrender and peace talks ("the lucky dog"), would also be staying on to cover the China theater.* For his part, Paul was determined to stay in China. He had turned down a job with the Pentagon and was hoping he could wangle another year with the OSS as it continued its postwar patching up with Chiang's government. That would give him a chance to see some more of the country and, he hoped, get to Peking, which he had to visit before he left or he would never forgive himself.

Of their old gang, he would be saddest to see Julia go. "Over the 18 months or more that I have known Julia I have become extremely fond of her," he reflected in a letter to Charles. "She is really a good friend, and though limited in relation to my concept of *la femme intégrale*, she still is understanding, warm, funny and darling. I hope you will meet her sometime as I believe that even in a U.S.A. context she will show up very well." She was so "companionable" in so many ways, and he counted her as a "real friend." He also felt deeply indebted to her. She had been such a comfort and had helped him over many a rough spot by dint of her "simple love and niceness." Her birthday was on August 15, and Paul had presented her with a sonnet penned in her honor:

How like the Autumn's warmth is Julia's face
So filled with Nature's bounty, Nature's worth.
And how like summer's heat is her embrace
Wherein at last she melts my frozen earth.
Endowed, the awakened fields abound

---

* Marjorie Severyns ended up marrying Al Ravenholt in Shanghai in 1946.

With newly green efulgence, smiling flowers.
Then all the lovely riches of the ground
Spring up, responsive to her magic powers.
Sweet friendship, like the harvest-cycle, moves
From scattered seed to final ripened grain,
Which, glowing in the warmth of Autumn, proves
The richness of the soil, and mankind's gain.
    I cast this heaped abundance at your feet
    An offering to Summer, and her heat.

Touched as she was by Paul's poetic tribute, Julia found it disheartening that "sweet friendship" was what he had in mind. For all his fine words about "heat" and her embrace melting his "frozen earth," he was still expounding in a platonic vein. Julia had done all she could to fashion herself in the mold of the "worldly" women Paul professed to admire. She had persevered, partly out of the desire to win him and, partly, just hopeful curiosity. She had looked to him as much more than a mentor, hanging on his every word with the intention of both becoming more cultivated and cultivating his interest. To that end, she had read what he read, had eaten what he ate, and had suffered what he suffered—commiserating with all his aches and pains, ups and downs, heartbreaks and setbacks. She had done all she could to impress him with her appreciation of art, music, and food, even to the point of convincing him she was a "gourmet"—a stretch for a woman who could barely fry chicken without starting a grease fire.

Still, at heart she worried she was "not the woman for him." He was a connoisseur and clearly found her lacking. Try as she might, she was "not intellectual." She did not excite him. When they finally went to bed, it was an act less of passion than of *com*passion. It was almost as if Paul, in his role as tutor, wanted to make sure she completed the lesson plan. Betty recalled Dick jokingly pointing out one evening that the poetry and novels Paul usually had tucked under his arm when he went to see Julia had given way to books about sex. "Perhaps he's catching her up?" he had quipped at the time.

Julia, always a realist, described what they shared as a "friendly passion," a mutual enjoyment of each other's company that fell somewhat short of Paul's lofty standards for love and marriage. He saw their affair as a natural expression of their close camaraderie, a condition inextricably rooted in "the limited and highly concentrated context of Kunming." It was an end-of-the-campaign fling. They were hardly the only couple that came together in those last crammed weeks of victory celebrations and drunken farewell dinners. In a snowstorm of confetti and swaying candy-colored paper lanterns, all differences of background, character, and expectation had been shoved aside for one imprudent night. As evidence of this, their clumsy lovemaking had not been a great success. In a letter to his brother, Paul admitted that he was so "exhausted" he doubted he "could even get an erection" even with the most seductive Chinese girl.

Julia was sufficiently disconcerted by his lackluster performance that it led her to wonder if she had made a mistake and they were, after all, a badly mismatched pair. "He is probably not the man for me as he is not constant nor essentially vigorous enough—which is hard to explain," she wrote in her diary, searching for a way to explain the feeling of inadequacy, though whether it was his or hers she could not be sure. "Perhaps it is his artisticness that makes him seem to lack a male drive. But his sensitiveness and the fact that we can talk about anything and there are no conventional barriers in thought communication make him a warm and loveable friend." Beyond everything, they had that bond, that deep sense of "companionship," and she knew only that she felt an overwhelming desire to protect it and nurture it. Wherever it led.

Meanwhile, the general state of confusion in the China theater delayed both their travel orders for several more weeks. Paul was headed to Peking for a little R & R. After that, barring any-last minute opportunities to stay on with the State Department in China, it was home to Washington. Julia, along with Rosie and Ellie, was scheduled to fly to Calcutta, where she was booked on a troopship for New York. It was just a matter of hanging on for their Hump clearances from Wedemeyer. Planes were few and far between, and there was nothing to do but wait.

With everyone gone and little work to do, Julia and Paul spent whole days together, just talking and trying to make sense of the past and the future. Neither of them had a job waiting or, for that matter, any clear idea where they would be living on their return. Julia very much wanted to know if their relationship had what OSS memos at the time termed "peacetime potentialities." Paul protested that he was too tired to even think about what came next. "I feel washed-out, and almost incapable of facing a new set of circumstances, people, responsibilities, and urgencies," he wrote Charles in mid-September. "The war's ending, the rapid change of plans, the slowing down of our pace . . . combine to let much gas out of my balloon. I feel suspended in a vacuum, with few plans, few interests, and no exuberance."

Julia persevered. She could see that he was worn out, and her sympathy and solicitousness in the weeks that followed endeared her to him more than ever. By the end of the month, a more serene-sounding Paul reported to Charles that he was benefiting from another sojourn to the Wenjen resort. "I'm sitting on a little knoll on top of a hill, above Hot Springs," he began, adding contentedly, "Julie, in pale blue slacks and dark blue sweater, is sitting beside me."

She was always by his side, a soothing presence, coaxing him out of his isolation and sadness. She was good for him. He had to admit he felt better about life—better about himself—when he was with her. Paul tentatively gave in to the idea of being with Julia. He agreed that the only way to measure the depth of their affection was to spend time together when they got back to the United States. They were mature adults—he was forty-three, she was thirty-three—and needed to make a mature decision. He wanted to see how they got on in a more quotidian setting, without the noisy, dramatic backdrop of the war as a distraction. He also wanted to meet her family in Pasadena (i.e., her father). If she immediately sank back into her old life and provincial level, it would never work. After Marjorie had broken his heart, Paul had sworn to his brother that he would never again rush headlong into another relationship. "Love," as he now conceived of it, involved "slow growth, many slowly formed bonds, tests by vicissitudes as well as pleasure, mutual sharing of esthetic experiences, humor, sensory things from food through music to passion, etc." Any truly lasting relationship, he concluded, would necessitate "a lengthy apprenticeship."

On October 8, Paul wrote Charles one more letter from Kunming. His departure date had been delayed again. There had been considerable excitement that last week as a minirevolution had broken out between the Generalissimo and Governor Long Yun, resulting in various Chinese soldiers taking pot shots at each other with the remaining OSS contingent caught smack in the middle. They had woken up at five in the morning to the sound of "machine guns hammering outside, artillery thudding, excited Chinese voices yelling, and running feet." Three fully armed Chinese soldiers invaded the girls' living quarters, giving Betty and Julia quite a scare. They heard later that afternoon that the Generalissimo had given orders to Tu Li-ming, commander of the Chinese Nationalist forces, "to reorganize the government of Yunnan," reported Paul. "So this is Chiang's party."

The uprising was carried out with surprising secrecy and efficiency and was mostly over by midday. Despite Long's surrender, there was a noisy battle that night at the governor's north barracks and more than five hundred Chinese soldiers were killed, with two hundred Americans pinned down in the cross fire just outside the city walls. After two long, boring days punctuated by random shooting it was announced that people could venture back into town, though there was a strict 8.00 p.m. curfew. He and Julia took the opportunity to enjoy a final feast at their favorite Peking restaurant in town. They had spring rolls, long-leaf cabbage and Yunnan ham, winter mushrooms with beet tops, and Peking duck. They topped it all off with a soup, which Paul, ever pedantic, explained was the traditional Chinese way to finish a meal. If there was anything bittersweet about this farewell banquet, he made no mention of it, noting only that the "eats" had been good.

9

INCURABLE ROMANTICS

Betty arrived in the capital on a chilly autumn afternoon, the first one from their Kunming detachment to reach home. Heppner had been so concerned for her safety that he had arranged for her departure on a Number 2 priority, unheard of for returning OSS personnel, and he took the extra precaution of sending along two paratroopers as an escort. Perfectly aware that this special treatment could only have been accomplished through some "substratum chicanery," she asked no questions and basked in the luxury of the full-service cabin with its reclining seats, drinks trolley, and hot meals. With the smug indifference of an old China hand, she experienced only the mildest guilt pangs upon learning that she was warming the seat of some poor colonel whose Number 4 priority meant he would be bumped at every stop along the way to Washington and would probably be en route for weeks. She soon got her comeuppance, however. After a brief layover in Karachi, she was informed they would be switching planes and making the rest of the trip on a lumbering hospital transport that had been on the Hump run for the last eighteen months and stank of stale cigarette smoke and disinfectant.

After allowing herself a day to get acclimated to civilian life, Betty took a cab to OSS headquarters. As soon as she stepped past the familiar security guard at the door, she noticed that something was wrong. Q Building was as squat and ugly as she remembered, but once she was inside it seemed like a shell of its former self. It took a few minutes before she realized it was the absence of noise and activity. The place was as hushed and still as a "mausoleum." She passed groups of men and women still in uniform, but all the swagger and urgency of old was replaced by the weary tread of returnees who had just flown across the Pacific and were waiting to be discharged. The executive order to terminate the OSS had taken a hammer to morale. Most OSS veterans had volunteered to go overseas and had performed above and beyond the call of duty, and their drawn faces bore the impact of their sudden dismissal. Betty could not help feeling like "the returning Confederate soldier looking over the burned-off ground that had once been his home."

A brisk, beautiful blonde named Kay Halle, apparently known to one and all as "Matta Halle," directed Betty to an interim office with a sleek desk, three phones, and a "new, noiseless typewriter." Whatever form the new intelligence agency was going to take, it was certainly a step up in office furnishings from the early days when she had shared a drafty room with several colleagues and fought over a single phone and battered Remington. While still in Kunming, Betty had been assigned to write the history of their OSS detachment in China, and she still had to put the finishing touches on it before turning it in. Before being issued her own walking papers, she was expected to write a report on the peacetime role of MO, though she had no idea what that encompassed. She only knew she planned to argue against throwing away all the foreign intelligence networks and contacts established during the war at great expense and loss of life. Given the speed with which the higher-ups were dismantling the organization, her recommendations would probably be filed away with scarcely a second glance or relegated to "some special OSS incinerator." It was like whistling in the wind.

Back in the familiar building, once filled with the echoing footsteps of colleagues on their way to war, she found it impossible not "to mourn the passing of the OSS." As for Donovan, he was already in pinstripes, having returned to his private law practice on October 1, reportedly let go in a letter from President Truman with little more than a pat on the back. "I felt a growing sense of loyalty to a brave and brilliant, if occasionally erratic, organization which had suddenly been disinherited by the government," Betty recalled. "I tried to be practical and tell myself that nothing is quite so moribund as a government agency suddenly shorn of its budget." Truman had announced that he wanted "a different kind of intelligence service," but she could not help thinking that scuttling the OSS was a terrible waste of valuable people and expertise. The war might be over, but anyone who had served in the CBI knew that the trouble had only just begun.

She was snapped out of her melancholy reverie by Matta Halle's repeated query: Did she know Jane Foster? When Betty nodded in assent, she was handed Jane's dossier. Thumbing through the stack of documents, she quickly realized they were all Jane's reports from the field to OSS headquarters. The last Betty had heard, Jane had been scheduled to drop into Java as soon as the declaration of peace was official. She had a vague recollection of seeing a leaflet advertising "Janey's Javanese Junkshop," requesting contributions of food and clothing for American women interred in Japanese prison camps in Batavia. Reading her description of the first secret meeting with Sukarno—"a handsome, dignified gentleman who spoke perfect English and invited visitors to set down to a dish of sherbet as soon as they arrived"—gave Betty a "vicarious thrill." It was vintage Jane, down to the last keenly observed detail. Her artistic friend had been brought into the OSS only because of her knowledge of the country and language skills but had acquitted herself with honor, carrying out an important assignment with great care and sensitivity. Her theater service record noted that she had done "an outstanding job on her specialty."

Betty felt a burst of pride: "Jane had done a first-rate job of reporting. Between the lines of formal reports I realized how much the return to her beloved Indonesia had meant to her":

> She wrote fervently of the tension which was growing between the Dutch Indies Civil Affairs group and the Indonesians. She

insisted that there was no master plan by Russians or defeated
Japs to overthrow Western imperialism in Asia, but it was rather
a natural eruption of the volcanic discontent which had been
rumbling for decades. The Asiatic countries were in a state of
ferment, and she found that throughout French Indo-China,
Burma, Malaya—and on a larger scale in India and China—the
people were following similar patterns of revolt against Western economic and political imperialism.

Betty was struck by the suggestion in some of Jane's reports that
MO tactics were being used by the United States' allies to try to influence public opinion in favor of the colonial prewar policy. Jane had
sent along a sample leaflet of the alleged declaration of war by the new
Republic of Indonesia, which had reportedly been distributed by native
extremists on the night of October 14, 1945, when the Allied military
administration was set up. The leaflet was "distributed clandestinely
along the Batavia waterfront," and a small native boy had brought a
copy of the declaration to the Hotel Des Indes, where Jane was dining
with a group of newspaper and magazine correspondents. Jane had immediately translated the leaflet, which called upon the Indonesians "to
declare a holy war against all Europeans, beginning with the Dutch."
It was signed "Republic of Indonesia." On hearing this, the assembled
journalists immediately hightailed it back to their offices, and the next
day the represented news outlets reported that the Republic of Indonesia had declared war. To Jane, the whole story seemed fishy, particularly as "the Dutch press was strangely silent on the subject. Nothing
was mentioned the next morning in the Batavia papers." No one was
ever able to find out who had issued the declaration, which was quickly
discredited, though never retracted in the press. When Jane finally
confronted Sukarno about "who might want to give Indonesians a bad
name," he declined to answer her question directly, but hinted that the
Dutch had the most to gain by spreading fears of a religious uprising.
The "phoney" declaration of war was a classic MO ruse. Betty recognized it as the same kind of tactic used by the Russians in propaganda posters and other psychological warfare material in their effort

to make inroads into Eastern Europe, Greece, and even Chinese Turkestan. Such incendiary leaflets were an ideal method of "propagating the faith," particularly when it would appear that they were Nazi-produced, when all along it was a Communist cover organization fomenting trouble. It was, Betty noted grimly, the same tried-and-true pattern that the OSS had perfected—create discord, then divide and conquer. Thanks to the war, everyone had received a crash course in subversion and was now playing the same game.

She inquired after Jane's whereabouts, excited at the prospect of a coffee-line reunion in the cafeteria, only to learn she was taking the slow route home aboard one of the "USS Unspeakables," as the overcrowded troopships were known. Still brooding over her second cup of coffee, Betty recognized Jan, the suave German-American agent who had been one of her first instructors. She asked his advice about the final report she was supposed to prepare on the postwar potential of subversion as a means of persuasion. Could he paint a scenario in which MO could be used to influence people's opinions and actions in peacetime? A ghost of a smile flickered on Jan's lips. "Well, let's see," he mused. "Want to start a whisper campaign about a hidebound Republican Wall Street lawyer [Donovan]? We can begin by sending, at absolutely no cost to him, copies of the *Daily Worker*. We shall also place his name on the mailing list of *The New Republic.*"

In answer to her raised eyebrows, he continued. Did she want to cause trouble in Japan, maybe upset the military brass serving under General MacArthur in occupied Japan? "Think of the fun you could have by sending a cable to some American government clerk at SCAP (Supreme Commander of the Allied Powers) headquarters in Tokyo electing him president of the 'MacArthur is *Not* a God Club' in Peoria."

His point was not lost on her. In spite of his playful tone, Betty detected the undercurrent of concern. There were ominous rumors floating around Q Building that State had closed its mind to the warnings of OSSers, some of whom were being identified as too biased—as in, too sympathetic to Mao and Chou En-lai in the civil war in China, as well as toward Ho Chi Minh and his efforts to unite Vietnam. The OSS had invested months of planning for greater cooperation with the

Communists in both countries, and in the end it had come to nothing. Now, with the policy concerns of Western Europe dominating Washington's interpretation of policy worldwide, OSS reports indicating the revolutionary ferment, the growing strength of Mao and Ho, and the dismal political and economic situation in both countries, were not well received.

Anti-Communism had become the dominant theme in world politics and the overriding policy issue. All other relevant political considerations had been put to one side. So it followed that it was much more important that Bulgaria and Rumania be ready for self-government and free elections than that the struggling republics of Southeast Asia be, even though the latter had never sided with the Axis powers. The fear was that, except for the atom bomb, there was nothing to stop the Russians from marching straight through to the Atlantic. If the new West German government were to falter economically, and if the Communist parties managed to gain entry into the governments of France, Italy, and the Netherlands in the next elections, the Russians would have a formidable stake in Western Europe.

For these and other reasons, OSS was increasingly out of step with the current climate and out of favor. Senior advisors and policy experts were being repudiated or reassigned to obscure posts. "The term Communism, applied in any sly, subversive manner to an individual or group, could become the kiss of death, the way America is thinking today," Jan told Betty, his tone no longer trifling. "I sometimes think that Moscow wanted to try for a split in our country over and above party lines when the Russian government gave its tacit blessing to the liberals in the Democratic party. Politics, of course, is a fine spawning ground for MO."

This was too much for her. She could not bear to think of the consequences of power-hungry nations unleashing "such forces of evil as MO" on the world at large. Suddenly, she wanted to go home to Hawaii and "sit under a coconut tree." Life was simpler there, everyone got along, and "the climate was just enervating enough to preclude fiery ideological clashes." She left for an early lunch and went to the nearest ticket office to book a flight for Honolulu.

By early 1946, Betty and Jane were roommates again, sharing an apartment in New York and trying to resume life as it had been before the war. They had corresponded over the holidays and agreed that it was impossible to sort out their futures while living under the same roof as their parents. (Even though, in Jane's case, the roof in question belonged to the elegant Fairmont Hotel.) They were both officially "severed" from the OSS and for the first time in three years free to do exactly as they pleased. It was both intoxicating and a little overwhelming. "It was hard to face up to things," explained Betty. "During the war, you made absolutely no decisions, they were all made for you. You did as you were told. The OSS was like a big wartime family—we all lived together in a house, ate all our meals together, and traveled together. It was not a normal way of living as an adult. . . . In the aftermath of the war, it was hard to get organized again and figure out where to live and find a way of living."

Leave it to Jane, with her myriad contacts and abundance of well-heeled friends, to know the son of William E. Dodd, the former ambassador to Germany, who happened to have a mansion-sized dwelling on Central Park West that he was happy to sublet. This suited Betty, who wanted to write and had lined up a job at *Glamour* magazine. She had also begun work on a book about her adventures as one of Donovan's operatives in the Far East.* Since there was no longer any need for secrecy, Donovan had no objection and even offered to read her manuscript at regular intervals and make suggestions. She frequently went to see him at his office at 2 Wall Street, and their relationship evolved from that of boss and employee to one of devoted friends. Donovan knew she was in love with a member of his firm and that she and Dick Heppner planned to marry as soon as they had obtained their divorces.

Betty and Jane shared the apartment with Heppner's cocker spaniel, who had been relieved of his duties as a member of the K-9 corps guarding the OSS installation in Kunming and shipped home with a

---

* As no censorship had yet been invoked on OSS files, Betty MacDonald's wartime memoir, *Undercover Girl,* was published in 1947.

formal letter classifying him as "K-9 First Class Sammy." Having spent his youth in the company of GIs, the pup had developed a taste for gin. Betty, who was besotted with the golden ball of fluff, catered to his every whim. In the evenings, when she and Jane had their dry martinis, she made one for Sammy, too, serving his in a saucer. On the nights she expected to be out late, she always left Jane a note: "Please be back early this evening and fix the martinis. Sam does not like to drink alone."

For her part, Jane was too preoccupied with trying to decide what she wanted to do with the rest of her life to worry about getting a job. She did not need to work, as she had managed to save quite a lot of her overseas pay. Her old friends had taken her up on her return to the city, and she was so busy reconnecting with people and running around that the months slipped by in a convivial, cocktail-infused blur. "Jane never seemed to have any money problems," said Betty, recalling that she had plenty of ready cash for fashionable clothes and restaurants and weekend getaways. "She was very social and hosted continual parties," Betty added. "Those were happy, happy days. Everybody came to visit us. The apartment was huge, and we had rooms to spare. OSS people were flowing in and out."

Jane still intended to write her book on Indonesia, but unlike Betty could never seem to find the time. Not that it kept her from complaining about the contemptible actions of the Dutch government to anyone who would listen. When she first got back to San Francisco, she was still boiling from her State Department debriefing, and more than a little of her outrage had spilled over into a December 31, 1945, interview she gave to her hometown paper. Under the headline "Trigger-Happy Dutchmen Started Shooting," Jane had provided what the *San Francisco Chronicle* called one "San Francisco woman's version of the uprising in Java." The paper quoted her at length on the atrocities— "an automobile's back-firing was enough to set off Dutch guns"—and noted that "Miss Foster believes the Indonesians' fight for freedom will continue to be bloody until the Republic is recognized." Even the traditionally liberal *Chronicle* felt that perhaps Jane's comments were a bit too contentious and took the precaution of including an opposing view from an official from the Netherlands Information Bureau, who blamed the ongoing violence squarely on "terrorism by extremist Indonesian groups."

Seizing the chance to stir the pot, *People's World*, a West Coast Communist newspaper, ran an exclusive interview with Jane repeating her charges that the Dutch had "forced the war" in Java. "JANE FOSTER of the U.S. Office of Strategic Services made this statement on her return to San Francisco from the East Indies," the paper trumpeted. "'Until the Dutch came, law and order was strictly enforced by the Indonesian republic. Then the Dutch ranged the streets, shooting anything that moved. They would throw Indonesians out of their homes and tear down the red-and-white republican flag.'" The paper quoted her as predicting insurrection: "'Now there will be plenty of fighting. Five million Indonesians are ready and able to fight. Another 45,000,000 will refuse to work at anything that helps Dutch rule. There will be a boycott of the Dutch. . . . Unless a settlement can be reached some way—through the United Nations perhaps—guerilla warfare will continue to rage.'" To make sure the press understood the seriousness of the story, Jane supplied copies of her report on Indonesia to one and all. Although the OSS had labeled it "Top Secret," she "did not attach any importance to that fact." Surely in peacetime those rubber-stamp restrictions no longer applied? Besides, it contained only her "own experiences and observations," along with information Sukarno and other Indonesian officials would want her to make public.

In a small city where everybody knows everybody, the outspoken statements made by the daughter of one of the Nob Hill swells were big news. After all, Harry Emerson Foster was from one of America's oldest families (a tenth-generation *Mayflower* descendent). An eminent conservative, he sat on the board of a number of hospitals and charities. As one of their own and an OSS officer just back from the war zone and POW camps, Jane was in demand. On January 11, 1946, she was persuaded to give a lecture at the Institute of Pacific Relations providing "an eyewitness account of the revolt in Indonesia." In her talk she argued passionately that the Dutch would never be strong enough to keep seventy million Indonesians under martial law indefinitely and the only viable alternative was that the old colonial power begin negotiations in good faith. A summary of her lecture was printed in *People's World,* along with her recommendation that the United Nations probe the situation to prevent more violence. Her remarks were sufficiently persuasive to give impetus to the formation of the San Francisco Committee for a Free Indonesia, as well as picket lines outside the British and Dutch consulates in San Francisco on several occasions.

Jane was scheduled to give a similar talk in February at the First Unitarian Church of Berkeley but had to cancel after the State Department raised holy hell about her remarks concerning the war in Indonesia. The State Department considered the public airing of those events, which Jane had observed while an employee of the U.S. government, and while on "confidential assignment" in Java, "a gross and embarrassing breach of security regulations." Not only that, but the Dutch government deemed her remarks at the Institute of Pacific Relations "offensive" and had lodged an informal protest. (Jane's FBI file reveals that her superiors at the OSS also suspected her of being the possible source of "classified information" contained in the article "Secrets of Siam," written by Edgar Snow and published in the January 12, 1946, issue of *The Saturday Evening Post.* The Foreign Office was so outraged by Snow's article that it arranged for two British officials to write rebuttals. It was felt that the publication of this information was "unfortunate" and might "jeopardize negotiations with the British." However, an internal investigation "failed to fix the responsibility for the leak" on Jane. While it was true that she and Snow were both in Bangkok at the same time, he had clearly obtained information from "numerous sources.")

Jane was not displeased to learn of the trouble she had caused. She was no longer a government employee, and no one in the State Department could stop her from speaking out about the injustices she had observed. From then on, she made Indonesia her mission. She took personally America's refusal to live up to the foreign policy promises of the war years. It hurt her to think she had failed all those people in Indonesia and Vietnam who had trusted her and believed in her and her country. They had listened to the speeches about freedom and democracy that had been broadcast all over the world from the newly formed United Nations Organization in San Francisco. Representatives of fifty countries had convened in her hometown to draw up the UN charter, which had been signed in June in the Garden Room of the very same Fairmont Hotel her parents now called home. It was too ironic for words.

She had made many of those same brave-new-world speeches, repeated the same promises—and for what? She could not believe America meant to deliver the Indonesian and Vietnamese to the race hatred and enslavement of the repellant colonialists and their puppet regimes. In Saigon, she had left behind any illusions she might have had about the possibility of peace or progress without America's active intervention. She was haunted by the last lines of Ed Snow's report from Indochina: "This is one of the reasons why some observers out here keep saying that America ended the war with greater prestige than any nation in history—and is losing it more rapidly than any nation in history."

That summer, her disgust at Washington's studied noninvolvement in Indonesia prompted her to write a long, irate letter to *The New York Times*. Taking issue with the paper's July 1 editorial "Danger in Indonesia," which blamed the failure of recent negotiations between the Netherlands authorities and Indonesians on the "divided character" of Sukarno's government, she wrote, "The Netherlands has refused to recognize the independence of Indonesia. It is on this point that negotiations have broken down." After a painstaking but concise analysis of events leading up to the present crisis, she reiterated that Sukarno's government had the full support of seventy million Indonesians and concluded tartly, "The real obstacle to peaceful settlement is the intransigence of a few politically powerful Dutchmen." She then took the *Times* to task for running such a misinformed article in the first place, closing with this parting shot: "The press of the United States has done a disservice to the cause of democracy by consistently presenting one-sided facts regarding Indonesia."

August presented Jane with a problem that left her so preoccupied she had to temporarily abandon her book on Indonesia, which still had not progressed beyond the outline stage. "The problem," as Betty put it delicately, "was trying to decide what to do about George."

For two years, Jane had managed to keep a tight lid on her private life. Now, suddenly confronted with the past, all her efforts to keep the personal and professional carefully partitioned no longer seemed to matter. She poured out the whole story to Betty in a rambling, unapologetic monologue—how she had had a lover before the war, a Russian Jew she had met during her radical phase, who had begged her to marry him before his regiment left for Germany. She had not wanted to at first, but he was sure he was going to die fighting for his country. In the end, she had relented, "weak creature" that she was. There was the ridiculous last-minute city hall ceremony, with just the two of them giggling while exchanging vows before a staid Washington justice of the peace. Jane never told anyone about the marriage, not even her parents. She had never changed her single status on the OSS records, noting that she had lied "if only by omission."

As the war went on, it was hard to believe it had ever really happened. When she fell in love with Manly, she had no guilt feelings. George was somewhere "on the other side of the world" and, if true to form, was probably not "sexually deprived." At one point, when she had not heard from him for a long time, she began scanning the casualty lists from the German offensive in the Ardennes and wondering if he was dead. Later, she learned he had survived the Battle of the Bulge and that his regiment of army engineers had helped to build the first bridge over the Rhine at Wesel, allowing Allied forces to cross with their tanks and trucks of supplies. When she finally reached San Francisco, she realized that after so much time apart he had grown rather "misty" in her memory. Looking at her elderly parents, she decided it was time to rectify her mistake while they were still none the wiser. She sat down then and there and wrote him a Dear John letter. George was very decent about the whole thing and sent her a release by return mail.

Only now he was in New York, fresh off a troopship, and had rung up and asked to see her. After receiving her letter, he had sent a terse reply explaining that with no one waiting for him at home he had decided to stay on in Europe. He had responded to an army circular looking for Russian-speaking officers to volunteer for liaison duty in Berlin or Vienna but instead had been assigned to the Military Intelligence

Service and sent to a training school in Oberammergau in Bavaria. After months of silence, he had dropped her a line stating that he would be coming to the States in the fall. Jane, in another moment of weakness, postponed her trip to Reno.

Betty could still remember the first time she met George Zlatovski. Jane had brought him by the house for a drink, and they were both pretty well lubricated by the time Betty joined them in the library. George was of medium height, wiry, with a narrow face, high cheekbones (Jane described them as "Mongol"), and a thin, aquiline nose. He had a slightly lopsided mouth that in repose made him look somewhat churlish. He wore his clothes well, with a certain Continental élan, and knew how to turn on a courtly Old World charm. Betty could appreciate that he might appeal to the ladies, but it did not take long for her to see that he had an enormous chip on his shoulder. "There was something about him," she said with an ambivalent shrug. "I had a feeling he wasn't quite up to her level."

Jane later told her that her husband had been born Alexander Mikhail L'vovich Zlatkovski but had opted for the more American-sounding name George Michael Zlatovski when his family moved from Russia in 1922, when he was twelve. (His family also dropped the first *k* in their last name.) The offspring of a doctor to nobility, he and his younger sister had enjoyed a life of privilege in prewar St. Petersburg; they had been raised with servants, dachas, private tutors, and music lessons. When the Russian Revolution began in 1917, his family fled to the Ukraine, returning to their devastated home three years later. His father was no Communist, but because he was deemed a "socially useful element" he was treated fairly well for a while. When he eventually fell afoul of the new Soviet authorities, the family followed the example of their cousins who had earlier settled in Duluth, Minnesota. George clearly held the decision to emigrate against his father, blaming him for a youth blighted by misery, poverty, and prejudice. Adapting to a new country and culture had been difficult. His mother retreated into silence and depression and died of tuberculosis a few years later. George became an angry, disaffected teenager who suffered the humiliation of being called "Trotsky" by classmates and was forced to dress up and play classical recitals at the local Rotary, Kiwanis, and Lions clubs for pocket money. His mother had wanted him to try for a scholarship to the Juilliard School of Music in New York, but in a desperate attempt to fit in with his midwestern peers he opted to study engineering at the University of Minnesota. He regarded it as the biggest mistake of his life.

Jane made no attempt to gloss over his left-wing politics. George had graduated in the midst of the Depression and with no chance at a job had drifted into various labor organizations, several of which were affiliated with the Communist Party. He quickly became radicalized and spent the next few years as an agitator, street-corner orator, and union organizer, mostly trying to enlist the support of unemployed immigrant steel workers.* In 1937, imbued with revolutionary ardor, he ran off to the Spanish Civil War to be a hero and fight the fascists with the Abraham Lincoln Brigade. He returned to New York one year later, disillusioned and broke. Like Jane, he had been married before, to a dancer he had met in Duluth named Kathleen O'Brien.

Jane met him shortly after she moved to New York in 1941, introduced by mutual friends at an antiwar rally sponsored by the American Peace Mobilization, the liberal answer to America First. Jane was immediately attracted to his dark, brooding looks, and to catch his eye she began attending various antiwar meetings and Communist Party fundraisers. A child of the Depression, she, too, had dabbled in left-wing politics after college but had succeeded mostly in infuriating her father. In 1938, while attempting to eke out a living doing political caricatures for Bay Area publications including *People's World,* she had joined the local chapter of the Communist Party. At the time, it had seemed to her like a way to take "a strong, uncompromising stand against the economic crisis, war, Fascism, Nazism, and colonialism." Her fellow travelers were almost all artists, most of whom were working for the Works Progress Administration (WPA), set up by Roosevelt's New Deal ad-

---

* George Zlatovski's FBI file notes that he was regarded as "too non-conformist" to gain admittance to the Duluth Communist Party and was described as "too selfish" and known for doing "a lot of talking."

ministration to put unemployed painters and sculptors to work decorating public buildings. Even though some of them were not very good artists, Jane thought it was a grand idea.

She liked to joke that neither she nor George were ever cut out to be Communist. He was too insubordinate—even by Party standards—and liked money too much. George was an awful snob, and part of Jane's appeal for him was her wealthy background and fine sensibilities. Jane, too, was "a bit of a snob." She considered all the Party rules and regulations a bore, and was disappointed that her comrades in arms were not exactly what one would call "jolly companions." Moreover, she was "useless" at Party tasks. Once, when told that every member was expected to sell the *Daily Worker* on street corners, Jane got all "gussied up" in her mink coat and Bergdorf Goodman suit and made rather a spectacle of herself in Union Square meekly offering the paper to passersby. She managed to sell only a handful of copies while earning a lot of queer looks, but she obstinately maintained it was better than going around "like one of the slouching, leather-coated characters who gave the Party a bad name." She and George "so hated this chore" that they took to dumping their allotted issues in the garbage and just pretended that the money they handed over the next morning was from paper sales. The Communist Party was not for her, and with the advent of the war her focus shifted to fighting the fascists.

The more Betty saw of George, the less she liked him, but the opposite was true of Jane. After a few weeks, it was apparent that their relationship was very much on again. They went out on the town night after night, racking up huge tabs in expensive restaurants and clubs, giddily spending their war savings. Each regarded the other as exotic and ungovernable without ever stopping to consider that their lack of anything in common might one day pose a problem. What united them as Catholic and Jew, according to George, was that they were both "incurable romantics," fueling each other's passions and propensity for martyrdom. It was an ill-considered union, in Betty's view, but they were too entangled to part. What could she say anyway? That she had a vague feeling of unease about George and "did not really trust him"? She and Dick had gotten married in June and were caught up in their own lives. Since moving out of the apartment she shared with Jane, she had seen less and less of her old friend. They moved "in very different circles."

Once they reunited, Jane and George fell in with the same careless bohemian crowd they had known before the war. At the center of their group were Martha Dodd Stern and her husband, Alfred K. Stern, a wealthy investment banker. The couple threw huge parties in their penthouse apartment in the Majestic on Central Park West, and all sorts of artists and intellectuals, rebels, and radicals came to eat their hors d'oeuvres and drink their liquor. Among the regulars at the Sterns' soirees were Lillian Hellman, Paul Robeson, Margaret Bourke-White, Clifford Odets, and Isamu Noguchi, along with members of the Soviet and Eastern European diplomatic set. Regarding the crowd of famous faces, one amused guest dubbed the Sterns' salon *"La Très Haute Société Communiste."*

Jane had been introduced to Martha at a concert at Carnegie Hall when she first moved to New York, and they quickly discovered they had much in common. (It was Martha's brother, Bill Dodd, Jr., who lent Jane his apartment.) Jane and Martha came from similar backgrounds: Martha was an "F.F.V." (as in first families of Virginia), had toured Europe with her parents, and, like Jane, had lived in Berlin during the 1930s, although the two did not know each other at the time. Martha, who was pretty, blond, and amorously adventurous, had written a surprisingly frank book, *Through Embassy Eyes,* chronicling her early infatuation with Hitler and her affairs with handsome Gestapo officers before she understood what was really happening in Germany. She eventually saw the light, switched to Communism, and became equally fervent about her new cause. Despite her Bolshie politics and love of all things Russian—the two swans that ruled the lake on the grounds of her Ridgefield, Connecticut, estate were named Vladimir Ilyitch and Krupskaya—she was cagey about her party affiliations. She boasted about slipping Nazi secrets to her Russian lover in the early days of the war, and, as far as Jane could tell, she "loved intrigue, both political and personal, for its own sake." She was always hatching plots, and she would create compromising situations between friends and then "slyly hint" about what she knew. Jane resented Martha's meddling in her relationship with George, and the degree to which he seemed at her beck and call, but continued to see her on the cocktail circuit.

In the fall, Jane announced her intention of getting married. As far as her parents were concerned, she was finally wedding her longtime beau, whom they had met briefly before the war. On September 26, 1946, she and George carried out the charade of their second nuptials—even taking themselves downtown to the New York Municipal Building and obtaining another license—all in the name of sparing her parents "the pain" of their secret elopement. Though if Betty had to venture a guess, she was pretty sure that given Mr. and Mrs. Foster's feelings about George's radical politics and his influence on their only daughter, they would have preferred the pain of a divorce. Since George was still in the army, he had to report back to Vienna at the end of his three months' leave. Jane, who was thrilled to have an excuse to get back to Europe, made plans to join him. Naturally she could not resist splurging on a week's holiday in her "adorable, adored Paris." Betty genuinely wished her the best. With all the disappointments and lost dreams of the war, there was something reassuring about knowing that for a few members of their detachment, at least, it had ended in a happily-ever-after.

By this time, Paul Child was back in Washington and, since the liquidation of OSS, officially an employee of the State Department. Paul was initially quite pleased, and not a little impressed, to find himself working for such a venerable institution. "Break out my striped pants and my *chapeau haut-de-forme,* my monocle, my gardenia, and my pearl gray spats," he had instructed Charles prior to leaving China. "I want to look reet when I arrive in Washington." The thrill faded quickly enough, though he enjoyed the executive-level position and freedom from drudgery. He had the catchall title of project director, which meant he was responsible for planning and executing all the visual media presentations—from short films, slide shows, diagrams, and exhibits to articles and brochures—required by the different departments, as well as for big meetings and international conferences. He had a large office, adequate staff, and all the supplies and specialized equipment he had dreamed of back in Kunming. If the job was not particularly creative or inspiring, at least it paid the bills. He planned to apply for another foreign post, preferably in Europe, when his life was more settled.

He was temporarily bunking with Charles and Freddie, and their three young children at their large home at 1311 Thirty-fifth Street in Georgetown. As much as he loved his brother, being back in the bosom of family was at times quite taxing. Paul had an extremely complicated, competitive relationship with Charles, and he spent most of his life defining himself in opposition to his identical twin. It was not that Paul resented his brother's good fortune; he did not. It was just that he could not help feeling left out or, more precisely, left behind: "This brings up the difference in our timetables," Paul once wrote, lamenting his perennial rear view of life's promise. Everything always happened to Charles "first": he was the first to marry, to get a government job, to merit a raise, to move to Washington, and, last but not least, to advance up the career ladder to an important new position (with UNESCO). "If you think back, or just wait for the future to unroll, you will see that I am right," Paul added. "You are always ahead."

Julia's fly-by visit in November on her way home to California was a salve to his wounded ego. There she was, the devoted friend featured in so many of his wartime letters, larger than life in the crowded sitting room, radiating admiration and affection for him and him alone. Just seeing her did him good.

Julia had traveled back on a packed troopship with Rosie Frame and was full of funny stories. It had been a long, boring trip, and naturally there was a certain amount of fraternization between the troops and female civilians on board. One night on the mild Indian Ocean, a young OSS officer, Bob North, and a secretary were caught in flagrante delicto on the top deck by the master at arms. In his haste to get away, North tossed most of their clothes down the steep ladder, swung his date—who was passed out cold—over his shoulder, and carried her to the women's quarters. Julia, who found him struggling to get into her cabin, relieved North of the half-naked girl, telling him with good-natured disapproval, "I'll take her from here." By the time they arrived in New York, she and Rosie were "tired and bedraggled" and smelled like they had come by "cattle boat." Thibaut de Saint Phalle, who was waiting on the pier to meet his fiancée, took one look at them and stopped by the nearest phone, called the Elizabeth Arden salon, and took them both directly there for a thorough beauty treatment.

During their brief reunion, Julia and Paul agreed to "pursue the plan" they had formulated on the hilltop at the Wenjen resort. What Paul had in mind was a waiting period of sorts, "to see what we looked like in civilian clothes and meet each other's friends and family, then see if we still felt the same way." He had managed to get through the war—no mean feat—but it had cost him dearly. Now he needed to give his depleted mind and body, to say nothing of his soul, time to heal. Over the Christmas holidays, he wrote her a long, ruminative letter, musing about her progress since he first met her "on the porch of the tea-planter's bungalow" in Ceylon:

> You have been emerging from the mists, indecisions, and attitudes of your past into a fuller and more balanced life. I am curious to know if your family will have noticed that you are indeed a newer, better Julie, a more emotionally stable Julie, a more thoughtful Julie, a darlinger, sweeter, and lovelier Julie— or are these perhaps qualities which you have always had and which it took my old eyes two years to see—finally?

Paul was too self-analytical not to "allow for the possibility" that he, too, had changed, and that it was perhaps he who had become more open and perceptive "and finally able to see the reality." That this "reality" might mean finally parting with his fixation on an impossibly idealized and unattainable woman (the Zorina) remains unstated if not unrecognized. What he does recognize, and pay homage to, is that both he and Julia were better people for knowing each other, and that "a relationship based on appreciation, understanding, and love can work that sort of double-miracle." He added: "Whether we do or do not manage to live a large part of our future lives together, I have no regrets for the past, no recriminations, and no unresolved areas of conflict. It was lovely, warming, fulfilling, and solid—and one of the best things that ever happened to me." He signed the letter "Affectionately, Paulski."

While Julia welcomed these sentiments, she found herself wish-

ing for less talk of regret and more in the way of resolution. She had
agreed to Paul's wait-and-see plan in theory but dreaded what it meant
in practice. She was impatient to get on with their courtship, and a long
hiatus spent in quiet reflection and renewal was the last thing she really
wanted. Moreover, returning to her father's home in Pasadena and her
prewar role as the spinster daughter cum caretaker—currently occupied by her sister, Dorothy—felt like a giant step backward. She needed
to move forward with her life, but with no job prospects and absolutely
no idea what she wanted to do professionally, she felt completely at sea.
Her OSS experience had improved her confidence and people skills,
though the only obvious career path it had prepared her for was some
form of administrative work, and she had made it clear on her government employment form that she would never have anything to do with
files again. She listed "public relations" as an alternative, for want of a
better idea, but that seemed far-fetched even to her. The one thing she
was sure of was that she did not want to lose Paul. But how was she
going to win him over when they were living on opposite coasts?

If Julia had learned anything about Paul during the war, it was how
much he cherished letters from friends and family, and she remembered the time and attention he had lavished on the Homeric offerings
he penned nightly for his brother, often reading long passages aloud to
her in her room after dinner. She knew he savored missives from old
friends and past flames, carefully tucked them away, and took them out
to read over and over on rainy days. Words, she decided, were the way
to his heart. If they had to be apart, then she would keep him close by
way of a persistent, intimate correspondence, an outpouring of love
and desire not even his defenses could withstand. As with everything
she did, Julia embarked on their epistolary romance in January 1946
with great gusto, infusing her letters with her irrepressible enthusiasm,
passion, and personality. Acutely aware that Paul was a very physical
man, the pages fairly tremble with her burgeoning sensuality:

Dearest Paulski:
Oh. I love hearing from you. I find myself haunting the mail-
box. When I read one of your letters I am engulfed with plea-
surable warmth and delight which glows in me. What have you

done to me, anyway—that I continue to long and languish for you? I want to know what you think about, what you would think about things here and people. I want to sit next to you, closely. Well.

Julia kept her tone buoyant and optimistic, describing busy days filled with the kinds of self-improving activities Paul would find commendable. She had bought a book on semantics, the philosophy of language, which she knew he had made a study of and considered crucial to any understanding of the deeper and hidden meaning of words and symbols. This had opened her eyes to the extent to which she was being "led around by words—slantings, loadings, judgements, inferences—but had never taken the trouble to see how."

Under Paul's influence, she was avidly reading the newspapers, with particular attention to the political pages and their conservative bent. "I am noticing things in the pages now, and with a sneer," she reported. "I have become insanely angry at the *LA Times* for being a biased and inadequate 'leading' paper in this every day more enormous community." For a more balanced view, she had subscribed to the daily *Washington Post* and Sunday *New York Times*. "I am going to make a detailed analysis of why the *LA Times* is inadequate—what news it misses and discolors. Then I am going to confront the Chandler family with the ineluctable facts, instead of raging at them with empty emotions. That will take at least two hours a day but will be very fruitful for me in (1) semantics, (2) general information, (3) newspaper techniques, (4) possible benefit to the community in improving the paper (very doubtful.)" She was closely following all the foreign news, and was intensely interested in Russian imperialism, which she understood to be "historic and crucial," with profound implications for the future of Europe, Asia, and the United States. "I wish you were here so I could sit in your lap and you could tell me *all* about everything and why," she wrote. "How little I know, to witness all of this intelligently—and it is the beginning of a new era, the end of an old regime and way of life."

To further address the grave shortcomings of her education, she was taking advantage of her leisure time to improve her mind. She had majored in history at Smith, but was too much of a "dilettante" in those days to concentrate on her studies. It was not until she joined the OSS, and found herself regularly in the company of academics—anthropologists, geographers, and historians—that she discovered that she "liked that type of person very much." Late in life, she had stumbled upon a whole new world and was ravenous to learn. To make up for lost time, she began reading everything she could lay her hands on, relying on Paul for guidance. At his suggestion, she read Henry Miller's *Tropic of Cancer*, a controversial novel based on the writer's youthful exploits in Paris, but confessed it was "too much of a stiff-prick forest" for her taste. As Paul insisted Miller was "a magnificent writer," she was attempting another of his works, *The Cosmological Eye*. She would return her "elementary book" on semantics and pick up the more advanced text he recommended. She had even started in on psychology, enthusing, "There is so much that is fascinating!" Ever his devoted protégée, she reported, "I have luxuriously surrounded myself with everything I am eager to know about." Piano lessons were also on the agenda, along with the promise to "practice laboriously." Knowing food was a subject dear to his heart, she concluded her letter with the description of a favorite delicacy and tried to tempt him with an invitation: "Now I am about to eat some cracked crab (would you care to join me?)." She signed the letter "Much loving and more so."

Determined to impress Paul with a fine homemade dinner the next time they met, Julia began taking cooking lessons. She studied under "two old English ladies" at the Hillcliff School of Cookery in Beverly Hills, dutifully attending classes three times a week. Paul responded with encouragement, observing drolly that he was sure she would one day make a superb chef "because you are so interested in food." Julia was not exactly at home in the kitchen. Unlike Paul's mother, whose taste buds were so exacting she once spent six months searching for the right coffee bean—and in the end roasted her own combination of three—Mama McWilliams had been no gourmet. She had relied on a family cook to get simple all-American fare to the table, raising her brood on baking-powder biscuits, Welsh rabbit, and roast beef. Julia lacked even the most rudimentary skills, admitting that her maiden effort with spoon and spatula resulted in a "debilitating kitchen experience." Her first forays—an array of breakfast dishes—were limited in scope, but her enthusiasm knew no bounds. After graduating from omelets to pancakes, she wrote Paul that she now considered Aunt Jemima mix to be "pedestrian," and boasted that her own recipe was an "experience in superbity," and that "a mediocre substitute will be but phlegm after a Julia McWilliams pancake has once been eaten."

Julia was not a natural, but with time and practice she began to improve. With characteristic honesty and self-deprecating humor, she kept Paul informed of her every success ("a light, delectable" béarnaise sauce) and failure (an exploded duck that set the oven on fire). It still took her hours to get dinner on the table, and she invariably wrecked the kitchen in the process, but it was progress. By the end of April, she professed herself "very pleased" with her latest kitchen feats, adding, "I do love to cook. I suppose it would lose some of its glamour if I were married to a ditch digger and had seven children, howsoever."

Reflecting on how much she had changed, Julia wrote Paul that she was finally "coming out of her cocoon and looking around at life as it should be lived." She mustered up the courage to tell her father that she would be moving out. Pasadena was "comfortable and lovely" but too contained. A sign of her newfound independence was the critical eye she turned on her beloved sister, Dorothy, or Dort, who was still unmarried and living at home. After four years of tending house for their widowed father, she struck Julia as "quite stale and stultified." Julia had argued vigorously against Dort's old-fashioned notion that as dutiful daughters their place was at home with "Pops." "I think girls should lead their own lives or they will be a pleasure to no one in the end," she asserted, adding that she had pointed out the obvious, which was that if they were "married and living in Oshkosh" he would have been alone anyway. He settled the question by announcing his intention to remarry.

Julia wrote Paul she thought she might look for work in Hollywood, and was planning to begin checking out opportunities shortly, after recovering from minor surgery on her neck. She did not rule out Washington or another government job, but her ambitions were bigger now and she would not settle for "any kind of job like Registry" nor less than four thousand dollars a year: "I want something in which I will grow, meet many people and many situations." In a subsequent letter, she noted with satisfaction that she had come a long way from the awkward twenty-five-year-old girl who was "so self-conscious that I actually hurt if I thought people were looking at me."

Even long distance, she remained Paul's biggest booster and was lavish in her praise of his talent and promising career. When he complained about his boss's attempts to undermine him, she reassured him that his worth would make itself apparent to his superiors: "Who is the most remarkable, charming, intelligent, and clever man to have but General Paulski?" Later, when he expressed interest in possibly working for UNESCO, which had a branch in Paris, she encouraged him to apply for a position. "It sounds like *the* place for you, my darling," she wrote, adding insightfully, "if you could find your niche, I should think you could find your life." After Paul reported to her a critical remark by Marge Kennedy, a former OSS colleague, to the effect that "everybody" in Kunming said he was "cold and uncommunicative," Julia leaped to his defense: "That is often a 'line' people take to ensnare the object into a passionate demonstration of warmth. With people you know, or think you will like, you are one of the most warm and personal people I have ever met—and that's what 'everyone' says." And when he took ill (a recurrence of dysentery) during a trip to New York, she worried about his health and suggested he come out west for a month to recuperate and regain his strength. He declined, citing his State Department work and ongoing job search.

While she was careful not to belabor the subject of their uncertain relationship, Julia made it clear that she was not spending her days and nights mooning over him. There are references to duck shooting with the boys, amusing dinner parties with friends, and late evenings that end with her tipsy ("but not swaying") after "fifty martinis." She is candid in answer to his query about potential suitors, owning up to not having met "a lot of nifty men." She immediately rescues herself from this potential humiliation by going on to say she had finally told her old standby, Harry Chandler, "who has been sucking around for years with $2 million and a thick head," to stop wasting his time. "I still like Paulski best," she teased, "but I ain't going around with my eyes shut."

Though she was too generous to toy with his affections, her own jealousy was easily aroused. When Paul wrote that Bartleman's latest predictions had them falling in love with other people, she replied hotly, "I think that woman, Bartleman, is really in love with you herself." On another occasion, after not hearing from him for a week, she made no attempt to hide her suffering. When his letter finally arrived, she berated him for not writing more often and admitted she was bereft at the idea that he had lost interest: "I was thinking, 'My G. that man has forgotten me, absence making heart grow fonder for someone else; my life turning to gall and emptiness; have my correspondings been *so* dreadful.' You see, you continue to have me, or it—you are under my skin."

Paul responded to Julia's letters with a steady stream of his own. They are tender in tone, though guardedly at first, the entertaining stories about work and gossip about old colleagues gradually giving way to more open expressions of how much he missed and adored her. He sent bundles of photographs, mostly of himself, as well as pictures of their favorite haunts in Kunming, his sketches and other artwork from China, anything he could think of to remind her of what their days together meant to him. He continued to worry that she might turn out to be a fusty old virgin or, worse, a prude, and urged her to read racy novels and books about sex. As the months passed, loneliness eroded his lifelong reserve and his letters echoed hers in longing and unconcealed desire. "You play a leading role in my fantasy life," he confided. In May, she replied by thanking him for the latest photograph of himself and confessed it made her "ache" to be with him. She wondered how it was that their six-month correspondence had the effect of making her want him more than ever: "Indeed I still think you are *the* nifty, and think so evermore. Why is that? Because we are having only a communion of minds, which, having had a taste of body, makes even words desirable and sweeter. I feel I am only existing until I see you, and hug you, and eat you."

In the spring, Julia wrote Paul that with her father about to head off on his honeymoon and her sister moving east "to have a try at NY," she was finally on her own. "This makes me really a fancy foot, free and loose." She renewed her invitation that he fly out to California for a visit. She proposed they drive slowly back across the country together—with "the excuse" that they were visiting friends along the way—perhaps ending up in Lopaus Point, Maine, where the Child brothers had built a rustic cabin. In any discussion, Paul's favorite term was "operational proof," by which he meant subjecting a theory to a test to see what happens. (His father had been a physicist, and Paul was sure that with his own love of logic and precision he would have made a good experimental scientist.) Well, what better way to see if they could stand each other's company over the long haul than a road trip? The close proximity would either confirm their compatibility or do them in. Paul agreed, and he applied for five weeks' leave.

When Paul arrived at Union Station in Los Angeles on July 7, Julia was pacing the platform. She was understandably nervous—and not just about their reunion. Paul would be meeting her father, and the traditional, old-guard Republican John McWilliams could be "very difficult" at the best of times, let alone when towering over the smallish, balding, mustachioed forty-four-year-old artist his older daughter had brought home from the war. Her worst fears were confirmed when it quickly became apparent the two men in her life did not get on. Paul's European style of dressing, particularly his soigné habit of tucking scarves into his open-neck shirts, rubbed the old man the wrong way. That Paul was also a Democrat and most likely responsible for the introduction of liberal rags like *The New York Times* into the McWilliams household, did not help.

Even more problematic was Paul's habit of trying to engage all those around him in philosophical conversations about everything from how the vastness of the West inspired the local architecture to what constituted a life well lived. Not only did they have nothing in common, but Paul and her father were almost diametrically opposed in their views of people, politics—everything. "My father was very conservative and nonintellectual," Julia recalled. As far as Pops was concerned, "intellectuality and Communism went hand in hand, so you were better off not being an intellectual." She loved them both but was resigned to the fact that they would never be friends. It was the first important step in what Paul would later describe as Julia's "divorce" from her father.

After a tense few days, Julia and Paul piled into her old Buick and made their escape. They spent the next month meandering through dusty small towns and sunburnt canyons, sticking to back roads and cheap motels. Although she had never been in a motor court before, she made the best of it, camping out without hesitation and preparing delicious meals under the most primitive conditions. She even surprised him their first night by pulling out eight bottles of her father's best whiskey, another of a gin, and a flask of mixed martinis. "Julie is a splendid companion, uncomplaining and flexible—really tough-fibered, a quality I first saw in her in Ceylon and later in China," Paul wrote his brother from Billings, Montana, adding, "She also washes my shirts! Quite a dame." A California girl at heart, Julia was in many ways much hardier than Paul, who fancied himself quite the mountain man despite a rather delicate constitution. Julia, on the other hand, had grown up in the West and spent her early years on horseback riding and hunting with her brother, John. As a strapping girl in her twenties, she had thought nothing of bagging sixteen ducks and bringing them home with just as many friends for dinner. She had no trouble peeing behind a bush or walking barefoot ("with rouged toenails") into a lumberjack's bar and downing a beer. She was from pioneer stock, sturdy and unpretentious, and completely at home with the rough country and male company she and Paul encountered on their travels.

As their journey neared its end, it was clear to Paul that Julia had passed all his tests with flying colors, even proving—much to his relief—to have "no measly Mrs. Grundyisms about sex." In his typical analytical fashion, he noted that she was much improved compared to his "findings of two years ago," and he sent his brother a summary of her better points entitled "The Good Julia." Above all, he recognized that Julia's finest quality was that she was always entirely herself, "a firm and tried character," with a boundless love of life and spontaneity that balanced his more sober, inward personality. "She never 'puts on an act,' or creates a scene," he wrote approvingly. "She has a deep-seated charm and human warmth which I have been fascinated to see at work on people of all sorts, from the sophisticates of San Francisco to the mining and cattle folk of the Northwest. She would be poised and at ease anywhere."

By the time they reached Maine, they were madly in love. No one was the least bit surprised when Paul declared his intention of getting married. "Well!" his brother and sister-in-law said in one voice. "We thought you'd never come out with it!" This time, Paul would brook no delay. Charles offered to have the wedding at Coppernose, their stately home in Bucks County, Pennsylvania, which had been in his wife's family for years. Plans were immediately put into motion. Barely a month later, on September 1, Julia and Paul exchanged vows in a small civil ceremony at the home of a neighboring lawyer; a garden party for family and friends followed. The reception was crowded with pals from their OSS days making champagne toasts and telling amusing anecdotes about the unlikely lovebirds.

10

OPEN SEASON

It was funny how they all ended up in Paris. What were the odds? So much had happened to them in the last few years, almost seven, between the end of the war in Kunming and sitting together in a café on the Left Bank. Of course, once they started talking and comparing notes, it made perfect sense. Julia and Paul had moved to France in the fall of 1948, when Paul took a job as exhibits officer with the United States Information Service. They had been there several years when an OSS colleague came through and mentioned that he had heard that Jane Foster was "somewhere in Paris" and he wondered where she was and what she was up to. Julia and Paul were horrified to think they had been living in the same city as their old friend all that time and had somehow remained ignorant of her presence.

They had last seen Jane in Washington shortly after they all got back from overseas, before she mysteriously "dropped out of sight." Her disappearance had aroused all sorts of speculation: "That's a name that's been in the mouths of all the ex-OSS-in-Ceylon people since the war's end," Paul wrote in his Paris diary, which continued to double as an intimate record of his daily life for Charles. "Mutual friends said

they'd heard she'd married a mysterious Pole after one week's acquaintance and that she couldn't even remember his name. She was reported
in Montevideo, in Brussels, but the most persistent rumor had her lost
behind the Iron Curtain because her husband was a Red. Ever since,
whenever we've seen any of our former OSS colleagues, the first thing
we've asked each other has been traditionally, 'Look—have you got any
dope on the whereabouts of Jane Foster?'" No one ever did. Discount-
ing the more fanciful stories they heard, Julia and Paul persisted in trying to find her, but she seemed to have vanished without a trace. No one
in their tight-knit little expat community had seen her, Julia recalled,
"so several people wondered about that."

Then, one brisk November afternoon in 1952, after tracking down a
particularly delicious omelet recommended by Julia's new pen pal Avis
DeVoto (who would soon become her literary agent), Julia and Paul were
prowling the art supply shops along the quay when he spotted a poster
in a store window and immediately recognized the drawing as one of
Jane's. He was certain it had to be her work, the style was "unmistakable."

Sure enough, the poster turned out to be an advertisement for an
upcoming exhibition of paintings by a "Jane Foster," and the small print
at the bottom gave the name and address of the art gallery. "So we hied
ourselves to the gallery," Julia recalled. The paintings were clearly Jane's:
they were modified abstractions, with unusual color combinations and
a sensuous feeling. As further proof, some of the subjects were Malaysian and Sinhalese. Confirmation came from the gallery owner, who
explained that Jane was now called Madame Zlatovski, that she lived
nearby at 32 rue Mazarine, and to the best of his knowledge she had
been there for some two and a half years. Paul scribbled a short note
and left it in care of the little man, who promised to pass it on.

Dearest Janie:
Ay Bong! (Sinhalese greeting, which roughly translates as "Hi
there!) We love your paintings; and we've always loved you,
too. We'd like to see you if you'd like to see us. Our telephone
no. is INV 92.90.

Paul and Julia Child

Paul only half expected to hear from her because of the "inexplicable suddenness with which she seemed to cut everybody off." Then again, if Jane was hiding, she would "never have had a poster stuck up with her name on it." He had to admit to being intensely curious about what had become of her. "If you'd been in Ceylon with OSS you'd know why this interested us," he informed Charles. "Everybody loved her, except a few people who hated her guts. We saw her, worked w/her, ate w/her, drank, sang, walked, talked and scrapped every day for almost a year." It was hard to be that close to someone and then just suddenly have that person vanish. If she had met with some accident or terrible fate, surely the news would have reached them.

She did not keep them in suspense for long. The following day was Sunday, and rather on the late side of morning Jane had rung to say yes, indeed, she was living in Paris and they must meet up at once. "She sounded exactly like the same familiar, warm, nice, outgoing, and enthusiastically vague Jane," Paul noted with satisfaction. "She was astonished to learn we'd been here for four years. She must be just as lazy, hazy, impractical & loveable as she was 7 years ago."

The next day, Jane came to lunch at their little third-floor apartment at 81 "Roo de Loo" (rue de l'Université), which was only a short stroll down Saint-Germain—"that euphoric boulevard"—from her place. They spent hours talking that first afternoon, catching each other up on the intervening years as the sky darkened and the shop lights came on and cast their rosy glow over the old city. Paul quickly filled Jane in on his marriage to Julia (she knew, of course, courtesy of Betty) and career moves. His job at the State Department had been eliminated by peacetime budget cuts in March 1947, and he had spent an anxious six months looking for work. During this enforced hiatus, he had taken up his painting and photography again and proudly told Jane about his one-man show in New York. When he was offered the post in Paris—the embassy was desperate for people with fluent French—he had grabbed it, and thank heaven for that because they were having the time of their life. The U.S.I.S. was essentially responsible for the propaganda campaign hitched to the great American money wagon that was the Marshall Plan, its mission being to check the spread of

Communism in Western Europe. Most of Paul's work involved staging U.S. government dog-and-pony shows, complete with art exhibits and banal photographs portraying "the American way of life." The job was fine as far as it went, and it involved opportunities for travel to international trade fairs, but the real treat was being back in Paris.

From her first bite of sole meunière, Julia had been smitten with the food in France. It was a revelation. She had worked diligently at her cooking prior to her marriage and during her two years as a Washington hostess, but it was not until they moved to Paris that she discovered the world of truly exquisite, glorious food. She was obsessed with what she rather grandiosely referred to as *"la cuisine française,"* enthusiastically trilling the words in her extraordinarily operatic, uniquely accented French. In a stroke of brilliance, Paul had pointed her in the direction of Le Cordon Bleu, and what had begun as a hobby had become her true passion and life's calling. She regaled Jane with stories about her rocky start at the famous French school of culinary arts. How after two trying days with rank beginners, she insisted on being transferred to the professional course, which was designed to turn out future restaurant chefs, only to discover that her classmates were eleven hopeless GIs. After six months, the "boys" still had not mastered the fundamentals and did not know "the proportions for a béchamel or how to clean a chicken the French way." Fed up with their lack of seriousness and their tortoiselike pace, Julia had dropped out and hired the school's legendary instructor, master chef Max Bugnard, to give her private lessons.

From then on, their life revolved around food. Julia spent her mornings in class and her afternoons "home-practicing" what she learned on poor Paul, who suffered through countless failed soufflés, galantines, and fondues. Weekends were devoted to scouring the local markets for the freshest fish, mouthwatering cheeses, baskets of mushrooms, and armloads of fragrant leeks. When she was not cooking, she was collating recipes, tapping them out, according to Paul, "like a determined woodpecker." He jokingly referred to himself as a "Cordon Bleu widower," but was unstinting in his praise of his wife's much-improved skills.

After a year of intensive training, Julia had felt ready to take the exam that was a prerequisite to receiving the legendary Cordon Bleu diploma. She was indignant on the subject of her trials and tribulations at the hands of Madame Elisabeth Brassart, the school's impossibly arrogant *directrice,* who had taken against her as a jumped-up American amateur and attempted to bar her from taking the final. It was only after Julia sent a letter containing dark threats that the American Embassy might take exception to the maltreatment of one of its own that she was grudgingly allowed to sit for the exam. Even then, Madame Brassart issued her only a certificate (not the real McCoy), since Julia had not technically completed the course. It took another year of letter writing and veiled threats before she extracted a signed diploma from the dreadful woman.

When she first arrived, Julia had only very halting, schoolgirl French. Discovering that after seventeen years of French classes she could neither speak nor understand the language, she had immediately enrolled in a Berlitz course. Before long, she was babbling away about pâtés and mousses and was proficient enough to continue perfecting her technique under Bugnard, as well as other leading Cordon Bleu chefs. She also joined Le Cercle des Gourmettes, a women's cooking club dedicated to haute cuisine. This was something of a rebel league in France, where the elite dining clubs and three-star restaurants were still the exclusive preserve of men, who staged magnificent feasts and preened in the company of their fellow culinary kings.

It was at Le Cercle that Julia befriended Simone Beck and Louisette Bertholle, two Frenchwomen who were excellent cooks and who shared her obsession with the craft—researching and codifying recipes, carefully recording the exact ingredients and precise steps that went into preparing the very best quiche lorraine, *canard à l'orange,* or *turbot farci braisé au champagne.* The two women had completed the manuscript of a collection of French recipes tailored for Americans and were looking forward to their next venture. Impressed with Julia's personality and resourcefulness, to say nothing of her Cordon Bleu pedigree, they invited her to be a partner in their own small cooking school. L'École des Trois Gourmandes opened for business in January 1952, initially operating out of Julia's ancient kitchen and teaching a handful of unknowing wealthy American women the basics of French cuisine. Paul moonlighted as their resident wine expert and kept the finances straight so that their tiny *"l'école"* cleared a profit. Inspired by their success, the partners decided to publish a teaching manual. Originally, their plan was to rework Beck and Bertholle's modest collection of recipes, but after reviewing the recipes and the confusing instructions, Julia persuaded them to embark on a much more ambitious French cookbook that would reflect her teaching style and a more informal "human approach."

Jane was vastly amused by the idea of the tall, white-aproned Professeur Julia lecturing a bunch of bored embassy wives on the proper way to prepare coq au vin. She admitted to rarely darkening the door of her own minuscule kitchen, adding that she and her husband were habitués of a bar/restaurant in their *quartier* called La Grignotière (The Nibblery). Waving away any suggestion she had intentionally distanced herself from her old pals, she said airily, "Oh well, I never write letters, you know—gave that up long ago."

She told them about her own unexpected marriage to George (they'd known each other "a long time") and their move in March 1947 to Austria, where he served with the U.S. Army of Occupation. He worked for "so-called Military Intelligence" as a liaison officer, mainly interviewing refugees— Hungarians, Ukrainians, Balts, and people of other Soviet nationalities—who had collaborated with the Germans during the war and were housed in temporary camps. Jane had landed a job with the information services branch of the army, where she had managed to parlay her propaganda experience in OSS into a senior position as head of the Austrian radio station in Salzburg, with considerable editorial influence and a staff of ninety-five. She explained how difficult she had found it in the beginning to work with her Austrian subordinates, the majority of whom had "all been Nazis" and had worked for the German *Rundfunk* (broadcasting system) during the war. In time her attitude had softened, as she saw the toll of defeat and desperate poverty in their faces. Her proudest moment was broadcasting the first postwar Salzburg Festival in 1947, which was transmitted by the Vienna station throughout Western Europe. She made Julia and Paul laugh with tales about how her rusty German got her in trouble, like the night she scandalized her staff and listeners alike by mispronouncing the name of Mozart's "Eine kleine Nachtmusik" (A Little Night Music), instead saying "Eine kleine Nacktmusik," which translated roughly as "A Little Naked Music."

She and George had spent a year together in Austria, squandering her salary on frequent weekends in Paris. It was formidably expensive because rationing was still on, but then she had always lived beyond her means. Her favorite motto was and always would be "Give me the luxuries of life and I'll do without the necessities!" Whenever they could, she and George hopped the Orient Express or Arlberg Express. They would take the night train after work on Fridays, arrive at Gare de l'Est in Paris first thing Saturday morning, live it up for thirty-six hours, and then sleep it off on the return trip to Salzburg on Sunday. At the end of 1947, George was sent to Fort Belvoir, in Virginia, before being demobilized. They had planned to reunite in Paris, but their four-month separation stretched to more than eighteen months when George landed a job in New York with an engineering consulting firm and decided to stay in the States and try to earn some money. What exactly went on during this period was unclear, but she implied that there had been some trouble in the marriage. Jane remained in Salzburg, where she had planned to meet up with her parents in June and accompany them on a three-month holiday in Europe.

When her parents returned to San Francisco at the end of the summer, Jane went to Paris and after much searching found a tiny garret she and George could just afford. George was finally able to join her in August 1949. He went back to school, courtesy of the GI Bill, completing a degree at the Faculté des Lettres, and was earning an "inadequate" salary working part-time for UNESCO writing a French-German-English glossary of engineering terms. Unable to obtain a work permit—all the available jobs went to French nationals—he had to settle for freelance jobs. Fortunately, she still had her two-hundred-dollar allowance from her father, which he sent by American Express each month. It was enough to get by on. "Poor George is full of neuroses," she said of her contentious, petulant spouse, suggesting he was not always the easiest to live with, "but he's a very nice guy, and he's learning to relax little by little."

For her part, Jane was taking art classes at the University of Paris and had received a commission from the French government to design some tapestries. She dismissed the latter as just a sideline, as her main interest continued to be her painting. Paul was green with envy at the mention of her small studio at the Académie de la Grande Chaumière, and Jane insisted that he and Julia come by and see it. After lunch, Paul hesitantly showed her the large study of Paris that he had labored over for many painful weeks. (He knew Jane could produce a picture in a day.) Although he always protested that he painted "just to please himself," he privately worried that his work was too old-fashioned and illustrative, and totally out of step with the times. Jane's genuine enthusiasm took him by surprise. "Don't touch anything," she said, "Leave it the way it is. It's wonderful!" As Paul reflected later, "She was unusually discerning and appreciative of my painting, which draws me to her in spite of the fact that she's almost a pure type of 'the instinctive woman'—a race I tend to rear away from out of self-protective cowardice." The years had not changed Jane a bit. She was "the same *Grand Naturelle,*" as earthy and impulsive as always. Her habits were as undisciplined and unregulated as they had been during the war. There was no telling what time she might drag herself out of bed. It was always best to phone after noon.

The following Saturday they dined "*chez* Jane" in her fourth-floor apartment in a crumbling seventeenth-century building overlooking the baronial splendor of the Bibliothèque Mazarine, the oldest public library in France. Jane lived in Vieux Paris, in the heart of the art district, almost directly across the Seine from the Louvre Museum. Around the corner on Quai Voltaire was Sennelier, the legendary art shop where Cézanne and Picasso bought their custom-made pigments. Her father had lent her the money to buy the two-bedroom apartment, and Jane had fixed the place up charmingly, stuffing the rooms with bibelots and shabby antiques salvaged from the Marché aux Puces (flea market). Blue denim draperies framed the windows overlooking the narrow streets below, and the stark white walls blazed with her brilliantly colored abstract paintings. As always, she had various animals about the place, including a black-and-white alley cat and a French poodle.

She introduced her husband, who struck Julia as "a small, short, funny fellow." Paul found George "shy and brainy" and felt he was completely in thrall to his charismatic wife. George let Jane do "all the talking" and just sat back and listened, though he managed to laugh at the appropriate places. "She has him completely mastered through the surging rush of her personality," Paul mused later. "He's helpless under its tumult. We think they've worked out a successful system of living together, though either Julie or I would recoil from it."

That night, they drank a lot of wine and stayed up late talking about old times. Julia and Paul told of seeing Cora DuBois and Jeanne Taylor, as well as Rosie Frame and her husband, Thibaut de Saint Phalle. Jane and George had dined with Betty MacDonald and Dick Heppner on their recent visit to Paris. They began reminiscing about their days in Kandy. Paul recounted the famous chipmunk-chasing escapade that had ended with Jane shimmying down the drainpipe after her runaway pet and being confronted by a "naked blimpish British colonel" spluttering with embarrassment. "The war was funnier than I thought at the time," wrote Paul, "and as we went back over it we damn near knocked ourselves out laughing."

After that, Julia and Paul saw Jane and George for dinner every few weeks. On several occasions, the Childs entertained at their own place and Julia cooked up a storm. Paul groused to his diary that he hardly felt it was worth "feeding them with finesse," given the pedestrian fare they dished up at their place. "They do a lot of cooking out of cans (the way most Europeans think most Americans do) because it's easier," he observed with distaste. "Jane really doesn't want to bother to prepare anything. George does most of the cooking and cleaning up anyway—seems like. Our first dinner at their place was lamb chops, boughten French fries, and canned peas. It ended with French pastries. Not too hard to prepare!" However, Paul chalked it up to "laziness rather than esthetic insensibility" and was inclined to be generous as Jane had such extraordinary taste in painting and photography, and her husband, though untrained, was not far behind her.

Paul and Jane had agreed to swap pictures, and he looked forward to having an original Foster on his wall. He was giving her a cubistic design he had done of Paris rooftops and chimney pots that she said she loved. "She is almost psychic in her appreciation of what one has done," he marveled to Charles. "She rushes up to a painting and puts her nose close to the surface—her face as eager as a child's, her eyes dancing—and begins to explore its surface like a quartering bird-dog, talking sense every minute. It rather takes my breath away." Unfortunately, one could not expect this affinity to extend to all fields. "They don't take food anywhere nearly as seriously as we do," he concluded, "though they like it so appreciate it."

One subject both couples took seriously was politics. Whenever they got together, they would work themselves up into a state about the anti-Communist hysteria gripping American domestic politics and the divisive 1952 elections, dominated by McCarthy's outrageous scapegoating and Richard M. Nixon's Red-baiting. America, they agreed, was going to the dogs. It was far better to be in Paris. Julia and Jane swapped stories about their fathers, both "congenital Republicans," as Julia put it, and stalwart supporters of McCarthy and Nixon.

Julia had been shocked but not surprised by a *Herald Tribune* article that September detailing Nixon's secret campaign slush fund that mentioned her father as one of the generous contributors. She had laughed aloud at the sight of his name on the front page—"John McWilliams, Pasadena rancher"—but it had been a mirthless laugh all the same. After Julia's father had provoked her into mounting a vigorous defense of Charlie Chaplin—whom McCarthy had accused of being involved with left-wing causes in the 1930s and ordered Immigration Services to "hold for hearings" if he tried to return to the United States—her brother had written asking her to cease and desist. It just upset the old man. Her stepmother, Phila, seconded the motion. Julia did as they asked but remained mutinous. As she later fumed to Charles and Freddie, "I'll bet I would have been a Communist at that period, too, if I had been an intellectual instead of a fairly well-to-do butterfly. Who knows."

Jane, who was coping with another extended visit from her own father—at that very moment ensconced at the fashionable Hôtel

Lutetia—understood Julia's muzzled anger. It was a condition she knew all too well. As Paul observed, "From her description, her father is the psychological spit and image of Mr. McWilliams: a California transplant from New Hampshire in his youth, wealthy, a retired surgeon, nice, extremely Right Wing Republican." It was uncanny how similar their backgrounds were. They decided the OSS must have made a point of recruiting the free-spirited daughters of rich, reactionary Californians.

While she often made light of it, Julia found the political climate in her home state truly dismaying. On her last visit to Pasadena, she had been so upset by the accusatory "soft on Communism" blather of her father and old family friends that she could not relax until she was back on French soil. She blamed Nixon, then California's freshman senator, for whipping people into a frenzy. As a member of the House Un-American Activities Committee (HUAC), Congressman Nixon had investigated the Communist sympathies in the movie industry and succeeded in jailing the Hollywood Ten, who included directors and screenwriters such as Edward Dmytryk and Ring Lardner, Jr. Many other famous figures, among them Elia Kazan and Lee J. Cobb, were pressured into testifying against their colleagues. Nixon had followed this onslaught with his famous interrogation of Alger Hiss, which led to the former State Department official's being convicted of espionage and sentenced to five years in prison.

Throughout the 1952 presidential race, Nixon—whom Paul called "the master of innuendo and slythytovery"—had toadied up to McCarthy and helped campaign against the Democratic candidate, Adlai Stevenson, smearing the Ivy League liberal as "a PhD graduate of the Cowardly College of Communist Containment." In the highly charged election, with the American public's paranoia amplified by the Soviet Union's acquisition of the bomb and the outbreak of the Korean War, Nixon's strategy worked; it won him national prominence and a place as Dwight D. Eisenhower's vice presidential candidate. Disgusted with Nixon's "dirty fighting," Paul had fumed to his brother, "I hate the stench that emanates from that political piggery where Senator Nixon does his wallowing." Julia, who had rather liked Ike in the beginning, was undecided ("a straw in the wind") as to which candidate to support, but by that November was so repelled by Nixon she voted the Democratic ticket by absentee ballot.

They had all been living abroad when McCarthy spearheaded his campaign to root Communists out of high office in 1950, but it had shaken the State Department to its very core, and the tremors could be felt throughout the entire far-flung diplomatic community. He had accused the State Department of harboring Soviet "fifth-columnists" and declared that he and his team of investigators were determined to ferret them out. His infamous "list" of "traitors," which seemed to keep growing, had resulted in the creation of the "Tydings Committee" (a subcommittee of the Senate Foreign Relations Committee, informally named for its chairman, Senator Millard Tydings). This subcommittee was authorized to conduct the State Department Employee Loyalty investigations.

Julia, Paul, and Jane knew countless people from their OSS days whose names had somehow ended up on the senator's list, including their close friends Cora DuBois and Jeanne Taylor, whose loyalty and patriotism were beyond reproach. Paul could not help wondering if the reason they were singled out was more personal than ideological: Cora was unorthodox in her private life and had begun a lesbian affair with Jeanne in Ceylon. The two women were now living as a couple (they had visited Paris the previous spring), and it seemed probable that someone with McCarthy's mentality might view their relationship as a "risk factor" leaving them open to blackmail or outside pressure to betray secrets. It was absurd, of course. Paul remembered Jeanne confiding in him about the hard time she had been given by the civil service investigators when she joined the OSS because she had once, five years earlier, signed a petition nominating some candidate for election in New York City who was a Communist and as a consequence been "suspected of all sorts of subversive and liberal ideas." Now, as then, it seemed to him "hardly possible that this sort of thing could be going on."

Looking back, Julia and Paul realized they had seen the dress rehearsal for McCarthy's brand of character assassination in late 1945, when President Truman fired Patrick J. Hurley, then the American ambassador to China. Hurley had attempted to cover his humiliation in a blaze of vitriol, attacking his embassy staff for undermining him and sabotaging U.S. foreign policy, charging that "the weakness in American foreign policy together with the Communist conspiracy within the Department" were reasons for "the evils that are abroad in the world today." Hurley had pointed a finger at their friend John Stewart "Jack" Service, along with a number of other veteran China hands, and implied that Service was subversive for being critical of Chiang and overly sympathetic to Mao. Hurley's statements kicked up a storm of controversy. Service was raked over the coals for allegedly sharing information with a correspondent from *Amerasia* magazine, a publication charged with being a front founded by the "millionaire Communist" Frederick Vanderbilt Field. Before the "*Amerasia* affair" was over, Service was recalled from Chungking, suspended, and hauled before a Senate hearing. The fact that most of the reporters they knew in China considered Hurley to be empty-headed to the point of advanced senility—Al Ravenholt thought he had "lost his mind"—and utterly unsuited for the delicate diplomatic role of mediating between Mao and Chiang, never seemed to get reported.

The charges against Service were eventually dropped, but in 1951 McCarthy fastened on the issue of the loyalty of the China hands and turned it into fodder for his fearmongering campaign. With the intensification of the Cold War and the Hiss and Rosenberg cases driving home the reality of Soviet espionage within the United States, America's hysteria reached fever pitch. The country needed someone to blame for its new vulnerability, and a good place to start was the painful reversal in China that had resulted in the establishment of the People's Republic under Mao while Chiang and his followers were forced to retreat to Taiwan. Looking for headlines, McCarthy put a pernicious spin on the old charges of "leftist leanings" among the Foreign Service officers and made the case that they had contributed directly to the "loss of China to the Reds." Service was accused of being a Communist sympathizer and summarily fired from his job for "doubt of loyalty." From then on, it was open season on the China hands.

Julia and Paul were extremely fond of Jack Service and his wife,

Caroline, and were appalled at what was happening to them. As a result of McCarthy's accusations, their friends now faced another round of intrusive security investigations, repeated questioning by Senate committees, and ruinous publicity. The loyalty standards were changed, and old cases in which Jack Service had been cleared were reopened, reportedly because of new accusations and evidence. Dick Heppner, working out of Donovan's firm, was helping to prepare his defense, but it was going to be a long, grueling process. Whatever the end result, Service's diplomatic career was most certainly destroyed.* "He was treated very shabbily," Julia recalled, noting that almost all their old State Department pals from China—among them John Paton Davies Jr., O. Edmund Clubb, and John Carter Vincent—were "drummed out of the Foreign Service by McCarthy's tactics."

Julia had read hundreds of reports from field agents across China and knew the importance of having experienced local operatives like Service and Davies, both of whom had been both born in China and were fluent in Mandarin. What made them "so invaluable," she argued indignantly, was that they loved the country, knew it intimately, and could "penetrate in" and gather deep intelligence far beyond anything the Washington experts could hope to glean from Kuomintang functionaries. The China hands candidly relayed the facts about Chiang and Mao as they saw them, facts that were later twisted to mean something quite different than they had at the time. Service's realistic reports from Chungking to the effect that the Communists were "here to stay" had proven true, but instead of acknowledging him for being right, McCarthy was pointing to his past statements as a reason to question his integrity.

John Carter Vincent, the latest of McCarthy's victims, was someone Julia and Paul particularly liked and respected. They had seen quite a

---

* It took Service fourteen years of legal wrangling to clear his name. In 1957, the United States Supreme Court ruled that his discharge was illegal, based solely on the unfounded action of the Loyalty Review Board, and his record was expunged. He was then reinstated and promptly banished to Liverpool, where he remained until his retirement in 1962.

lot of him in recent years while he was minister to Switzerland. Vincent had been a senior State Department advisor in Chungking and a sharp critic of Chiang's government, and McCarthy was clearly bent on making him an object lesson. Accused of being a former member of the Communist Party, he was forced to retire in 1952, and was vilified during six days of interrogation by HUAC. Many of the journalists who covered the hearings were shocked by the shameful spectacle. "Vincent all but had a light shined in his eyes and was beaten by a rubber hose," Joseph and Stewart Alsop reported in their *New York Herald Tribune* column.

Julia would later recall that period as "a disgusting era." The State Department was too weak to defend its own people, and instead bowed to McCarthy's pressure and the howls of powerful anti-Communists in Congress and agreed to set up its own Loyalty Review Board to carry out internal investigations. Ironically, Dean Acheson, by then secretary of state, had personally overseen the publication in 1949 of the White Paper on China, which concluded that the wartime reporting of the China hands had been balanced and had had no impact on the failed U.S. intervention in the Chinese civil war, but because of the angry backlash, its findings were largely ignored. In the end, Acheson was willing to toss a few men to the lions in order to satisfy the mob and protect the reputation of the institution as a whole. When, after months of closed-door sessions, the Loyalty Review Board recommended Service and Clubb be discharged from the State Department, Acheson did not object. Julia and Paul were crushed. It was a travesty of justice.

Julia believed the lack of leadership on the part of the president— on everything from the Korean War to McCarthy's mudslinging—had deeply shaken people's faith in their country, but everyone in Washington was too scared of a "political blunderbust" to speak out. "My moral and spiritual point is this," she declared in a letter to Charles. "The McCarthyites have reaped what they have sown; because they let ethics and honesty and morality out of the window they've let tragedy in the door, and the end result is a just payment."

To lift their spirits, Julia and Paul decided to throw a dinner party to usher out 1952. The party would very probably mark the end of their stay in Paris, as the government appropriations for Paul's position had run out and he had been told to expect a transfer in the coming year. In some ways it was just as well, as he had found his job increasingly frustrating. The USIS's propaganda programs, particularly his own elegant if "unimportant" art exhibits, were so minor and trivial he felt they were nothing more than "a drop in the bucket" and all but useless in trying to penetrate the Iron Curtain. "The vigor and force of Communism's electric current is burning up and changing the world," he wrote with grim certaintly in his diary. "Karl Marx should have been christened Pandora." Hoping for a promotion and a more challenging and vital assignment, Paul had finally worked up the nerve to take the Foreign Service exam. Then came the hard knock: not only had he failed it, but the examiner could not understand why he was considering a career change at such a late date. Paul received it as a snub, confiding in Charles that it was as good as being declared "not eligible for membership in The Club." To cap it all off, the humiliation was painfully public. Most of their friends knew he had taken the exam and were waiting with bated breadth to hear the outcome. *Merde!*

It had been a discouraging year for Julia, too. After much sweat and toil, and hundreds of hours at the typewriter, she had sent off her sample chapter on French sauces to the publisher, Sumner Putnam, the head of Ives Washburn, only to have it critiqued as too unconventional. Now Avis DeVoto was helping Julia and her coauthors shop for a new publisher for their cookbook, a frustrating business to say the least. Julia had turned forty that August and was feeling decidedly middle-aged. It did not help that her sister, Dort, who had only married the previous June, had promptly become pregnant. The baby girl, born that spring, was named Phila after their stepmother. She was a darling, and Julia could see that Dort was blossoming in the role of mother, describing her tellingly to Charles and his wife as "a real woman now with breasts full of milk." Her heart was full of joy for her sister, but there was also a beat of regret.

Julia and Paul threw themselves into the preparations for their New Year's Eve party, inviting all their closest friends, including Jane and George. Paul covered the table with a deep pink cloth, and he crafted a festive centerpiece out of fruit and surrounded it with a ring of holly. Julia cooked a "whiz bang" boeuf bourguignon. The snow fell heavily outside, but they were cozy and gay, and the last guests did not leave until two in the morning. Julia and Paul spent most of the next month holed up against the cold and fog of the Paris winter, devoting their weekends to lovingly crafting the 250 handmade Valentine's Day cards they sent to their dearest friends and scattered wartime colleagues. "We have finally tracked down Jane Foster (Mrs. George Zlatovsky)," Julia reported on the card she sent out to Ellie Thiry and Basil Summers. "She is still as much fun as ever, and doing wonderfully good paintings. They've been here for three years, but everyone thought she was lost."

In February, Paul was told he was being transferred to Marseille. With Julia's work and book partners based in Paris, they returned often, and always made a point of stopping by Jane's apartment for a drink and a visit. "Every time we went to Paris we would see her," Julia reported to her OSS colleagues. As usual, they traded bits of gossip about mutual friends before moving straight to politics. The news on both fronts was distressing.

A number of journalists they had known well during the war had seen their careers come to an abrupt halt. Ed Snow, who had written favorably of Mao, had come under suspicion, been questioned by the FBI, and asked to disclose the full extent of his Communist activities. While he had not been subpoenaed, the Washington whispering gallery had him as good as tried and guilty. After he quit the conservative *Saturday Evening Post* over a disagreement with his editors, Snow found that all opportunities for work had suddenly evaporated. Jane heard he had moved to Switzerland. To avoid being similarly blacklisted, Teddy White, who had by then broken with Henry Luce and *Time*, had moved to Paris and was playing it safe, avoiding anything related to China and churning out upbeat stories about America's efforts to rebuild Europe through the Marshall Plan. His book *Thunder Out of China* had been a huge best seller in 1946, but with the country now in the fevered grip of McCarthyism, he was under a cloud of suspicion and being monitored by the FBI. "I hate only a very few people," Julia raged in a letter to a friend. "One being Madame Brassart, head of Cordon Bleu, who is a nasty, mean woman; McCarthy, whom I don't know; and Old Guard Republicans, whom I see as little as possible."

That's when the stories about the book burning began. Both Ed Snow and Teddy White were on McCarthy's target list. They were blacklisted authors whose works had to be expelled from the USIS libraries. In March, McCarthy's two investigators, Roy Cohn and David Schine, descended unannounced on the Paris embassy. "These two men are young lawyers—about 26—typical Fascist bully-boy types, v. reminiscent to one chap here of Hitler's Gestapo agents—filled w/ the euphoria of 2nd-hand power and riding roughshod over everybody," Paul wrote Charles.

> It seems clear that they came not so much to investigate as to make it appear to their constituents and followers in the States that they were in Europe collecting on-the-spot facts. The three concepts which they brought with them—and which they are out to make the public believe—are: (1) USIS is following a pro-Communist line, as proved by either titles or authors of books in our libraries. (2) USIS is wasting the taxpayer's money by featherbedding, duplication of effort & empire building. (3) The personnel of USIS & other agencies abroad is riddled by people who are security risks, either because they are followers of the Party line, or because they are sex perverts.

The next day, after a rude interview with the ambassador in their hotel bedroom, during which they forked scrambled eggs and made idle accusations, they abruptly took off for Bonn. The upshot, as far as Paul could tell, was "25 minutes of insolence, unproven charges, and threats to embassy officials, men who were older, wiser, more experienced, and certainly more devoted to the interests of the United States than they were." Apparently, more such visits were to be expected.

As the summer months went by, the atmosphere in the Marseille office grew increasingly strained. Since McCarthy decided to attack the USIS, Paul had seen its monthly book purchases shrink from 20,000 to a meager 1,592. At the same time, he had been ordered to compile a list of all the volumes on its shelves so that they might be reviewed and then either removed, refiled, or destroyed. Another "undercurrent of anxiety," Julia recalled, was the retrenchment being ordered by the congressional bean counters, who were allocating more and more money to the military and steadily cutting back on the postwar goodwill programs. It was all part of what Julia described in an irate epistle as the increasing "yellow-bellyism in Washington." Meanwhile, Paul was getting very disgruntled. He was no "yes-man," and he hated carrying out McCarthy's mad purge of their little Marseille library. "He's emasculating and stamping the life out of the Information Program," Paul lamented to Charles. "He's a dirty and astute demagogue, advancing himself, like a surfboard rider, on a wave of fear."

McCarthy's Red scare was fueled by names. All he had to do was set his sights on an institution for its leaders to begin turning on their own. Even at USIS, which Julia described as a "stepchild" organization and "not really part of the brotherhood," the chilling effect made itself felt in the constant rumors about missed promotions, arbitrarily denied appointments, and exile to remote posts. No one, it seemed, was above suspicion or immune from scrutiny. Paul, with his long history of leftist politics and many artist friends who were avowed Communists, had to tread carefully. In the current "better safe than sorry" climate, it would take only a word for him to be out of a job. Julia expressed her growing anxiety in a letter to Avis DeVoto, who had become a close friend and confidante. "I am terribly worried about McCarthyism," Julia wrote. "What can I do as an individual? It is frightening. I am ready to bare my breasts (small size though they be), stick out my neck, won't turn my back on anybody, will sacrifice cat, cookbook, husband, and finally self. . . ."

Julia had first written to Avis's husband, Bernard DeVoto, a well-known columnist, after reading his meditation on the shortcomings of stainless steel knives. Julia, who was of like mind, had sent him a French carbon steel paring knife and a note, initiating an exchange of letters that grew into a steady correspondence. She had turned to Avis for advice because she knew that Bernard had stood up to McCarthy in the past. He had done so most notably in his "Easy Chair" column in the October 1949 issue of *Harper's*, in which he, after being interviewed by the FBI, dared to mock the prying, snooping style of the HUAC squad in its hunt for closet Communists. In "Due Notice to the FBI," DeVoto, taking a page from one of his wife's cookbooks, imagined how a grilling of a Republican presidential candidate might proceed:

> Does Harry S. Dewey belong to the Wine and Food Society? The Friends of Escoffier? Has he ever attended a meeting of either group? Does he associate with members of either? Has he ever been present at a meeting of any kind, or at a party, at which a member of either was also present? Has he ever read A. Brillat-Savarin's *The Physiology of Taste*? Does he associate with people who have read it? Has he ever been present at a meeting or a party at which anyone who has read it was also present?

Halfway through the article, DeVoto abandoned his farce and told his readers that he was fed up. The Red-baiting had "gone too far." McCarthy and his henchmen were dividing the country into "the hunted and the hunters." He ended by publicly declaring that he was done answering questions: "From now on any representative of the government, properly identified, can count on a drink and perhaps informed talk about the Red (but non-Communist) Sox at my house. But if he wants information from me about anyone whatsoever, no soap."

The FBI had been furious and opened a file on DeVoto. In a speech about Adlai Stevenson, the Democratic presidential candidate in 1952, McCarthy took aim against DeVoto, who worked for the campaign, attacking him as a Communist sympathizer who in 1947 had led a Boston delegation from the American Civil Liberties Union protesting the ban on a speech by the wife of Gerhardt Eisler, a Communist who had disappeared behind the Iron Curtain. McCarthy went so far as to try to cast DeVoto's activities in a questionable light by quoting the Communist *Daily Worker*. DeVoto calmly maintained he could be anti-Communist and still want to uphold the freedom of speech as guaranteed by the Constitution. He told reporters at the time that he had done nothing then that he would not do for the senator, adding, "I think the United States will survive both McCarthy and the Communists." It was a politically brave response, but it earned DeVoto the special antipathy of both McCarthy and J. Edgar Hoover, who instructed the FBI to keep the writer under close watch and dig for dirt. Avis DeVoto, who knew what her husband's flair for controversy had cost—the headlines, hate mail, and constant attacks from critics on the right—warned Julia that if Paul valued his diplomatic career they should keep out of the line of fire.

Try as she might, Julia could not keep a lid on her indignation. Anger came at a boiling rush when she read in March 1954 that McCarthy's witch hunt had reached her alma mater, Smith College. A Mrs. Aloise B. Heath of the so-called Committee for Discrimination in Giving had accused five faculty members of being associated with organizations that were "Communist fronts" in a mailing alerting alumnae to the presence of "traitors" on campus. Mrs. Heath also accused the college of "knowingly harboring" the turncoats and insinuated that there were others, as yet unnamed, who were trying to subvert the young minds at the school. She also suggested people withhold donations to the college as they were being used to fund Communists. In classic McCarthyesque style, the accusations, made by an anonymous group of alumnae without any supporting evidence, were released to the public before any attempt was made to ascertain the facts or allow Smith's president the opportunity to reply.

Taking her cue from Bernard DeVoto, Julia took a strong, principled stand in her letter to Mrs. Heath, who happened to be the sister of William F. Buckley and sister-in-law of L. Brent Bozell, who had coauthored a defense of McCarthy as a patriotic crusader against Communism. Julia sternly chastised her fellow alumna for acting as an informer without any proof and for failing to employ "proper democratic methods" in dealing with "charges of this grave nature":

This is the theory of the "end justifying the means." This is the method of the totalitarian governments. It makes no difference how you do it: lie, steal, murder, bear false witness, but use any

method fair or foul as long as you reach your goal. . . . In Russia today, as a method of getting rid of opposition, an unsubstantiated implication of treason, such as yours, is often used.
But it should never be used in the United States.

She pointed out that in this fraught period of history, it was im-
perative that young people learn to "sift truth from half-truth, demagoguery from democracy, totalitarianism, in any form, from liberty."
To that end, she was sending Smith College a copy of the letter, along
with a check doubling her annual contribution to the alumnae fund.
She added, acidly, "For the colleges harbor the 'dangerous' people, the
people who know how to think, whose minds are free."

Smith's president, Benjamin F. Wright, stated that he had "complete
confidence" in his staff and objected to the anonymous group's sneak
attack on the college. In May, the five accused faculty members were
dragged before the Massachusetts Un-American Activities Committee.
By the time the hearings were over and all the testimony heard, the subcommittee charged with the investigation had found no evidence of illegal or disloyal activity, and the matter was dropped. Julia was pleased
to discover that Mrs. Heath's strategy backfired, at least to the extent
that as a result of her poisonous letter more loyal alumnae poured more
money into Smith's coffers than ever before. But the damage to the reputations of teachers, and that of the college, could never be undone.

In a rare act of open defiance, Julia sent a copy of her letter to her
father. She was motivated in part by pride, for it had taken considerable courage on her part to speak out, and in part by sheer pique at
his continued confidence in a "desperate power-monger" she believed
was destroying a country that had come out of the war the strongest,
most unified nation on earth. No doubt some of her rancor stemmed
from the memory of her own thoughtlessness and political naïveté and
a time not so long before when she might have failed to recognize the
danger inherent in McCarthy's Red scare, with its reckless innuendo
and ad hoc retribution. It pained her to think that her dear old Pop was
"right in there with them [the McCarthyites]."

Not surprisingly, her father took a dim view of her exercise in moral outrage and did not mince his words, scolding his daughter for "supporting the Communist line." In letter after letter, he pounded away at his favorite paranoid theme. "These people with red badges have to be exposed," he insisted. "It's a hard, dirty job that has to be done and it takes a rough-and-ready person like McCarthy to do it. In his zeal he gets out of bounds now and then but that's our business." He was convinced that Julia and her husband were "falling right into the plan the Reds [were] developing—that of creating dissension and distrust among their enemies." They had fallen prey to the "socialistic element in Europe" and would do well to come home for a refresher course in real American patriotism. Paul literally felt ill at the thought and had to lie down.

In October, Paul was transferred again. He and Julia fit in a quick visit with Jane, stopping in Paris for a few hours en route to their new post in Bonn. It was a merry occasion as always, full of drinks, toasts to the future, laughter and talk. There was nothing memorable to eat, of course, but the company more than compensated for the lack of food. Paul and Julia were a bit pressed for time that afternoon and kept an eye on the clock. In their hurry to be off, grabbing up coats and bags and calling hasty *adieus* over their shoulder, they never dreamed of what was to come. How were they to know that disaster lay just around the corner? That what Bernard DeVoto had once called "the avalanching danger" of rumor, insinuation, slander, and malice hung over them all? The quiet men with credentials were closing in. They never heard them coming.

11

THE NIGHTMARE

It was a languid Sunday morning in mid-August and Paris was half asleep on its feet. Julia and Paul had just finished a delicious meal at Les Deux Magots and were lingering at their table, too content to move. Tired of dull, stodgy Bad Godesberg, they had decided on a brief holiday "to break loose from the rhythms of life in Germany." They knew it was silly to go to Paris at that time of year, "the very nadir of *La Morte Saison*" when any Frenchman with sense flees the city, but Julia's birthday fell on the fifteenth and they wanted to celebrate "*la Naissance de Julie*" in their beloved city. After brunch, Paul had left Julia sitting in the sun, toying with her beer, while he ran off to take a few quick photos of Place Furstenberg, a charming little square hidden in the heart of Saint-Germain-des-Prés. When he returned, whom should he see but George Zlatovski, talking intently to Julia, one hand furiously stabbing the air with a lit Gauloise. They both turned to look at him as he approached, and in that moment Paul detected an atmosphere of such gravity that he asked immediately why Jane was not there. With an impatient gesture, George resumed his tale, but the angry torrent of English and French was almost impossible to follow.

"I must confess to being sort of confused by what he said," Paul wrote Jane afterward. "He didn't want to repeat the whole story again, and gave me only a brief fill-in. Later on, Julie wasn't clear on all the details." Paul outlined the little he knew: that the previous fall, Jane had flown to San Francisco on a moment's notice after being informed that her mother was dangerously ill; that exploratory surgery had happily proved this to be false; that she had been about to return to Paris when State Department authorities suddenly seized her passport; and that she had been stranded in the United States ever since. George had conveyed the extreme anguish and hardship Jane had endured for the last nine months: "that you have to live apart from your husband, your apartment, your clothes, your paintings, and your normal life." Choosing his words with enormous care, aware that prying eyes might pick apart every line, Paul wrote, "And that the reason they won't give your passport back is that you have been presented with a long list of accusations of subversive activities." He continued:

> What is this all about, and why? We both want to know. We really don't know anything about your political affiliations, or about your life before OSS, or, for that matter, about your Paris life either. But we've always been terribly fond of you, and consider you our friend. And we are terribly sorry you are in this predicament. If you are assumed guilty and are expected to prove your innocence, then have you gotten in touch with the American Civil Liberties Union? They are, from what we have read, supposed to help out people in just such a situation.

Jane's passport troubles had come as a complete surprise to Julia and Paul. They were genuinely heartsick at the idea that she was going through this political torment all on her own, without even her husband by her side. Charlie Chaplin's case had received massive publicity in Europe—McCarthy's demagogic attacks on his patriotism had driven the actor and his family into exile in Switzerland—and they were by now all too familiar with the State Department's efforts to restrict the travel of anyone suspected of being a Communist sympathizer or of having participated in any so-called Communist-front groups. Their friend Teddy White had also had his passport taken away the previous summer after the McCarthyites branded him a subversive, and he had been forced to hire a lawyer and battle the State Department to get it back. That Jane should now find herself the target of such suspicions was incredibly sad but, given the poisonous mood in Washington, hardly unexpected.

Julia and Paul could not believe she was guilty of more than her usual impudence and imprudence. She had always been too cavalier, and too careless—about her money, work, affairs, everything. Irreverent, irrepressible, and utterly lacking in propriety, that was Jane. It was all too easy to imagine how she might have gotten herself in a jam with "McLeod's boys,"* or McCarthy's, or any one of a number of official investigative bodies. Moreover, she was their friend, and they were not about to start jumping to conclusions because her name cropped up in some FBI file. They had seen too many colleagues have their names blackened by spurious charges to desert Jane because of vague suspicions about her supposed Communist connections.

Over the past year, Julia had been revolted by the sight of colleagues who would "cringe" in fear before McCarthy's men, and she was determined never to be one of those people "who just cravenly fell down in front of them." She would not be intimidated. She and Paul would stand by their friends—and their principles—no matter what the cost. Without making too much of a point of it, Paul attempted to express their sympathy and solidarity, and concluded his note to Jane by encouraging her to get in touch: "We would very much like to hear from you, if you feel like writing us about yourself." He signed it, "Love from both of us, and keep your chin up." They sent it to the New York

---

* Determined to avoid a repeat of the Alger Hiss case on his watch, Secretary of State John Foster Dulles appointed R. W. Scott McLeod the first-ever assistant secretary of state for security and consular affairs in 1953. During his four-year tenure, McLeod fired some three hundred State Department employees on the suspicion that they were Communist sympathizers.

address George had provided, but were not at all confident of its ever reaching her. In these days of secret loyalty investigations, letters were often intercepted.

What they did not tell Jane—or, for that matter, mention to George at the café—was that Jane's situation had hit home in a very personal way. Just that past spring, their own world had been turned upside down by similarly nebulous charges. Out of the blue, Paul had been dragged back to Washington in April and forced to endure a full security inquiry, hours of interrogation at the hands of two FBI agents, and all the indignity and injury that came with being under suspicion. And throughout the entire ordeal, the one question that had haunted them was, Why? What was the investigation's raison d'être? What did the State Department authorities have on him? Was it something from his past? Or someone? Paul did not really have any enemies, so he and Julia could not believe he was "being attacked by a revenge-seeker." In the course of being questioned, Jane's name had come up more than once, but then so had many others—the FBI had harped on Charles Child's leftist leanings—and in the end Paul could not be sure what any of it meant. After weeks of trying to analyze every angle, he had taken Julia's advice and given up trying to make sense of it all, and had just tried to put the episode behind him.

Now, with terrible certainty, Paul realized his case was inextricably linked to Jane's. When the State Department confiscated her passport in December 1954, it must have been the culmination of an aggressive investigation. Any cursory check of her wartime service record and close colleagues would have turned up his name and set the bureau machinery in motion checking out the new lead.* The FBI had worked fast. Four months later, Paul was in the hot seat, defending

---

* Paul was essentially correct: among the many affidavits and character references Jane provided to the State Department on January 24, 1955, was a list of her American friends in Paris, including Julia and Paul. It was on the basis of that information that the USIS initiated an investigation of Paul Child "to determine the nature and extent of his association with Jane Foster Zlatovski and her husband, George."

his reputation and swearing for all he was worth that he was a loyal American.

Both Julia and Paul felt sick. At one level, they were furious with Jane. If not for her big mouth, messy bohemian lifestyle, and utopian beliefs, none of this would have happened. At the same time, they were enormously fond of her and genuinely feared for her future. As Julia wrote late that night, "I think she undoubtedly joined a lot of hair-brained 'humanitarian' causes in the '30's, as she would be a perfect fall guy for that sort of thing. . . . and a thoughtless fool in many ways. I can see her as an unwitting tool . . . but it is hard to picture her as an enemy agent." They were much less certain about what they thought of George. "Wouldn't know about him," Julia commented, but ventured a guess that his political sympathies lay to the far left. They imagined that, being a Russian-Jewish immigrant, he might have reacted against being treated like a Jew, and could well have joined the Party. Based on what a journalist friend had told them, most of the American volunteers, like George, who were with the Loyalist forces in the Spanish Civil War were recruited by the Communists. Apart from what Jane had told them, they had no real knowledge of George's background or affiliations. It was all just conjecture on their part. And it was hardly fair to judge the man in his present mood. The government's persecution of his wife had made him "as un-American as anybody can be, and deeply embittered," Julia conceded, adding, "a frightful advertisement for us."

One of the theories that had occurred to Paul when he was sweating it out in Washington was that it all had to do with J. Robert Oppenheimer, the director of the Manhattan Project and so-called Father of the Atomic Bomb, who had had his security clearance revoked in 1954 after a loyalty-security hearing revealed his Communist ties. One of the accusations made against him was that as a physics professor at Berkeley before the war, Oppenheimer had been a member of a "discussion group" that was identified as a secret underground unit of the Communist Party, along with his friend and fellow faculty member Haakon M. Chevalier, a professor of French literature. Chevalier had reportedly approached Oppenheimer about sharing nuclear secrets with the Russians. Knowing that Chevalier had since moved to Paris (in part because of his own passport troubles), and frequented the same arty, left-wing intellectual circles as Jane and George, Paul saw exactly how the FBI could have pasted together the names and facts and arrived at their incriminating conclusion. "What I suspect," he noted, "is that the Oppenheimer investigation revealed to them the name of Haakon Chevalier; his name, and his connection, produced the Zlatovsky [sic] couple; and their name and connections produced my name as a friend."

As Paul saw it, "the McLeod boys" would have written a report and handed it over to the FBI, which already had Haakon Chevalier marked down as an active Communist, and that was all they would have needed for the old guilt-by-association match-up. Jane and George, even though neither worked for the government, would now be fair game. The same went for himself and Julia. FBI agents have "the professional investigator's habit of following *every* lead, no matter how tenuous," Paul reasoned. "Their job (as defined by somebody) must be to try to locate every Communist, and get as much of a line on them as possible—all their connections, habits, changes of address, and modes of life, etc.— *just in case*. Of course: they tell you nothing. So this speculation." *

Despite their mixed feelings, Julia and Paul mustered their courage and carefully drafted their letter of support to Jane, fully cognizant of the ramifications. If it was "intercepted by the FBI," it could cause them real problems: Paul's name would be flagged, his file reopened, and more questions asked. His career would never survive a second inquiry, of that they were sure. It stunk, but there it was. But no matter how they looked at it, they felt they had to hold the line against the stampede of reckless and unsubstantiated accusations that was wreaking havoc with all their lives and destroying the reputations of perfectly good and harmless people. As Paul told Julia after his FBI interview, he did not like a country where people in power could dictate "what we must and mustn't believe, what we can say, and who we can have

---

* In August 1955, an FBI field agent in Paris reported that confidential French sources indicated that George Zlatovski was "believed to have been in contact with Haakon M. Chevalier and Robert Oppenheimer."

as friends." Jane was innocent until proven guilty in a court of law, and that was all they needed to know.

After wrestling with their decision for days, Julia felt it was necessary to inform her father of their political stand. She did not want him opening the newspaper one morning and reading their names on one of McCarthy's infamous lists. The least she could do was give him fair warning. Steeling herself against an imagined blast of scorn, she explained their position with characteristic fortitude and forthrightness. "Ah me," she began, "we are in the midst of composing a letter which may be the death knell of our work in the government, but we don't see that we have any other choice." She continued:

> We cannot with decency turn our back on a former colleague. Besides, is it not part of our duty, as U.S. citizens, and members of a democratic system we are trying to preserve, to help people out if they have gotten on the wrong trolley . . . Prodigal Son, and all that? What good is our famous "way of life" otherwise. . . . The way things are going now, we shall probably be thrown out on our ear as being people about whom "reasonable doubts of loyalty" can be entertained. An ironic end, but we're stuck with it. What would you have done?

Julia added a grace note: "Of course, this letter is not only a presumed comfort to Jane, but an affirmation to ourselves that we are not cowards."

She never sent the letter. After much agonized debate back and forth, she slipped it into a drawer and hoped against hope that events would soon render it superfluous.

It was another two months before they heard from Jane: "Well, the Nightmare is over, thank God." She was back breathing "the wonderful free air of *La Belle France*" and feeling better with each passing day. She thanked them profusely for their letters, particularly that first one to New York—"that was really fine"—and admonished them for taking the risk of writing someone as dangerous and disreputable as herself. "You are in no position to associate with Typhoid Mary," she chided, noting that while she was under suspicion in America she was about as popular as someone carrying the "Black Plague." She apologized for her long silence, and explained that she and George had intentionally not alerted them to what was happening because "knowing what good people you are, we knew you'd stand by and being a friend of mine was, at that moment, no recommendation for advancement in the State Department."

The letter was classic Janie, a dense, furious, and at times morbidly funny account of her harrowing saga. She began by confirming what George had already told them—"you have the outline right"—and launched into an indignant version of how the State Department heavies had descended on her parents' apartment at the Fairmont on her fourth day back in the United States and impounded her passport without giving "any reason." This sounded somewhat disingenuous, as surely Jane must have known she was vulnerable to attack given the Red hysteria and her radical past, but they granted that she had probably been aghast that the government would take such extreme action against her. Jane had always thought of herself as an invincible rebel, able to speak her mind and come and go as she pleased. Stripped of her passport, she was suddenly powerless. In one stroke, the government had humbled her. With no papers, she was stuck, a tethered goat.

When Jane told her father what had happened, he just scowled. "Well, what did you expect?" He had never approved of her liberal ideas, and his stony expression told her he thought she was about to pay the price for her poor judgment. By mutual agreement, they did not tell her mother until she came home from the hospital. Even then, she took the news badly. "[Her] only thought was for her own," Jane wrote in her memoir. "Communism, Schmomunism, she did not care." Her mother had no time for politics and stopped voting after the 1928 election when Al Smith, the first Roman Catholic to seek the presidency, lost to Herbert Hoover. There was never any question that both her parents would stand by her. She might be a problem child, but she was their only child and they would do everything they could, spend any amount of money necessary, to help her get back her freedom and return to Paris.

Once she had recovered from the initial shock, Jane consulted Abe Fortas, a prominent attorney with the influential New Deal firm of Arnold, Fortas & Porter, whom she had gotten to know during the war. Fortas explained that the State Department had essentially extended its customary discretion over issuing passports, which was confirmed by a 1926 law, to control all international travel by Americans. In 1941, it was made illegal to leave or enter the country without a passport, a law that became permanent with the passage of the Immigration and Nationality Act of 1952. With the advent of the Cold War, the State Department had begun asserting this traditional control as a way of denying passports on the basis of individual political beliefs. What's more, the Internal Security Act of 1950 explicitly prohibited the issuance of passports to members of the Communist Party, and the State Department had taken to denying a passport to anyone who refused to file an affidavit denying Party membership. In short, Jane would have to sue the State Department to get her passport back.

Fortas, much in demand in those days, was already busy representing Owen Lattimore, who was the most visible of the China hands accused of being "pro-Red" and who had been singled out by McCarthy as "the top Russian espionage agent in the United States." Fortas referred her to another capable attorney, and Jane arranged to meet with him in Washington. Loath to take yet another plane, she opted to travel by train. To break up the journey, she planned to spend a few days in Chicago at the home of George's older sister, Helen, who was married to Michael Tenenbaum, a brilliant metallurgist, and had two daughters, Susan and Anne. Jane had never met them before, but there was nothing like disaster to drive you into the arms of family.

Shortly after the train left the Oakland station, Jane fell into conversation with a U.S. Air Force captain who was seated in the compartment directly across from her. She accepted his offer of a drink, and they passed a few hours in casual conversation. They talked about the usual things—what they had done during the war, people they might know in common. Jane prattled on about her friend Paul, a painter, who was now working for the State Department in Germany. She was well into her second whiskey and soda by the time she realized that her companion was not making idle chitchat but methodically working his way through what had to be the standard FBI template for interviewing a potential subversive. He was asking what she later came to think of as "the four liturgical questions" as she heard them repeated over and over again, always in the same order, like a schoolboy catechism: (1) "What do you think of God?" (2) "What do you think of Communists?" (3) "What do you think of China?" (4) "The last question (and why did the silly asses never change their order of questions?) was always 'What do you think of Alger Hiss?'" After dinner, while sitting and smoking, she was joined by a group of Italian air force officers who were overjoyed to find someone who spoke their native language and knew their *bel paese*. As they chatted away in Italian, Jane saw the friendly FBI agent hovering nervously in the doorway, until he lost his composure and burst out, "What are they saying? What are they telling you?" He was desperate to know what to put in her file.

When Jane got off the train in Chicago, George's sister took in the attractive group of uniformed men in her compartment and looked ready to salute. "Really, Jane," she murmured, "you do pick them up. You must have loads of sex appeal." In no mood to play the femme fatale for her midwestern in-laws, Jane brutally tromped on Helen's harmless quip. "It's not my sex appeal nor my beauty nor my charm," she said through clenched teeth. "The American is a *Spitzel* (German for informer or spy) and his mission is tailing me."

While Helen was naturally distressed to hear of Jane's political problems—the family already knew more than they wanted to about George's ideological baggage—this did nothing to dispel her view of Jane as her wealthy, glamorous relative fresh from Europe. "My mother was more than a little in awe of her," recalled Helen's daughter, Susan Tenenbaum. "Jane was terribly elegant compared to what we were used to in Flossmoor, Illinois. Her clothes were fabulous, all bought in Paris, and she was petite and wore them well. She had all these scarves and hats and went around looking very pulled together. We thought she was terribly chic. She used to always say to me, 'Give me a thousand dollars of your father's money, and I will make a woman of you.'"

While in Chicago, Jane announced she was going to see Su-Lin.

Helen generously offered to drive her, saying that she would love to meet Jane's friend. "You can't," Jane told her dramatically. "She's stuffed." Su-Lin was the small, burping panda cub she had babysat in Shanghai in 1936 before it was smuggled to America. Sadly, Su-Lin had not thrived in captivity and had succumbed to pneumonia at the age of two. An autopsy later revealed that she was really a he, but Jane persisted in thinking of Su-Lin as a doomed little girl, tragically torn from a hollow tree in China's Szechuan province by greedy American collectors. The family accompanied Jane to the Field Museum of Natural History, where the popular panda's body was on display. "Jane just stood there, staring at Su-Lin behind the glass case," Susan recalled, "sobbing her eyes out." Even as a young girl, she sensed Jane's tears were as much for herself as for the dead bear.

When Jane got to Washington, she learned that her new lawyer had arranged for an informal hearing before Ashley Nicholas, deputy director of the Passport Division of the State Department. Nicholas was "a hideous creature who looked like a tarantula," she told Julia and Paul, and then, just "to show the nightmarish quality of it all," she cited all the nefarious activities he suspected her of:

> They accused me of such things as being an active communist at Mills College in 1934–35, and of having joined the Communist Party in the Indies . . . although I didn't go to the Indies until 1937! They also accused me of having circulated a Communist petition in India! Can't you see me circulating a petition around the Queens Hotel! Anyway, you get the drift. They accused me of <u>nothing</u> in all the years I've been in Europe, and told my lawyer they had absolutely nothing against me since I've lived in Paris.

She maintained that of the seven charges they came out with "only two" were factually correct: she was a member of the Washington Bookshop, now apparently suspected of being a Communist front, and in 1941 she had once picketed the White House with the American Peace Mobilization, also now on the attorney general's list of Red organizations. According to Jane, all they had dredged up was her youthful flirtation with radicalism, now fifteen years out of date. The Catholic Church and the Communist Party—they were the only two organizations she had ever belonged to, and she had pretty much abandoned both by the age of thirty. Despite all the inaccuracies and unsubstantiated charges, they denied her application.

Feeling defeated and dejected, Jane returned to the coast to wait for the formal hearing before the Board of Passport Appeals of the State Department, better known to penitents as "the Holy Office." By then, Jane told Julia and Paul, she was "a physical and mental wreck." Her father suggested a family vacation in La Jolla, as he thought the sea air might do her some good. As the weeks dragged by, Jane became increasingly isolated and depressed. She avoided getting in touch with any of her old friends. She knew she would not be doing them any favors by showing up at their door trailing the "keystone cops," as she referred to her various shadows. While she was detained in the United States, George was summoned to the American Embassy in Paris, where officials demanded he surrender his passport. He refused, but as it had expired some months before it was a somewhat empty gesture. In any case, it meant that he could not join her. She had been desperately afraid he would try to rush to her rescue only to end up having his passport withheld as well. Then they could have begun deportation proceedings against him, but as the only place he could have been sent back to was Russia—and that was clearly impossible—he probably would have ended up a stateless citizen in detention.

There were gaps in her narrative—events that she omitted, in part out of embarrassment, in part from "unadulterated horror." One sorry episode was when, out of sheer desperation, she, George, and their lawyer in Paris cooked up a plan for her to slip across the border into Mexico, get a quickie divorce, and marry a French friend who was single and willing. If all went well, she would for a brief time even have had the title of *comtesse*. "It would have been what the French call a *mariage blanc* (unconsummated)," she recalled later. "We would have been divorced afterwards and I would have remarried George for the *third* time. Oh God!" It was a sign of how bleak things looked that her father agreed to go along with the scheme. Jane met her parents at the Biltmore Hotel in Los Angeles, and they spent countless hours reviewing the different ways she could slip unnoticed into Mexico. Finally, it was decided that they would take a family holiday in La Jolla, and her parents would proceed from there to Ensenada and retain a local lawyer on her behalf. Inevitably, the over-the-border gambit blew up in their faces. They later worked out that the hotel room must have been bugged, because the men "with mirrors on the rims of their glasses" were on to them from the start. The FBI must have had the last laugh when her parents, in their naïveté, hired a complete shyster to obtain her divorce—they paid a five-hundred-dollar retainer, with the promise of another five hundred—only to have him turn around and try to blackmail them for more.

Things went rapidly downhill from there. "Then the Nightmare really began," as Jane informed Julia and Paul.

We were all, separately and collectively, followed around by the Secret Police . . . whether it was FBI or McLeod's boys I don't know. The young men, all looking like instructors in English Lit. at some fourth rate college, in sports jackets and gabardine topcoats. Thank God they did it to my mother and father—one funny thing was my reactionary father's rage at the thought that his not inconsiderable taxes were going to support his harassers—otherwise everyone would have said I'd just gone off my rocker. Anyway, from then on, for five solid months they never left me alone—day or night.

No longer making any attempt to disguise their assignment, the agents broke into her hotel room repeatedly and searched its contents, reserved rooms adjacent to hers, and left tape recorders lying out on their windowsills in plain view. Once, when she was sitting on the beach, four men in a parked car began calling her names—yelling "Spy! Spy!" at the top of their lungs. On another occasion, she was in a coffee shop when a square-jawed navy captain sauntered over to her table with studied ease and offered to give her a lift to Tijuana in his huge, brand-new Buick. Talk about too good to be true! That was when she realized the game was up. They were just waiting for her to run. The minute she committed a criminal offense—as opposed to a political one—they could snap on the cuffs and call it a day. They wanted to destroy her morale, to push her over the edge. The only thing that kept her going was her anger and her determination not to let them win.

In March, she took the train across the continent again for her hearing before the Board of Passport Appeals. At nine o'clock in the morning, she and her lawyer entered the State Department building together and were ushered into a large room decorated with the requisite American flag. Assembled behind a long table were three men. At each end, young attorneys representing the appeals board sat poised for action, a thick stack of documents in front of them. Jane and her lawyer were seated at a table clear across the room, as far from the others as possible. She stood up and took the oath, swearing before God to tell "the whole truth and nothing but the truth." Then she lied.

Was she "a member of the Communist Party"?

"No."

Was she "ever a Communist"?

"No."

She admitted, according to court records, that during a brief period between May 1941 and January 1942 she had embraced with enthusiasm what she then "conceived to be the Communist ideology" and that she had attended "all manner of meetings, particularly because [her] own abhorrence of war coincided with the then expressed views of those espousing the Communist cause."

At one o'clock, they adjourned for lunch. Jane and her lawyer scrambled over to the Willard Hotel, where Jane fortified herself with two martinis. The questioning continued all afternoon. Her interrogators produced a list of names of former friends and acquaintances and demanded to know if any of them were Communists: Martha Dodd Stern? Her brother, Bill Dodd? Before the war had she rented a room in Georgetown from the Dodds' friends Susan B. Anthony (grandniece of the famous suffragette), an editor for the *Washington Star,* and her husband, Henry Hill Collins, Jr., a political activist? Was she aware that they were Communists? Jane maintained that she knew nothing of the sort. She was hardly going to inform on her friends, who might or might not be card-carrying members of the Party, for all she knew. Moreover, it was clearly a trick. The slightest admission that she had consorted with known subversives would drive the last nail into her coffin. There was nothing to do but assert her ignorance over and over again.

"It was a real inquisition," Jane reported to Julia and Paul. "They produced no witnesses, no evidence, just interrogated me for eight solid hours." She told them how the lawyers had dredged up more obscure incidents from the past in a deliberate attempt to make her look guilty. With no supporting evidence, they claimed that in 1942 she had been working for the "Second Front." They cited an even more absurd incident, stating that in 1934 she had once said that "happiness was to be found in the Communist Party." As to the latter, Jane admitted it was entirely possible: "I probably was drunk at the time."

When it was over, Jane fled Washington. She went to New York, she told Julia and Paul, and "holed up in a hotel room." She stayed at the Essex House, but it was infested with badly dressed "whey-faced agents." She moved to a cheap dive downtown on Waverly Place. She kept to herself and waited. "Afraid to go out," she explained. "Every time I did, the boys in gabardine coats were after me. . . . Afraid to call anyone for fear I would get them in trouble by associating with them." She made herself physically sick with worry. She could not eat or sleep. When she forced herself to eat something, she vomited it up. She grew so weak that when she got out of bed her knees buckled and she collapsed.

On March 29, after she had spent two weeks locked in her hotel room, her lawyer called to say that the appeals board had handed down its decision: it was negative. As Jane put it to Julia and Paul, "I had been finally and irrevocably turned down on the grounds that I 'had joined the Communist Party in the 1930's and had for many years thereafter followed the Communist Party line.' Period." The following day, Secretary of State John Foster Dulles, acting on confidential information presented to him by the FBI, approved the decision. It was "not in the best interests of the United States" to allow her to leave for France.

As a last resort, Jane made an appointment to see Mrs. Ruth B. Shipley, the ogress in charge of the Passport Division of the State Department, described by *Time* magazine in 1951 as "the most unfirable, most feared" woman in government. Jane thought Mrs. Shipley more than lived up to her terrifying reputation, with her long, narrow face and autocratic manner, enthroned in her expensively appointed office and surrounded by opulent baskets of flowers. She stood at the far end of the enormous room and made Jane traverse the length of it before her, "the way Mussolini used to do with visitors." When Jane extended her hand in greeting, Mrs. Shipley deliberately put her arms behind her back, as if she were afraid of catching something. Not too proud to beg by this point, she pleaded with the woman to give her back her passport and allow her to go home to Paris, adding plaintively that the only reason she had ever left was because she thought her mother was "very sick."

"Don't blame your mother!" Mrs. Shipley barked. "Never blame you mother!"

Surprised by her vehemence, Jane replied, "What do you mean? Of course I don't blame my mother. I blame you, frankly." Needless to say, the rest of the visit did not go well.

It was one setback too many. Jane was exhausted. Her nerves were shot. What drove her to the brink of despair, she wrote Julia and Paul, was that she was flat out of options: "There I was—with the one suitcase I came with, no husband (Georgie couldn't come . . .), no home, no work, and, had it not been for my father, no money." That was when she "really snapped." Her father ("no fool he") diagnosed her fragile state and sent her to see Dr. Harold E. Wolff, a leading Cornell neuropsychiatrist and, as it turned out, an expert in the field of Psychosomatic Medicine at Medical School. His assistants, various young doctors known as the "Wolff pack," looked Jane over, ran a battery of tests, and within twenty-four hours had her checked into New York Hospital. "They were wonderful," she reported. They provided the respite she needed to regain her strength. Their tests actually turned up a few physical ailments along with her obvious mental disorders, and she underwent minor surgery on a gland under her armpit. They assured her that she was not "a paranoiac," that various agents were "all around the hospital" but they would not let them in. For the time being, she was safe. She spent her days assiduously working on her paintings, trying to keep her mind off her problems. She gave three pictures to her brother-in-law when he came to visit, including a self-portrait he found "disturbingly dark." Jane stayed in the hospital for five weeks, by which time the psychiatrists had "unwound her" sufficiently that she was starting to "make some sense."

Even in the midst of her breakdown, Jane had the wherewithal to feel outraged when the investigators turned their smear tactics on her family. After all they had put her through, she found the attack that was hardest to bear was the one on her father. She had heard it quite by accident while listening to Walter Winchell's broadcast on the radio, which she tuned into Sunday nights in the hospital as a form of self-flagellation. She had been half listening to the trademark machine-gun introduction when she suddenly realized that Winchell was talking about her: "*Rat-tat-tat-tat. Rat-tat-tat-tat.* Good evening, Mr and Mrs America. Watch for the initials JF in the Cutter scandal. I repeat the initials JF. I'll give you the name later."

That summer of 1955, Cutter Laboratories, where her father served as medical director, had been engulfed in scandal when a batch of Salk's vaccine—a newly developed polio vaccine manufactured by Cutter—resulted in a number of cases of polio-related paralysis and the deaths of several children. The public panicked, and Cutter's vaccine was immediately recalled. Federal virologists crawled all over the California-based family firm to determine the cause of the problem, and a number of high-level health officials were fired. Her father, who had strongly opposed the manufacture of the Salk vaccine as premature and had pushed for further testing, had been overruled, but his name was dragged through the mud with those of all the others. Then the FBI had the bright idea that perhaps Jane had sneaked into Cutter and contaminated the vaccine. The FBI greatly added to her father's woes by repeatedly questioning the company director, Robert Cutter, one of his oldest friends, as to whether or not Jane could be the culprit. It was crazy, of course—they were wildly shooting in the dark, hoping to bring her down—and beyond cruel.

In time, she got her strength back, and her will to fight. She fired her first lawyer, on whom she had squandered five thousand dollars, and hired Leonard Boudin, a well-known civil liberties attorney and "passport specialist." Her mother had come across his name in recent newspaper reports about the case of Dr. Otto Nathan, a leading economist, who had sued the State Department and won. In her enterprising way, Eve Foster, with her refined whisper of a voice, had somehow managed to get Nathan on the phone, explain that her daughter was in the same situation, and ask about his lawyer. Nathan had not only recommended Boudin highly, he had offered to meet Jane and do what he could to help.

Jane had been well enough to meet him at a Schrafft's in Midtown. Nathan was little, wore gold-rimmed glasses, and spoke with a thick German accent. After fleeing the Nazis—he became a naturalized U.S. citizen in 1939—he joined the faculty of Princeton University and struck up a close friendship with the Nobel Prize–winning physicist Albert Einstein. The State Department had denied his application for a passport for years on the grounds that he had been a member of various Communist-front groups and that this made his travel "undesirable." It all became a matter of international import because Nathan was the sole executor of Einstein's estate, and following the physicist's death in April it became urgent that he be allowed to attend a conference on relativity in Switzerland in order to preserve some of Einstein's important papers. Jane thought Nathan was "a loveable little man," and she was inordinately grateful to him for his kindness.

Boudin, Nathan's lawyer, was a supremely confident being. Just staring up at his handsome, intelligent face, she felt better. He had just won a series of victories in the courts, arguing that the ban on travel by American citizens whose political views were not in accordance with those of the State Department was unconstitutional. In June, he had managed to get the courts to recognize that the State Department's Passport Office, in the person of Mrs. Shipley, had been operating as "a law unto itself," consistently denying Americans their passports "without hearing, evidence, specific reasons, or appeal." Boudin made the Passport Office's improper regulations the main focus of his legal attack in Nathan's case. He argued that his client had been denied due process, and the judge agreed, ordering the State Department to set up and submit for his approval a proper legal procedure. When the State Department failed to do so, the judge ordered it to grant Nathan his passport forthwith. The State Department appealed, but before the case reached the court of appeals, the department suddenly issued Nathan his passport, ostensibly on the grounds that it had reversed its decision as to the danger he posed society. Boudin maintained it was more likely that the State Department wanted to avoid risking a higher-court precedent that would undercut its powers.

When Boudin first came to see Jane in July, they talked strategy. He told her he would essentially be taking the same tack as in the Nathan case. He had decided not to "fool around" with the State Department and intended to go right to the courts. They would file suit against the secretary of state and ask the court for a preliminary injunction preventing the State Department from withholding her passport pending her suit. Jane was "shaking like an aspen leaf" at the very prospect of a trial, but Boudin was optimistic. He said the "log-jam" of cases was breaking up and predicted that he would make rapid progress.

On August 3, Boudin appeared before Judge Burnita S. Mathews of the U.S. District Court for Washington, D.C. Two weeks later, the judge summoned Boudin and the lawyer representing Secretary of State Dulles. Jane, who had reentered the hospital for another small operation and some psychiatric follow-up, was not present but had it all straight from Boudin, who described the horse trading that took place in the judge's chambers and led to her case being dismissed:

> [Judge Mathews] told them first informally, that she was going to find for me, that the State Dept. had committed an illegal act in taking my passport, and that they had produced no evidence to support their charges, and that even the charges all dated from long before my residence in Europe. That therefore "grievous injury" had been done me, and she was not even going to order State to give a quasi-judicial hearing as had been done in the Nathan and Foreman cases, but would order State to issue me a passport immediately!

This would have made legal history and set a precedent, as it had never been done before. It would also have seriously limited the State Depts. right to issue passports. It threw the Dept. of Justice lawyers into a tizzy and they asked for five minutes to talk to Boudin before the decision was formally issued. They told him that if he would withdraw his motion for a preliminary injunction (forcing State to issue the passport) I would have my passport in three days!

Boudin accepted the deal. Jane went on to explain that if he had refused the deal the State Department would have appealed and she would have had to wait many more months. It went without saying that her attorney was concerned about what another delay might mean in light of her mental state. As a result, she was a free woman, and her case, *Zlatovski v. Dulles,* was no more than a footnote in Boudin's files. She added that her esteemed attorney believed the State Department wished to avoid the publicity that the judge's decision would have elicited, particularly as Jane's story "did not show them in a very good light" and they were "getting nervous."

What actually transpired behind closed doors, however, was very different from what either Jane or her lawyer believed. Judge Mathews had ruled that unless the State Department produced additional "derogatory information" about Jane, particularly information dated more recently than 1948, she was going to grant her a passport. The court forced the secretary of state's hand. Faced with having to disclose that she was the subject of the top-secret "Mocase" investigation and risk exposing the identity of their double agent, the government had to give Jane back her walking papers. Dulles could not risk jeopardizing the decade-long investigation of an international Communist conspiracy. The bureau had expended considerable time and effort on the case: apartments, offices, and hotel rooms had been bugged, paid informants employed, and dozens of agents had pursued leads across the country, as well as in Canada, France, Germany, Mexico, and Puerto Rico. Many more agents were chasing down investigative leads arising from the case. Dulles did not want to let her go, but it was the lesser of two evils.

On Monday morning, August 22, Jane marched into the State Department building in New York and walked out an hour later with a brand-new passport. It was only temporary, valid for three months, and marked with various stamps declaring her questionable status like a subversive's stigmata, but she did not care. Determined to celebrate, she booked a suite at the Plaza Hotel, where she had often stayed with her parents in happier times, and threw a victory party. She invited everyone who had been kind to her in the hospital—her various doctors and psychiatrists—as well as her lawyers. Even Otto Nathan came to wish her well. At the end of the evening, one of her doctors confided that the FBI had demanded to see her medical records. When the doctors refused to "break the seal of the confessional," the FBI had gone over their heads to the hospital administration. Instead of forcing the doctors to cooperate, New York Hospital had unleashed its lawyers, who insisted on protecting her rights as a patient. She did not know what they said to the agency, but from the day she left the hospital "the boys in gabardine coats" had left her alone.

Two days later, she left for Paris. After all she had been through to get that "damned" passport, the Air France official barely gave it a second glance. As soon as she was safely home, she cabled Julia and Paul: ARRIVED PARIS YESTERDAY LA VIE RECOMMENCE.

In the fall, Julia and Paul made another sojourn to "*La Belle France*" and had a chance to see Jane, fresh from the wars of loyalty review. She had been shaken to the core, but was still defiant. They had been vastly relieved when they received her telegram telling them she was safely back in Paris. It stood to reason that the U.S. authorities would never have let her leave the country if they had anything on her, so Jane was probably in the clear. As much as they were dying to hear all about what she had been through, Julia and Paul did not pester her for details. She was still a bit fragile and protested that she did not want to spoil their visit with her sad *histoire,* but promised to send a blow-by-blow account of her battle with the state department.

Jane's epic, single-spaced four-page letter describing all that had transpired reached Julia and Paul in Bad Godesberg in late October. "Forgive me for probably boring you with such a lengthy saga but I thought you'd like to have the story," she wrote in conclusion. "I hope you don't mind, Paulie, if I loathe your employer, the U.S. State Department, with a towering and terrible loathing. They took practically a year out of my life, uselessly and senselessly—wrecked my health, I am still under a doctor's care—and for what? My dear, grateful country. The only decent thing about it is that I appreciate now how much I love our life here. . . . I go around grinning like a Chessy cat with sheer joy." Striving to end on a positive note, she added, "But there are some really wonderful Americans and you are right on the top layer."

One of the last things George told them that August afternoon at Les Deux Magots was that he planned to apply for French nationality. His lawyer had advised that it might take four to six months. As soon as the paperwork was finalized, Jane was going to apply for it, too. By becoming his little French wife, and giving up her American citizenship, she hoped to evade the long arm of the law and put her passport problems behind her once and for all. As Jane put it to them, "then I can really say—J'ai choisi la Liberté."

Only days after Jane's letter arrived, Paul received official confirmation that he had been cleared. On October 25, 1955, Charles M. Noone, chief of the Office of Security at the USIA, wrote to inform him that after his interview with the special agents Sanders and Sullivan in April, his "case had been considered" and "a favorable decision reached under the provisions of executive Order 10450." That was it—six months of fear and tribulation dismissed in a six-line memo. Still, Paul was grateful to have the documented proof of his innocence. It wasn't much, but it might help him sleep more soundly. His own vivisection at the hands of the FBI had just begun to fade from memory when Jane's missive had come, and her frightening description of her ordeal had brought it all back, along with the anxiety and fitful nights.

12

THE TASTE OF ASHES

Try as they might, Julia and Paul were never really happy in Bad Godesberg. The best that could be said about their last year there was that they were boringly productive, with Julia toiling over recipes for "the Book," as she had taken to calling her ever-expanding manuscript, and Paul traveling more than usual while overseeing seven major international exhibits. After his triumphant return from Berlin, still glowing from the stellar reviews for his show on the U.S. Space Program, Paul heard he was being transferred back to Washington. They had not expected to be uprooted again so soon but were secretly elated to be getting out of Cold War Germany. They were tired of Bonn and the USIS mission, which was a "dumping ground" for the worst sort of career diplomat and beset with office intrigues and personnel woes. Julia could not wait to see the back of Paul's alcoholic boss, old "Woodenhead," who had given him "poor marks" for administration in his latest efficiency review. After all Paul's hard work, it seemed particularly petty and disappointing.

Julia, who was proud of her husband, as well as fiercely protective, believed his superiors' grudging attitude revealed the residual doubts that still lingered in the wake of his loyalty hearing. Even though Paul had been exonerated, the stain on his record was permanent—those "unremovable smirches" he had rightly feared when he first realized he was under investigation. The very suggestion that he might be a "treasonous homosexual" irked him still. In a pointed repudiation of his cowardly accusers, Julia and Paul posed gloriously naked in a tub of suds for their 1956 Valentine's Day card, with only a mound of bubbles covering her breasts. The tongue-in-cheek inscription read: "Wish You Were Here."

It was a bold gesture, and it revealed just how dissatisfied they had become with the narrow constraints of government life. They "despised" John Foster Dulles and his crony, Scott McLeod, for driving the ablest men out of the State Department and stunting, if not destroying, the careers of so many of their friends. Sadly surveying the evidence of disarray all around them, they could not help feeling they had stayed in the Foreign Service too long. The world had changed. No one seemed to have any sense of purpose anymore. The only people who seemed to get ahead in the increasingly polarized political climate were the "brainless bureaucrats," the kind Paul said could be relied on to "never rock the boat." The Woodenheads always survived.

At the end of October, Julia and Paul headed back to the United States, stopping off in Paris for a last hurrah. They booked into the Hôtel Pont Royal, where they had lived when they first arrived, and spent ten days running around frantically trying to see all their friends and fit in their many favorite restaurants. It was a bittersweet time, full of wonderful dinners, warm memories, and difficult farewells. No matter how busy they were, Julia and Paul would almost certainly have called on Jane before leaving the country, if only to check on her progress and try to cheer her up. There is no record of their visit, in part because Paul's diaries for that period were lost.* By all accounts,

---

* Paul's personal papers, along with most of his correspondence covering June 1954 to December 1955, as well as from October 1956 to March 1959, mysteriously went missing. He noted that no one could come up with a satisfactory explanation of how or why they were lost.

it would have been a disheartening visit. Jane was in terrible shape. The last two years had not been kind to her. Nothing about her situation was any clearer. She could not banish her private fears about the FBI's intentions and the feeling that the bureau was still after her. She was convinced she was being followed again, though by which agency she did not know. The "Wheyfaces," as she called the agents trailing her, seemed to be French, but "that did not mean anything as the CIA had a number of 'natives' in their employ." Her marriage had suffered during her long absence, and George's increasingly brazen womanizing was a constant source of arguments and upset. She was nervous, depressed, and drinking too much. "She and George had always had a pretty well-lubricated lifestyle," recalled her niece, Susan Tenenbaum. "But with all the pressure she was under, I think she really hit the bottle. From what I understand, she was in a very bad way."

Just before Christmas, Jane attempted suicide. She swallowed a handful of Nembutal pills and washed them down with whatever she was drinking that night. She was rushed to the hospital, her stomach was pumped, and she spent a month in care. In her memoir, she noted bleakly that an attempted suicide is "a cry for help, but no help was forthcoming."

Julia and Paul were unaware of the depth of Jane's despair. They were worried about her and empathized with her misery and frustration but had no reason as yet to believe the crisis would not pass. The State Department had furnished her with a new passport and permitted her to return to France, and there was every indication her case could be resolved in the near future. There were even signs that the acrimonious political climate at home was beginning to improve. Ever since the nationally televised Army-McCarthy hearings, when counselor Joseph N. Welch famously called the senator to account—"Have you no sense of decency, sir?"—McCarthy and his nasty sidekicks, Cohn and Schine, had been finished. Finally embarrassed by McCarthy's excesses, the Senate had voted overwhelmingly to censure him, 67 to 22. These days, he was drunk by noon, his mad rants recognized for what they always had been—the ravings of a crazy, dangerous fanatic. With his reign of terror at an end, the reactionaries in Congress were quieter and their Red-hunting activities somewhat curtailed. Even Jane's nemesis, the dreaded Mrs. Shipley, had retired.

In the meantime, the French authorities had given Jane *une carte d'identité*, which allowed her to function perfectly well within the country. And there were worse places to be marooned indefinitely than Paris. It was hard, at times, for them not to feel a bit weary of Jane's dramatics, especially when they were always left with the uneasy sense that there was more to it all than she was saying, that she was concealing the worst of her sins. They did not know what folly she had committed and could only hope for her sake that it fell short of anything Dulles and his posse would feel obliged to pursue across the ocean.

Preoccupied with their homecoming and the busy holiday season spent back in the bosom of the Child clan, they had little time to ponder Jane's fate. They had settled back into their former home at 2706 Olive Avenue, in Georgetown. The old three-story house looked rather neglected after being rented out for eight years, and they were determinedly whipping it into shape. Betty MacDonald, who dropped by to see them shortly after their return, sat in the kitchen and watched in amazement while Paul drew on the wall precise outlines of every one of Julia's polished copper pots and iron skillets in an effort to impose order on her unruly mass of equipment. Inside each penciled circle, he wrote: "Please Replace." Laughing at the memory, Betty said, "Julia was awfully messy, and that was something he couldn't stand."

They spent a pleasant afternoon talking and exchanging bits of news about old friends. In the course of catching up, Julia and Paul told Betty about Jane's trials and tribulations. Betty was sorry to learn of Jane's ongoing FBI investigation but was not surprised. The FBI had questioned her about Jane's politics back in 1948 and Betty had told them that while her OSS colleague was a "liberal," and had gotten into trouble for her outspoken support of the Indonesian revolutionary government, Jane was "entirely loyal." Like many OSS veterans, Betty and her husband had also had their share of problems with the FBI. "Hoover was no friend of Donovan's and did his best to destroy what was left of his reputation after the war," she recalled. "The FBI hounded all the people that had worked for him in the Far East. Lots of people recruited by the OSS had been Communists or socialists at one time.

Donovan and Dick spent days throwing out papers and going through the files to get rid of things that might be incriminating. They destroyed the records to keep them out of the hands of the FBI." Betty had been home working one afternoon when two agents in dark suits and fedoras knocked on the door of her New Jersey home and announced they had orders to search the place. "They went through the library and removed two books: *Mein Kampf* and *The Little Red Book,* full of quotations from Chairman Mao." She was never questioned by the FBI but remembered all too well "the feeling they were watching you." Thinking of Jane, she added, "Those were horrible days, not knowing why it was happening or what they were after."

Julia reassured herself that post-McCarthy Washington was a somewhat saner place. The country was on the mend after a virulent period. It was "now the land of Nixon-lovers, 'Elvis the Pelvis,' and other strange phenomena." Perhaps that was why she was not more disturbed when the FBI came around to Olive Avenue that winter asking about Jane. Unflappable as always, Julia answered their questions; she was polite but firm. A brief note in her date book on February 14, 1957, reveals that when they asked if she thought Jane could be engaged in subversive activities, she told them she did not "think someone that funny and scattered could be a spy." Her cool self-possession was such that she took the agents' house call in stride, dismissing the visit as perfectly "pleasant."

A few months later, while Julia and Paul were still trying to become acclimated to Washington's tropical heat and humidity, they awoke on a sultry July morning to stunning news. Splashed across the front pages of all the newspapers were pictures of Jane and George along with giant headlines proclaiming them to be Russian spies: "U.S. COUPLE ACCUSED OF SPYING FOR RUSSIA: Linked to International Ring." "2 EX-AIDES OF U.S. INDICTED AS SPIES," proclaimed *The New York Times,* "Former Intelligence Officer and Wife, Once in OSS, Named as Soviet Agents."

The opening lines of the *Washington Post*'s lead story took their breath away: "An American couple was indicted today as alleged members of a global spy ring personally organized in the Kremlin by Stalin's late secret police boss, Lavrenti Beria." The story went on to say that on

July 8 a federal grand jury had accused George and Jane of transmitting secret information on American intelligence and U.S. installations abroad to Moscow intelligence. A dozen Russian nationals were named as coconspirators in the case. Although espionage was not an extraditable offense, the U.S. Attorney's Office was working to convince the French government to return the Zlatovskis to America to stand trial. It added that the pair faced "a possible death penalty under the charges."

Paul ran out and bought every newspaper he could lay his hands on. He and Julia spent the morning poring over the stories in a state of shock. According to the complicated picture presented in the indictment, Jane and George were minions in a spy ring that had flourished "since 1940 and right up to this day." They were charged with working for a Lithuanian-born Soviet agent named Jack Soble, a small-time importer of bristles and animal hair, who had been recruited by Beria to set up the Soviet intelligence cell. In January 1957, the Justice Department arrested the ringleaders, Jack Soble and his wife, Myra, and in April the two pleaded guilty to "receiving and obtaining" U.S. defense secrets. Another member of the ring, Jacob Albam, arrested at the same time, also pleaded guilty. The plea deal got them out of a tougher conspiracy charge that carried the death penalty. In return, the Sobles were being "cooperative" and were reportedly "talking their heads off" about the inner working of their spy network. As a direct result of the secret Soble testimony, which the grand jury had been listening to since January, Jane and George were indicted on five counts of spying. Bench warrants had been issued for their arrest.

A total of thirty-eight "overt acts" of espionage were listed in the indictment. The *Post* story summarized the five main accusations against the Zlatovskis:

- That the wife passed to Soviet agents a "report on Indonesia" based on information obtained while employed in the OSS.

- That "information relating to the national defense of the United States" was given to "a representative of the intelligence service of the U.S.S.R."

- That Mrs. Zlatovski turned over information "concerning the personnel and operations of intelligence units of the U.S.A., including biographical data on American intelligence agents."

- That George Zlatovski transmitted to Soviet agents "the names of certain persons who had fled to Austria" from satellite states.

- That in December 1949, both defendants traveled to Austria "to obtain compromising information regarding the personal lives, specifically, the sexual and drinking habits, of the personnel assigned and attached to American installations in Austria."

The last part of the story read like something straight out of Hitchcock, with all the cloak-and-dagger characters and international rendezvous of a noir thriller. According to the indictment, Jane and George, when not taking orders from Soble, did jobs for the "mysterious Boris Morros," as the *Times* called him, a Russian-born Hollywood producer who was secretly working as a double agent. Morros, who was sixty-two, had reportedly been forced to work as a front man and courier for Soviet intelligence in an effort to protect his aged parents and in 1947 went to the FBI and offered his services as a counter-espionage agent. Morros testified that Jane, code-named "Slang," was an active agent, handing off her valuable reports to him for delivery to Soviet representatives. George, code-named "Rector," was not as useful, mostly gathering information on refugees, and was once ordered by Soble to go to Yugoslavia to observe conditions and make a report on what he found for the Soviet secret police. Morros, who claimed the Soviets had given him money for monthly payments to the Zlatovski "team" between December 1949 and October 1950, operated as the go-between and detailed meetings among himself, the Sobles, and the Zlatovskis in New York, Washington, Vienna, Paris, Zürich, and Lausanne. The *Times* story ended with a glum image of Jane barricaded in her Left Bank apartment, declining to comment: "I can't tell you anything, you will have to speak to my lawyer."

The later editions of the newspapers carried a new set of banner

headlines—FRANCE GRANTS ASYLUM—and included quotes from
George. He declared the charges to be false and ridiculous, telling the
Washington *Evening Star,* "The French have given us political asylum.
We are their guests. We can say nothing which would embarrass our
hosts." The story went on to quote a Foreign Ministry official denying
asylum had been granted, saying the issue was still being discussed.
George, who was photographed peering out of the doorway of his
apartment on rue Mazarine, was described as "dark and youthful," with
his brown hair in a neat crew cut. He wore a pale, thin silk robe open to
the waist and a pair of straw slippers. The walls of the living room, just
visible behind him, were hung with vivid abstract paintings, which he
explained had been done by his wife before "her health broke over this
business." Jane was nowhere to be seen. When asked to respond to their
many questions, George told them angrily, "You people have already
made up everything you want to, so why should I say anything more?"
adding, as he closed the door, his voice barely audible over the barking
of the couple's poodle, "I am sorry to be rude, but I wish you would
leave me alone." When asked by another reporter about the grand jury
indictment, he said tersely, "They've been reading too many stories of
junior G-men."

Julia and Paul were stunned by what they were reading. It was impossible to take it all in. If there was any truth to the charges, Jane and
George were villains of the first order. Not only had they been conspiring against their country for years, but their treasonous services to
Moscow were supposedly motivated by their long-hidden personal ani-
mus for America and everything it stood for. It was the same McCarthy
madness, being replayed with tragic familiarity. Or was it? The implications left them almost speechless with fear and horror.

Over the next few days, everything they knew about Jane was
played out in the pages of the newspapers in lurid fashion, from her beginnings as a wealthy, convent-educated socialite to her drift into San
Francisco's "avant-garde" art scene and eventual indoctrination into
New York's "parlor pink" Communist circles. The conservative papers
like the *Washington Post and Times-Herald* and *Chicago Daily Tribune*
were merciless and gave every fact a sinister twist. The stories explained
that Jane had been a target of the FBI as far back as the early 1940s,

when she had worked for the Board of Economic Warfare, which had been revealed in many congressional investigations as "a haven" for Communists. She then "shifted her base of operations" to the OSS, "also exposed in later years as Communist-ridden." Jane reportedly delivered her OSS report on Indonesia to her "Red spymasters" in 1949, and then she and her husband began shuttling back and forth between Vienna and Zürich, "providing a flow of secret information to the Russians on American personnel in Western Europe."

As the summer weeks passed, Jane and George remained front-page news. Adding to the sensational nature of the stories was the fact that the Sobles had been interviewed about their connection to Julius and Ethel Rosenberg, who had been found guilty of being KGB spies and were the first civilians ever executed for espionage in the United States. Jack and Myra Soble both denied knowing the Rosenbergs as well as many of the Russian members of the ring. The prosecutors theorized that the Sobles and the Zlatovskis were probably part of a small cell that did not interact with the others. The newspapers also seized on the connection to another infamous case of espionage: that of the admitted Russian spy Elizabeth Bentley, who had turned against her Moscow superiors and in July 1948 enthralled congressional investigators by spilling the secrets of her work as a courier for spy rings in New York and Washington. Her testimony had helped to convict Alger Hiss and expose Jack Soble. Jane promised to be another "blond spy queen," and every new development in the case was played out like the latest steamy chapter in a long-running summer fiction serial.

The country was again in the grips of spy fever, and the papers worried breathlessly about whether or not Jane and George would be extradited to the United States to stand trial for their crimes against their country. Before their fate was decided, the United States would have to formally request extradition for the pair in accordance with French administrative and legal procedures. Typically, the French Ministry of Justice would order the couple's arrest. The case would then be submitted to the Chambre des Mises en Accusation, the French equivalent of a grand jury, which would hear all the facts and have three to four weeks to reach a decision. The prospects did not look good, however, as the

Franco-American extradition treaty of 1911 did not cover the crime of espionage and specifically barred extradition on political charges. French officials had further raised doubts by explaining that the United States would have to prove that the Zlatovskis had engaged in "criminal activity" before France would agree to send them back to stand trial. Assistant U.S. Attorney General William F. Tompkins, in charge of internal security, was flying to Paris to press for their return. He insisted that his staff was exploring every possible loophole and cited a promising lead concerning a 1927 extradition statute. The French authorities were conducting their own investigation to determine whether or not they should prosecute the couple. Some papers speculated that the extradition could become an international incident, with the U.S. government having to bring North Atlantic Treaty Organization pressure to bear to pry the accused pair loose.

Inevitably, the House Un-American Activities Committee got in on the act, expressing outrage that a spy had been allowed to slip through the FBI's fingers. Representative Francis E. Walter of Pennsylvania, the chairman of HUAC, told a throng of reporters in Washington that the courts had put Dulles in "an untenable position," and said the situation pointed to the "loose passport practices which are spearheaded by court decisions." He called on the House to "pass remedial legislation." Other right-wing senators weighed in, with Roman Hruska, Republican of Nebraska, insisting that Jane's escape to France illustrated the dangers of the liberals' campaign against security safeguards in government. "A Communist suspect who has been indicted for espionage was able to move about Europe for two additional years on an American passport and is now outside the jurisdiction of the United States," Hruska said. "I hope that the French government will extradite the Zlatovskis and that there will be an early trial so that the details of current Soviet espionage can be made known to the American people."

Meanwhile, Boris Morros was basking in all the publicity, apparently relishing his role as the daring double agent. Morros, who made his first public bow at a news conference in Washington on August 12, turned out to be a balding, roly-poly former musician, whose ostensible claim to fame was having composed "The Parade of the Wooden

Soldiers."* A suave Slavic charmer, Morros liked to brag about his days as a child prodigy in Russia and claimed to have arrived in the United States at age sixteen, when he was already conducting the Russian Imperial Symphony. He boasted of having scored the music for over four hundred films and claimed that, as musical director for Paramount Pictures, he persuaded the great Leopold Stokowski to make his first motion picture. He then turned producer, making the 1939 Laurel and Hardy comedy *The Flying Deuces,* the 1942 romantic comedy *Tales of Manhattan* with Rita Hayworth and Henry Fonda, and the 1947 musical bomb *Carnegie Hall.*

According to Morros, the Russians pressured him into becoming a spy in 1945, and so he disappeared from Hollywood and spent twelve years posing as a millionaire Russian spy and recruiting important, well-to-do Americans to steal secrets for the Kremlin. What the Russians did not know, however, was that he was actually serving as a U.S. counterspy and feeding them only secret documents "approved" by the FBI. He claimed he had done so at great risk to his own life and at great expense to his career. Fooling everyone—including his wife, family members, and friends—for all those years "didn't come easy," Morros boasted in a lengthy prepared statement that was released to the press. "I hated everything they stood for and when I had to express myself to high Russian officials and the American spies employed by them in terms of supporting their vicious ideology I really had to do a more realistic acting job than any of the players whom I ever directed in Hollywood."

Morros supplied the newspapers with a wealth of colorful anecdotes about his thrilling escapades and close shaves. (Bureau agents, apparently bemused by his braggadocio, referred to him as their "special special agent.") He claimed to have gotten to know Jane extremely well and said she had always accepted him at face value, except one night in Paris, when she had been drinking heavily and leaned across

---

* In fact, the jaunty march, originally known as "The Parade of the Tin Soldiers," was composed by Leon Jessel in 1905.

the restaurant table and said, "Boris, somehow I don't believe you're a Communist." Another Russian agent, "a prominent American woman," also became suspicious of him and confided her doubts to the second secretary of the Russian Embassy in Washington. Subsequently, while in Munich, the FBI sent Morros a one-word coded wire—CINERAMA—alerting him that he had been compromised and his life was in danger. Morros managed to charm the Russians into believing that the American woman who had squealed on him was merely jealous. He had a narrow escape, hastening to take a plane to New York, where his grand jury testimony indicting the Sobles effectively ended his run as a counterespionage agent. The government paid for his services, but Morros did not disclose the sum. He stated that with his undercover work now over, he was hoping to resume his movie career.

In the days that followed, the case took another bizarre twist. Outraged members of HUAC clamored to hear more from Morros about the "missing link" in the Sobles' domestic espionage ring. After a three-hour closed-door session with the Morros, HUAC's chairman, Francis Walter, announced that the "prominent American woman" who tried to tip off the Russians was none other than the ex-ambassador's daughter, Martha Dodd Stern. He added that Morros's statement established that Martha and her husband, Alfred Stern, were "part of the Soviet apparatus." Earlier that spring, the Sterns, who had been living in Mexico, had failed to appear after being subpoenaed by the grand jury investigating the Sobles and been cited for contempt and fined $50,000. On July 21, just days after the Zlatovski indictment, Martha and Alfred Stern, accompanied by their eleven-year-old son, Robert, suddenly upped and fled to Prague. Traveling on black-market Paraguayan passports, they boarded a 1 a.m. flight to Amsterdam via Montreal and then flew on to the Czech capital. The wealthy couple apparently astonished prosecutors by ducking behind the Iron Curtain and managed to take much of their substantial fortune with them.

The Sterns' lawyer, Paul O'Dwyer, who made an unsuccessful effort to have the subpoena quashed, admitted years later that he could not blame his clients for being too scared to appear in court. "The Justice Department, at that time, was finding the most underhanded ways of getting indictments," he explained. "They were very apprehensive. They believed that Morros would say one thing and they would say another, and that would be an indictable offense. [To hand down an indictment, a grand jury does not have to be convinced of guilt beyond reasonable doubt, only persuaded there is sufficient evidence to warrant a trial.] All the rules about the defendant being innocent until proven otherwise—all those rules went out the window because of the atmosphere in which these trials took place." O'Dwyer never doubted for a minute that their lives were at stake. "I am firmly of the belief that knowing how Boris Morros was acting, that if the government had taken the Rosenbergs and electrocuted them, they would have electrocuted Martha and Alfred."

On September 6, the Sterns held a press conference in Prague to denounce the "fascist" practices of the United States. Martha, as brash and beautiful as ever, opened her remarks by making a preemptive strike against Morros, saying that her husband had been subjected to a "campaign of character assassination" and felt compelled to reply. Morros's accusations were the "fantastic inventions of a Hollywood imposter" employed by the United States government to "destroy or silence those people who dare dissent." The allegations, she continued, were motivated by revenge for the failure of his music company, when in fact the fault lay with his own "incompetence." She added that her and her husband's long progressive record was well known, and they were "proud" to be in the United States' tradition of protest. The government was persecuting them because the ruling elite was "deathly afraid of . . . peaceful economic and political competition with the socialist countries."

Three days later, on September 9, the Sterns were indicted for espionage in absentia. Morros, the principal witness against them, testified before the grand jury that he was told by his Russian superiors to set up the Boris Morros Music Company in December 1943, and that the Sterns would be investing $130,000. He was supposed to look after the legitimate end of the music-publishing business in Hollywood, while the Sterns took over the New York office as a front for their espionage activities. Morros became irritated with Alfred Stern as a partner, explaining that he was extravagant, once billing the company $5,000 for a payoff to another Russian agent. They also argued over the song "Chattanooga Choo-Choo." Apparently Mr. Stern did not like the title, though, as Morros was quick to point out, it was a hit anyway. Still, Alfred and Martha Stern served a useful purpose, as the Soviets needed independently wealthy Americans who could travel without raising questions and could easily pass information over the border.

Morros testified that Martha Stern's role was to sound out prospective agents and arrange for their introduction into active espionage cells. She was charismatic and persuasive, and knew how to play on people's weaknesses and desires, occasionally resorting to blackmail when necessary. She had roped her own husband and brother into working for the Soviets before moving on to friends and colleagues. It was Martha Stern, Morros stated, who introduced him to Jane, whom she claimed to have mentored, and personally "guaranteed" the latter's devotion to Russia.

That fall, in a series of articles in *The Philadelphia Inquirer*, Morros told his tales of derring-do to Rep. Francis E. Walter, who wrote it up as the "First Official Story of the Man Who Fooled the Kremlin." The pudgy counterspy was characterized as "a sensitive, dynamic, extremely intelligent man with a fantastic memory." A Russian agent, Morros confided, never did anything by accident. Everything was by design; even the most innocuous acts had a hidden meaning—"a hand to shake, a kiss, a match to light a cigaret . . . " That was how it was with Martha and with Jane, casual encounters that led him to a ring "up to their eyeballs in red espionage." The pulpy prose was accompanied by macabre cartoons depicting Morros fending off shadowy spies and foiling the advances of mysterious beauties. And so it went on and on, with the flamboyant, self-mythologizing Boris Morros beaming in the spotlight, granting exclusive interviews, and clearly loving being back in show business.

While they were being vilified in the American press, Jane and George were besieged in Paris. The bottom had dropped out of their world six months earlier. Like Julia and Paul, they had awoken one morning to devastating news. It was January 26, 1957, just days after Jane got out of the hospital, when they read in the *Herald Tribune* that Jack and Myra Soble had been arrested in New York as "Soviet spies." They had known the Sobles for years. Jane and George quickly made the connection between the newspaper article and the recent reappearance of CIA agents outside their home. There had also been the terse phone call the previous day requesting their presence at the American Embassy "at eleven o'clock tomorrow morning." Panic stricken, they had immediately phoned their lawyer. They took a taxi straight to his office in the Seventh Arrondissement and observed that they were followed the entire way by two cars, four men in each. They attempted to explain their predicament to their French lawyer, the "tragic-comedy of errors," as Jane later put it, laying out how their friendship with this couple would inevitably link them to some sort of "crime" in America. He listened, concluded there was little he could for them at present, but managed to make them feel somewhat calmer.

As soon as Jane and George stepped into the street, they were surrounded. It was the same eight men they had seen in the cars earlier that morning. Terrified that they were about to be abducted by the CIA, Jane began yelling for help. Their lawyer, roused by her terrified screams, came rushing downstairs, coatless and still in his slippers. He reassured her that the officers were French police, attached to the Direction de la Surveillance du Territoire (DST), or counterintelligence unit, and that she and George were obliged to go with them. By law, they could be detained for twenty-four hours and questioned. At the end of that period, they had to be released or formally charged. She was put in one of the cars, George in the other, and they were driven to the DST headquarters near the Élysée Palace. They were led across the huge courtyard of a nineteenth-century building and deposited in separate waiting rooms. Jane was taken to a small room occupied by two men, each seated at a desk before an identical typewriter. A short, round officer, who looked like "a hairless teddy bear," took charge of her interrogation.

At the outset, his questions ranged widely, from when she had joined the Communist Party to whether she knew the famous Soviet spy Richard Sorge (she had no idea who he was) to her familiarity with a long list of Russian names. The only person she had ever heard of was Lavrenti Beria ("Who hadn't?"), the notorious head of Stalin's secret police who was executed for his crimes against the state in 1953. As the interrogation progressed, the questions cut to the heart of the matter—her relationship to the Sobles, the Sterns, and, to a lesser degree, Boris Morros, whom the short French policeman referred to as "Maurice Borrós." Jane began by being defiant and obstructionist, convinced that they were going to try to pressure her into listing American Communists and "demand names." She was not being brave, she noted in her memoir, as she was "in no sense a Communist sympathizer by 1957" and had "no ideology" to sustain her. She simply had a deep-seated "hatred and contempt for snitches" going back to her days at the convent school.

When it became clear that the officers were not interested in her Communist ties, only in her connection to the espionage ring, she "put her head on the desk and bawled." When they presented her with copies of every letter she had ever written to Soble, including a receipt for the repayment of a $1,800 loan to him, she sobbed harder. Faced with this feminine display of hysterics, the French officers became "extremely solicitous." They asked whether she would like some champagne, whiskey, beer, or fruit juice. Understanding the root of her distress, they also brought her a copy of the French civil code and pointed out the relevant passage barring extradition for political offenses, adding that "espionage was an eminently political offense." The short, round policeman then prodded her to talk, saying, "You might as well tell the truth. Soble is talking in America."

Jane gave him a withering look. All she felt in that moment was frustrated rage. She did not have to be told Soble was talking. She already knew he would say anything he had to in order to avoid the same fate as the Rosenbergs. She also knew of his "mental deterioration" over the last few years, and of his wife, Myra's, "stupidity." She could only imagine how easily they could both be manipulated to "say anything the Americans wanted."

The real problem was not Soble but Boris Morros, a lying, self-

aggrandizing clown of a Hollywood mogul, who, she only now realized, much too late, had been playing a far more complicated game
than she had ever imagined. Morros was in the business of peddling
hearsay and innuendo, and he had handed her and George over in a
neat package tied up with string. Jane could not help wondering if it
had been Morros, pulling strings behind the scenes, who had been responsible for getting her passport restored. "Morros, who did not want
to lose his highly profitable meal ticket. He had been eating high on
the hog, off the FBI/CIA, and was undoubtedly telling them . . . George
and I could lead them directly to the top echelons of the KGB."

It was by then one or two in the morning, and she was exhausted.
She must have looked wrung out because the policeman took her into
another room, furnished with a Napoléon III sofa upholstered in "hideous green rep," and brought her an inedible sandwich. He placed a
hand on her arm and said, *"Écoutez-moi bien, madame. La France vous
a donné l'abri et le refuge. Et vous refusez maintenant d'aider la France?"*
(Listen to me well, madam. France has given you shelter and refuge.
And do you now refuse to help France?)

It was a masterstroke of interrogation. She had been on the verge
of breaking. By invoking her beloved France, he unlocked her tongue.
If she had any allegiance left it was to the country she now called home
and desperately wanted to go on calling home for the rest of her days.
France had a long history of welcoming political refugees, and it was
her last, best hope. In that moment, she roused herself to make one
more attempt to clear her name. Never one to "do things by halves,"
once she started to talk she could not stop.

She told the DST "everything"—about her "reasons for joining the
Communist Party and those for leaving it"; about the early days, before
the war, when she was an "open member" of the Party and picketed
the White House, signed petitions, and sold the *Daily Worker* on street
corners. Her interrogator appeared surprised by the last and returned
to it repeatedly, as if this menial task did not fit with his information
about her as a high-level Soviet operative. She thought that she could
see the dawning realization that she and George "were either the victims of the Americans, or of the Russians, or of both, or, at the most,

'*lampistes*'—a term meaning literally railroad employees who swing lanterns when a train pulls out and, by extension, the lowest of the low, who are made to pay for the mistakes or misdeeds of their superiors."

She told of meeting the Sobles through Martha Stern in New York and how, after Jack Soble expressed interest in the Indonesian conflict, she had given him a copy of her OSS report to read. She described her gradual alienation from the Sterns, whom she had not seen since leaving New York ten years earlier. She outlined her relations with Jack Soble, the money she had lent him for his business back in 1947, and her efforts to collect it some years later when she learned he was in Paris. She talked about his odd demeanor, dramatic mood swings, and strange insistence that she meet his successful Hollywood producer friend Boris Morros, all the while going on about "what a fabulous man he was." When Morros had offered her husband a job managing his art-house theater on rue du Faubourg Montmartre, they could not resist taking him up on it. George, "the eternal student," had been unable to find steady work in the pinched French postwar economy, and this seemed like the answer to all their problems.

"Boris Morros was an outstanding confidence man," Jane recalled, explaining how he had taken them to the theater and introduced them to the "principal" owner, a White Russian émigré and son-in-law of Rachmaninoff. "Had we the brains of a gnat between us, we would have realized that all Boris Morros had proved was that the theater really existed and nothing more." When Morros proposed selling them a 10 percent interest in the business for $4,000 (approximately $30,000 today), Jane, against her "better judgment," allowed herself to be persuaded. She asked her father to advance the sum and wrote Morros a check on her Swiss bank account. He had at once paid out a month's salary in advance, and George, "in the euphoria of the moment," had proposed that they all go on holiday, inviting the Sobles and Morroses to join them at the Salzburg Festival. Jane's doubts about Morros faded in light of his obvious celebrity in music circles, especially when he called his "good friend" Yehudi Menuhin, the famed violinist and conductor, and got them tickets to the sold-out performance of *Don Giovanni*. When they returned to Paris a week later, however, Morros promptly vanished into obscurity, and they discovered that the art-house theater really belonged to the White Russian. There never was any partnership or job. It was a "pure swindle on the part of Boris Morros."

Then began what Jane described as the "great battle" to get her money back. When they learned from the theater owner that Morros was negotiating to buy a film in Vienna, George dashed off to confront him and wound up punching him in the face and breaking his two front teeth. Morros, who was never down for long, proposed making restitution in the form of a 50 percent interest in his new acquisition, a quasi-Russian propaganda film called *Marika*. As soon as George phoned Jane with the news of this new venture, she hopped a train to Vienna and put a stop to it. When she threatened legal action, Morros agreed to pay her back the full amount when he returned to Paris in a few weeks. Months passed. Sometime in the winter of 1950, Morros telephoned to say he had the money and would meet them in Zürich, together with the Sobles. Jane and George arrived to find that the $4,000 had been deposited in her Swiss account. "Undoubtedly," she noted with grim hindsight, "it came from the FBI/CIA." They had lunch at the Baur au Lac hotel, and then she and George headed back to Paris with "no intention of ever seeing any of them again."

The problem was, she did see Morros again. Feeling "bored" and lonely with George away in Italy, she succumbed to his dubious charms. Thinking he might have "amusing stories" to tell, she agreed to meet him for lunch at the Hôtel Plaza Athénée. At one point during the meal, he pulled out a notebook and asked her to write something for him. "Anything," he prompted. "Hieroglyphics. Anything in your own handwriting." Naturally, she refused, "but the request seemed so bizarre that I did not realize it was a provocation." Later, when they were walking down rue du Faubourg Saint-Honoré, he stopped in front of the Lanvin store to admire some ties, then asked if she would pick out a dozen for him and send them via airmail as he was leaving for the United States that afternoon. "I have absolute confidence in your taste," he cajoled. This time Jane had the sense to ask for the money up front. Morros demurred.

At some point in the interrogation, around four or five in the morning, the DST officers asked for permission to search Jane and George's apartment in their presence. Jane agreed and signed the release. She had told George that she was cooperating fully, and he had followed suit. When they brought him to her, his voice was hoarse from the hours of talking and smoking. The police drove them to rue Mazarine. Upon entering the apartment, they were assaulted by their poor poodle, Maggie, who had been locked up for sixteen hours. George, accompanied by a DST officer, took the dog for a quick walk. Then Jane and George sat on the sofa while the policemen went through their desk drawers, letters, and papers. Jane gave them her last remaining copy of the now "famous" OSS report on Indonesia.

When the interrogation resumed, the questions focused on her relations with Bill Browder, brother of Earl Browder, the former leader of the American Communist Party. Jane admitting knowing Bill Browder and explained that she had been introduced to him by Martha Stern before the war and they had met on several occasions for drinks at various Greenwich Village bars. She recalled that he had told her she would be more helpful to the Party if she was "more discreet, and that Martha reiterated this more than once." She explained that she did not "understand his reasoning" but welcomed the suggestion as a way to get out of selling papers and other Party tasks that were not her idea of fun. When she went to Washington in 1942, he had introduced her to a young woman who would help her "keep in touch with the Party." Jane never recalled the woman's ever asking anything about her work or anything important but remembered that she had once brought a message from Browder telling her not to accept an overseas assignment from the OSS. Presumably, Browder was directing her into underground operations, much as he had done with Whittaker Chambers twelve years earlier, but she was not as receptive. As usual, Jane said, she "rebelled and refused to comply."

The French police seemed very interested in this "shadowy woman" from fifteen years before and asked Jane if she could pick her out in any of the photographs they supplied. She could not. A little while later, the short, round policeman gathered all the typed pages of her statement into a neat stack and asked her to initial them. The interrogation had lasted precisely twenty-four hours, "the legal limit." She and George were free to go, although they would be called back for additional questioning. It was then explained to them that the fact that they were not being arrested meant that their case would not be remanded to a grand jury for a hearing.

The DST interrogations continued sporadically for several more weeks. The short, round policeman was joined by a half-dozen others with varied expertise, who proceeded to comb through their documents and compare and analyze their answers to see if their stories matched. In order to satisfy the French authorities, Jane and George agreed to tell everything they knew about Soviet espionage in France and anyone they knew who was involved in Communist causes and fronts. In the end, Jane admitted to passing on some material but claimed she had never been more than a dupe and had been unaware at the time of the Sterns' collusion with Soviet intelligence. According to FBI records, the French service advised that Jane felt Martha had "led her to become involved in espionage on the belief that she was working for international Communism on an ideological basis." Once Jane was caught in the Stern-Soble web, she found it difficult to extricate herself. She could not go to the authorities at that point because all of her friends were Communists and she could not bring herself to inform on them. Angry at having been made a tool of the NKVD (Soviet secret police under Stalin) and the mess it had made of her life, Jane gave the French police chapter and verse on the clandestine activities of her former comrades. Ironically, after years of standing on principle, she was naming names. She told herself it was not the same thing, but in the end she did it for the same reason as all the others—to save her own neck.

In her memoir, Jane is circumspect about the extent of her disclosures to the DST. She never acknowledged taking part in any espionage, and even attempted to insinuate that the French authorities did not think she was particularly guilty, suggesting that the reason she and George were allowed to go free was that neither of them impressed the DST as nearly slick enough to have pulled off the sophisticated covert operation outlined in the indictment:

It seemed highly unlikely to the DST that the Russians would recruit open Communists like George and myself and, knowing that Boris Morros was a double or triple agent and an *agent provocateur,* the DST began to consider the possibility that the so-called *Stern-Soble-Zlatovski* "spy network" was, in reality, a simple *réseau bidon,* i.e. false network, immobilizing a large part of the CIA while the Russians did their dirty work through agents who really were *agents.*

Like most rationalizations, this argument had an element of truth to it. The Stern-Soble network was a fairly sorry, minor-league operation, and Jane and George among the most underemployed and unreliable of recruits. While Jane understandably preferred to trivialize their contribution, implying that the French had let them walk because of their utter incompetence and unimportance, the fact remains that they were released because they cooperated and provided valuable information about illegal Soviet activity within France. They purchased their liberty the same way Elizabeth Bentley had bought hers a decade earlier—by betraying those who had betrayed them.*

In March 1957, Jane had another breakdown. The weeks of relentless questioning and demeaning admissions were too much for her. She entered a *maison de santé*—a French euphemism for "not exactly nuthouses but rest homes for people with nervous depressions." She underwent what was fashionably known in those days as a *cure de sommeil,* a treatment that involved being pumped so full of tranquilizers she was "in a constant state of somnolence." Her worried parents, who had flown to Paris to provide moral support, made the arrangements and footed the bill.

Jane had been in the hospital about two weeks when she was informed that two high-ranking American officials, Assistant Attorney

---

* It is worth noting that Bentley, too, claimed she had been working for the Communist Party of the United States and initially had no idea that she was spying for the Soviet Union.

General William Tompkins and Special Assistant Attorney General Thomas B. Gilchrist, were waiting at the DST headquarters to question her about the Sobles. Despite being woozy on whatever drug cocktail she had been given that morning, she got dressed and went to meet them. When she walked into the room, the first words out of Tompkins's mouth were "Mrs. Zlatovski, we would like you to come back to America for a few days to testify in the Soble case." She refused. Much to the Americans' irritation, she persisted in speaking French, drafting one of the DST officers as interpreter. They explained that they had brought a U.S. Air Force plane specially to take her to New York, and she would travel round-trip in comfort. She insisted on having their re marks translated. Then she refused again, in French, and waited for her meaning to be conveyed. She would not say a word in English. It was a small act of rebellion, the only one she could manage under the circumstances. At the end of their tense exchange, she asked to be driven back to the *maison de santé.* Jane talked the driver into stopping off at a bistro along the way, and they both had an aperitif. It was "very human and very French."

When she got back to the hospital, she climbed into bed and slit her wrists. As political protests go, it was remarkably effective. When she woke up, both arms were bandaged up to her elbows and the special attorneys had been sent home. She had lost a lot of blood, but she had made her point. She would rather die by her own hand in France than return to the United States to die in the electric chair. From then on, a special nurse was assigned to stand guard in her room, but she had no more visits from the police.

A confidential memorandum from the American Embassy in Paris to the director of the FBI, dated May 28, 1957, reveals the diplomatic stalemate she had achieved: "In view of Jane Zlatovski's attempted suicide and her mental attitude, the Zlatovskis have not been reinterviewed." Shortly after the attorney general issued the indictment, and while the American papers were having a field day running the most dramatic parts of Morros's testimony, Tompkins flew back to Paris to again formally request their extradition. Another memo from the American Embassy to the FBI, dated July 24, reflects that Tompkins again returned home empty-handed. The embassy official reiterated the view that no useful purpose would be served in trying to question the Zlatovskis "because of their knowledge of the United States' trying to obtain their return, and because Jane might attempt suicide again."

In the meantime, the French authorities had reached their decision. A high official in the Quai d'Orsay, the French foreign office, summoned the Zlatovskis for a meeting. As Jane was still too ill to go, George met with *monsieur le ministre,* who gave him his assurance that the French government would never allow them to be extradited. The French authorities' official recalcitrance made the headlines in the following day's *Herald Tribune:* "PARIS REFUSES TO GIVE U.S. TWO ALLEGED SPIES."

By the time Jane returned from the hospital a few weeks later, a mob of hostile reporters was permanently camped outside their building on rue Mazarine. They swarmed the sidewalk, staircase, and landing and "acted like a pack of jackals," she recalled, incessantly ringing the doorbell, banging on the door, and shouting insults. Even the "respectable" papers were venomous, offering large bribes to the housekeeper and printing rumors and ill-informed scuttlebutt. Jane became a virtual prisoner in the apartment. Not that it mattered terribly. The drugs in the hospital had left her in such a weakened state that she was in for a long recovery. She stayed inside and out of sight. Apart from George's initial comments to the press, they decided to grant no interviews. They kept silent and waited for the furor to die down.

While she was recuperating, her New York lawyer, Leonard Boudin, sent her a copy of the indictment. She read through the five counts and all thirty-eight charges, spelled out "in barbarous, presumably legal language" over twenty pages. "It was THE BIG LIE," she wrote in her memoir. "For all its gobbledegook, lies, errors, imprecisions, contradictions and sheer nonsense, it was devastating. How *does* an individual fight THE BIG LIE? We were utterly helpless against the judiciary of a powerful government, which wanted another Rosenberg case."

She also learned that in exchange for turning state's evidence—and presumably their promise "to reveal a vast Soviet spy network"—the Sobles had gotten off relatively lightly: Jack was sentenced to seven years and Myra to five and a half, though in return for all her assistance her sentence was reduced again and she served only four years. According to press reports, while awaiting trial Jack Soble was kept in the psychiatric ward at Bellevue Hospital. Directly after being transferred to the Lewisburg Federal Penitentiary after sentencing, he swallowed a handful of nuts and bolts stolen from the machine shop. He was then transferred to a medical facility for federal prisoners and later received shock treatments. Jane thought the prosecutor must have been "greatly relieved" to have Jack Soble's guilty plea, as he would have been a pathetic sight on the witness stand.

To her family and friends, Jane would angrily hold forth about the "glaring inaccuracies and discrepancies" contained in the thirty-eight charges and how most of them were based on innuendo and "sheer ignorance." To begin with, she argued, counts 1 through 8 did not even mention either her or George by name and had to do with other members of the ring. Counts 9 and 10 alleged she had met Soble in December 1945, when she was still aboard the "USS Unspeakable" on her way home from the war, as could easily be corroborated by the ship's manifest. She actually met Soble six months later, in April or May 1946. Counts 14 through 18 had her traveling to Paris "five times" between May 1948 and February 1949 to meet with unnamed Soviet agents, when she was there only twice, and the second time was to meet her parents—"those two well-known spies, Dr. and Mrs. Harry Emerson Foster"—with whom she traveled through Europe for the next few months until returning to Paris in March 1949, at which point Paris became her permanent home.

The twenty-ninth charge, which received the greatest share of titillating press coverage, alleged that in December 1949 she and George had gone to Salzburg to report on "the sexual and drinking habits" of the American personnel in Austria. By that time, both she and George were civilians, and all they did was relax for a few days, visit old friends, and attend midnight Mass in the church of Sankt Wolfgang. "As for 'sexual and drinking habits,' if the Russians were interested, all they had to do was ask any Austrian bartender or chambermaid."

By far the best "gem" of prosecutorial invention, in her view, was the line in count 4 of the indictment: "Mrs. Zlatovski fled from justice in or about the month of April 1947 and departed from the United

States." It was hard to see how boarding the U.S. passenger lines on a
legal passport to join her husband, who was working for U.S. military
intelligence "in the American-occupied zone of Austria" amounted to
fleeing. And what was she supposed to be "fleeing from in 1947"? No
charges were ever filed against her until a decade later.

For all that she would rail against the indictment as a "scurrilous
document" and quibble endlessly about specific dates and details,
several of which were demonstrably wrong, Jane could not deny the
damning chain of association outlined in the charges: that she knew
the Sterns very well, had once considered them close friends, and that
it was at their apartment in the Majestic that she had met both the
Sobles and Boris Morros. Nor could she dispute that she had socialized
with the Sobles and Morros later in Paris, lent them money for business
ventures, and traveled with them or to meet them on more than one
occasion, spending time with them in Salzburg, Vienna, and Zürich.
It strained credulity to the breaking point to believe she had never had
so much as an inkling of anything unusual, let alone illegal. But then, if
anyone ever lived in a bubble, it was Jane. Wittingly or unwittingly, she
had surrounded herself with companions who were not only Communists but were actively involved in Soviet espionage and determined to
lead her and her husband down that same path. Considering what little
regard she had for this unsavory crew, her willingness to become so
intimately involved with them reveals a record of bad judgment and indiscretion on a colossal scale. To the charge of stupidity, Jane observed
ruefully in her memoir, she had no defense:

Gertrude Stein wrote in her *Autobiography of Alice B. Toklas,*
"Every time a genius entered the room, a bell went off in my
head." With me, it's always been the opposite. Every time an
evil or disaster-boding person entered the room, a bell would
go off in my head. Unfortunately, I never paid attention to it. I
was still trying to be all sweetness and light, and thought there
was something wrong with me and that I was being irrational.
The minute I laid eyes on Boris Morros, the bell started clang-
ing loudly.

The best argument in Jane's favor was her apparent lack of guile or premeditation. If she was the Sterns' protégée, as Boris Morros contended, and from early 1941 was being carefully groomed to become an undercover agent, why would she have listed Martha Dodd Stern, a leader of the Soviet spy ring, as a character reference on her 1943 employment application for the OSS? For that matter, why would the Soviets have picked someone as unabashedly antiestablishment as Jane to be a mole? She was so unguarded about her radical activities that the Civil Service Commission, which investigated all prospective government employees, had insisted on a special hearing in September 1943 to address all the "derogatory information" that had been discovered. During the hearing, Jane had again cited her friendship with Martha, mentioning their common interest in music and painting and that they saw each other "socially at concerts and parties." If Jane knew Martha was at the red-hot center of a secret Soviet intelligence conspiracy, it would seem like very poor tradecraft to flaunt their relationship and invite the investigators to talk to her. (Martha begged off, claiming to be too ill to be interviewed in person, told the investigators by phone that Jane was a "very sweet person.") At the time, Jane also candidly listed as "social acquaintances" Charles Flato, her boss at the Board of Economic Warfare, and Dr. Susan B. Anthony and her husband, Henry Hill Collins Jr.—all Communist sympathizers she seems to have had no qualms about advertising as friends. Surely she could have come up with a more conservative list of pals if she wanted to be considered for a sensitive government job? Or at least have done a better job of covering her tracks? Instead, she left a trail of Communist ties that the FBI followed like bread crumbs and later used to bolster its case against her.

Jane's FBI file reveals that she turned up on the bureau's radar again in the spring of 1948 because of her connection to Jack Soble. A "known Soviet agent," Soble was the focus of the "Mocase" investigation and the FBI was listening in on his calls, reading his mail, and checking out anyone who crossed his path. J. Edgar Hoover immediately ordered a "complete and exhaustive investigation to determine the present contacts and activities of the Zlatovskis," bringing all the investigative techniques of the bureau to bear, including "technical and microfilm surveillance, physical surveillance, and mail and trash recovery." The investigation turned up the usual Communist Party sympathies and friends until July 1949, when a "Confidential Informant" (Boris Morros) suddenly identified Jane and George as "active in Soviet intelligence."

The FBI files reveal that Morros was immediately fascinated by Jane, and saw her as ripe for the picking. In the course of vetting her, he reported reams of gossip about Jane picked up at the Sterns's parties, detailing her upper-crust background, reactionary father, youthful so-journ to Russia, marital infidelities, and sexual attractiveness. George's pro-Russian sympathies, lack of money, and drinking habits were duly noted but of less interest. He was apparently never viewed as having much potential, and Soble wrote him off as a "parasite." Morros re-ported to the FBI that Soble praised Jane as one of their "best agents" and supported this claim by explaining she had gathered information on Americans in Austria but "destroyed the notes" when her Soviet contact failed to show, although she managed to pass along a report on "the Marshall Plan in Paris."

In the hundreds of reports in her FBI file,* and in all the hours of testimony, there was never any definitive evidence that Jane know-ingly crossed over from ordinary Communist Party work to outright espionage—becoming a significant source, serving as a courier, or pass-ing valuable military secrets to Soviet intelligence—other than the word of Morros and Soble. There was also never any explanation as to how, as an employee of the Austrian radio service and later as an unemployed painter, Jane gained access to important classified information. An FBI memo reveals that after four weeks of investigation in Austria, the bu-reau was unable to discover any derogatory information and reported Jane had an excellent reputation among her colleagues in Salzburg.

Jack Soble was repeatedly interviewed in prison, and what emerges from his vague, rambling, and often jumbled recollections is that he

---

* The FBI made some but not all of Jane Foster's massive file—more than 60,000 pages—available. In addition, some documents are censored, and in some cases so many names and sentence fragments have been blanked out that the reports are virtually incompre-hensible.

and his wife were far from brilliant intelligence masterminds. They were very ordinary people, originally forced into spying to help their family members still trapped in the Soviet Union—they managed to get eighteen relatives out, along with a baby boy they adopted—and were threatened and tormented by the NKVD (and later the NKGB) at every turn. In their desperate efforts to keep their masters happy, they fed them a steady diet of scuttlebutt, secondhand information, and whatever low-level reports their various informants, mainly relatives, could lay their hands on. At one point, Soble admits that while he obtained various kinds of information from Jane and George, he could not recall what and "must have" told the Soviets it was "military information" even though it was nothing of the kind.

Even Myra Soble's sworn statement proved too vague to corroborate their allegations against Jane and George. For example, she stated she "did not know if Jane ever prepared any reports on [words deleted] or any other United States personnel at Salzburg." While she believed Jane was providing reports to her husband, Myra "never saw any of these reports" and did "not know what was in them." She testified to the same ignorance in reference to George's work. The reason she believed they were both "furnishing reports" to the Russians was that otherwise they would not have been paid $150 a month. She later added, however, that Jane and George stated that Morros had cheated them out of a $4,000 "investment in a theater enterprise" and that Morros had paid them back $150 a month for a while and then stopped. The Zlatovskis blamed her husband for "the swindle," and she never saw them again after the spring of 1951. The apparent contradictions in her testimony were never addressed.

There was no love lost between the Sobles and the Zlatovskis, and Myra volunteered all kinds of seamy details about Jane's personal life—mentioning her affair with "a black man," multiple abortions, and her drunkenness—in an attempt to cast her in the worst possible light. Neither of the Sobles was able to present any physical evidence or any document to substantiate their allegations. The one classified document Jane was specifically accused of handing over to Jack Soble was the OSS report on Indonesia that she had previously disseminated to the press, discussed in a series of interviews and one public lecture, and summarized in a *New York Times* letter to the editor. According to Morros, Soble claimed the OSS report was useful to Moscow in the "UN debate on Indonesia," but this seems highly unlikely as the report was old news by then and the political situation in Indonesia had changed considerably. Given the extent to which Boris Morros might have been tempted to embellish these nuggets for his bureau employers, and Jack and Myra's desire to dress up their statements to impress their Soviet handlers and later in their bid for leniency, it was impossible to gauge the verisimilitude of any of their accounts.

The major underlying problem with the government's case was that Morros, the FBI's counterspy, was himself a very questionable character, whose self-serving version of his own activities the authorities knew from the outset to be exaggerated and extremely unreliable. From the very first statement he made to the press when he came in from the cold—that patriotic sentiment had inspired him to call the FBI on July 14, 1947, and offer his services—Morros was prevaricating, blurring the line between fact and convenient fiction. FBI documents reveal unequivocally that it was the FBI's Los Angeles field office that first contacted Morros in 1947—not the other way around—and that he was interviewed on July 14, 16, and 18 about his connections to the Soviet intelligence official Vasily Zarubin. It was only *after* Morros realized the FBI knew of his involvement with Soviet espionage operations that he decided to cooperate fully to avoid prosecution. FBI records indicate he may also have angered his bosses at the NKVD and was running scared, providing additional impetus to ingratiate himself with the American intelligence service. His business setbacks—he had filed for bankruptcy twice—may also have motivated him to seek a new career as a counterspy.

Internal memos between D. M. Ladd, assistant director of domestic intelligence, and Hoover further reveal that the FBI had grave concerns about Morros's personal and financial integrity, and agents were ordered to maintain close tabs on him to be sure he would not end up double-crossing the bureau. In the end, however, the FBI was so eager to develop Morros as an informant that it overlooked the dubious incidents in his past, leaving open the question of what lies he might have told and misdeeds he might have committed in the name of his new

employer, to say nothing of the damage caused by his overblown allegations of Soviet espionage.

Morros's veracity became a critical issue for the Justice Department
in January 1957, when the U.S. attorney Thomas Gilchrist was about to
impanel the grand jury and bring Boris Morros in to testify. Before calling on the double agent, Gilchrist's office had queried the bureau about
"available information concerning Boris Morros that would reflect on
his credibility," including the extent of his "compensation or expense
money." Gilchrist did not get the answers he had hoped for, however,
and had to delay the proceedings while he dealt with what the FBI's
director disclosed about their star witness.

Hoover's memo revealed that the FBI knew of at least three instances when Morros had been less than truthful. First, Morros had
had not made full disclosure about his initial contact with the FBI in
1947. Second, he had reported to his FBI handlers in 1955 that he had
met with Jane Foster in Paris in November 1954. The FBI, aware that
she was in the United States at that time, "repeatedly interrogated" Morros about the meeting in Paris, but he insisted that it took place. The
agents were not too concerned, as they believed it was possible Morros
was confusing the meeting with one that took place months earlier.
Still, it raised doubts about his memory, if not his honesty. Third, and
far more incriminating, Morros had forged business contracts showing
that he had the rights to the score of the opera *War and Peace,* which
he had attempted to exploit in the United States for financial gain. In
the summer of 1955, the Leeds Music Company of New York, which
had obtained the rightful title from the noted Russian composer Sergey
Prokofiev, filed a complaint with the FBI. Under pressure, Morros had
reluctantly agreed to make restitution and paid the company the sum
of $40,000.

As far as the FBI was concerned, the matter was closed. The more
troubling implications of Morros's veniality were ignored. (There were
also allegations concerning Morros's relations with the USIS in Vienna,
as well as with a firm called Metal Import Trust of Zürich, which the
FBI chose not to pursue.) The three incidents were judged insufficient
to call into question Morros's ten-year relationship with the bureau or
impeach the vast bulk of his testimony, which had been corroborated

by agents and other sources over the course of countless separate investigations. To assuage Gilchrist's concerns, Hoover sent the U.S. attorney a second memo detailing all the evidence substantiating Morros's
claims.*

Jane's parents considered the charges preposterous and believed
the government's case was a pack of lies supplied by a paid informant
with the improbable name of Boris Morros. From the perspective of
her sturdy Yankee father, the fact that Morros was a Hollywood producer was reason enough not to believe a word out of his mouth. None
of it made any sense. Not long after the indictment was handed down,
Harry Foster got a call from the American Embassy in Paris asking him
to come in for an informal chat. "Will I be able to go out again?" he had
inquired in a skeptical drawl.

"Oh, Dr. Foster!" the voice on the line spluttered, feigning shock.
When he reluctantly met with embassy officials, they pleaded with him
to use his influence to persuade Jane to return to the United States to
testify. They told him it would be for the best. He would not hear of it.

George's family also rejected the espionage charges and regarded
the pair as victims of a savage game of Cold War politics. His sister,
Helen, stood by him and sent money to help pay the legal fees. "The
family always viewed the charges against them as trumped up," explained Helen's daughter, Susan. She added that, if anything, they always held George to be the more accountable of the two. "Everyone
knew he was a loose cannon. I wouldn't put it past my uncle to thumb
his nose at the world in ways that were not judicious and possibly bor-
dered on the treacherous." Either way, she could not imagine that he
was ever much more than a nuisance. He had been engaged in one kind
of political mischief or another since his days as a union organizer in
the 1930s. His big mouth and back-parlor posturing had gotten him
into trouble too many times for anyone to trust him with anything re-
motely important. As for Jane, Susan always had the sense that she had

---

* This included the corroborating evidence supplied by the then top-secret Venona decrypts described in the appendix of this book.

made herself an easy target. She was "vulnerable"—by virtue of her easy way with money, readiness to embrace anyone who flouted convention, and fondness for alcohol. "She liked the high life and her party-loving friends," Susan reflected. "I don't think she was very particular about who she surrounded herself with. Jane and George drank too much, more than they could hold. It's possible that one or both of them may have been used."

Julia and Paul did not know what to believe. On the face of it, the government's case against Jane appeared overwhelming. Yet experience had given them a very jaundiced view of the FBI's so-called evidence. It was now clear to them that Paul's loyalty hearing had been an ugly sideshow to a much larger investigation. The FBI had lumped him in with Jane in their Washington-to-Paris web of conspiracy, and because he was a fellow artist they were all too ready to believe he was also a flagrant fellow traveler. Had he not shouted his innocence from the rooftops, called every friend he had, and enumerated his father-in-law's right-wing bona fides, he might have ended up another casualty of their reckless hunt for coconspirators. He and Julia hated even to think how close he had come to being pulled into the "Mocase" morass.* They also understood that Jane's choice of exile did not necessarily implicate her. It was less an admission of guilt than an expression of sheer terror. They had all seen what a grueling process these hearings were and the toll they had taken on much tougher people. It was not hard to see why Jane did not have the stomach for it.

Julia and Paul recalled that on one of the last times they had seen Jane in Paris she had speculated that all her problems with the State Department might have been the result of her sharply worded criticisms

---

* In the search of the Zlatovskis' apartment on January 26, 1957, the French police took George's address book, which listed Paul Child as a contact. This information was forwarded to the FBI, which requested that George "be questioned concerning the subject [Paul]." A memo from the Paris legation to the director of the FBI in March 1957 states that a review of the Zlatovskis' statements revealed that Paul Child was in the OSS, then with the American Embassy and USIS, and "the possibility exists that the subject is a covert operative with the CIA."

of U.S. policy in Indonesia and Indochina at the end of the war. When she returned from overseas, she had been angry and disillusioned and had spoken out passionately against the Dutch and French efforts to reclaim their former colonies, warning that it was not in America's interest to support their European allies in this unjust cause, which would result in guerilla warfare for years to come. She had *anticipated* revolution, saying precisely what Washington policy makers did not want to hear at that combustible moment in history, when they feared revolution could spread like wildfire across Southeast Asia, consuming Thailand, Burma, Malaya, and the whole Indonesian archipelago. State Department officials, angered and alarmed by her ad hoc support of nationalism, had accused her of a breach of security. She had broken rank, and her intemperate remarks had created friction with their European allies at a time when American diplomacy was focused on cementing relations and resisting the Communist challenge. Looking back at everything that had happened since then, Jane could not help wondering if she had made powerful enemies in the defense establishment. If her dissenting views had aroused the first stirrings of suspicion and disapproval, planting the seeds that led to her loyalty investigation and eventual indictment.

Jane's suspicions were borne out in late 1957 when the House Committee on Un-American Activities began investigating her wartime activities in Indonesia. The notion that one of the OSS's agents in Indonesia was a spy fit in perfectly with HUAC's theory that all the policy difficulties in that part of the world derived from communist subversion of the U.S. government. A leading proponent of this argument, Major General Charles Willoughby, MacArthur's former chief of intelligence, charged that the current crisis in Indonesia could be "traced directly to communist subversives who had 'induced the United States Government to champion Sukarno,'" whom he labeled a Japanese collaborator and communist sympathizer.*

---

* Andrew Roadnight, *United States Policy Towards Indonesia in the Truman and Eisenhower Years* (New York: MacMillan), p. 154.

Every time Julia and Paul had been confronted with the possibility of Jane's suspect loyalty in the past two years, they had rejected it. Every instinct they had told them she was not capable of such duplicity. In all the time they had known her, Jane's utopian beliefs and assorted political causes had never amounted to anything in the way of the ideological commitment it would take to become a traitor. The only thing she had ever seemed really committed to was her painting—and having a good time. They decided to stick by their earlier conclusion: Jane might be indiscreet, but she was not dishonest. "We talked about it and Julia and I shared the same feeling," Betty recalled. "Jane might have been foolish at times, she might have said things that were unwise, and kept company with all kinds of crazy characters. So what? That would be entirely in character for her. But a spy, definitely not."

The idea that she could be a traitor was absurd. "Jane was a wonderful person who had done so much during the war," Betty insisted. "The idea that anyone could suspect that she wasn't 'a loyal American' was just incredible to me." In the hellish months that followed the indictment, Betty received several letters from Jane. "They were very sad, full of the things the FBI was doing to her and how unhappy she was. They were still trying to prove she was guilty. But Jane had been framed. There was nothing to prove."

Jane's friends and former colleagues were divided as to her culpability. There were plenty of people who had no trouble believing she was subversive and were quick to say they had never trusted her. A number of her old OSS colleagues, however, kept faith with her and sent letters expressing their support and offering assistance. Jane never received them. "She was very hurt by it," Susan recalled. "It seems many of their letters were 'lifted,' so they never heard from many of their friends and family members all during that dreadful time. It made them feel abandoned. Jane was so angry about it that she cut herself off from everyone. She refused to call or write anyone from home. It was a typical act of arrogance on her part."

Jane was resigned to life in exile. She was a fugitive from justice in her own country and a political prisoner in France, unable to venture beyond its borders without risking arrest and extradition. It was the peculiar, precarious existence of the stateless. The first months were the most difficult. In late 1957, the French authorities asked Jane and George to surrender their identity papers and offered them a choice: they could leave France for whatever country would have them or agree to live for an "unspecified period" in the *département* of Gard, in southern France. The Gard was where the French administration banished persons under *assignés à résidence* (forced residence orders) while their legal cases were under review. It was also where the French regularly stowed members of parliament who had misbehaved or were being penalized for one reason or another. Jane and George had not been accused of any crime, but they were "guests" of a foreign government and this was an invitation they could not refuse. Of course, they opted for the Gard and rented a house in the Cévennes region in which to wait out their sentence.

After being banished for almost a year, they were allowed to return to Paris to pick up the pieces of their life. Their French identity cards were restored, and they went back to being "ordinary people again." After initially feeling terribly humiliated by their outlaw status, Jane had come to learn that the French did not attach the same disgrace to political dissidents. Being labeled a Communist carried no social stigma; in some circles, it was almost a badge of honor. They were warmly received by their neighbors and local shopkeepers on rue Mazarine and quietly protected as old residents of their *quartier*. Jane's parents wanted to hire a new set of lawyers to see if they could get the indictment quashed, but she told them not to bother. It would be throwing good money after bad. "Simply to be accused of being Soviet spies in the climate of the 1950s was to be automatically found guilty by the courts and the press, even on the testimony of a madman, Soble, and of a psychopathic liar, Morros." She had no hope of rehabilitation and did not want it.

Jane turned her back on America. She refused to see old friends. She severed all her ties with the past. Betty stopped receiving letters. After a Christmas card with a brief, scribbled note, she heard nothing more. She knew of no one from their old gang who was still in contact with Jane, not even Julia and Paul. She was not sure, in all honesty, how hard they tried to keep in touch. Betty's husband had just been appointed to a big job; as deputy assistant secretary of defense for international security affairs, he had to tread carefully. He wanted her to be careful, too. "Julia was braver," she said. "Perhaps, because of her work, she could afford to be. But Paul had a government job. Jane made him nervous and with good reason. He knew he had to steer clear of the whole situation. That's just the way it was then."

In 1959, Paul received another transfer abroad, this time to Norway. It would be their last post. After two uneventful years in Oslo, Paul decided he wanted to retire. He was sixty years old and fed up with working for a government bureaucracy he had never really liked in the first place. He was done scaling the career ladder. He knew perfectly well he would advance no higher. He wanted to devote himself full-time to his painting, photography, writing, and music, which he had relegated to weekend hobbies for too long. Julia, who was tired of moving her kitchen every few years, was more than ready to try another way of life. "We decided we would take a gamble," recalled Paul. "We said, 'O.K., we'll quit and we'll go back home and be Americans and we'll see what happens." They did not have much in the way of savings left and were not certain what they would live on. Julia could give cooking lessons, and perhaps, if her book was well received, she could become a food writer for a magazine and he could take the pictures to accompany her articles. For Paul, it was all part of the adventure. "You never know what's going to happen unless you do it," he challenged Julia. "It's all theory until you subject it to the 'operational proof.'"

They decided to settle in Boston, Paul's old home base, because California at that point "seemed so far away." They found an old clapboard house in Cambridge they could just afford. It had formerly been owned by the Harvard philosopher Josiah Royce and so would provide a good, solid intellectual foundation for their new life. Paul threw himself into designing an elaborate kitchen / cooking laboratory he called Julia's "war room," while she put the finishing touches on her opus, now ten years in the making. The original manuscript had run to 850 pages, so huge that even after Julia and her two coauthors reluctantly hacked it down to 684 pages it was still rejected by Houghton Mifflin as overly long and formidable for the average American housewife. Julia had just about given up hope when Alfred A. Knopf agreed to publish it in all its unwieldy glory. Paul helped her with the proofreading and indexing and took hundreds of photographs from which a sketch artist made the final drawings for the book. *Mastering the Art of French Cooking* came out in the fall of 1961. It created an immediate sensation. The book received overwhelming praise and was hailed by the *New York Times* food critic Craig Claiborne as "the most comprehensive, laudable, and monumental work on the subject." An appearance at Boston's public television station, WGBH, four months later to promote the book led to her being asked to tape three pilot programs on cooking. The result was the development of her popular television series *The French Chef.*

Julia, who had been in search of a career her whole life, stepped eagerly into the limelight. Her "bigness," once the cause of so much grief, made her a natural star. Paul stayed in the wings, becoming her protective manager as well as "prime dishwasher and baggage carrier." They made a splendid team. Julia, acknowledging his "enormous" contribution, never spoke of her work except in the plural. "We do everything together," she would tell journalists fascinated by their devoted partnership.

Reflecting on her late-in-life success, Julia would often say, "The war made me." She was very nostalgic about her years overseas with the OSS, when she finally came into her own, fell in love, and first tasted the spicy Indian curries and savory Chinese dishes that awakened her senses and her deep affinity for food. Yet she was never inclined to romanticize the past, remaining characteristically clear-eyed and forthright about the demagoguery that had blighted the postwar period. She and Paul had escaped relatively unscathed, but too many friends had not been as fortunate. For all that those years had brought them, they could never look back on that time, and Paul's "shameful episode," without bitter regret, like "the taste of ashes" in their mouths.

EPILOGUE

JANE FOSTER lived in exile in Paris for another two decades. It was a quiet, cosseted existence, underpinned by a generous monthly income from her indulgent parents. She moved to an ancient, elegant apartment at 10 rue Chanoinesse on Ile de la Cité, an island in the very heart of medieval Paris, just steps from Notre Dame. In time, she acquired a second home, a fifteenth-century stone cottage in the Dordogne region in southwestern France. Jane created a small studio in her apartment and continued to paint and to exhibit her work. She kept up with a few old friends, meeting them for drinks on Tuesdays at Harry's Bar. She never lost her taste for the finer things in life. She was always beautifully dressed in Chanel and Dior, her once-unruly mane of blond curls coiffed to perfection. George, who had always been nattily attired, wore hand-tailored suits, Burberry coats, and Gucci shoes. In his later years, he carried a brass tipped cane. They frequented five-star restaurants and entertained lavishly at home, where Jane took wicked pleasure in laying her table with copious settings of family silver and then waited to see which of her guests knew what to do with the ice cream fork. They were by all accounts convivial hosts, and loved to discuss current affairs and trade gossip. The one rule that was always observed was that no one made any reference to the past unpleasantness. "It all receded into myth," recalled Susan, a frequent visitor to the Ile de la Cité apartment in the 1960s and 1970s. "And it was never spoken of."

Despite her claim to have followed the example of Sara and Gerald Murphy, the wealthy, handsome members of the so-called Lost Generation who famously remarked, "Living well is the best revenge," Jane's comfortable expatriate life never afforded her much in the way of happiness or satisfaction. She defiantly declared she would "never go home again" but at the same time was haunted by the tenuousness of her fugitive status. For years she suffered from the recurrent nightmare that she was trapped on a ship or plane headed for the United States and unable to get off or turn back, unable to save herself from the terrible fate that awaited her there. When she awoke, "seized by terror," it would come as a huge relief to find herself safe and sound within the familiar four walls of her Paris bedroom. "The worst part of the dream," she wrote obliquely, "was that I always realized that I did it myself and that nobody forced me." She did not find much solace in her marriage. She and George continued to drink and squabble, and close friends were often dismayed by his surly moods and violent outbursts. The two separated for a time, then drifted back together. They were miserable together, but they had shared the same lifeboat too long to know how to survive apart.

Then, in 1970, as her eighty-eight-year-old father lay dying in a San Francisco hospital and her eighty-year-old mother, who was already sick with cancer, was left to cope on her own, Jane suddenly wanted nothing more than to be allowed to return home. Her longtime New York attorney, Leonard Boudin, and the lawyer her parents retained from a white-glove San Francisco firm, both warned her not to risk traveling to the United States. There was still a warrant out for her arrest. In jail, she would be of no help to her ailing parents. Her mother called and begged her not to come. Desperate, Jane asked Boudin to contact the Justice Department to see if there was anything that could be done to improve her legal standing.

After ordering a review of the case, Chief Judge Sydney Sugarman of the United States District Court for the Southern District of New York requested advice from the FBI and the Department of Internal Security on any changes that might have occurred in the intervening years. The FBI advised that it had received identical inquiries concerning the

Zlatovskis in Paris and the Sterns in Prague. As the bureau regarded the two cases as "intrinsically tied together" from the very inception of the conspiracy, all aspects of their situations would need to be considered together. More than thirteen years had elapsed since the indictment, and both of the principal witnesses against the subjects—Boris Morros and Jack Soble—had since died. A FBI memo dated August 4, 1970, stated, "While it would appear difficult to sustain prosecution against these subjects in the absence of the aforementioned witnesses, the existence of the outstanding indictment appears to be a major deterrent against the return of these persons to the U.S." While it was "doubtful" that Jane could be prosecuted successfully, the bureau noted that Myra Soble was still alive and living in New York, and of sound mind, and her testimony could "possibly be of value." The memo concluded that in view of the subjects' past history and activities, "the Bureau would consider their presence in the U.S. to constitute a grave danger to the internal security." The Justice Department informed Boudin that the indictment would not be dismissed. If his client attempted to reenter the United States, she would be arrested upon arrival.

The news came as a terrible blow to Jane. It meant she would be unable to say good-bye to her father, who had seen her through such terrible times and, whatever his private reservations, had been unwavering in his support. She saw it as a final act of cruelty by a heartless country. When the Greek actress Melina Mercouri, who had been stripped of her Greek citizenship and was on the wanted list for her opposition to the military dictatorship in her country, had petitioned for the right to return to Athens to attend her father's funeral, even the "Fascist junta colonels ruling Greece," Jane wrote scathingly, "still had the decency to give her a twenty-four-hour safe conduct." That the "non-fascist American government" refused to extend her the same courtesy was something she would "never forget nor forgive." Jane's mother buried her husband in June 1971 and a few weeks later underwent surgery. She survived and rallied sufficiently to fly to Paris, where she remained until her death two years later. In 1976, Jane and George again petitioned to return to the United States, to no avail. Then, to their surprise and relief, after two decades of legal maneuvering they were granted

French citizenship. It meant they could at last fulfill their long-held desire to travel. They celebrated by taking a drunken cruise through the Greek islands.

Jane had been able to keep going as long as she had her parents, but with their deaths she lost the last remaining ballast in her life. Even though she inherited a substantial sum—she was convinced a government conspiracy lay behind the maddeningly slow probate—she grew increasingly melancholy. She withdrew from the world and devoted herself to her painting. When she was diagnosed with macular degeneration, and could no longer see to paint, she lost all interest in living. After a routine operation on her leg for phlebitis, from which her doctors fully expected her to recover, she refused to walk or make any effort to get better, despite the danger of developing a blood clot. She spent her days sitting by the window of her apartment brooding. She dictated her memoir from that perch, finishing the last chapter just before her death from thrombosis on September 24, 1979. "She willed herself to die at age sixty-seven," said Susan. "She was a very bitter, unhappy woman at the end."

After the funeral, held at the small side chapel of Notre Dame, Susan had tea with Jane's closest friend and former nurse, Mazella Swarbrick, and received an appalling account of George's behavior. His womanizing, which had always been a problem, continued unabated, and he had invited all kinds of companions back to the apartment. He had "opened Jane's closets to his *putains* [whores]," she reported with disgust, and allowed them to paw through her finery. All of her beautiful clothes, her minks and jewels, were gone. Jane, of course, had left no will—when had her affairs ever been in order?—and George had taken malicious pleasure in dispersing her belongings at whim. It was George who arranged for the posthumous publication of Jane's memoir, *An UnAmerican Lady,* by the London publisher Sidgwick & Jackson in 1980. He personally oversaw the editing process and approved the title and provocative cover, a photograph of Jane superimposed on the American flag. His involvement, however peripheral, places a question mark by her memoir—already a highly selective set of revelations—as a reliable record of Jane's experience.

In any autobiography, there are usually reasonable doubts about the credibility of the author's account of the most controversial events, but in Jane's case there is compelling evidence that she refused to confront the truth about herself at the most fundamental level, her denial and self-delusion casting doubt on her whole story. A passionate idealist, she had spent her whole adult life cultivating an image of herself as a humanitarian, an individual of great heart and deep principle. She had joined the Communist Party for the best of reasons, believing she could help make the world a better place. She had joined the OSS in much the same spirit and had volunteered for dangerous assignments, fully committed to the idea that the liberation of the poor and oppressed was something worth fighting for. But in her eagerness to devote herself to the cause of the downtrodden, she blithely put her faith in the hands of a group of Communist Party activists, even when their ideological fervor and conspiratorial arrangements caused her to have doubts. She was so determined to prove her commitment—to prove she was not just another wealthy dilettante who had latched onto the proletariat cause—and so eager for their acceptance and approval that she turned a blind eye to what was going on until it was too late to turn back.

It is impossible to read her saga without being haunted by one question: When Jane told the DST she had been deceived by Martha Dodd Stern and Boris Morros and deliberately misled into working for the Soviets under the guise of doing odd jobs for the Party, was she telling the truth? Or was it, at least in part, a case of wishful thinking? Surely she was too intelligent, and too sharp, not to have seen through them eventually. And when she finally realized she was working for the NKVD, did she allow herself to be further drawn into its scheme rather than risk incriminating herself and her entire circle of friends? For all her wit and charm and generosity of spirit, the woman who emerges from the final chapters of her book seems tremendously insecure, lonely, and adrift, a rudderless vessel. She knew she had fallen in with bad company but was incapable of breaking away. Instead, she blundered on, lying to herself and others, at all times her own worst enemy.

On the last page of her memoir, she identifies herself with the martyrs of the McCarthy era, whose lives were "scarred and ruined" by the anti-Communist hysteria and by the people who had created it, "motivated by their greed for notoriety, money, and, above all, power." There is no doubt that in their relentless drive to root out spies in America, McCarthy and his followers did more harm to the country, and the constitutional liberties they held so dear, than the handful of conspiracies they managed to unmask. In numbering herself among the persecuted, however, Jane was attempting to obscure her own culpability under the cover of a greater tragedy. Nothing can undo the damage done by McCarthy's assault on the State Department and the ravaging effects of the fear and hatred he unleashed. But at the same time, no one was more to blame for Jane's foolishness and misguided loyalties and ultimate naïveté in allowing herself to be hustled and entrapped by the unscrupulous Boris Morros than she herself. Jane was never an archvillain, smuggling out nuclear secrets and imperiling the security of the nation, but she was not as innocent as she pretended. To the end, she clung resolutely to her vision of herself as a victim, a hapless dreamer who stumbled into a den of traitors, rewriting history the way alcoholics excuse the previous night's transgressions, always making someone else responsible for leading them astray.

While Jane never confessed in her memoir to engaging in espionage, she does acknowledge an ambiguous form of guilt in a telling quote from Aeschylus's *Prometheus Bound:*

> With open eyes, with willing mind I erred. I do not deny it.
> Mankind I helped but could not help myself. Yet I dreamed
> not that here in this savage solitary gorge, on the high rock,
> I should waste away beneath such torments.

A snob to the core, Jane, in a final act of unreconstructed bourgeois class consciousness, arranged to be buried in the famous Père Lachaise Cemetery, home to a who's who of painters, poets, and musicians and known as "the grandest address in Paris." After George died in 1985, his ashes were added to her crypt.

JULIA and PAUL CHILD made Cambridge, Massachusetts, their home for the next thirty-two years. After three houses in Washington, two in Marseille, one in Paris, one in Bonn, and one in Oslo, they never wanted to move again. Once Paul had installed Julia's immense *batterie de cuisine*, with every pot and pan hung in its place on the green pegboard lining the kitchen walls, everything from cheese graters to colanders and sieves sorted, and more than seventy-five separate pieces of equipment meticulously arranged in a fashion "suitable for framing," it was impossible to imagine ever doing it again. Her now-famous kitchen is on display at the Smithsonian National Museum of American History in Washington, D.C.

For a late starter, Julia went on to become a phenomenal success. The first volume of *Mastering the Art of French Cooking* has sold more than thirty million copies to date, and she went on to coauthor a hefty sequel, as well as eight more cookbooks. Her *French Chef* television series ran on PBS for ten years and turned Julia into a household name—and the quintessential television chef. What made Julia so appealing, apart from the fact that she was a natural ham, was that she was something entirely new and unexpected: with her commanding physical presence, intelligence, and operatic voice, she was a whisk-wielding, apron-clad marvel. She credited her incredible ad-libbing skills to the years she spent attending embassy cocktail parties with Paul, where she learned to disarm the stuffiest foreign diplomats with her down-to-earth American humor and entertaining anecdotes. She never developed an ounce of smugness about her enormous popularity. Nor did she ever consider moving to commercial television or cashing in on her name by accepting any kind of product sponsorship. "We have no desire for mink coats, yachts, or Cadillacs," she once explained. "We're perfectly happy just the way we are." They did allow themselves one big splurge: in 1965, flush from the royalties of her first book, Julia and Paul built their dream house in Provence, in the small town of Plascassier above the hills of Cannes. For the next two decades, they spent six months of every year at "La Peetch," short for La Pitchoune (The Little One), as they called their French hideaway.

Julia inspired legions of television chefs, a classic *Saturday Night Live* parody—which she loved and kept a copy of by her television set—and the musical *Bon Appétit!* starring Jean Stapleton. An absolute original, Julia did not take kindly to imitators. One fan she reportedly did not approve of was the blogger Julie Powell, with her mission to cook every recipe in *Mastering the Art of French Cooking*—a stunt on which Powell based a best-selling book, *Julie and Julia: 365 Days, 524 Recipes, 1 Tiny Apartment Kitchen,* which in turn inspired a movie. The Nora Ephron film, which also drew on Julia's memoir, *My Life in France,* written with her nephew Alex Prud'homme, charmingly evokes the Childs' marriage, with Meryl Streep and Stanley Tucci as Julia and Paul.

Julia was continually grateful that she had found true love, and that it in turn had led her to a second love affair with cooking and to such a joyous career. Paul was content in his supporting role, making himself quietly indispensable. Every morning, he and Julia would sit at their kitchen table and discuss the workday ahead, discussing plans for her new show and downing oceans of lapsang souchong. Despite their disparate personalities, what they had in common was their slow, careful approach to work and their dedication to perfection. After hours of laboring over scripts and shooting scenes for *The French Chef* at WGBH, they would often slip away to Joyce Chen, their favorite Chinese restaurant in Cambridge. Julia rarely cooked anything Asian style, believing that a lifetime was barely long enough to learn the French cuisine, but she confessed she could happily "live on Chinese food." It reminded her and Paul of the old days, and all the wonderful meals they shared in Chungking when they were courting.

They remained devoted to each other. Even during the most hectic years of book promotion, they were rarely apart. When Paul, who was ten years her senior, began to fade with age, Julia faithfully took him on the road with her, and always made sure he had a front-row seat at her cooking demonstrations. He would watch the clock, advise her to speak louder, and lead the applause. After a series of strokes in 1989, he entered a nursing home in Fairlawn, Massachusetts. Their forty-eight-year partnership ended with his death in 1994 at the age of ninety-two. Julia lived another decade, returning to her native California in her last years, and died on August 13, 2004, two days before her ninety-second birthday.

There is no evidence that on their many trips to Paris Julia and Paul ever saw Jane again. Nevertheless, in the hundreds of interviews she gave over the course of her career, Julia never said a word against her former OSS colleague. As the former head of the Registry, she was much too disciplined at keeping secrets to let anything slip. As a friend, she was far too loyal to speak out of turn or sit in judgment. Not until 1991, in a lengthy oral history interview for the Association of Diplomatic Studies and Training, did Julia open up about her relationship with that "fascinating and amusing girl, Jane Foster," reminiscing about her fondly for a few minutes before adding matter-of-factly, "who turned out to be a Russian agent."

BETTY MACDONALD became a widow quite without warning in May 1959 when her husband, Richard Heppner, died of a heart attack at age forty-nine. Betty, who worked in a variety of government jobs after the war, joined the CIA as an operations officer and continued to work for the agency until her retirement in 1973. By then, she had married Frederick B. McIntosh, a veteran World War II fighter pilot, and settled in Leesburg, Virginia. In addition to her wartime memoir, *Undercover Girl,* she wrote the highly praised *Sisterhood of Spies: The Women of the OSS,* published by the Naval Institute Press in 1998. She has also penned two children's books, *Inky* and *Palace Under the Sea.* For many years she served as editor of *The OSS Society Newsletter.* In the early 1980s, while in Paris on business, Betty decided to look up Jane. She discovered she was too late and instead had a brief, awkward visit with George. He was perfectly polite but struck her again as "a strange man" and not particularly to her liking. She soon made her apologies and left to pay her respects at Jane's grave. To this day, Betty remains unshaken in her conviction that her friend and former OSS colleague was never a spy.

MARTHA DODD STERN and her husband, ALFRED, remained in exile for the rest of their lives. Fleeing to Prague, they reportedly requested permission to live in Moscow but after a brief sojourn in Russia and Eastern Europe returned to the Czech capital. By all accounts, they enjoyed a privileged life in Prague, where they lived in a sprawling three-story villa and were treated as local celebrities. A KGB document indicates that from 1963 to 1970 they made their home in Havana, after Martha fell in love with the romance of the Cuban revolution. The Sterns eventually became disappointed with the Cuban political scene and disillusioned with life in such a desperately poor country and returned to Czechoslovakia. In November 1972, they walked into the American Embassy in Prague and applied for passports. They retained Leonard Boudin, petitioned to return to the United States, and began protracted negotiations to avoid prosecution and imprisonment on their return. The Sterns, according to their lawyer, were getting on in age and were no longer happy with life behind the Iron Curtain. The Justice Department took the position that if the Sterns wanted to return to the United States, then they needed to cooperate as witnesses: they would have to agree to meet in a neutral country and tell the FBI all they knew about Soviet espionage operations in America during the 1940s and 1950s. The FBI field office in New York emphasized to Washington that the accused spies could furnish worthwhile information and "every effort should be made to obtain the Sterns' story prior to their entrance in the United States."

The Sterns refused to talk. But their passport application placed the government in something of a quandary: with the main witnesses against them deceased and with no way to sustain a prosecution for espionage conspiracy, the State Department had no real grounds for denying them passports. In an effort to strengthen its case against the Sterns, the FBI considered approaching Jane and George Zlatovski to see if they would agree to be interviewed. If they were amenable, the bureau could send a special agent acquainted with their case to Paris to question them "concerning their knowledge of the Sterns and Soviet espionage operations in the U.S." Jane and George would be offered immunity in return for their testimony. In the end this strategy was vetoed and the matter dragged on for years without resolution.

In 1979, the twenty-two-year-old indictment against the Sterns was finally dropped, in part due to the couple's advanced age and the absence of witnesses against them. Their lawyer, Victor Rabinowitz, Boudin's longtime partner, described the indictment as "a very grave injustice of the McCarthy era," and the dismissal, the result of almost ten years of talks with the FBI and the Justice Department, as "a belated effort to set things straight." The Sterns never exercised their right to return. Their statements to the FBI indicated their dread of any publicity that might revive interest in their infamous case. They were "too old," Martha wrote a friend, "to pull up roots."

When the Sterns learned that Jane had written a memoir, they considered suing to stop its publication until their lawyers convinced them there was little they could do. They were very unhappy with Jane's portrayal of them but took consolation in the book's poor sales and inability to find a publisher outside England. Alfred Stern died of cancer in Prague in 1986. Martha Dodd Stern remained in exile and died in 1990. Their son, Bobby, whose childhood was blighted by their life in exile, developed a "nervous condition" that was later diagnosed as schizophrenia. Dr. Judd Marmor, an eminent Los Angeles psychiatrist who saw Bobby at the Sterns' request, later wrote them that despite his biochemical vulnerability, their son "must be considered one of the unfortunate victimized innocent bystanders of the whole miserable McCarthy era."

BORIS MORROS chronicled his adventures in a melodramatic book, *My Ten Years as a Counterspy,* published by Viking Press in 1959. He immediately began negotiating to sell the film rights, and it was made into a pseudodocumentary-style, anti-Communist propaganda film, *Man on a String,* starring Ernest Borgnine as "Boris Mitrov," an even more fictionalized version of the FBI's "special special agent." The book also helped spawn a television series, *The Spy Next Door.* Morros's life did not have the happy ending he had scripted: a few months after he was unmasked as a counterspy, his wife, Catherine, filed for legal separation. In October 1957, she alleged cruelty against him in her Superior Court suit for separate maintenance and charged that Morros had even failed in recent years to provide support for his ninety-eight-year-old father, the same man he had theoretically become a Soviet agent to protect. Morros died of cancer on January 8, 1963. *The New York Times* reported his age as seventy-three, while other newspapers gave it as sixty-eight. As Jane observed in her memoir, "it is absolutely typical of his whole lying life that no one, probably not even the FBI/CIA, ever knew the true facts about him. Undoubtedly he himself no longer knew truth from fiction." One thing is certain: Morros knew how to market himself as a spy—whether it was to Moscow, Washington, or Hollywood—and he played his part to the hilt.

JACK and MYRA SOBLE: After their arrest in January 1957 as Russian spies, Jack and Myra Soble were questioned scores of times by the FBI, and were persuaded to testify against friends and family members in their espionage ring in return for drastically reduced sentences. Nearly four years later, on November 30, 1960, their statements led to the indictment of Jack's brother, Dr. Robert A. Soblen (he reportedly added an *n* to his name to differentiate himself from his physician-wife), on espionage charges. Soblen, a fifty-nine-year-old psychiatrist, pleaded not guilty to conspiring to obtain material relating to national defense for the Soviet Union, both during World War II and thereafter. Jack Soble, one of the government's main sources of allegations against Jane, would be the prosecution's star witness, which meant that for the first time his testimony would be exposed to the rules of evidence in a court of law. (As the Sobles had both made deals, and both the Sterns and the Zlatovskis had declined to return to the United States to stand trial, the government had never had to show any proof of their crimes.) That, during his years in jail, Jack Soble had suffered a mental breakdown, twice attempted suicide, and received twenty shock treatments before being found "mentally competent" to testify against his brother apparently did nothing to diminish the government's faith in his credibility.

On June 19, 1961, the case *United States v. Dr. Robert A. Soblen* opened to a packed federal courthouse at Foley Square in New York, featuring the first public appearance of a principal player in what one newspaper called "the biggest spy ring smashed in this country since atom spies Julius and Ethel Rosenberg went to the chair." It turned out that the defendant, Dr. Soblen, was in an advanced stage of lymphatic leukemia, and appeared frail and heavily medicated in his wheelchair. Jack Soble testified at length about their political activities in Lithuania in the 1920s and 1930s, and later in Germany, where they joined the

Communist Party and supported its "Trotskyite wing," and sometime in 1940 begun gathering information for the Soviet Union, employing many family members in their ring. Under cross-examination by the defense counsel Joseph Brill, Jack Soble admitted to being a desperate man forced to take desperate measures. When asked, for example, if he had done the things reported in the sensational *Journal-American* articles detailing his exploits with Martha Dodd Stern and Jane Foster, he denied both their accuracy and their authorship, and explained he had agreed to their publication sight unseen because he needed the money. He also admitted to making up material for Boris Morros to feed to the Russians, fearing that Morros would make good on his threat to expose him to the FBI if he did not give him the reports, which Soble described as "lies and wrong things about what I did in this country."

After nearly four weeks of trial, during which the defendant's condition worsened to the point that he was too weak to take the stand, the defense rested without calling a single witness and asserted that the government had failed to present a prima facie case. In just a little over an hour, the jury brought in its guilty verdict. On August 7, the day of sentencing, two former OSS men—H. Stuart Hughes, a Harvard professor of history, and Herbert Marcuse, a Brandeis professor of philosophy—came forward and raised serious doubts about some of the key testimony in the trial concerning information about the atom bomb project, which Soblen was accused of passing on to the Soviet Union. They argued that it could not have come from the two low-level German refugees then employed in the Biographical Records section of the OSS. Both professors offered to testify at a new trial. Judge William B. Herlands asserted that Soblen could request a new trial after sentencing and then proceeded to hand down a life sentence, stating firmly, "A spy is a spy no matter what his health may be."

On August 31, 1962, Jack Soble was paroled for "good behavior" after serving five and a half years. A week later, his brother, who had jumped bail and fled the United States for England, and was in Brixton prison awaiting extradition, committed suicide by taking an overdose of drugs. Robert Soblen had made a dramatic entry into England on July 1 after an earlier attempt to seek asylum in Israel failed and he was forced by Israeli authorities to leave. As his chartered El Al flight returning him to New York neared London, Soblen cut his wrists and stabbed himself in the stomach; he later stated that this was not a suicide attempt but a carefully designed ploy to enter Britain, where he had hoped to prove his innocence. Jack Soble had five years to think about what he had done to his brother before he died in 1967.

Myra Soble served only four years. Afterward, she took an assumed name and made a new life for herself in New York City, where she was employed at an accounting firm. On July 5, 1991, she received a full pardon from President George H. W. Bush. Myra Soble died in 1992.

THEODORE H. WHITE was officially cleared of all charges of subversion two days before Christmas 1954, just three weeks after Senator McCarthy's methods were condemned by the full Senate. Although he was granted a spotless new passport, "with all the dirty restrictions of the old wiped out," he did not immediately recover his self-confidence and former zeal. He was sufficiently traumatized by the loyalty-security hearing that he did not write anther word about China between 1954 and 1972 and wrote only four articles about Vietnam. For years, he also deliberately avoided reporting about foreign policy and defense— loaded topics during the Cold War. In his memoir, *In Search of History,* he castigated himself for ignoring those subjects because "too much danger lurked there; and for that shirking I am now ashamed."

White returned from his "wilderness" years in France and threw himself into analyzing domestic American politics, becoming one of the country's foremost historians with *The Making of the President, 1960* and the series of books that followed. He died of a heart attack in New York in 1986. Looking back on the ultimate impact of McCarthyism, White observed that its "warping effect" not only affected his own life but affected the country for decades to come:

> McCarthy's most lasting effect on American history may well have been on its foreign policy—for a direct line runs between McCarthy's terrorizing of the Foreign Service of the United States State Department and the ultimate tragedy of America's war in Vietnam . . .

The wrong done by the McCarthy lancers, under McCarthy leadership, was to poke out the eyes and ears of the State Department on Asian Affairs, to blind American foreign policy. And thus flying blind into the murk of Asian politics, American diplomacy carried American honor, resources, and lives into the triple-canopied jungles and green-carpeted hills of Vietnam, where all crashed.

APPENDIX

In the summer of 1995, the CIA and the National Security Agency (NSA) released the first group of "Venona" decrypts, translations of coded Soviet intelligence messages dealing with espionage operations in America between 1940 and 1948. "Venona" was the fanciful code word assigned to the highly classified government project, which began in 1943 and was formally closed in 1980, in order to limit access to the cryptanalytic breakthrough that finally made it possible to crack the Russian secret code. Approximately 2,900 Soviet diplomatic telegrams, intercepted by the U.S. Army's Signal Intelligence Service (a precursor to the NSA), have now been painstakingly decoded and deciphered, allowing experts to read portions of the secret cables. The majority of the KGB communications were translated and made available to the U.S. government by 1945, which meant that intelligence officials were in possession of evidence about a wide variety of Soviet espionage operations—everything from the Rosenbergs' atomic spying to the Soble ring—that was not made public at the time of their controversial cases. The release of so much new evidence has inevitably led to a certain amount of revisionism in terms of the guilt of many of the accused Soviet spies from that era, and analyzing and interpreting the full meaning of the Venona haul will doubtless keep historians, journalists, and authors busy for years to come.

The deciphered Venona cables pertinent to Jane Foster's case suggest she lied in her memoir about the purely social and happenstance nature of her contacts with Martha Dodd Stern, Jack Soble, and Boris Morros. A telegram from Vasily Zarubin, a KGB general operating in the United States under the alias Zubilin, informed Moscow in June 1942 of a possible new source: [UNRECOVERED CODE GROUP] LIZA [MARTHA DODD STERN], WE ARE CULTIVATING THE AMERICAN JANE FOSTER WITH A VIEW TO SIGN- ING HER ON. SHE IS ABOUT 30 YEARS OLD AND WORKS IN WASHINGTON IN THE DUTCH [TWO UNRECOVERED CODE GROUPS] TRANSLATOR OF MALAY LANGUAGES. . . . SHE IS A FELLOWCOUNTRYWOMAN [COMMUNIST PARTY OF THE SOVIET UNION, OR CPSU, MEMBER]. SHE IS DESCRIBED BY THE FELLOWCOUNTRYMEN [CPSU] AS A [UNRECOVERED CODE GROUP], DEDICATED PERSON. In subsequent Venona messages from 1943 and 1944, Jane, identified by her code name "Slang," is described as providing information, but these memos are incomplete and extremely vague. It is impossible to tell if Jane was simply being indiscreet and talking about information gleaned from her job that the author of the memo felt would be of in- terest to Moscow or actually "reporting" the information to her Soviet handler.

There are only a handful of Venona decrypts referring directly to Jane, and while incriminating they are not conclusive evidence that she was a Soviet spy. To begin with, the translations are woefully incom- plete: the cryptanalysts were able to decipher only portions of the coded telegrams, leaving gaps that could alter the meaning of the messages. In addition, all of the messages are secondhand accounts by Zarubin or another Soviet handler reporting to the KGB about what various American sources—Martha Dodd Stern or Jack Soble or Morros—said or claimed to have done. As a result, inaccuracies abound. For example, Morros's report in one cable that Jane told him she was recruited by Martha Dodd Stern in 1938, when she was actually still in Batavia, was wrong and demonstrates the danger of hearsay. Morros was either mis- taken or misinformed. Adding to the confusion, they all were assigned code names, and these code names changed over time and are often only half deciphered, so the cryptanalysts made educated guesses as to their identities.

The decrypts are also ambiguous and open to interpretation. The Zarubin telegram from 1942 is speculative in nature, merely outlining their plan to recruit Jane in the future. While Zarubin was later convinced Jane was working as an agent and passing them information, the reports are still all secondhand, and Jane's state of mind—whether she was under the impression she was helping the Sterns and the Communist cause or was fully cognizant that she was serving Soviet intelligence—is unclear. Finally, given all the testimony on record from the Sobles and other Soviet recruits to the effect that they were under enormous pressure to keep Moscow supplied with information, and Jack Soble's admission under oath in the Soblen trial that he told Morros "lies" just to keep him happy, there is no way to be certain of the accuracy or verisimilitude of these messages. They all had an obvious interest in exaggerating their progress to their Soviet handlers, and their inflated claims about new recruits and espionage coups may have been closer to empty boasts than actual achievements.

Apart from the Venona decrypts, a wealth of new material about Soviet espionage has also come to light in recent years from the notebooks of a former KGB officer, Alexander Vassiliev, who was permitted unprecedented access to Stalin-era intelligence archives in 1993. Sorting through Vassiliev's extensive notebooks of transcribed KGB material, two historians, John Earl Haynes and Harvey Klehr, have provided a thorough and carefully constructed account of Soviet intelligence operations in the United States during the 1930s and 1940s. These official communications include much new material about the Soble ring and the activities of the double agent Boris Morros. There are KGB memos referring to Jane and George, confirming the Venona cables and again implicating the pair as members of the Soble network. In one KGB memo, Zarubin listed "'Slang,' Jane . . . of the Far Eastern Department of the 'cabin' [OSS]" as one of the sources recruited under his watch. In a later retrospective memo dated 1957, he wrote, "On a lead from 'Liza' the agent 'Slang' was recruited, followed by 'Slang's' husband, the agent 'Rector,' who once worked for American counterintelligence in

Austria." The authors go on to observe that the notebooks reveal that the KGB developed "more than a dozen sources in the OSS," eleven of whom were "secret Communists" who came to the KGB via the American Communist Party, which is the same route Jane followed.

The Vassiliev notebooks, like the Venona transcripts, provide a fascinating glimpse into the inner workings of Soviet espionage, but it is impossible to simply accept the claims of the KGB authors or their American sources as fact. They were all too adept at spinning their successes and failures to have any of their accounts taken at face value. Once again, Vassiliev's access was partial and restricted, and, as Haynes and Klehr are careful to note, "even contemporaneous documents can sometimes mislead because their author didn't correctly understand the events he was reporting for some reason, harbored prejudices and assumptions that distorted what was reported, or for self-promotion or self-protection distorted what actually happened."

In spite of all these caveats, the existence of multiple documentary sources describing Jane Foster and George Zlatovski as Soviet assets establishes that they were deeply enmeshed in the Soble espionage ring. How they became caught up in the Soviet network, and whether or not there were mitigating circumstances, is another matter. The fact remains that in her book Jane never acknowledged even being aware of any Soviet espionage, let alone becoming a participant, and lied about the true nature of her complicated relationship with the Sterns, the Sobles, and Boris Morros. Even at the end of her life, she was too accustomed to half truths and evasions to permit herself to be completely candid. By writing a memoir about her wartime service and postwar travails, Jane hoped to have the last word about her fascinating life. Unfortunately, her flawed and incomplete account raises more questions than it answers.

95

VENONA
~~TOP SECRET~~

LIZA = mother Dodd Stern 20/8/64 c

USSR

Ref. No: ⬛⬛⬛⬛ (of 11/6/1957)

Issued : ⬛⬛⬛ /30/4/1964

Copy No: 204

2nd RE-ISSUE

PROPOSED RECRUITMENT OF SEVERAL AGENTS
INCLUDING "UCN/29" AND JANE FOSTER (1942)

From: NEW YORK

To: MOSCOW

No: 854   16 June 42

To VIKTOR.[i]

Reference No. 2359.[a]

The signing on of "UCN/29"[ii] was delayed because of his prolonged absence and the necessity for checking additional information. He arrived today and we shall report results.

[1 group unrecovered] "LIZA"[iii], we are cultivating the American Jane FOSTER[iv] with a view to signing her on. She is about 30 years old and works in WASHINGTON in the Dutch [2 groups unrecovered][B% translator] of Malay languages. FOSTER is a FELLOWCOUNTRYWOMAN[ZEMLYaChKA],[v]

[86 groups unrecoverable]

[D% .....SK] was given [1 group unrecovered].

Her vetting was carried out by us. She is a FELLOWCOUNTRYWOMAN. She is described by the FELLOWCOUNTRYMEN[ZEMLYaK] as a [1 group unrecovered], dedicated person.   .....TER[vi] has also been reported on favourably by "F.N"[vii] who is a friend.

We intend to sign her on with a view to making use of her connections and [2 groups unrecovered] [B% her] [1 group unrecovered] SOUTH AMERICA our tasks [1 group unrecovered]. We urgently request approval.

No. 552   MAKSIM[viii]

<u>Distribution</u>   [Note and Comments overleaf]

w.f.21   M.H. file

95

~~TOP SECRET~~

2

Note: [a] Not available.

Comments: [i]   VIKTOR : Lt. Gen. P. M. FITIN.

[ii]   UCN/29 : Unidentified cover-name. See also NEW YORK's No. 253
                  of 19th February 1943   ) and No. 955 of
                  21st June 1943   .

[iii] LIZA   : Unidentified cover-name. First occurrence in this
                  lane.

[iv]   FOSTER : Later given the cover-name "SLANG". **Employed by
                  Netherlands Study Unit: later by BEW, then by OSS.**

[v]   FELLOWCOUNTRYWOMAN: Member of the Communist Party.

[vi]   ...TER : The full name cannot be FOSTER. It will however be a
                  fairly short name since TER is preceded by a single
                  group probably of one or two syllables.

[vii] FAN   : Unidentified cover-name. First known occurrence.

[viii] MAKSIM : Vasilij ZUBILIN, Soviet Vice-Consul in NEW YORK.

For those who are interested in reading more about Soviet espionage against America during this era, I recommend the following:

Benson, Robert Louis, and Michael Warner, eds. *Venona: Soviet Espionage and the American Response, 1939–1957.* Washington, D.C.: National Security Agency / Central Intelligence Agency, 1996.

Haynes, John Earl. *Red Scare or Red Menace?: American Communism and Anticommunism in the Cold War Era.* Chicago: Ivan R. Dee, 1996.

—— and Harvey Klehr. *Early Cold War Spies: The Espionage Trials That Shaped American Politics.* New York: Cambridge University Press, 2006.

——. *Venona: Decoding Soviet Espionage in America.* New Haven: Yale University Press, 1999.

—— and Alexander Vassiliev. *Spies: The Rise and Fall of the KGB in America.* New Haven: Yale University Press, 2009.

Klehr, Harvey, John Earl Haynes, and Kyrill M. Anderson. *The Soviet World of American Communism.* New Haven: Yale University Press, 1998.

Klehr, Harvey, John Earl Haynes, and Fridrikh Igorevich Firsov. *The Secret World of American Communism.* New Haven: Yale University Press, 1995.

Lamphere, Robert J., and Tom Shachtman. *The FBI-KGB War: A Special Agent's Story.* New York: Random House, 1986 / Macon Ga.: Mercer University Press, 1995.

Romerstein, Herbert, and Eric Breindel. *The Venona Secrets: Exposing Soviet Espionage and America's Traitors.* Washington, D.C.: Regnery Publishing, 2000.

Sibley, Katherine A. S. *Red Spies in America: Stolen Secrets and the Dawn of the Cold War.* Lawrence: University Press of Kansas, 2007.

Weinstein, Allen, and Alexander Vassiliev. *The Haunted Wood: Soviet Espionage in America—the Stalin Era.* New York: Random House, 1999.

West, Nigel. *Venona: The Greatest Secret of the Cold War.* New York: HarperCollins, 1999.

NOTES

Sources frequently cited have been identified by the following abbreviations:

EM Elizabeth P. McIntosh, aka Betty MacDonald, interviews by the author.

ET Eleanor Thiry, unpublished diary and private family letters.

FAP Foreign Affairs Oral History Project, Foreign Service Spouse Series, Julia Child Interview, November 7, 1991. Frontline Diplomacy, Manuscript Division, Library of Congress, Washington, D.C.

FBI Federal Bureau of Investigation, U.S. Department of Justice, Record/Information Dissemination Section, Records Management Division, Washington, D.C. All documents are referred to by case file number and name of subject.

JC Julia Child Correspondence, Julia Child Papers, Arthur and Elizabeth Schlesinger Library on the History of Women in America, Radcliffe Institute for Advanced Study, Harvard University, Cambridge, MA.

PC Paul Child Correspondence, Julia Child Papers, Arthur and Elizabeth Schlesinger Library on the History of Women in America, Radcliffe Institute for Advanced Study, Harvard University, Cambridge, MA. All of Paul Child's quotations from his letter-diaries to his twin brother, Charles—which cover years of his life and many thousands of pages—and letter-diaries to Julia during his security check in Washington will be referenced by the carton and file folder for that specific time period.

OSS/FIR   OSS Field Intelligence Reports, Jane Foster, Theater Officer Correspondence, Draft Histories, RG 226, box 21.

SMITH   Oral History Interview with Julia McWilliams Child, Smith College Centennial Study, conducted by Jacqueline Van Voris, October 10, 1972.

SS   Elizabeth P. McIntosh, *Sisterhood of Spies*. Annapolis: Naval Institute Press, 1998.

ST   Susan Tenenbaum, Jane Foster's niece by marriage and closest surviving relation, interview.

UG   Elizabeth MacDonald, *Undercover Girl*. New York: Macmillan, 1947.

UL   Jane Foster, *An UnAmerican Lady*. London: Sidgwick & Jackson, 1980.

1. Special Inquiry

All Paul Child quotes in this chapter are drawn from his letter-diaries to Julia Child from 1955 found in PC, carton 2, folder 46.

All of the references to Paul Child and Julia Child background checks, and details of Paul Child's FBI interrogation, including the agents' questions and his answers, are drawn from FBI case file 123–192, Paul Child.

The same FBI reports, plus some additional memorandums, can also be found in summarized form Paul Child's Department of State / USIA dossier, case file IOS-4454.

Additional sources are identified below.

1 "REPORT SOONEST . . .": PC, carton 2, folder 46.
1 "head of the . . .": FAP, p. 7.
2 "Woodenhead the First": ibid., p. 9.
3 "horrified": SMITH, p. 25.

3 "To think of . . .": PC, carton 2, folder 71.

3 "Woe—how did we . . .": Noël Riley Fitch, *Appetite for Life* (New York: Anchor Books, 1999), p. 218.

4 "had enough of that . . . : ibid.

5 "a peculiarly depressing . . .": James B. Conant, *My Several Lives* (New York: Harper & Row, 1970), p. 577.

5 "rampant right wingery . . .": PC, carton 2, folder 71.

6 "dear old Pop": ibid.

6 "good-hearted . . .": ibid.

7 "still working . . .": "McCarthy Charges Reds Hold U.S. Jobs," *Wheeling Intelligencer,* February 10, 1950.

7 "security risks": Conant, *My Several Lives,* p. 563.

7 "positive loyalty": Gary May, *China Scapegoat* (Washington, D.C.: New Republic Books, 1979), p. 269.

8 "vague, but dirty": PC, carton 2, folder 69.

8 "two young bloods": ibid.

8 "during most of . . .": ibid.

8 "a desperately dangerous . . .": PC, carton 2, folder 71.

8 "Eisenhower appears . . .": ibid.

9 "Quite a number . . .": FAP, p. 5.

9 "ever meet up . . .": PC, carton 2, folder 65.

9 "You have no . . .": ibid.

9 "After the events . . .": Fitch, *Appetite for Life,* p. 215.

10 "SITUATION CONFUSED": PC, carton 2, folder 46

11 "It would have . . .": ibid.

11 "SITUATION HERE . . .": ibid.

19 "Paul is being . . .": Fitch, *Appetite for Life,* p. 225.

19 "As soon as . . .": FAP, p. 7.

20 "hyperpatriotism": *Washington Post and Times-Herald,* April 19, 1955.

21 "You are finer . . .": PC, carton 2, folder 46.

21 "A horrible experience": FAP, p. 7.

23 "INVESTIGATION . . .": PC, carton 2, folder 46.

2. Initiation

24 "Look, just what . . .": UG, p. 2.

24 "That was . . .": EM.

25 "a wild, messy . . .": PC, carton 1, folder 28.

26 "whispered overtures": UG, p. 4.

26 "on the spot": EM.

26 "This is not . . .": ibid.

27 "to do something . . .": ibid.

27 "terrible, terrible . . .": ibid.

27 "the Japanese came to us": SS, p. 198.

27 "sent off somewhere": EM.

28 "ever considered . . .": UG, p. 4.

28 "hadn't described . . .": ibid., p. 3.

28 "something like . . .": Elizabeth P. McIntosh Papers (AFC/2001/001/ 30838), Veterans History Project, American Folklife Center, Library of Congress.

29 "overcome by . . .": UG, p. 4.

29 "caused trouble": UL, p. 57.

29 "study painting . . .": ibid., p. 58.

30 "silent and . . .": ibid., p. 59.

30 "three-kinds of . . .": ibid., p. 61.

30 "wide-eyed . . .": ibid., p. 62.

30 "romantic idea": EM.

31 "probably have . . .": UL, p. 89.

32 "My mother . . .": ibid., p. 91.

32 "You girls . . .": UG, p. 4.

35 "at the very . . .": ibid., p. 1.

35 "a large proportion . . .": UL, p. 106.

35 "hardly beloved": ibid.

36 "sneeringly said . . .": ibid.

36 "MO Manual . . .": UG, p. 7.

36 "when done right . . .": ibid., p. 2.

37 "Morale operations include . . .": ibid., p. 7.

37 "blow cover . . .": ibid.

38 "Our black radio . . .": ibid., p. 8.

38 "If it worked . . .": EM.

38 "It takes all kinds . . .": ibid., p. 8.

38 "It was . . .": ibid.

39 "pistols, machine . . .": UL, p. 108.

39 "understood nothing": ibid.

39 "The first thing . . .": ibid.

39 "I did not join . . .": ibid.

41 "mental hazard . . .": UG, p. 45.

41 "Besides . . .": ibid., p. 49.

41 "a half-consumed pint . . .": ibid.

42 "After ten minutes . . .": UL, p. 109.

42 "It was permissible . . .": UG, p. 45.

42 "a charming . . .": ibid., p. 46.

42 "leaving Kilroy . . .": ibid.

42 "by what sounded . . .": ibid., p. 47.

43 "The idea . . .": UL, p. 109.

43 "neurotic intellectual": ibid., p. 109.

43 "open-face-sandwich . . .": UG, p. 39.

44 "whether to salute . . .": UG, p. 6.

46 "Safecrackers . . .": Dan Pinck, interview by the author.

46 "a weird . . .": UL, p. 106.

46 "elephant laboring . . .": UG, p. 20.

47 "From a pathetically . . .": ibid., p. 38.

48 "The Japs, we . . .": ibid., p. 54.

49 "admirably adapted . . .": ibid., p. 31.

49 "inherited from Eve . . .": ibid.

50 "crept up . . .": ibid., p. 11.

50 "a singularly . . .": ibid.

50 "The professor . . .": UL, p. 111.

51 "Why not . . .": UG, p. 14.

51 "cast suspicion . . .": ibid.

52 "We were flat . . .": ibid.

3. Late Start

53 "five major . . .": UG, p. 18.

53 "stomach-full . . .": PC, carton 1, folder 28.

53 "Brooks Brothers . . .": ibid.

54 "a princeling": Philip Ziegler, *Mountbatten* (New York: Harper & Row, 1986), p. 221.

54 "rather confused . . .": UL, p. 117.

55 "the most important . . .": ibid.

55 "suspicious of . . .": E. Bruce Reynolds, *Thailand's Secret War* (Cambridge, U.K.: Cambridge University Press, 2005), p. 125.

55 "door to India . . .": UG, p. 18.

56 "to obtain New York . . .": Reynolds, *Thailand's Secret War,* p. 125.

56 "full operational control . . .": ibid., p. 126.

56 "other complications . . .": UL, p. 117.

56 "with a monumental hatred": ibid.

57 "his wife, his child . . .": ibid.

57 "keeping China . . .": Ziegler, *Mountbatten,* p. 241.

57 "a blend of . . .": Edmond Taylor, *Awakening from History* (Boston: Gambit, 1969), p. 347.

57 "We must take orders . . .": ibid., p. 18.

58 "bursting to blab": ibid., p. 20.

58 "highly developed . . .": ibid., p. 26.

59 "the distilled reports . . .": ibid.

59 "lady novelist": SMITH, p. 17.

59 "social butterfly": PC, carton 2, folder 58.

60 "too long": FAP, p. 7.

60 "good impression": National Archives, OSS Records, Julia Child.

61 "a cross between . . .": UG, p. 21.

61 "fish-squeezing unit": SMITH, p. 28.

61 "Julia was a woman . . .": Fitch, *Appetite for Life,* p. 85.

62 "a plain person": FAP, p. 7.

62 "The idea of going . . .": ibid., p. 28.

63 "never been anywhere . . .": ET, diary.

63 "We presented . . .": ibid.

64 "Julia, Rosie . . .": Thibaut de Saint Phalle, interview by author.

64 "I never would . . .": ibid.

65 "The times when . . .": ibid.

65 "Easter Sunday . . .": ibid.

66 "a killing train ride . . .": Fitch, *Appetite for Life,* p. 92.

66 "number three air . . .": UG, p. 39.

67 "Just think . . .": Alexander MacDonald, *My Footloose Newspaper Life* (Bangkok: Post Publishing, 1990), p. 80.

67 "We were just so . . .": EM.

67 "*C'est la guerre*": Alexander MacDonald, *My Footloose Newspaper Life,* p. 80.

67 "problems": PC, carton 1, folder 28.

67 "designed to test . . .": UG, p. 40.

68 "It took all . . .": UL, p. 109.

68 "from the hip . . .": UG, p. 51.

69 "We had been . . .": ibid., p. 52.
69 "the professionals . . .": UL, p. 107.
69 "Foster, here's . . .": ibid., p. 111.
70 "several boxes . . .": UG, p. 52.
70 "wouldn't hear . . .": ibid.
71 "did not mind paying . . .": UL, p. 112.
71 "OSS girls bound . . .": UG, p. 53.
71 "wishful packing": ibid.
71 "disemboweled . . .": ibid., p. 54.
72 "recalled the era . . .": ibid., p. 56.
72 "One of them . . .": UL, p. 112.
73 "The following will . . .": UG, p. 60.
73 "The prospect of . . .": ibid., p. 61.

4. A Fine Sort

75 "Breakbone fever": UL, p. 78.
75 "Toonerville Trolley": ibid., p. 113.
76 "cubbyhole . . .": ibid., p. 114.
78 "red from head . . .": ibid.
78 "the drains of . . .": ibid.
78 "Delhi Belly . . .": PC, carton 2, folder 49.
80 "lonely . . .": ibid.
80 "Zorina": ibid.
81 "a new and interesting . . .": PC, carton 2, folder 50.
81 "Janie is . . . Bohemienne": ibid.
84 "Young lady, may . . .": UL, p. 121.
84 "a little bit . . .": Vicki Constantine Croke, *The Lady and the Panda* (New York: Random House, 2005), p. 133.
85 "as it was forbidden . . .": UL, p. 70.
85 "Mrs. Harkness would emit . . .": ibid.
85 "fascinating . . .": FAP, p. 7.
85 "She was terribly funny . . .": ibid.
86 "probably the most beautiful . . .": Ziegler, *Mountbatten,* p. 279.
86 "Lovely Louis . . .": UL, p. 123–124.
86 "the mangy British lion": ibid., p. 125.
87 "He had the . . .": ibid., p. 123.
87 "the jolliest girl . . .": Fitch, *Appetite for Life,* p. 101.

87 "having a genius . . .": UL, p. 134.
87 "bagging the beasts . . .": PC, carton 2, folder 49.
87 "an Oxford don . . .": ibid.
88 "When the waters . . .": UG, p. 144.
88 "For use in salt . . .": ibid., p. 145.
88 "mad scientist": UL, p. 116.
88 "the fascination of a . . .": ibid.
90 "by drinking . . .": PC, carton 2, folder 50.
90 "to undermine the . . .": UL, p. 118.
90 "a phenomenal memory . . .": ibid.
90 "I would look . . .": ibid.
91 "could have cared . . .": UL, p. 119.
91 "We would parachute . . .": ibid.
91 "Why don't we . . .": ibid.
91 "wasting the taxpayers' . . .": ibid., p. 118.
92 "disconcerted . . .": Carleton Scofield, University of Missouri at Kansas City Archives, Carleton F. Scofield Papers, diary, August 14, 1944.
92 "wiles of the . . .": Reynolds, *Thailand's Secret War,* p. 229.
93 "the contagions of . . .": Taylor, *Awakening from History,* p. 352.
93 "little more than . . .": ibid.
93 "Damn it, why . . .": Scofield, diary, August 19, 1944.
93 "It may be . . .": SS, p. 212.
94 "At present . . .": ibid.
94 "tactless . . .": ibid, p. 213.
94 "uncoordinated . . .": UG, p. 133.
94 "To those red-blooded . . .": ibid, p. 132.
94 "Oh, What a . . .": Eldridge, *Wrath in Burma,* p. 263.
95 "put their imagination to work . . .": Alexander MacDonald, *My Footloose Newspaper Life,* p. 85.
95 "Madison Avenue ad men . . .": ibid.
97 "Each side cheated . . .": Taylor, *Awakening from History,* p. 351.
97 "high-echelon personnel": UG, p. 121.
97 "easy targets . . .": UG, p. 121.
98 "OK, Alec . . .": UL, p. 126.
98 "hell-raising . . .": PC, carton 2, folder 50.

5. Instant Fame

100 "Donovan's here . . .": Alexander MacDonald, *My Footloose Newspaper Life,* p. 86.

100 "quasi-royal procession": UL, p. 122.

100 "It meant we . . .": ibid.

100 "Sounds promising . . .": Alexander MacDonald, *My Footloose Newspaper Life,* p. 86.

100 "How about . . .": ibid.

101 "They're messages . . .": ibid.

101 "It seems a . . .": ibid.

101 "instant fame": SS, p. 220.

102 "Jane, really!": ibid.

102 "the same freckled . . .": UG, p. 132.

102 "on a boondoggling . . .": ibid.

102 "so clean it . . .": ibid., p. 133

103 "reached the saturation point": Fitch, *Appetite for Life,* p. 100.

103 "by holding a . . .": UL, p. 124.

103 "Stilwell knew . . .": ibid.

104 "the old sourpuss": ibid., p. 124.

105 "fantastic": PC, carton 2, folder 51.

105 "as a casual . . .": ibid.

105 "though where she . . .": ibid.

105 "of course, I am not . . .": ibid.

105 "except that all . . .": ibid.

106 "And there's . . .": UG, p. 141.

106 "I took this . . .": ibid.

107 "Chop says he . . .": ibid., p. 134.

107 "the care and training": ibid.

107 "shield them from . . .": ibid.

107 "Hindus no beef . . .": UL, p. 120.

107 "so no one's . . .": UG, p. 136.

108 "wilted when . . .": ibid.

108 "He says he's . . .": ibid., p. 137.

108 "the mute . . .": ibid.

108 "They don't like . . .": ibid.

109 "The subs go over . . .": UG, p. 144.

109 "subversive bone . . .": ibid., p. 135.

109 "they never knew . . .": ibid., p. 136.

110 "It could be just . . .": Alexander MacDonald, *My Footloose Newspaper Life,* p. 87.

110 "When the station . . .": UG, p. 144.

110 "The Thai foreign . . .": Alexander MacDonald, *My Footloose Newspaper Life,* p. 88.

111 "nerve center": Fisher Howe, interview by the author.

111 "fool-proof locator system": SS, p. 217.

111 "one of those you have . . .": ibid.

112 "If you don't . . .": ibid.

112 "exuberant and . . .": Fitch, *Appetite for Life,* p. 98.

112 "Julia was so . . .": EM.

112 "It was already . . .": EM.

113 "Wish I were . . .": Fitch, *Appetite for Life,* p. 98.

113 "Julia, the 6'2" . . .": PC, carton 2, folder 50.

113 "a warm and witty . . .": ibid.

113 "she says . . .": ibid.

114 "heavily in love": PC, carton 2, folder 51.

115 "best birthday . . .": ibid.

115 "Your confusion . . .": ibid.

115 "but not one of . . .": UL, p. 130.

116 "a bit of an . . .": ibid.

116 "be true to each other": ibid.

116 "unevenly, of course": ibid.

116 "There was a lot . . .": EM.

116 "No one else . . .": UL, p. 130.

116 "fleet-footed couriers": Manly Fleischmann letters, FBI case file 100-35543, Jane Foster Zlatovski.

116 "I can hardly tell . . .": ibid.

116 "the U.S. armed forces . . .": UL, p. 130.

117 "It is not necessary . . .": Manly Fleischmann letters, FBI case file number 100-35543, Jane Foster Zlatovski.

117 "red-and-white dressing gown . . .": UL, p. 130.

117 "the only child . . .": Windmiller, *International Journal of Intelligence and Counterintelligence* 8 (1955), p. 111.

119 "straight-backed Groucho . . .": UL, p. 127.

119 "Two years . . .": Lord Louis Mountbatten, *Personal Diary . . . 1943–1946* (London: Collins, 1988), p. 61.

119 "a useless organization": UL, p. 129.

120 "modestly advised Mountbatten . . .": Geoffrey T. Hellman, "Curator Getting Around," *The New Yorker,* August 26, 1950.

120 "never forgave . . .": UL, p. 129.

120 "Get the Commander . . .": ibid.

6. The Great White Queen of Bali

122 "a sad, ugly . . .": UL, p. 132.

122 "cesspool . . .": ibid.

123 "Something was always happening . . .": ibid.

123 "I'm sorry . . .": ibid.

123 "purple with rage . . .": ibid., p. 133.

124 "the war would . . .": ibid.

124 "negligence and/or . . .": ibid.

125 "Rumors were . . .": ibid., p. 134.

125 "Oh, Gregory . . .": ibid., p. 135.

125 "mostly devoted . . .": UL, p. 136.

126 "a vast eyeball-searing . . .": ibid.

126 "I'm writing . . .": ibid.

126 "How we celebrated . . .": ibid., p. 138.

126 "I quickly . . .": ibid., p. 139.

127 "The Indonesians were in full . . .": ibid.

127 "What could possibly happen . . .": ibid.

128 "confidential plan": UG, p. 145.

128 "peace-time covert . . .": E. Bruce Reynolds, "Staying Behind in Bangkok," *Journal of Intelligence History* 2, no. 2 (Winter 2002), p. 24.

128 "covert development . . .": ibid.

128 "Here's luck!": UL, p. 140.

129 "cherished wish . . .": ibid., p. 139.

129 "He made the . . .": ibid., p. 29.

129 "1.1 billion enemies . . .": Geoffrey Gunn, "Origins of the American War in Vietnam," *Asia-Pacific Journal: JapanFocus,* May 9, 2009.

130 "the Draconian Thailand . . .": UL, p. 140.

130 "the quiet shelving . . .": ibid.

131 "It was a bittersweet . . .": UL, p. 141.

131 "sat on the beach . . .": ibid.

131 "Well, kid . . .": Manly Fleischmann letters, FBI case file 100-35543, Jane Foster Zlatovski.

132 "a lovely surprise": UL, p. 141.

133 "Jane, those . . .": ibid.

133 "How could you . . .": ibid., p. 142.

133 "She was pure . . .": ibid., p. 86.

134 "We could distinctly see . . .": ibid., p. 142.

134 "the dreaded Japanese . . .": ibid.

135 "occasionally seemed . . .": ibid., p. 143.

135 "explosive": OSS/FIR, Jane Foster, "Current Political Situation," September 20, 1945.

136 "That'll l'arn 'em": UL, p. 143.

136 "The pilots had . . .": ibid., p. 144.

136 "The prisoners were": ibid., p. 143.

137 "case in point": ibid.

138 "Some of the . . .": ibid., p. 145.

139 "You're not . . .": ibid.

140 "the only flag . . .": OSS/FIR, Jane Foster, "Current Political Situation," September 20, 1945.

140 "Americans were the only . . .": UL, p. 145.

140 "In the event . . .": ibid., p. 145.

140 "increasingly tense": OSS/FIR, Jane Foster, "Current Political Situation," September 20, 1945.

141 "The city is . . .": ibid.

141 "the great mass . . .": ibid.

142 "to resist by force . . .": ibid.

142 "With a supreme lack . . .": UL, p. 146.

142 "ambiguous . . .": OSS/FIR, Jane Foster, "Current Political Situation," September 20, 1945.

143 "It looks as if . . .": ibid.

143 "precarious": ibid.

143 "waiting (like dopes)": OSS/FIR, Operational, Jane Foster to Lloyd George, September 25, 1945.

144 "All in all . . .": ibid.

144 "would drive . . .": Frederick E. Crockett, "How the Marble Began in Java," *Harper's Magazine,* March 1946, p. 281.

144 "The broadcast was . . .": ibid.

144 "no authority . . .": ibid.

145 "liked the Dutch":

146 *"status quo ante bellum"*: UL, p. 149.

146 "no information . . .": Crockett, p. 282.

147 "Her days were . . .": Timothy Lindsey, *The Romance of K'Tut Tantri and Indonesia* (New York: Oxford University Press, 1997), p. 165.

148 "sounded like the . . .": UL, p. 149.

148 "war wounds": ibid., p. 190.

148 "What the hell . . .": Crockett, p. 283.

148 "The lieutenant insisted . . .": ibid.

149 "swilling whiskey . . .": UL, p. 151.

149 "in light of . . .": OSS/FIR, Military Attache Report, Colonel Kenneth Kennedy, Military Intelligence Division, October 11, 1945.

149 "We are of the opinion . . .": ibid.

150 "salivating at . . .": UL, p. 150.

150 "Incidents continue . . .": OSS/FIR, Jane Foster, Situation Report, October 15, 1945.

150 "an undisguised . . .": ibid.

150 "quite appalled . . .": ibid.

151 "a complete stalemate": ibid.

152 "brutal conduct": Crockett, p. 283.

152 "The peoples of . . .": ibid.

152 "the rattle of . . .": UL, p. 152.

152 "Jane, have . . .": ibid.

153 "fat Dutch sergeant": ibid.

153 "GET FOSTER . . .": UL, p. 152.

153 "Public opinion . . .": ibid.

153 "OK, Jane . . .": ibid.

154 "HAD NOT . . .": UG, p. 298

154 "PEACE OF WORLD . . .": ibid.

7. Chickens Coming Home to Roost

156 "the remnants of sugar . . .": UL, p. 153.

158 "apparently enjoying . . .": Archimedes L. A. Patti, *Why Vietnam?* (Berkeley: University of California Press), p. 317.

158 "Cochinchina is . . .": ibid., p. 320.

159 "mistaken identity": ibid., p. 322.

159 "not doing their stuff": OSS/FIR, Memorandum for the President, Representative in Kandy to Donovan, September 28, 1945.

159 "Basically, the situation . . .": UL, p. 154

160 "[Miss Foster] felt . . .": Department of State Memorandum, "Conditions in Saigon," December 12, 1945.

160 "It was apparent . . .": ibid.

160 "Boycotts and . . .": ibid.

161 "The general situation . . .": Gunn, "Origins."

161 "the single immediate . . .": ibid.

161 "on the par . . .": UL, p. 154.

161 "to get the French back . . .": *Vietnam: A Television History*, "The Roots of War (1945-1953)," written and produced by Judith Vecchione for American Experience. WGBH Educational Foundation, 1983/2007.

162 "the best journalist": UL, p. 154.

163 "practically all": ibid.

163 "If there is anything . . .": Edgar Snow, "Secrets from Siam," *Saturday Evening Post*, January 12, 1946.

164 "as secret as La Guardia . . .": Reynolds, *Thailand's Secret War*, p. 303.

165 "But I had . . .": UL, p. 155.

165 "stern self-discipline . . .": ibid.

165 "Of all the . . .": ST.

166 "There was no . . .": UL, p. 155.

166 "to swipe . . .": ibid., p. 154.

167 "A sixteenth-century . . .": ibid., p. 155.

167 "We are all slightly . . .": OSS/FIR, Operational, Jane Foster to Lloyd George, September 25, 1945.

168 "it was so fitting": UL, p. 155.

168 "although he, too": ibid.

168 "physically push": UL, p. 156.

168 "It showed . . .": ibid., p. 159.

169 "Darling, do you . . .": ibid., p. 160.

169 "the heavy-duty thinkers": ibid.

169 "No longer in . . .": ibid.

170 "The Japanese . . .": ibid.

171 "a gentleman of . . .": UL, p. 161.

171 "there are . . .": ibid.

171 "Sukarno is a traitor . . .": ibid.
172 "I've just come . . .": ibid.
172 "Don't you remember . . .": ibid.

8. Whispers in the Willow Trees

174 "more icicle than . . .": PC, carton 2, folder 56.
175 "Balm in Gilead . . .": ibid.
175 "It's dirty beyond . . .": ibid.
175 "bawling like . . .": ibid.
176 "of becoming magnificently . . .": ibid.
177 "dangerous thinker": SS, p. 230.
177 "with an eager mind . . .": PC, carton 2, folder 56.
177 "a great solace": ibid.
178 "Paul Child . . .": Thibaut de Saint Phalle, interview by author.
178 "the underside of . . .": ibid.
178 "incandescant . . .": ibid.
179 "slightly disintegrated": ibid.
179 "The atmosphere is . . .": PC, carton 2, folder 57.
180 "appeals from . . .": ibid., p. 170.
180 "The warlords . . .": EM.
180 "the Chinese . . .": UG, p. 162.
181 "ambush discipline . . .": ibid., p. 164.
181 "Lack of patriotism . . .": ibid., p. 165.
181 "The warp and woof . . .": PC, carton 2, folder 57.
183 "struck off into . . .": ibid.
183 "Perhaps you will . . .": ibid.
184 "love at first sight . . .": ibid.
184 "Marjorie continues . . .": ibid.
184 "A good many . . .": ibid.
185 "We were pulled . . .": EM.
185 "We talked . . .": EM.
185 "how could it be . . .": PC, carton 2, folder 57.
186 "So now, as before . . .": ibid.
186 "These prison wires . . .": ibid.
187 "We talked about . . .": ibid.
187 "morale-building . . .": ibid.

187 "He was terribly . . .": UG, p. 149.

187 "It was fortunate . . .": PC, carton 2, folder 57.

188 "Do you realize . . .": ibid.

189 "They were an . . .": Thibaut de Saint Phalle, interview by author.

189 "running a very complicated . . .": Calvin Tomkins, "Good Cooking," *The New Yorker,* December 23, 1974.

189 "A wonderful 'good scout' . . .": PC, carton 2, folder 57.

189 "The China theater . . .": EM.

189 "They were always . . .": EM.

189 "never liked the idea . . .": PC, carton 2, folder 57.

189 "He sort of . . .": EM.

190 "plunge headfirst . . .": PC, carton 2, folder 57.

190 "a great whisper . . .": UG, p. 218.

190 "to be light for . . .": PC, carton 2, folder 57.

190 "placidly hoeing . . .": ibid.

190 "rather stay alive . . .": ibid.

191 "something terrible . . .": UG, p. 220.

191 "Until that time . . .": ibid.

191 "All the toilets . . .": PC, carton 2, folder 57.

192 "as a purely . . .": ibid.

192 "That's a big rat . . .": ibid.

192 "melting like . . .": UG, p. 221.

192 "a tough people . . .": PC, carton 2, folder 57.

192 "The sudden ending . . .": ibid.

194 "Never mind . . .": Maochun Yu, *OSS in China* (New Haven: Yale University Press, 1996), p. 289.

195 "a lack of good . . .": ibid., p. 240

195 "keeping order . . .": ibid.

195 "It discourages . . .": PC, carton 2, folder 58.

195 "victory hullabaloos . . .": ibid.

196 "perhaps the God damned war . . .": ibid.

196 "important work . . .": National Archives, OSS Records, Julia Child

196 "There was a sudden . . .": UG, p. 227.

196 "I was in love . . .": EM.

197 "pitch-fork out": PC, carton 2, folder 57.

197 "Over the 18 . . .": ibid.

197 How like the . . . : ibid.

198 "not the woman . . .": Fitch, *Appetite for Life,* p. 124.

198 "Perhaps he's catching . . .": EM.

198 "friendly passion . . .": Fitch, *Appetite for Life,* p. 124.

199 "the limited and . . .": PC, carton 2, folder 57.

199 "exhausted . . .": ibid.

199 "He is probably . . .": Fitch, *Appetite for Life,* p. 124.

200 "I feel washed-out . . .": PC, carton 2, folder 57.

200 "I'm sitting on . . .": ibid.

200 "Love . . .": ibid.

201 "machine guns . . .": ibid.

9. Incurable Romantics

202 "substratum chicanery": UG, p. 262.

203 "mausoleum . . .": ibid., p. 294.

203 "the returning . . .": ibid.

203 "new, noiseless . . .": ibid., p. 295.

203 "to mourn the . . .": ibid.

204 "a handsome . . .": ibid., pp. 297–298.

205 "The leaflet . . .": ibid., pp. 300–301.

205 "the Dutch press . . .": ibid., p. 301.

206 "Well, let's see . . .": ibid., p. 303.

207 "The term . . .": ibid.

207 "such forces . . .": ibid., p. 304.

208 "It was hard . . .": EM.

209 "Please be back . . .": UL, p. 167.

209 "Jane never . . .": EM.

209 "Trigger-Happy Dutchmen . . .": *San Francisco Chronicle,* December 31, 1945.

210 "forced the war . . .": *People's World,* January 5, 1946.

210 "did not attach . . .": UL, p. 166.

210 "an eyewitness account . . .": Jane Foster, "Revolt in Indonesia," Institute of Pacific Relations, San Francisco, CA January 11, 1946.

211 "confidential assignment . . .": FBI case file 100-35543, Jane Foster Zlatovski.

212 "This is one of the . . .": Edgar Snow, "No Four Freedoms for Indo-China," *The Saturday Evening Post,* February 2, 1946.

212 "The Netherlands . . .": Jane Foster, letter to the editor, *The New York Times,* July 15, 1946.

212 "The problem . . .": EM.

213 "if only by . . .": UL, p. 110.

213 "on the other . . .": ibid., p. 130.

213 "misty . . .": ibid., p. 164.

214 "There was something . . .": EM, interview by author.

214 "socially useful element . . .": Zlatovski, "The Autobiography of an Anti-Hero," Minnesota Historical Society, Minnesota Public Library, p. 26.

215 "a strong . . .": UL, p. 82.

215 "too non-conformist . . .": FBI case file 100-35543, Jane Foster Zlatovski.

216 "a bit of a . . .": ibid., p. 83.

216 "gussied up . . .": ibid., p. 96.

216 "incurable romantics . . .": Zlatovski, "The Autobiography of an Anti-Hero," p. 1.

216 "did not really . . .": EM.

217 "In very different . . .": EM.

217 "*La Très Haute Societé* . . .": Katrina Vanden Heuvel, "Grand Illusions," *Vanity Fair,* September 1991, pp. 219–25, 248–56.

217 "loved intrigue . . .": UL, p. 97.

218 "adorable, adored . . .": ibid., p. 170.

218 "Break out my . . .": PC, carton 2, folder 57.

219 "This brings up . . .": PC, carton 2, folder 58.

219 "I'll take her . . .": John K. Singlaub with Malcolm McConnell, *Hazardous Duty* (New York: Summit Books, 1991), p. 115.

219 "tired and . . .": Thibault de Saint Phalle, *Saints, Sinners, and Scalawags* (Brookline, N.H.: Hobblebrush Books, 2004), p. 161.

220 "pursue the plan . . .": SMITH.

220 "to see what . . .": ibid.

220 "on the porch . . .": Fitch, *Appetite for Life,* p. 129.

220 "allow for . . .": ibid.

220 "a relationship based . . .": ibid.

221 "Dearest Paulski . . .": JC, carton 2, folder 45.
The letters that follow from JC to PC, January to June 1946, are contained in JC, carton 2, folder 45, and only the sources of quotes drawn from elsewhere will be identified.

223 "dilettante": SMITH.

223 "liked that type . . .": ibid.

225 "everybody": JC, carton 2, folder 45.

226 "You play a leading role . . .": Fitch, *Appetite for Life,* p. 131.

227 "operational proof . . .": FAP.

227 "very difficult . . .": SMITH.

227 "My father was very . . .": ibid.

228 "divorce . . .": PC, carton 2, folder 58.

228 "Julie is a splendid . . .": PC, carton 2, folder 58.

228 "no measly . . .": ibid.

228 "a firm and . . .": ibid.

229 "Well!": PC, carton 2, folder 58.

10. Open Season

230 "somewhere in Paris": FAP.

230 "dropped out of sight . . .": PC, carton 2, folder 68.

230 "That's a name . . .": ibid.

231 "so several people . . .": FAP.

231 "unmistakable": PC, carton 2, folder 68.

231 "So we hied . . .": FAP.

231 "Dearest Janie . . .": PC, carton 2, folder 68.

232 "inexplicable suddenness . . .": ibid.

232 "If you'd been . . .": ibid.

232 "She sounded . . .": ibid.

233 "the American way . . .": PC, carton 2, folder 60.

233 "the proportions for . . .": ibid., folder 65.

233 "tapping them out": ibid., folder 68.

233 "Cordon Bleu widower": ibid., folder 65.

235 "human approach . . .": ibid., folder 66.

235 "Oh well, I never . . .": ibid., folder 68.

235 "a long time": ibid.

235 "so-called Military . . .": UL, p. 174.

235 "all been Nazis": ibid., p. 176.

236 "Give me the . . .": ibid., p. 185.

236 "Poor George is full . . .": PC, carton 2, folder 68.

237 "just to please . . .": ibid., folder 65.

237 "Don't touch . . .": ibid., folder 69.

237 "She was . . .": ibid.

238 "a small, short . . .": FAP.

238 "shy and brainy": PC, carton 2, folder 68.

238 "naked blimpish . . .": ibid.

238 "feeding them with finesse": ibid.

239 "She is almost . . .": ibid.

239 "congenital Republicans": PC, carton 2, folder 68.

239 "John McWilliams . . .": ibid.

239 "I'll bet I . . .": ibid, folder 66.

240 "From her description . . .": ibid., folder 68.

240 "soft on Communism . . .": ibid., folder 66.

240 "the master of innuendo . . .": ibid., folder 68.

240 "a PhD graduate . . .": ibid.

240 "dirty fighting . . .": ibid.

241 "suspected of all . . .": ibid., folder 48.

242 "the weakness . . .": E. J. Kahn, *The China Hands* (New York: Viking Press, 1975), p. 238.

242 "millionaire Communist . . .": Herbert Romerstein and Eric Breindel, *The Venona Secrets* (Washington, D.C.: Regnery Publishing, 2000), p. 57.

242 "lost his mind": Stephen R. MacKinnon and Oris Friesen, *China Reporting* (Berkeley: University of California Press, 1987), p. 143.

242 "doubt of loyalty": "China Hands," Association for Diplomatic Studies and Training, *Frontline Diplomacy—Country Readers—China.* Arlington, Va.: ADST Foreign Affairs Oral History Program, 2000.

243 "He was treated . . .": FAP.

243 "so invaluable . . .": ibid.

244 "Vincent all but . . .": Gary May, *China Scapegoat* (Washington, D.C.: New Republic Books, 1979), p. 224.

244 "a disgusting era": FAP.

244 "My moral and spiritual . . .": PC, carton 2, folder 66.

245 "unimportant": ibid., folder 65.

245 "The vigor and . . .": ibid.

245 "not eligible for . . .": ibid., folder 68.

245 "a real woman . . .": ibid.

246 "whiz bang": ibid.

246 "We have finally . . .": ibid., folder 69.

246 "Every time . . .": EAP.

246 "I hate only a . . ." Fitch, *Appetite for Life,* p. 182.

247 "These two men . . .": PC, carton 2, folder 69.

247 "25 minutes . . .": ibid.

248 "undercurrent of . . .": PC, carton 2, folder 46.

248 "yellow-bellyism . . .": ibid.

248 "He's emasculating . . .": ibid., folder 69.

248 "stepchild . . .": FAP.

248 "I am terribly . . .": Fitch, *Appetite for Life*, p. 204.

250 "I think the . . . Edwin R. Bayley, *Joe McCarthy and the Press* (Madison: University of Wisconsin Press, 1981) p. 111.

250 "Communist fronts": Aloise Buckley Heath, *Will Mrs. Major Go to Hell?* (New York: Arlington House, 1969), p. 134.

250 "proper democratic . . .": Julia Child to Mrs. Heath, March 12, 1954, Smith College.

251 "sift truth . . .": ibid.

251 "For the colleges . . .": ibid.

251 "desperate power-monger": PC, carton 2, folder 71.

251 "right in there . . .": ibid.

252 "supporting the . . .": Julia Child with Alex Prud'homme, *My Life in France* (New York: Anchor Books, 2006), p. 200.

252 "These people with . . . : ibid.

252 "the avalanching danger": Bernard DeVoto, "Due Notice to the FBI," The Easy Chair, *Harper's Magazine*, October 1949.

11. The Nightmare

253 "to break loose . . .": PC, carton 2, folder 46.

253 "the very nadir . . .": ibid.

254 "I must confess . . .": ibid.

254 "that you have . . .": ibid.

254 "And that the . . .": ibid.

255 "cringe": FAP.

255 "who just cravenly . . .": ibid.

255 "We would very . . .": PC, carton 2, folder 46.

256 "being attacked . . .": ibid.

256 "to determine . . .": USIA case file 105-4454, Paul Child.

257 "I think she . . .": PC, carton 2, folder 46.

258 "What I suspect . . .": ibid.

258 "the professional . . .": ibid.

258 "intercepted by . . .": PC, carton 2, folder 46.

258 "what we must . . .": ibid.
258 "believed to have been . . .": FBI case file 100-35543, Jane Foster Zlatovski.
259 "Ah me . . .": ibid.
259 "Well, the Nightmare . . .": ibid.
260 "you have the . . .": ibid.
260 "Well, what did . . .": UL, p. 20.
260 "[Her] only thought . . .": ibid., p. 29.
261 "the top Russian . . .": Joanne Cavanaugh Simpson, "Seeing Red," *Johns Hopkins Magazine,* September 2000.
262 "the four liturgical . . .": UL, p. 22.
262 "really, Jane . . .": ibid., p. 24.
262 "My mother . . .": ST.
263 "You can't": ibid.
263 "Jane just . . .": ibid.
263 "a hideous . . .": UL, p. 27.
263 "to show the nightmarish . . .": PC, carton 2, folder 46.
264 "the Holy Office": ibid.
264 "a physical . . .": ibid.
264 "unadulterated horror": ibid.
264 "It would have . . .": UL, p. 29.
265 "with mirrors . . .": ibid., p. 30.
265 "Then the Nightmare . . . : PC, carton 2, folder 46.
265 "Spy! Spy!": UL, p. 30.
266 "a member of . . .": ibid., p. 35.
266 "conceived to be . . .": HUAC Memorandum, September 12, 1962, From Don Sweeney to Francis J. McNamara, Re: Jane Foster Zlatovski v. Secretary of State, J. B. Matthews Papers, Duke University Rare Book, Manuscript, and Special Collections Library, Durham, N.C.
267 "It was a real . . . PC, carton 2, folder 46.
267 "holed up in . . .": ibid.
267 "whey-faced agents": UL, p. 41.
267 "Afraid to go out": PC, carton 2, folder 46.
267 "I had been . . .": ibid.
267 "not in the . . .": HUAC Memorandum, September 12, 1962, From Don Sweeney to Francis J. McNamara, Re: Jane Foster Zlatovski v. Secretary of State, J. B. Matthews Papers, Duke University Rare Book, Manuscript, and Special Collections Library, Durham, N.C.

268 "the most unfirable . . .": *Time*, 1951.

268 "the way Mussolini . . .": UL, p. 36.

268 "very sick": ibid.

268 "There I was . . .": PC, carton 2, folder 46.

269 *"Rat-tat-tat-tat . . . "*: UL, p. 43.

270 "a loveable little . . .": ibid., p. 40.

270 "a law unto itself": Leonard B. Boudin, "The Right to Travel," *Nation*, July 30, 1955.

271 "fool around": PC, carton 2, folder 46.

271 "shaking like an . . .": UL, p. 45.

271 "log-jam": PC, carton 2, folder 46.

271 "[Judge Mathews] . . .": ibid.

272 "did not show them . . .": ibid.

272 "derogatory information": HUAC Memorandum, September 5, 1962, Honorable Gordon H. Scherer to Francis J. McNamara, Director, Re: Jane Foster Zlatovski v. Secretary of State, J. B. Matthews Papers, Duke University.

273 "break the seal . . .": UL, p. 48.

273 "the boys in gabardine . . .": PC, carton 2, folder 46.

273 "ARRIVED PARIS . . .": ibid.

273 "Forgive me . . .": ibid.

274 "then I can really say . . .": ibid.

274 "case had been . . .": USIA case file 105-4454 / FBI case file 123-192, Paul Child.

12. The Taste of Ashes

275 "dumping ground": FAP.

275 "poor marks . . .": Julia Child, *My Life in France*, p. 224.

276 "Wish You Were Here": JC, Papers, Schlesinger Library, Radcliffe Institute, Harvard, carton 2, folder 47.

276 "brainless bureaucrats": FAP.

277 "that did not mean . . .": UL, p. 218.

277 "She and George . . .": ibid.

277 "a cry for help . . .": UL, p. 218.

278 "Julia was awfully . . .": EM.

278 "liberal . . .": FBI case file 100-35543, Jane Foster Zlatovski.

278 "Hoover was no . . .": ibid.

279   "now the land of . . .": Julia Child, *My Life in France,* p. 224.

279   "think someone that . . .": Fitch, *Appetite for Life,* p. 237.

279   "U.S. COUPLE ACCUSED . . .": *Los Angeles Times,* July 9, 1957.

279   "EX-AIDES OF U.S. . . .": *The New York Times,* July 9, 1957.

279   "An American couple . . .": *The Washington Post and Times-Herald,* July 9, 1957.

282   "FRANCE GRANTS" . . . *Washington Daily News,* July 9, 1957.

282   "The French have . . .": *Evening Star,* July 9, 1957.

282   "They've been . . .": Reuters, July 9, 1957.

282   "parlor pink": *Washington Daily News,* July 9, 1957 .

283   "a haven": *Chicago Daily Tribune,* July 11, 1957.

283   "shifted her base . . .": ibid.

284   "an untenable . . .": *The Washington Post and Times-Herald,* July 11, 1957.

284   "A Communist suspect . . .": ibid.

285   "approved": *The New York Times,* August 13, 1957.

285   "didn't come easy . . .": *The New York Times,* August 13, 1957.

285   "special special agent": *Time,* January 12, 1959.

286   "Boris, somehow . . .": ibid.

286   "a prominent American . . .": ibid.

286   "missing link": *The New York Times,* August 17, 1957.

286   "part of the Soviet . . .": ibid.

286   "The Justice Department . . .": Katrina Vanden Heuvel, "Grand Illusions," *Vanity Fair,* September 1991.

288   "guaranteed": *The New York Times,* September 10, 1957.

288   "a sensitive, dynamic . . .": Francis E. Walter, "The First Official Story of the Man Who Fooled the Kremlin," *The Philadelphia Inquirer,* September 29, 1957.

288   "a hand to shake . . .": ibid., October 2, 1957.

289   "at eleven o'clock . . .": UL, p. 218.

289   "tragic-comedy . . .": ibid.

289   "a hairless teddy bear": ibid., p. 222.

290   "put her head . . .": ibid.

291   "Morros, who did . . .": UL, p. 46.

291   "*Écoutez moi* . . .": ibid, p. 224.

291   "do things by . . .": ibid.

292   "what a fabulous . . .": ibid., p. 200.

292   "Boris Morros was . . .": ibid., p. 209.

293   "pure swindle . . .": ibid., p. 211.

293 "Undoubtedly . . .": ibid., p. 212.

293 "amusing stories . . .": ibid., p. 213.

294 "more discreet . . .": ibid., p. 226.

296 "It seemed highly . . .": ibid., p. 224.

296 "not exactly . . .": ibid., p. 227.

297 "Mrs. Zlatovski . . .": ibid., p. 228.

297 "In view of . . .": FBI case file 100-35543, Jane Foster Zlatovski.

298 "because of their . . .": ibid.

298 "acted like a . . .": UL, p. 232.

298 "It was THE BIG . . .": ibid., p. 233.

299 "glaring inaccuracies . . .": ibid., p. 234.

300 "Gertrude Stein . . .": ibid., p. 200.

301 "socially at concerts . . .": Civil Service . . . FBI case file 100-35543, Jane Foster Zlatovski.

301 "complete and . . .": FBI case file 100-35543, Jane Foster Zlatovski.

303 "did not know . . .": ibid.

304 "UN debate on Indonesia . . .": ibid.

305 "available information. . . .": John F. Fox Jr., "In Passion and in Hope," (Ph.D. diss.) University of New Hampshire, 2001), p. 16.

306 "Will I be able to . . .": UL, p. 241.

306 "the family always . . .": ST.

307 "She liked . . .": ibid.

307 "be questioned concerning . . .": FBI case file 123-192, Paul Child.

307 "the possibility exists . . ." ibid.

308 "traced directly": Andrew Roadnight, *United States Policy Towards Indonesia in the Truman and Eisenhower Years* (New York: MacMillan, 2002), p. 154.

309 "We talked about it . . .": EM.

309 "Jane was a . . .": ibid.

309 "She was very . . .": ST.

310 "ordinary people . . .": UL, p. 244.

310 "Simply to be accused . . .": ibid., p.232.

311 "Julia was braver": EM.

311 "We decided . . .": SMITH.

311 "seemed so far away": FAP.

312 "the most comprehensive . . .": Craig Claiborne, review of *Mastering the Art of French Cooking*, by Julia Child, *The New York Times*, October 18, 1961.

312 "prime dishwasher . . .": FAP.
312 "enormous": Donna Lee, "The Man Behind Julia Child," *Boston Herald American Magazine,* May 10, 1981.
312 "We do everything together": ibid.
312 "shameful episode": Julia Child, *My Life in France* (New York: Anchor Books, 2005), p. 215.

Epilogues

313 "It all receded . . . ST.
314 "never go home again": ibid.
314 "seized by terror": UL, p. 245.
315 "intrinsically tied . . .": FBI case file 100-35543, Jane Foster Zlatovski.
315 "Fascist junta . . .": UL, p. 245.
316 "She willed herself . . .": ST.
316 "opened Jane's . . .": ibid.
317 "scarred and ruined . . .": UL, p. 246.
318 "With open eyes . . .": ibid., p. 33.
319 "suitable for framing . . .": PC, carton 2, folder 73.
319 "We have no . . .": SMITH.
319 "We're perfectly happy . . .": Calvin Tompkins, "Good Cooking," *The New Yorker,* December 23, 1974.
321 "fascinating and . . .": FAP.
321 "a strange man": EM.
322 "every effort should . . .": FBI case file 100-57453, Martha Dodd Stern.
322 "concerning their . . .": FBI case file 100-35543, Jane Foster Zlatovski.
322 "a very grave . . .": *International Herald Tribune,* March 24, 1979.
323 "it is absolutely . . .": UL, p. 238.
324 "the biggest spy ring . . .": Walter Schneir, "The Soblen Trial," *The Nation,* August 26, 1961.
325 "lies and wrong things . . .": ibid.
325 "less than a year . . .": ibid.
325 "A spy is a . . .": ibid.
326 "with all the dirty . . .": Theodore H. White, *In Search of History* (London: Cape, 1979), p. 391.
326 "too much danger . . .": ibid., p. 392.
326 "warping effect . . .": ibid., p. 395.

BIBLIOGRAPHY

Archival Sources

Arthur and Elizabeth Schlesinger
Library History of Women in
America, Radcliffe Institute for
Advanced Study, Harvard
University, Cambridge, Mass.

Julia Child Papers
Paul Child Papers

Federal Bureau of Investigation,
Department of Justice,
Washington, D.C.

Paul Child
William Donovan
Boris Morros
Jack Soble
Martha Dodd Stern
George Zlatovski
Jane Foster Zlatovski

U.S. Department of State Bulletins

Jane Foster
Richard Heppner

Rare Book, Manuscript, and Special
Collections Library, Duke
University, Durham, N.C.

J. B. Matthews Papers

Hoover Institution on War, Revolution,
and Peace, Stanford, Calif.

Jane Foster Papers
Joseph W. Stilwell Papers
Albert C. Wedemeyer Papers
Raymond A. Wheeler Papers

Library of Congress, Veterans History   Elizabeth P. McIntosh Papers
    Project, American Folklife Center,   Martha Dodd Papers
    Washington, D.C.

U.S. National Archives and Records   OSS Records/R6226
    Administration (NARA),   SEAC Records
    College Park, Md.   State Department Records

National Cryptologic Museum,   Venona Decrypts
    Fort Meade, Md.

OSS Society, *The OSS Society Newsletter*   OSS Personnel

Harry S. Truman Library,   Dean Acheson Papers
    Independence, Mo.   Manly Fleischmann Papers
                                                 Harry S. Truman Papers

University of Missouri at Kansas City   Carleton F. Scofield Papers
    Archives   Edgar Snow Papers

University of New Mexico, The Center   Leendert Kamper Affidavit
    for Southwest Research, Albuquerque

Woodrow Wilson Center, Cold War   Vassiliev Notebooks
    International History Project,
    Washington, D.C.

Private Collections / Unpublished Manuscripts

John F. Fox, Jr. "In Passion and in Hope: The Pilgrimage of an American Radical, Martha Dodd Stern and Family, 1933–1990," Ph.D. dissertation, University of New Hampshire, 2001.

Julia McWilliams [Child] Datebook/Diary, excerpts courtesy of Noël Riley Fitch.

Eleanor Thiry [Summers] Wartime Diary and Correspondence. Courtesy of Chris Summers.

George Zlatovski, "The Autobiography of an Anti-Hero," Minnesota State

Historical Society, Minnesota Public Library, quoted with permission of
Susan Tenenbaum.

Oral Histories

"China Hands," Association for Diplomatic Studies and Training. *Frontline
Diplomacy—Country Readers—China*. Arlington, Va.: ADST Foreign Affairs Oral History Program, 2000.

John Cady, Oral History Interview, OSS, Research Analyst 1943–1945, interview by Richard D. McKinzie, July 31, 1974, Harry S. Truman Library,
Independence, Mo.

Julia Child, Foreign Affairs Oral History Project, Foreign Service Spouse Series, Frontline Diplomacy, interview by Jewell Fenzi, November 7, 1991,
Manuscript Division, Library of Congress, Washington, D.C.

Julia McWilliams Child and Paul Child, Smith College Centennial Study,
interview by Jacqueline Van Voris, October 10, 1972.

Elizabeth P. McIntosh, Veterans History Project, Frontline Diplomacy, interview by Leslie Sewell, Library of Congress, Washington, D.C.

Interviews by the Author

Walter Joseph Patrick Curley II, 2010
Thibaut de Saint Phalle, 2011
Noël Riley Fitch, 2010
Fisher Howe, 2010
Judith Jones, 2011
Elizabeth P. McIntosh, 2009–2011
Walter Mess, 2010
Dan Pinck, 2010
Sylvia Ripley, 2011
Basil Summers, 2009
Susan Tenenbaum, 2009–2011

Films and Videotapes

The French Chef. Boston: WGBH Boston / PBS, 1963. Produced by Russell
Morash.

Government Girls of World War II. Washington, D.C.: The History Project, 2006. Produced, written, and directed by Leslie Sewell.

Vietnam: A Television History. Boston: WGBH Boston / PBS, 2007.

Government Documents

U.S. Congress. House Committee on Un-American Activities. *Hearings Regarding Communism in the U.S. Government—Part I.* 81st Cong., 2nd sess., 1950.

U.S. Congress. House. Committee on Un-American Activities. *International Communism (Espionage).* Excerpts of Consultation with Counterspy Boris Morros (August 16, 1957), Reprint of Series of Articles by Representative Francis E. Walter Appearing in the *Philadelphia Inquirer.* 85th Cong., 1st sess., September 29–October 3, 1957.

U.S. Congress. House. Hearings Before the Committee on Un-American Activities, House of Representatives *Investigation of Soviet Espionage.* 85th Cong., 1st sess., October 7, 8, and 9 and November 20, 1957.

U.S. Congress. House. Committee on Foreign Affairs. *Denial of Passports to Persons Knowingly Engaged in Activities Intended to Further the International Communist Movement.* 85th Cong., 2nd sess., July 17 and August 14, 15, and 18, 1958.

Articles

Becker, René. "Julia: A Love Story," *Boston Magazine.* July 1992, 52–55, 121–123.

Boudin, Leonard B. "The Constitutional Right to Travel." *Columbia Law Review* 56, no. 1 (January 1956): 47–75.

———. "The Right to Travel: A Significant Victory." *Nation,* July 30, 1955, 95–97.

Crockett, Frederick E. "How the Trouble Began in Java." *Harper's Magazine,* March 1946, 279–284.

De Graaf, Bob. "Hot Intelligence in the Tropics: Dutch Intelligence Operations in the Netherlands East Indies During the Second World War." *Journal of Contemporary History* 22, no. 4 (1987): 563–584.

DeVoto, Bernard. "Due Notice to the FBI," The Easy Chair. *Harper's Magazine,* October 1949, 65–68.

"Everyone's in the Kitchen," *Time,* November 25, 1966, 74–87.

Gunn, Geoffrey. "Origins of the American War in Vietnam: The OSS Role in Saigon in 1945." *Asia-Pacific Journal: JapanFocus,* May 9, 2009.

Hellman, Geoffrey T. "Curator Getting Around." *The New Yorker,* August 26, 1950.

Lee, Donna. "The Man Behind Julia Child." *Boston Herald American Magazine,* May 10, 1981.

McMahon, Robert J. "Anglo-American Diplomacy and the Reoccupation of the Netherlands East Indies." *Diplomatic History* 2, no. 1 (January 1978): 1–24.

McMillan, Richard. "British Military Intelligence in Java and Sumatra, 1945–46." *Indonesia and the Malay World* 37, no. 107 (March 2009): 65–81.

Ripley, S. Dillon. "Incident in Siam." *Yale Review* 56 (Winter 1947): 272–276.

Reynolds, E. Bruce. "Staying Behind in Bangkok: The OSS and American Intelligence in Postwar Thailand." *Journal of Intelligence History* 2, no. 2 (Winter 2002): 21–48.

Roadnight, Andrew. "Sleeping with the Enemy: Britain, Japanese Troops, and the Netherlands East Indies, 1945–1946." *History* 87, no. 286 (April 2002): 245–268.

Schneir, Walter. "The Soblen Trial." *The Nation,* August 26, 1961.

Simpson, Joanne Cavanaugh. "Seeing Red." *Johns Hopkins Magazine,* September 2000.

Snow, Edgar. "No Four Freedoms for Indo-China." *Saturday Evening Post,* February 2, 1946.

———. "Secrets from Siam." *The Saturday Evening Post,* January 12, 1946.

Tomkins, Calvin. "Good Cooking." *The New Yorker,* December 23, 1974.

Vanden Heuvel, Katrina. "Grand Illusions." *Vanity Fair,* September 1991.

Walter, Francis E. "Chronicle of Treason." *Philadelphia Inquirer,* March 3–9, 1958.

———. "First Official Story of the Man Who Fooled the Kremlin." *Philadelphia Inquirer,* September 29–October 3, 1957.

Whitmore, Hank. "Julia and Paul." *Parade,* February 28, 1982.

Windmiller, Marshall. "A Tumultuous Time: OSS and Army Intelligence in India, 1942–1946." *International Journal of Intelligence and Counterintelligence* 8, no. 1 (Spring 1955): 105–124.

Newspapers and Periodicals

Associated Press
Boston Herald
CBI Roundup
Chicago Daily Tribune
The Evening Star
Foreign Affairs
Harper's Monthly
International Herald Tribune
Life
Los Angeles Times
The Nation
New York Journal-American
Pacific Newsletter
New York Herald Tribune
The New Republic
The News (San Francisco)
The New Yorker
The New York Times
Newsweek
People's World
The Philadelphia Inquirer
San Francisco Chronicle
The Saturday Evening Post
The Times (London)
Time
United Press International
U.S. News and World Report
Washington Daily News
The Washington Post and Times-Herald

Books

Aldrich, Richard J. *The Hidden Hand: Britain, America, and Cold War Secret Intelligence.* Woodstock, N.Y.: Overlook Press, 2002.
——. *Intelligence and the War Against Japan: Britain, America, and the Politics of Secret Service.* New York: Cambridge University Press, 2000.

Aline, Countess of Romanones. *The Spy Wore Red: My Adventures as an Undercover Agent*. New York: Random House, 1987, Jove Books, 1988.

Alsop, Joseph W., with Adam Platt. *I've Seen the Best of It: Memoirs*. New York: W. W. Norton, 1992.

Alsop, Stewart, and Thomas Braden. *Sub Rosa: The OSS and American Espionage*. New York: Ryenal & Hitchcock, 1946.

Bayley, Edwin R. *Joe McCarthy and the Press*. Madison: University of Wisconsin Press, 1981.

Benson, Robert Louis, and Michael Warner, eds. *Venona: Soviet Espionage and the American Response, 1939–1957*. Washington, D.C.: National Security Agency / Central Intelligence Agency, 1996.

Bentley, Elizabeth. *Out of Bondage: The Story of Elizabeth Bentley*. New York: Ivy Books, 1988. First published 1951 by Devin-Adair.

Brown, Anthony Cave. *The Last Hero: Wild Bill Donovan*. New York: Times Books, 1982.

Brysac, Shareen Blair. *Resisting Hitler: Mildred Harnack and the Red Orchestra*. New York: Oxford University Press, 2000.

Caldwell, Oliver J. *A Secret War: Americans in China, 1944–1945*. Carbondale: Southern Illinois University Press, 1972.

Chalou, George C., ed. *The Secret War: The Office of Strategic Services in World War II*. Washington, D.C.: National Archives and Records Center, 1992.

Chambers, Whittaker. *Witness*. Chicago: Regnery, 1970. First published 1952 by Random House.

Child, Charles. *Roots in the Rock*. Boston: Little, Brown, 1964.

Child, Julia, with Alex Prud'homme. *My Life in France*. New York: Alfred A. Knopf, 2005; Anchor Books, 2006.

Conant, James B. *My Several Lives: Memoirs of a Social Inventor*. New York: Harper & Row, 1970.

Croke, Vicki Constantine. *The Lady and the Panda: The True Adventures of the First American Explorer to Bring Back China's Most Exotic Animal*. New York: Random House, 2005.

Davies, John Paton, Jr. *Dragon by the Tail: American, British, Japanese, and Russian Encounters with China and One Another*. New York: W. W. Norton, 1972.

Dennis, Peter. *Troubled Days of Peace: Mountbatten and South East Asia Command, 1945–46*. New York: St. Martin's Press, 1987.

Dodd, Martha. *Through Embassy Eyes*. New York: Harcourt, Brace, 1940.

Dunlop, Richard. *Donovan, America's Master Spy*. Chicago: Rand McNally, 1982.

Eldridge, Fred. *Wrath in Burma*. New York: Doubleday, 1946.

Evans, M. Stanton. *Blacklisted by History: The Untold Story of Senator Joe McCarthy and His Fight Against America's Enemies*. New York: Crown Forum, 2007.

Fenn, Charles. *At the Dragon's Gate: With the OSS in the Far East*. Annapolis, Md.: Naval Institute Press, 2004.

Fenzi, Jewel, with Carl L. Nelson. *Married to the Foreign Service: An Oral History of the American Diplomatic Spouse*. New York: Twayne, 1994.

Fitch, Noël Riley. *Appetite for Life: The Biography of Julia Child*. New York: Doubleday, 1997; Anchor Books, 1999.

Foster, Jane. *An UnAmerican Lady*. London: Sidgwick & Jackson, 1980.

Gouda, Frances, with Thijs Brocades Zaalberg. *American Visions of the Netherlands East Indies / Indonesia*. Amsterdam: Amsterdam University Press, 2002.

Haynes, John Earl. *Red Scare or Red Menace?: American Communism and Anticommunism in the Cold War Era*. Chicago: Ivan R. Dee, 1996.

———, and Harvey Klehr. *Early Cold War Spies: The Espionage Trials That Shaped American Politics*. New York: Cambridge University Press, 2006.

———. *Venona: Decoding Soviet Espionage in America*. New Haven: Yale University Press, 1999.

———, and Alexander Vassiliev. *Spies: The Rise and Fall of the KGB in America*. New Haven: Yale University Press, 2009.

Heath, Aloise Buckley. *Will Mrs. Major Go to Hell?* New York: Arlington House, 1969.

Hellman, Lillian. *Scoundrel Time*. Boston: Little, Brown, 1976.

Herring, George C. *From Colony to Superpower: U.S. Foreign Relations Since 1776*. New York: Oxford University Press, 2008.

Hough, Richard C. *Mountbatten, Hero of Our Time*. London: Weidenfeld & Nicolson, 1980.

Howe, Fisher. *Which Reminds Me: Things to Remember in a Long and Happy Life*. Privately printed, 2010.

Jakub, Jay. *Spies and Saboteurs: Anglo-American Collaboration and Rivalry in Human Intelligence Collection and Special Operations, 1940–45*. New York: St. Martin's Press, 1999.

Joiner, Lynne. *Honorable Survivor: Mao's China, McCarthy's America, and the Persecution of John S. Service.* Annapolis, Md.: Naval Institute Press, 2009.

Kahin, George McTurnan. *Nationalism and Revolution in Indonesia.* Ithaca, N.Y.: Cornell University, 1952; Southeast Asia Program Publications, Cornell University, 2003.

Kahn, E. J., Jr. *China Hands: America's Foreign Service Officers and What Befell Them.* New York: Viking Press, 1975.

Klehr, Harvey, John Earl Haynes, and Fridrikh Igorevich Firsov. *The Secret World of American Communism.* New Haven: Yale University Press, 1995.

Klehr, Harvey, John Earl Haynes, and Kyrill Anderson. *The Soviet World of American Communism.* New Haven: Yale University Press, 1998.

Koke, Louise G. *Our Hotel in Bali: How Two Young Americans Made a Dream Come True—a Story of the 1930s.* Singapore: January Books, 1987.

Lamphere, Robert J., and Tom Shachtman. *The FBI-KGB War: A Special Agent's Story.* Macon, Ga.: Mercer University Press, 1995. First published 1986 by Random House.

Lilley, James, with Jeffrey Lilley. *China Hands: Nine Decades of Adventure, Espionage, and Diplomacy in Asia.* New York: PublicAffairs, 2004.

Lindsey, Timothy. *The Romance of K'Tut Tantri and Indonesia.* Kuala Lumpur; New York: Oxford University Press, 1997.

MacDonald, Alec. *A Wandering Spy Was I.* Kearney, Nebr.: Morris Publishing, 1997.

MacDonald, Alexander. *Bangkok Editor.* New York: Macmillan, 1949.

———. *My Footloose Newspaper Life.* Bangkok: Post Publishing, 1990.

MacDonald, Elizabeth. *Undercover Girl.* New York: Macmillan, 1947.

MacKinnon, Stephen R., and Oris Friesen. *China Reporting: An Oral History of American Journalism in the 1930s and 1940s.* Berkeley: University of California Press, 1987.

Marks, Leo. *Between Silk and Cyanide: The Story of SOE's Code War.* London: HarperCollins, 1998.

May, Gary. *China Scapegoat: The Diplomatic Ordeal of John Carter Vincent.* Washington, D.C.: New Republic Books, 1979.

———. *Un-American Activities: The Trials of William Remington.* New York: Oxford University Press, 1994.

McIntosh, Elizabeth P. *The Role of Women in Intelligence.* McLean, Va.: Association of Former Intelligence Officers, 1989.

———. *Sisterhood of Spies: The Women of the OSS*. Annapolis: Naval Institute Press, 1998.

McMahon, Robert J. *Colonialism and Cold War: The United States and the Struggle for Indonesian Independence, 1945–49*. Ithaca, N.Y.: Cornell University Press, 1981.

Merrill, Hugh. *The Red Hot Typewriter: The Life and Times of John D. MacDonald*. New York: Thomas Dunne Books / St. Martin's Minotaur, 2000.

Merry, Robert W. *Taking On the World: Joseph and Stewart Alsop, Guardians of the American Century*. New York: Viking, 1996.

Mills, Francis B., with John W. Brunner. *OSS Special Operations in China*. Williamstown, N.J.: Phillips Publications, 2002.

Milton, Miles E. *A Different Kind of War*. Garden City, N.Y.: Doubleday, 1967.

Morros, Boris. *My Ten Years as a Counterspy; as Told to Charles Samuels*. New York: Viking Press, 1959.

Mountbatten of Burma, Louis Mountbatten, Earl. *Personal Diary of Admiral the Lord Louis Mountbatten, Supreme Allied Commander, South-East Asia, 1943–1946*. Edited by Philip Ziegler. London: Collins, 1988.

O'Donnell, Patrick K. *Operatives, Spies and Saboteurs: The Unknown Story of the Men and Women of World War II's OSS*. New York: Free Press, 2004.

Olmsted, Kathryn S. *Red Spy Queen: A Biography of Elizabeth Bentley*. Chapel Hill: University of North Carolina Press, 2002.

Painter, Charlotte. *Gifts of Age: Portraits and Essays of 32 Remarkable Women*. San Francisco: Chronicle Books, 1985.

Patti, Archimedes L. A. *Why Vietnam?: Prelude to America's Albatross*. Berkeley: University of California Press, 1980.

Pincher, Chapman. *Treachery: Betrayals, Blunders, and Cover-ups: Six Decades of Espionage Against America and Great Britain*. New York: Random House, 2009.

Pinck, Dan. *Journey to Peking: A Secret Agent in Wartime China*. Annapolis: Naval Institute Press, 2003.

Price, Ruth. *The Lives of Agnes Smedley*. New York: Oxford University Press, 2005.

Rabinowitz, Victor. *Unrepentant Leftist: A Lawyer's Memoir*. Urbana: Illinois University Press, 1996.

Rand, Peter. *China Hands: The Adventures and Ordeals of the American Jour-*

nalists Who Joined Forces with the Great Chinese Revolution. New York: Simon & Schuster, 1995.

Reynolds, E. Bruce. *Thailand's Secret War: The Free Thai, OSS, and SOE During World War II.* Cambridge, U.K.: Cambridge University Press, 2005.

Roadnight, Andrew. *United States Policy Towards Indonesia in the Truman and Eisenhower Years.* New York: Macmillan, 2002.

Romerstein, Herbert, and Eric Breindel. *The Venona Secrets: Exposing Soviet Espionage and America's Traitors.* Washington, D.C.: Regnery Publishing, 2000.

Saint Phalle, Thibaut de. *Saints, Sinners and Scalawags.* Brookline, N.H.: Hobblebush Books, 2004.

Schneir, Walter. *Final Verdict: What Really Happened in the Rosenberg Case.* Edited by Miriam Schneir. Brooklyn, N.Y.: Melville House, 2010.

Schulzinger, Robert D. *A Time for War: The United States and Vietnam, 1941–1975.* New York: Oxford University Press, 1997.

Service, John S. *Lost Chance in China: The World War II Dispatches of John S. Service.* Edited by Joseph W. Esherick. New York: Random House, 1974.

Shapiro, Laura. *Julia Child.* New York: Lipper/Viking, 2007.

Sibley, Katherine A. S. *Red Spies in America: Stolen Secrets and the Dawn of the Cold War.* Lawrence: University Press of Kansas, 2004.

Singlaub, John K., with Malcolm McConnell. *Hazardous Duty: An American Soldier in the Twentieth Century.* New York: Summit Books, 1991.

Smith, Nicol. *Burma Road.* Indianapolis: Bobbs-Merrill, 1940.

Smith, R. Harris. *OSS: The Secret History of America's First Central Intelligence Agency.* Berkeley: University of California Press, 1972.

Snow, Edgar. *Journey to the Beginning: A Personal View of Contemporary History.* New York: Random House, 1958.

Taylor, Edmond. *Awakening from History.* Boston: Gambit, 1969.

Terraine, John. *The Life and Times of Lord Mountbatten.* New York: Holt, Rinehart & Winston, 1980. First published 1968 in London by Hutchinson.

Troy, Thomas F. *Donovan and the CIA.* Frederick, Md.: Aletheia Books, 1981.

Tuchman, Barbara W. *Stilwell and the American Experience in China, 1911–45.* New York: Macmillan, 1970.

United States War Department, Strategic Services Unit, History Project. *War Report of the OSS (Office of Strategic Services).* New York: Walker, 1976.

Vellacott, Kathleen. *Ticket to Burma.* London: Shakespeare Head, 1952.

Wasserstein, Bernard. *Secret War in Shanghai.* Boston: Houghton Mifflin, 1999.

Weinstein, Allen, and Alexander Vassiliev. *The Haunted Wood: Soviet Espionage in America—the Stalin Era.* New York: Random House, 1999.

West, Nigel. *Venona: The Greatest Secret of the Cold War.* New York: HarperCollins, 1999.

White, Theodore H. *In Search of History: A Personal Adventure.* New York: Harper & Row, 1978 / London: Cape, 1979.

———, and Annalee Jacoby. *Thunder Out of China.* New York: William Sloane Associates, 1946 / London: Gollancz, 1947.

Yu, Maochun. *OSS in China: Prelude to Cold War.* New Haven: Yale University Press, 1996.

Ziegler, Philip. *Mountbatten.* New York: Alfred A. Knopf, 1985; Harper & Row, 1986.

ACKNOWLEDGMENTS

This book is deeply indebted to those writers who came before—the diarists, letter writers, and memoirists whose voices imbue almost every word with the emotional veracity, urgency, and complexity of their wartime experiences and the aftermath. Facts can always be researched and assembled, but the absurd twists and turns of fate, and the astonishing extremes of history that allow a period of unprecedented courage and idealism to devolve into a frenzy of fear and hate, cannot be adequately rendered without a record of the human toll. First and foremost, I must thank Elizabeth P. McIntosh (Betty MacDonald) for serving as my trusted guide through this troubled time. Not only did I rely on her two excellent books about the OSS, I took full advantage of her marvelous memory over the course of many interviews—and countless telephone queries—during the three years it took to complete this project. Her compassion, wisdom, and wonderful good humor have colored and shaped every page. I dedicated this book to Betty because it is every bit as much her story as it is Jane's, Julia's, and Paul's. To that end, I am also grateful to Susan Tenenbaum, Jane Foster's niece by marriage and closest surviving relative, for her willingness to share her family saga and unflinching honesty in facing some of the more uncomfortable truths.

No writer could have asked for a better archive than the one left to the Schlesinger Library by Julia and Paul Child. I wish to thank the library's long-suffering staff, Lynda Leahy and Elle M. Shea, for helping me to navigate the tremendous store of correspondence, diaries, personal papers, clippings, photographs, and videotapes, as well as Diana Carey, for coping with my many photo requests. My gratitude also to Athena Angelos for her work at the Library of Congress. I must also thank the author Noël Riley Fitch, who conducted extensive interviews with Julia Child for her excellent biography, *Appetite for Life*, for helping to fill in some gaps and making available some private diary entries not in the archive. She generously shared many of her impressions of Julia, as well as her attitude about the security investigation and Jane's culpability, and I am most grateful for her insight. Also, Susy Davidson, coordinator of the Julia Child Foundation, for granting access to certain photographs.

For access to unpublished collections thanks are also due to Chris Summers for the wartime letters and diary of his mother, Eleanor Thiry; also to Susan Tenenbaum for the private papers of Jane Foster, as well as access to a trove of her artwork, and the unpublished manuscript of George Zlatovski's autobiography.

In the writing of this book I am indebted to those people who particularly helped me along the way: Charles T. Pinck, president of the OSS Society; his father, OSS veteran and historian Dan Pinck; Fisher Howe; Walter Curley; Walter Mess; Basil Summers, now sadly deceased; and John F. Fox, Jr., FBI historian. I was incredibly fortunate to be working for the fourth time with my indefatigable researcher, Ruth Tenenbaum (no relation to the Tenenbaums in this book), who fell in love with this project and did so much more than I could have asked—and dug up so much more than I would have believed possible—that I owe her far more than I can ever repay. I also benefited from having the best assistant, Cavelle Sukhai, who keeps my world running even when I disappear into my writer's cave for months on end. A very special thanks goes to the multitalented Mary Tavener Holmes, who commented on this work in progress, encouraged my every step of the way, and generally tried to keep me sane. I would also like to acknowledge Perri Peltz for her kindness and support. Having such loyal friends (and I include all the tennis girls) is what makes such a lonely endeavor possible.

As always, I am profoundly grateful to Kris Dahl, my literary agent, a friend and advisor for two decades. None of my books would have seen the light of day without my brilliant editor, Alice Mayhew, who somehow always manages to drag me over the finish line, and then days later convinces me that the next one will be no problem. Her enthusiasm and vision have been a driving force in my work. A team of gifted people at Simon & Schuster contributed to this book, including the attention of Alice's assistant, Rachel Bergmann, dedication of Roger Labrie, careful copyediting of Janet Fletcher, and astute art direction of Michael Accordino.

Finally, for their unfailing support, I would like to thank my husband, Steve Kroft, and son, John. They showed great love and forbearance in listening to me go on and on about Julia, Paul, and Jane for three years, particularly when the present was imposing on their lives, there were so many pressing matters at hand, and I was always stuck in the past. Thank you.

INDEX

Photo Credits